THE DRAGON'S GIFT

THE DRAGON'S GIFT

THE REAL STORY OF CHINA IN AFRICA

DEBORAH BRAUTIGAM

OXFORD
UNIVERSITY PRESS

OXFORD
UNIVERSITY PRESS

Great Clarendon Street, Oxford OX2 6DP

Oxford University Press is a department of the University of Oxford.
It furthers the University's objective of excellence in research, scholarship,
and education by publishing worldwide in

Oxford New York

Auckland Cape Town Dar es Salaam Hong Kong Karachi
Kuala Lumpur Madrid Melbourne Mexico City Nairobi
New Delhi Shanghai Taipei Toronto

With offices in

Argentina Austria Brazil Chile Czech Republic France Greece
Guatemala Hungary Italy Japan Poland Portugal Singapore
South Korea Switzerland Thailand Turkey Ukraine Vietnam

Oxford is a registered trade mark of Oxford University Press
in the UK and in certain other countries

Published in the United States
by Oxford University Press Inc., New York

British Library Cataloguing in Publication Data

Data available

Library of Congress Cataloging in Publication Data

Data available

Typeset by SPI Publisher Services, Pondicherry, India
Printed in Great Britain
on acid-free paper by
Clays Ltd, St Ives plc

ISBN 978–0–19–955022–7

1 3 5 7 9 10 8 6 4 2

For David

ACKNOWLEDGMENTS

"His 'gifts' were tangible and generous," a South African newspaper commented when Chinese President Hu Jintao signed several aid agreements during his 2007 visit to Mozambique. But for many people, the "gifts" borne by the Chinese dragon are more mysterious than tangible, and much more ambiguous than simply generous. As the first impressions of China's rising engagement began to harden into conventional wisdom, a troubling picture arose, based on a sometimes sensational mix of fact and fiction, all circulating rapidly through cyberspace. The scale of the Chinese presence, and the obvious concerns this raised in Africa, Europe, Japan, and the United States, pushed me to return to a topic I first began to study in the 1980s. This book is the result: my effort to sort the myths of Chinese aid and economic engagement from the realities, and provide a more balanced, historically grounded, and complex picture of a phenomenon that became central to African development in the first post-millennium decade.

This book relies on nearly three decades of scholarship, but most recently on field research in South Africa, Nigeria, Tanzania, Zambia, Mauritius, Mozambique, Sierra Leone, and Zimbabwe, as well as interviews in Washington, Beijing, and Europe. I have learned from many people who know a piece of this puzzle, but especially from Phillip Snow, Ian Taylor, Daniel Large, Lucy Corkin, Qi Guoqiang, Li Baoping, Zhang Jun, Zhou Hong, Zha Daojiong, Li Anshan, He Wenping, Paul Hubbard, David Shinn, Jamie Monson, Chris Alden, Adrian Davis, Gregor Dobler, Sanusha Naidu, Mike Morris, and Adama Gaye. I acknowledge with great appreciation the many other people in China, Africa, Europe, and the US who asked questions when parts of this book were presented at seminars and conferences, or who shared their insights and experiences with me. I am particularly grateful to Anne Brautigam, Richard Brautigam, David Hirschmann, Carol Wise, and an anonymous reviewer who read the entire manuscript. Others read chapters and offered helpful advice, including David Leonard, Albert Keidel, Jamie Monson, Carol Lancaster, Julia Strauss, Martha Saavedra, and several anonymous reviewers of the proposal. Any errors are of course my sole responsibility.

I thank the German Marshall Fund of the United States, the Smith Richardson Foundation, and American University for funding portions of the research. My international team of research assistants deserves special thanks: Arthur Taillu, Remidius Ruhinduka, Dominic Liche, Hans Hobbs, Hu Di, Liang Xingni, Medesse Raissa Sonou, Lijia Gong, Meghan Olivier, Vanessa Alvarez, Melissa Klink, Hala Hanna, Ritodhi Chakraborty, Zu Yiming, Paul Colombini, and especially Tang Xiaoyang.

For their critical roles in bringing this project to print, I thank my editor at Oxford, Sarah Caro, who approached me with the idea, and Daniel Large, who first invited me to return to the topic of China and Africa. Mick Moore gave the book its title. Above all, I thank David Hirschmann, whose contributions to this book, but more importantly to my life, are beyond measure.

Deborah Brautigam

CONTENTS

Conclusion: Engaging China

LIST OF FIGURES

The Changing Face of Chinese Engagement in Africa

For three days in November 2006, China's capital city was host to delegations from forty-eight African states gathered for the Beijing Summit of the Forum on China–Africa Cooperation. As the African leaders strode up the red carpet of the Great Hall of the People to shake hands with China's President Hu Jintao, the streets outside were filled with billboards saluting "Amazing Africa." Hu's opening speech brought waves of applause as the Chinese leader outlined a plan for a new "strategic partnership" and a deepening of "economic cooperation" with African countries. Over the next three years, the Chinese pledged to double aid, ratchet up concessional finance for trade and infrastructure and allow duty-free entry for many African exports. China would set up a fund for investment in Africa, build a hundred rural schools and thirty hospitals, and establish up to five trade and economic cooperation zones across the continent. This strategic partnership with Africa would be based, they said, on "win-win cooperation."[1]

Newspapers around the world filled with stories on the summit. Soon, think-tanks, universities, foundations and aid agencies began to organize meetings to try and understand what seemed to be an exciting – or perhaps worrying – new turn for African development. I attended many of these meetings. My 1998 book on Chinese aid and African development was one of the few resources for people trying to understand what a doubling of Chinese aid and the other pledges might mean for the continent.[2]

At a conference in an ivy-covered building at Harvard University, Ndubisi Obiorah, a soft-spoken Nigerian human rights activist, told us of civil society's concerns about China's poor record on governance, social and environmental responsibility and the risks this posed for African countries. But as we strolled in the hallways during a break, Ndubisi told me that part of him welcomed China's interest: "You remember," he said, "a few years ago, *The Economist* did a cover story on Africa: 'The Failed Continent.' My friends and I, we talked about that for weeks. It was depressing: 'Africa, the failed continent!' And now China comes, and they are talking about business, about investment, about win-win cooperation." He smiled a bit ruefully: "Who knows? Maybe this change will be good for Africa."

China's Rise in Africa

The Beijing Summit focused attention on development in a part of the world that had seen far more than its share of dispiriting headlines. It forced the West to focus on something new: Chinese aid and other forms of economic engagement were sharply on the rise in Africa. China was on track to become the African continent's largest trading partner, outpacing Britain and the United States. Nearly 900 Chinese companies had invested in Africa by then – in factories and farms, retail shops and oil wells. Li Ruogu, head of China's Export Import Bank (Eximbank), predicted six months after the summit that his bank would commit $20 billion over the next three years to finance Chinese exports and business in Africa (including North Africa).[3] By comparison, World Bank loan commitments to countries in Africa over a similar three-year period (2006 to 2008) totaled just over $17 billion.[4]

Though much of the West only began to focus on it after the Beijing Summit, China's accelerated move into Africa was by then already a decade long, building on forty-five years of aid that the Chinese promised almost from the start would be based on "mutual benefit." China has given aid to every country in Africa save one: Swaziland, which alone has never switched allegiance from Taiwan. Official aid is still regarded by China as a sensitive area, a state secret. This shroud of secrecy has helped to intensify concerns both in Africa and in the West. Much attention has focused on the multi-billion dollar, resource-backed loans offered for infrastructure in countries recovering from conflict, particularly Angola and the Democratic Republic of the Congo (DRC). Others have condemned China's policy of engaging with all countries that grant it diplomatic recognition, and its pledge not to interfere in domestic affairs, which has meant that the leadership actively engages dictators shunned by many other governments: in Sudan, for example, or Zimbabwe. As the debates unfolded in conference rooms, blogs, and media outlets in the West and in Africa, and as rumors of a huge new aid program created a mix of alarm and anticipation, it was obvious that debaters, bloggers, and journalists were drawing conclusions with only scant information.

The Chinese press painted a consistently rosy picture of friendship and mutual benefit. African leaders were almost uniformly positive about the benefits of China's embrace. Journalists in Africa and in the West were much more skeptical. Myths sprang up and were rapidly accepted as facts: the Chinese were targeting aid only to countries with rich natural resources and questionable governance, and giving Africa three times as much aid as all the West combined! China was a "rogue donor" operating completely outside the rules and making governance worse. Chinese aid was "toxic," a highly placed US foreign policy pundit told his audience. The Chinese "stifle real progress while hurting ordinary citizens."[5] They import all their own workers for their projects, it was said. Some claimed the Chinese were using prison labor. Others predicted that China would manipulate debt relief for political leverage.

In the waves of misinformation and hasty conclusions, it became very clear that no one was answering the central questions: what *are* the Chinese doing in their new wave of aid and economic cooperation across Africa? What will this mean for poverty and development in Africa? And what will it mean for the West and our own approach to development and aid? This book takes on that challenge.

China and Africa: Mutual Benefit?

On the small Indian Ocean island of Mauritius, crews from Beijing Construction Engineering Group operate the bulldozers tearing up sugar-cane fields to construct low-income housing units financed by a Chinese concessional loan. An exception in Africa, Mauritius has more than forty years of vibrant, multi-party democracy and no natural resources to speak of, save an interesting volcanic landscape, beautiful beaches, and rich soils that support a sugarcane crop that was for nearly two centuries the lifeblood of the economy. French tourists heading for a beach holiday sometimes find themselves lining up for their bags beside Chinese businessmen. Some of the latter may work for Huawei Technologies, a leader in information technologies and one of China's flagship companies. With encouragement from the Mauritian government under its efforts to re-invent Mauritius as a "cyber island," Huawei moved its Africa research, finance, and administrative centers to Mauritius, anchoring one of the modern "cyber towers" near the national university.

Others waiting for their bags may be on a delegation invited by China's Shanxi province Tianli Group, operator of a high-tech spinning mill in Mauritius, where textiles form another key sector of the economy. By the time of the November summit, Tianli and the Mauritian government were close to concluding a deal for Mauritius to host one of the proposed special economic cooperation zones. Two weeks after the billboards were removed from the Beijing streets and the city emptied of its African visitors, Tianli arrived in Mauritius with a delegation of officials and twenty Chinese firms interested in investing.

"We understood that the Chinese were interested in Mauritius nine or ten months ago," Finance Minister Rama Sithanen told me when I met him in Washington the following April. "I set up a team, the Minister of Land, the Board of Investment, etc., so that we could put a package together." He laughed. "Tianli negotiated very hard. There were thirty or so conditions, it was very complicated. They wanted zero tax, but we are a low tax country already, only 15 percent, that's lower than Singapore and Hong Kong. They accepted this, but then we had to give them a very good deal on the land." Tianli designed an advertising campaign to attract Chinese companies, and the Mauritian government negotiated the politically sensitive issue of compensation for the 250 small farmers who had leased the government-owned land, and would have to be given alternative farming sites.

Rama Sithanen was back in Beijing in July, accompanying Prime Minister Navin Ramgoolam and a public–private delegation. Sithanen and the Chinese deputy Minister of Commerce, Liao Xiaoqi, initialed an agreement for an aid package of $117 million – triple the amount of aid offered in the country's last agreement with China.[6] As an upper-middle-income country, Mauritius received little aid from the West. The government appreciated the Chinese aid, most of it in the form of concessional loans that would finance infrastructure, but they were more enthusiastic about the potential investment. "We have never targeted a market like this, we have always been Eurocentric," declared Raju Jaddoo, the director of the Mauritius Board of Investment. "People in Mauritius talk non-stop about the double taxation treaty between India and Mauritius. But this opening toward China is much bigger."[7]

Zambia's Chambishi copper mine had been closed for more than ten years when China Non-Ferrous Metals Corporation (CNMC) bought 85 percent of the mine in 1998 for $20 million, investing another $130 million for its rehabilitation.[8] CNMC were pioneers. By the end of 2005, more than 160 Chinese companies had invested in Zambia. A thousand Zambians were employed at Chambishi alone. The Chinese investors had complaints, as a Zambian newspaper reported: "the Zambian government's rigid control over expatriate staff, high transportation costs due to its landlocked position and poor infrastructure, discriminatory incentives, complicated labour relations laws, frequent strikes by workers, and poor local industries were not helping investors."[9] But Zambians had complaints too.

The Chambishi joint venture marked the start of a steep learning curve for the Chinese.[10] In April 2005, as many as fifty-one factory workers were killed in an explosion at the Chinese-owned BGRIMM explosives plant on the grounds of Chambishi mine. The Chinese were widely accused of lax safety standards, and observers linked the disaster with the high rate of fatalities in China's own mines. Yet as one investigative journalist pointed out, the problem of mine safety in Zambia was not uniquely Chinese. In fact, in the year up to October 2005 there had been only one fatality inside the Chinese mine itself, while more than twenty workers had died inside Mopani copper mines, a Swiss–Canadian–Zambian joint venture.

The Chinese company paid funeral costs and compensation of some $10,000 per employee killed, but the BGRIMM explosion also helped facilitate Zambia's National Union of Miners and Allied Workers' efforts to organize workers at the Chinese mine. The following year, in a protest over wages, workers on the night shift at Chambishi vandalized equipment at the mine and attacked a Chinese manager. The next morning, as a fracas at the gate turned into a riot, a worker was shot and wounded by security guards. When rumors spread that he had been killed, another group of miners stormed the Chinese residential compound, where, apparently, a panicked manager with a gun shot and wounded another five miners.

The Chinese connection grew into a heated issue in the Zambian presidential elections in September 2006. Opposition Patriotic Front candidate Michael Sata, who had visited Taiwan at the invitation of its government, seized on the anti-Chinese feeling. Aid and investment from China were Trojan horses, he told Zambians. "You recruit Chinese doctors and they end up having Chinese restaurants in town. They are just flooding the country with human beings instead of investment and the government is jumping," he charged. "We have to be very careful because if we leave them unchecked, we will regret it. China is sucking from us. We are becoming poorer because they are getting our wealth."[11] The late Zambian President Levy Mwanawasa countered: "The Chinese government has brought a lot of development to this country and these are the people you are demonstrating against?"[12]

After concerns about local demonstrations kept China's President Hu Jintao from visiting Chambishi to inaugurate the Zambia–China Economic and Trade Cooperation Zone in February 2007, Zambian Minister of Mines Dr. Mwansa chided the people of Chambishi for their militant stand. Hu Jintao had promised that China would invest at least $800 million in the Zambia–China economic zone, creating thousands of local jobs. Mwansa reminded the people of Chambishi that the copper-processing factories planned by the Chinese would help Zambia to industrialize, and move away from simply exporting raw copper concentrate.[13]

In July 2007, Mwansa and President Mwanawasa visited Chambishi to preside over the launch of the Chinese company's new social responsibility plan. A spokesman for the Chinese firm announced that they were supporting renovations at the Sino-Zam Friendship Hospital (another Chinese aid project), and repairing local roads, building bus shelters and public recreation facilities, and giving money for local education and women's empowerment.[14] "As more and more Chinese companies are established in this area, we will see a flourishing and vigorous economic zone in the near future," the spokesman pledged, adding "More value-addition and revenue will be left locally." Then President Mwanawasa took the microphone: "You people of Chambishi should know better. This mine here was run by a South African company which failed. The Chinese came and you have seen what is happening. Don't be cheated to lose your employment, because your children will suffer."

China is also active in West Africa's fragile conflict zone. More than twenty years ago, as a student, I spent a year in West Africa interviewing local people and Chinese aid workers, studying China's approach to aid, and visiting Chinese projects deep in the interior. I returned often after that. By coincidence, three weeks before Charles Taylor invaded from the north, setting off more than a decade of civil war, the US Agency for International Development (USAID) sent me to northern Liberia to talk to village women for a project they hoped to fund on horticulture exports.

That was my last visit to Liberia for many years, but I remembered how the rainy season churned up the roads carved into the rusty, iron-saturated soil, making a thick soup that regularly trapped four-wheel-drive vehicles seeking to venture into the wet green forests. And I often wondered what had happened to the Chinese projects I had studied in West Africa. Were the bridges, rice fields, and feeder roads still operable? Was the Chinese hydropower project still producing electricity for Kenema and Bo? What happened to the joint ventures that the Chinese government was starting to nurture nearly two decades ago?

Poverty and Prosperity

If you could travel by satellite directly across the African continent on a clear night, the vastness of African underdevelopment would hit you with stunning effect. In South Africa, a sprawl of light would mark Johannesburg and a smaller glow would be Cape Town. Between the border of South Africa, and up to the curve of the continent around the Bay of Benin, would be velvety black, broken only by the unruly spread of Lagos. At night, most of Africa is truly in the dark.

The majority of the world's poor do not live in Africa: for the moment, that dubious distinction still belongs to South Asia with its relatively larger population. But as we are reminded by rock stars such as Bono and Bob Geldolf, and university stars like professors Paul Collier and Jeffrey Sachs, Africa is home to most of the *desperately* poor – a large share of the "bottom billion" who have scant access to primary schools, clean water, sanitation, or opportunity.

The reasons for African poverty are complex and still debated. Three decades ago, it was commonplace to blame the ravages of colonial exploitation for Africa's poor progress.[15] Yet the political and economic success of former British colonies like Botswana and Mauritius, both relatively prosperous democracies, and similar outcomes in Japan's former colonies Korea and Taiwan, ensured that colonialism itself was no longer enough of an explanation.

For the past thirty years, most African countries have suffered at one time or another from a combination of low prices for their exports, mountains of debt, and a series of painful austerity measures and liberalization programs known as "structural adjustment" and imposed by international financial institutions in return for access to new loans. Although growth rates turned up in many African countries after the start of the new millennium and poverty fell somewhat, the economic crisis that began in 2008 ensured that most would fall far short of the Millennium Development Goal (MDG) targets by 2015. Innovations such as the "green revolution" that enabled rural Asia to produce food surpluses have not been widely successful in Africa, and many governments across the continent have not provided clear and credible support for job-creating investment. On measures of the quality of governance, African countries still lag behind the rest of the world in accountability, rule of law, and transparency.[16]

During the same three decades, Chinese leaders cast aside the socialist economy of Mao Zedong, and embarked on a gradual economic transition with spectacular economic results. Beginning with agricultural reforms first tried out in the province of Sichuan, China's policymakers unleashed market incentives in a country where, not long before, being labeled a "capitalist running dog" would have brought discrimination, rejection, and abuse.

In 1980, I journeyed through China just as the first wave of reforms was taking hold. After waiting weeks in Taipei and then Hong Kong for our rare individual visas, a friend and I traveled by train through the Lion Mountain tunnels, and across the miles of rice paddies that would later become the factory-dense Special Economic Zone of Shenzhen. Between Guangdong and Shanghai, we met two students from Benin and Sudan whose studies in China were sponsored by the Chinese government. A young soldier in the People's Liberation Army and his new wife shared our compartment for half a day, on their honeymoon. The train passed dozens of small grey villages, stopping sometimes at towns where small, sleepy donkeys rested beside the platform. There were no shops, no markets, and no restaurants. We could still make out the faded calligraphy of slogans: "Serve the People" and "Tireless Struggle," painted across the sides of the dusty brick buildings. I asked the young soldier whom he had served during his time in the countryside. He laughed and pointed to himself.

When Deng Xiaoping brought China out of the chaos of the Cultural Revolution, and set the country on the path to what the Chinese still call a "socialist" market economy, he famously said that ideology no longer mattered: "Black cat, white cat, as long as it catches mice it's a good cat." He also said: "to get rich is glorious." At first in fits and starts, the market economy came alive. Deng Xiaoping's Open Door policy invited in foreign investment, skills, and new technologies, and sent students abroad to soak up the latest thinking at cutting-edge universities in the West. Chinese entre-preneurs flourished, but more unusually, through a mix of market and plan, the state sector gradually created its own business leaders, encouraging them to develop global brand names and seek profits abroad.

China now has the second-largest economy in the world. It is the world's workshop, not only for toys and garments, the first stages of export manu-facturing, but for laptop computers, iPods, and digital medical devices. China's coming out party – the summer Olympics of 2008 – showed the world what the country had become. When I first visited China, there was widespread equality, but everyone was equally poor. Between 1981 and 2001, as economists Shaohua Chen and Martin Ravallion report, China reduced the proportion of people living in poverty from 53 percent to only 8 percent.[17] Yet inequality has risen as rapidly and as sharply as the economy has prospered. I have seen beggars sitting on the curbs of the prosperous shopping streets of Beijing's Wanfujing District. In summer and winter, the city is usually blanketed in dense yellow smog, the contribution of hundreds of ill-regulated factories. The rains that wash the air and give temporary blue skies are highly acidic. Many of China's streams and lakes have been rendered useless for fishing, and contaminants have entered the ground-water in most urban areas.[18]

These costs of rapid industrialization are starting to be taken seriously by China's leaders today; for many Africans, these costs are invisible. They see the face of China's prosperity: the confident traders that arrive to sell goods, the increasing numbers of Chinese tourists traveling to Africa, delegations of Chinese business leaders investigating potential profits. And many of them find this face very attractive. The idea of China as a model for prosperity has captured the imagination of many ordinary Africans, although others fear the threat of competition from the Chinese industrial juggernaut, and the rise of Chinese traders competing at the entry level in local African markets. On the one hand, we see excitement and anticipation; on the other, unease about Chinese aid and state-sponsored economic engagement. Yet, overall, I frequently hear comments like this, from a thoughtful Nigerian diplomat in Beijing: "The Chinese have an advantage of not having a colonial hangover. Whatever the Chinese do for Africa is very credible in our eyes. You have to understand this. We think maybe we can learn something from the Chinese."

A Different Kind of "Aid"

Not long ago, I attended a conference on the future of foreign aid organized by Oxford University. We gathered in Rhodes House, one of the Oxford buildings donated by Cecil Rhodes. Rhodes was the nineteenth-century founder of the De Beers diamond company, and the man who pushed the British Empire north of the Limpopo River in South Africa, all the way to Lake Tanganyika, grabbing present-day Zimbabwe and Zambia. Rhodes once said, "I would annex the planets if I could; I often think of that. It makes me sad to see them so clear and yet so far."[19]

Former President of Mozambique Joaquim Chissano, winner of the first Mo Ibrahim prize for excellence in African leadership, opened the conference with a frank speech calling for change in the aid system. He castigated the "never-ending litany of seminars and workshops...of doubtful value" and the pressures for political reform with sometimes destabilizing consequences. He charged that donors had "systematically dismissed" African needs for infrastructure, and generally ignored the need for development of the local private sector: "We should devise innovative ways to leverage aid to attract private sector resources in order to nurture and support the emergence of robust entrepreneurial classes that have a strong stake in the national economies," Chissano said.[20]

Despite nearly sixty years of aid, wealthy countries still do not have a way to ensure that their assistance will actually promote development (economic, social, sustainable, people-centered – however it is defined) and reduce poverty.[21] Official donor agencies and non-governmental organizations (NGOs) operate on the base of a mix of theory and practice, and the mix changes regularly. Periodic evaluations and a large industry of academic and professional reviews, meetings, and publications create new knowledge about what seems to work and what does not, and incentives for reinventing the "recipe" for effective aid. From an early occupation with infrastructure and industry, to, later, integrated rural development programs and (briefly) basic human needs, we shifted to structural adjustment, then governance and democracy, Grameen Bank-inspired microfinance, conditional cash transfers, and so on. Convictions about how aid can best foster development change regularly. And yet in Africa the continually changing recipe has yet to make much of a dent in ending poverty.

China's aid and economic cooperation differ, both in their content and in the norms of aid practice. The content of Chinese assistance is considerably simpler, and it has changed far less often. Influenced mainly by their own experience of development and by the requests of recipient countries, the Chinese aid and economic cooperation programs emphasized infrastructure, production, and university scholarships at a time when the traditional donors downplayed all of these. Chinese loans for infrastructure were intended to reduce the high costs of production (although contracts were tied to Chinese firms and the bidding was not very transparent). Subsidies for productive joint ventures were supposed to create employment, local capacity, *and* demand for Chinese machinery and equipment. Preferential loans for buyers of Chinese goods, and tariff-free access for commodities from low-income Africa emphasized trade over aid. Popular rotating health teams staffed local hospitals again and again, for decades.

China is different as a donor and strategic partner because it is also a developing country, and its development success (explicitly, its rapid economic transformation *and* its reduction of poverty) give it a great deal of credibility as a partner with relevant recent experience. As Liberia's former Finance Minister Antoinette Sayeh commented, "Clearly, for us, in Africa, we have a lot to learn from China, beyond its financial capacity to assist. China has made the most progress over the past several decades in reducing poverty. That experience is of great interest to us."[22]

China, Aid, and the West

While China's new role as a major source of finance was welcomed in the corridors of power in Africa, it sparked considerable concern in Europe and the United States. Some saw China primarily as a competitor unburdened by the kind of social, environmental, and governance standards increasingly applied to finance from the West. The president of the European Investment Bank, a public funding agency, angrily accused the Chinese of "unscrupulous" behavior after losing contracts to Chinese banks. The International Monetary Fund and the World Bank watched Chinese banks stepping in to compete directly with their own offers of finance. The former president of the World Bank criticized the Chinese for ignoring environmental and social safeguards in their loans.[23] Wealthy countries complained that Chinese companies were gaining business by tying aid to exports, a form of export promotion that the richer countries themselves had agreed to sharply reduce.

Although China has become increasingly transparent about many aspects of its governance and policymaking, aid figures remain state secrets. The Chinese government releases only the barest of information about the quantities of aid it gives. There are no official figures on aid allocations to individual countries or regions, no breakdown by sector or purpose. The tradition of secrecy fuels misunderstandings, rumor, and speculation. The media assume (mistakenly) that China's *aid* program is huge. Some report that China gives aid mainly as a "quid pro quo" in exchange for access to natural resources like oil (this is largely incorrect). "Rogue regimes" – Sudan and Zimbabwe – feature as notorious examples of typical countries enjoying large amounts of "no strings attached" aid from China (in fact, they get very little *aid*).

The lack of transparency about Chinese loans has also deepened concerns that Chinese banks are "free-riding" by extending loans to low-income countries recently freed of crippling debt. Many assume that the Chinese do not demand proper accounting of funds and worry that the lack of conditions on governance will worsen corruption in a region already plagued by official malfeasance. Oxford University professor Paul Collier, former head of research at the World Bank, declared in his book *The Bottom Billion*: "In the bottom billion [governance] is already unusually bad, *and the Chinese are making it worse*."[24]

In 2005, under the Paris Declaration, the major donor organizations committed to reform their own approaches to aid, in an effort to increase its effectiveness. As a newly significant source of finance for Africa, China's role is particularly important for the development agenda of the World Bank, and the leading nations that make up the Group of Eight (G-8) and the Organization for Economic Cooperation and Development (OECD, a members-only club of advanced industrialized nations, based in Paris). All of these organizations admit to operating largely in the dark in their assessment of the risks and opportunities presented by China's aid and development finance.

What they do not realize is that China's engagement in Africa often simply repeats patterns established by the West, and especially Japan *in China*. As China emerged from the chaos of the Mao years and opened its own door to foreign aid, loans, and investment from the West and Japan, Chinese leaders saw how aid could be mixed with other forms of economic engagement. They observed how wealthy countries ensured that aid would benefit both the donor and the recipient. The content of their aid reflects what they believe worked for their own development. And, surprisingly, much about the way they give aid reflects what they learned from all of us.

What is Foreign Aid?

Defining what counts as "foreign aid" should be fairly straightforward. It is not. Most people have a general sense that *foreign aid* is funding given from governments to promote economic and social development in less-advantaged countries. They would not normally include military aid in this definition (nor does this study) but what about road repairs or a school rebuilt by a peacekeeping force? What about funds sent abroad by non-governmental organizations like Save the Children? Government subsidies to promote exports or subsidies to promote private investment do not seem to be aid, but what if the subsidized exports are buses that will be used for public transport? What if the subsidies will be used for joint ventures and technology transfer to boost the opportunities for small and medium enterprises in developing countries? Are these "aid"?

Between 1960 and 1972, the traditional donors wrestled with these questions in order to develop a definition that would enable them to record and compare their core development aid in a consistent manner. Member countries of the Development Assistance Committee (DAC) of the OECD now report their aid on the basis of an agreed definition of official development assistance (ODA).

ODA comprises funding from governments to developing countries (those with a per capita income below a regularly adjusted threshold) and to multilateral institutions such as the United Nations Development Program or the World Bank. This funding has to meet two criteria. First, the purpose of the funding must be primarily to promote economic development and welfare in the recipient country. Second, it must be given on a concessional basis. Export credits do *not* generally qualify as ODA, nor do grants and subsidies to support private investment. In Chapter 6 we will return to this definition when we try to figure out how much aid China has given to Africa, and how this compares with other actors.

This standard definition of ODA provides the starting point for this study. However, I go beyond this definition to include a range of instruments used by the Chinese government to mediate its economic engagement in Africa. These other programs are often mislabeled as "aid" in the media. They need to be disentangled from the official aid program, and viewed for what they are: part of the portfolio of tools used by an activist, developmental government with a clear vision of what it needs to do to promote its national goals overseas. And in viewing them for what they are, we have a chance to reexamine the conventional wisdom that excludes these kinds of activities from the portfolios of most traditional donors.

Why Do Countries Give Aid?

Washington, DC: A television set flashes a picture of a brown-skinned toddler with a dirt-smudged face and large, startled eyes. A disembodied voice and a telephone number appeal on her behalf for contributions to the

Red Cross or another NGO, hard at work responding to another natural or man-made disaster. In a White House office a budget official is coordinating with the State Department, putting the final touches to a supplementary appropriations request for a record level of aid to Iraq and Afghanistan. Down the street, a smartly dressed representative from the US Department of Commerce answers a phone call from an American engineering firm at its Advocacy Center inside the World Bank.[25]

With some small changes, these pictures might also have been taken in Beijing. Like the US, China gives aid for three reasons: strategic diplomacy, commercial benefit, and as a reflection of society's ideologies and values. The broad brush-strokes of foreign aid policy are set by political leaders, who shape aid as one of many instruments of foreign policy.[26] These leaders can sometimes influence decades of aid practice through the bold gestures or ideologies of the moment: A former US President, Jimmy Carter, locked the United States into large transfers of aid to Egypt and Israel after a hand-shake at Camp David. The ideas of British Prime Minister Margaret Thatcher and US President Ronald Reagan deeply influenced aid for several decades, helping to shape a more conservative, market-oriented agenda.

However, the wishes of even strong leaders translate through a filter of three kinds of pressures – state, societal, and international – to arrive at the specifics of aid policy. State influences are key. The United States Agency for International Development is housed in the State Department, reflecting foreign aid's utility as an important diplomatic tool. Conversely, China's two main aid windows are housed respectively in the Ministry of Commerce and the China Export Import Bank, both tasked primarily with building China's domestic economy.

In the West, NGOs like Oxfam, Save the Children, and Bread for the World lobby parliaments to attach earmarks to the aid budget reflecting their changing concerns. Unions and businesses push to ensure that a large portion of the goods and services purchased by aid budgets continue to be home-grown. Chinese citizens donated thousands of Chinese renminbi (translated as "the people's money") to the Chinese Red Cross after the Christmas 2004 tsunami tragedy in Southeast Asia.[27] But compared with the West and even Japan, societal interest groups figure much less as a factor in shaping China's aid. Private and semi-private commercial inter-ests are a growing factor in the determination of Chinese assistance, particularly at the provincial levels. However, in China state interests (political, commercial, and bureaucratic) overwhelm the societal influences on aid.

The third set of pressures on aid policy in any country comes from the global aid regime. In 1960, in its fashionable Paris neighborhood not far from the Eiffel Tower, the OECD established the Development Assistance Committee (DAC) to help monitor and negotiate rules on aid. As with regimes that set rules and norms in other areas – international finance, arms control, or global climate change, for example – the aid regime is marked by largely voluntary rules and norms that have evolved to foster cooperation and shared standards. The DAC has worked to set norms of transparency and regular reporting, targets for aid and standardized definitions, and has built a consensus on mutual learning, external review, and best practices for aid effectiveness.

The aid regime is also influenced by changing ideas about development: the mix of foreign and domestic inputs that is believed to produce growth, reduce poverty, enhance equity and the broad-based sustainability of change. Here, Chinese ideas provide a significant contrast with ideas in the West. In 2004, Joshua Cooper Ramo, former foreign editor at *Time* magazine and a talented pilot (the holder of two US air speed records), coined the term "Beijing Consensus" in a trenchant analysis of China's development ideas.[28] Ramo argued that China's mix of pragmatism and idealism was an alternative model, rivaling the central tenets of a "Washington Consensus" rooted in the ideas championed by Margaret Thatcher and Ronald Reagan.

The comparative performance of China, with its five-year plans and emphasis on experimentation rather than certainties, stands as a rebuke to the Washington Consensus policies. Liberalization, privatization, and structural adjustment never quite achieved legitimacy as a development model in Africa, even before the world's faith in the market was severely tested in the global economic crisis that began in late 2008. Today's Chinese model is still a government-guided model, even if it now resembles the government guidance of Singapore, Taiwan, or Japan at an earlier date more than it does the heavy hand of Mao Zedong. China's variety of experiences make me hesitate to agree with Joshua Ramo that China has one identifiable model today. But this is not the first time developing countries have been attracted by what they saw as China's development model, as we shall see in the next chapter.

Issues and Themes

This book brings together issues and themes that first engaged me as a young American teaching English in Asia, and later as a graduate student doing surveys in rice-growing villages of West Africa. Traveling by lumbering public buses, and watching white Land Cruisers pass at odd intervals, each marked by the name of a donor or a relief agency, I would ponder the contrasts: why are some countries so rich and some so poor? When does aid help and when might it make things worse? Nearly thirty years later, these questions continue to motivate me as a scholar, professor, and development practitioner, and I have added others: Why do countries give aid? What effect does aid have on growth, governance, and poverty?

No matter how one approaches China's engagement in Africa, the contrast between China's rise and the poverty of much of Africa is never far from the surface. This book is not about that contrast, although it frames the study much as Mount Kilimanjaro frames the landscape of Tanzania's border region. China's rise *does* enter into the question of China's aid, of course. The Chinese model has attracted other nations since the time of the founding of the People's Republic. The possibility of links between China's domestic experience and its economic embrace of Africa explain much of the warm welcome Chinese leaders have received across much of Africa, and the country's credibility as a development partner and a giver of aid. Yet the concerns are also widespread, and not just in Africa or the West.

Why does China give aid? The conventional wisdom is: to get access to resources. Yet as I hope this book will make clear, this is *at best* a partial and misleading answer. Fundamentally, foreign aid is a tool of foreign policy. China is not an exception. All donors give aid for a variety of political, commercial, and moral reasons. Understanding the balance between these motives gives us one of the keys to unlock the black box of China's aid program.

The following pages scroll back to the program's origins and then move forward to document major policy shifts. Under China's leader Mao Zedong, aid helped the Communist Party in Beijing to overcome the continued international influence of its rival, the Kuomintang, which governed the breakaway province of Taiwan. Their civil war became a diplomatic war, fought in the halls of ministries of foreign affairs across the third world. Ideology and political strategy were then the primary thrusts behind China's extensive aid program.

Yet, as I hope Chapters 2 and 3 will make clear, after Mao died China's aid and economic engagement in Africa were shaped by two new (but related) influences. First among these was *its own experience as an aid recipient* and host to foreign investment. After China opened to the outside world and began to receive aid and investment from the West, and particularly from Japan, Chinese policymakers learned a new model of how aid could also serve China's own development goals. The second influence was a pattern of state-sponsored engagement more characteristic of *the East Asian developmental state* than of a communist dictatorship.

Chalmers Johnson, formerly of the University of California, Berkeley, coined the term "developmental state" in 1982 to describe Japan's once meteoric rise.[29] It has since been applied across East Asia to describe late-industrializing states that set clear development goals and use a wide array of instruments (particularly finance) to nurture their companies, but at the same time push and pull them to meet those goals. China's growing number of state-sponsored tools for external economic engagement, including aid, began to reflect this familiar regional model, particularly in the recent push to "go global" or "walk out." Chapters 4, 5, and 6 explain how Chinese aid works, and answer the question of how much aid China gives to Africa.

What is China actually doing in its aid program and its developmental state embrace of Africa? What will China's new wave of aid and economic cooperation mean for African development? The book tackles these questions in Chapters 7 through 11. Critics have laid serious charges at China's door: their aid and engagement in Africa "stifles progress," and hurts ordinary citizens. Is this true?

The focus of Chapters 7 and 8 is industry: will China catalyze or crush African manufacturing? Some of China's African factories began as aid projects and became joint ventures. Later, using aid and other tools, the Chinese state pushed its manufacturers to move offshore to invest in almost every country in Africa at a record pace. But China's role here illustrates the difficult paradox at the heart of Africa's industrialization challenge, particularly in the "easy" sectors of leather, auto parts, and textiles profiled in these chapters. Could Chinese factories pushed by Beijing serve as catalysts for Africa's long-delayed industrial transition? Or will the trade liberalization that allowed Chinese exporters easy access to the markets of Africa create fatal competition for African factories?

Agriculture, the subject of Chapters 9 and 10, was the foundation of China's own development, and it is where most of Africa's poor still currently live on the margins of subsistence. The Chinese state, its companies, and even private Chinese farmers are intensely engaged in rural Africa. Chinese multinational seed companies see Africa as a new frontier, while Chinese volunteers are building small-scale Chinese-style rice paddies and fish ponds in hundreds of villages. Aid mixes with investment in ways that excite African leaders, who view their vast lands as another untapped resource, but deeply worry critics.

Chapter 11 focuses directly on the myths and realities behind the idea that China is a "rogue donor." Does China's non-interference policy provide cover for pariah regimes in Sudan and Zimbabwe? Has China's growing presence in Africa worsened efforts to build good governance, improve human rights and reduce corruption? Are the Chinese leading a "race to the bottom" in social and environmental issues? Does their active support for Chinese business present unfair competition? The answers to these questions are bound to surprise some readers. Taken aback by the wave of criticism and fear that greeted their rapidly growing visibility in Africa, Chinese leaders have begun to actively debate and adjust their engagement. Still, China is unlikely to move toward linking aid to governance or human rights, or to pull back quickly from business practices that long characterized investment from the West and Japan. What will this mean for Africa's traditional partners? Will developing countries be able to use Chinese engagement as leverage in building new relationships with other donors? Will the traditional donors change? Who will blink first?[30]

Approaches and Analysis

This book responds to the lack of systematic analysis of China's aid and state-sponsored economic cooperation activities in Africa. Anyone seeking to understand this topic faces a daunting challenge. As I have noted, the

Chinese do not publish any official reports, figures, or evaluations of their aid, although they are more open about their overall economic cooperation. Chinese scholars have made some progress in describing the operations of the aid program and some of the reforms over the past few decades, but the scarcity of funding for fieldwork means that most Chinese scholars have relied on information made available to them in Beijing.

Journalists have given us quick sketches, but these impressions are often very partial, and sometimes, even in the best newspapers, surprisingly wrong. Chinese journalists do not enjoy freedom of the press. Other journalists are more balanced in their presentation, but lack the background to distinguish between foreign aid and the broader range of economic cooperation activities sponsored by China's developmental state. Such a differentiation is important if we are going to understand how China operates as a donor, and how Chinese aid and economic cooperation affect development.

I have used two complementary approaches to try to understand the impact of China's aid and state-sponsored economic engagement. First, I have done fieldwork in Africa – multiple times. I did field research across Africa: in countries where China's presence was longstanding (Tanzania and Zambia), in resource-rich states (Zimbabwe and Nigeria), in countries recovering from war (Sierra Leone and Mozambique) and in high-performing countries with better governance (Mauritius and South Africa). The book also draws on my earlier field research on Chinese aid and the influence of Chinese business networks. I have spent time at the sites of dozens of Chinese projects and investments (old and new), interviewed Chinese and African officials and Chinese aid workers, and spoken with many ordinary Africans. To piece together the history of China's early engagement, I sifted through the dusty, discarded files of the ministries who were China's partners on these projects. To track the changes in China's aid, I traveled several times to Beijing, spoke to Chinese aid officials there, and combed through the thin annual reports on aid from China's Ministry of Commerce[31] and the small but growing Chinese literature on aid.

But the research does not depend only on case studies and fieldwork. My second approach uses a collection of data on Chinese aid assembled by a team of research assistants to draw a broad portrait of the scope of aid in Africa over time and to test some of the common assumptions about Chinese aid. The data and case study evidence allow me to dispel many of the myths:

the Chinese are *not* new donors in Africa. They did *not* prove an unreliable partner, "dumping" Africa after Mao died, returning only as their resource hunger grew. Their aid program is certainly large and growing but not enormous. They are undoubtedly interested in gaining access to Africa's petroleum, minerals, and other natural resources but there is little evidence that aid is offered exclusively, or even primarily, for that purpose. From the evidence, China's aid does *not* seem to be particularly "toxic"; the Chinese do not seem to make governance worse, and although it is popularly believed that aid comes with "no strings attached," economic engagement usually *does* come with conditions, some of it even (indirectly) governance-related.

In the final analysis, the developmental impact of Chinese aid and economic cooperation will almost certainly vary country by country and sector by sector. The deciding factor in each case is likely *not* to be China, but individual African countries and their governments. In relatively well-governed, stable countries, Chinese aid and investment are likely to provide net gains. Democratic pressures and civil society watchdogs will push to ensure that costs of competition or displacement are spread across society, and governments with an eye on the ballot box will be choosier when presented with the options for engagement offered by Beijing. In highly corrupt, unstable, authoritarian countries where governments are far less accountable, China's engagement (like that of any other country) is much less likely to produce broad gains.

Like the Japanese, the Chinese believe that the best antidote to conflict and instability is sustained economic development. This is the strategy they adopted at home, and this is the theme of China's current strategic engagement in Africa. They also believe that Africans will accept that aid can be offered in a frank exchange, as part of a relationship of mutual benefit. This makes aid less a one-way offering of alms (as Chinese premier Zhou Enlai explained in 1964), and more a practical investment in a mutually profitable future. This is the promise. The book examines just how well Chinese aid and economic cooperation live up to this promise, and what the growing prominence of China might mean for Africa and its traditional development partners in the West.

CHAPTER I

Missionaries and Maoists: How China's Aid Moved from "Red" to "Expert"

The imperialist countries of the West...are plundering the recipient countries in the name of "aid."   *Xinhua*, February 6, 1968

Foreign aid as we in the West know it today has its origins in the missionary outposts of the Victorian age and the development and welfare funds set up in the last decades of the colonial period. As a child, I heard stories of my mother's missionary aunt Bethel, who became a doctor and married an ornithologist. The two of them headed to the Himalayan foothills of northern India to teach, deliver medical care, and (in his case) study birds. In the 1950s, on a birding holiday, Bethel and her husband Robert trekked through Nepal – at the time a Shangri-La off limits to most visitors. The king of Nepal later invited the two intrepid missionaries to move to the Kathmandu Valley and build Nepal's first Western hospital.[1] Other missionaries built secondary schools and even colleges. Fourah Bay College, established in 1827 as an Anglican missionary school, became the nucleus of the University of Sierra Leone, West Africa's first Western-style university. South Africa's University of Fort Hare was founded by missionaries as the South African Native College in 1916.

Hospitals, clinics, schools, and orphanages were typical missionary activities. The first colonial development programs were similar. In 1923 the

French belatedly began programs to improve health care and hygiene in their African colonies. They built clinics and maternity centers and bought ambulances. In Britain, the hotly contested Colonial Development Act of 1929 broke with the tradition that colonies needed to be completely self-financing. Britain set up a fund to finance equipment imports and economic growth projects in agriculture, railways and roads, electricity, and mineral resources.[2]

Britain increased the pot of money in the 1940 Colonial Development and Welfare Act, and added social services to the list of fundable projects. The colony of Mauritius used a grant to eradicate malaria in the 1950s. Montserrat built hurricane-resistant housing. Other colonies established water supply and sanitation systems. These belated efforts did little to erase the stain of an unwelcome colonial domination. Yet it is interesting that, on average, today's developing countries that were once British colonies are ahead of their peers on economic and social indicators, something that may in part reflect this belated investment.[3] When World War II ended, the age of colonial empires and missionaries was in its twilight. A decade later, the charitable thrust behind the missionary activity was transformed in the rise of NGOs. The funds set up by the colonial development and welfare acts became the nucleus of bilateral foreign aid. These colonial and missionary origins still influence aid from much of the West today.

China's foreign aid has different origins. The Chinese are fond of recounting how their Ming Dynasty fleet sailed to the coast of East Africa several times between 1418 and 1433 under the direction of Muslim admiral Zheng He. Chinese archives record this as a truly mighty fleet, with some 28,000 men and sixty-three vessels, each at least six times larger than the three small ships sailed by Colombus. The Chinese did not colonize the lands of Africa. As a Chinese diplomat said, they took "not an inch of land, not a slave, but a giraffe for the emperor to admire." The doctors and pharmacists carried on each of Zheng He's giant ships also took back African herbs and local medicinal compounds, perhaps to combat a series of epidemics raging in China at that time.[4]

In a modern twist on the Zheng He story, in 2002 Chinese experts traveled to the ancient town of Lamu on an island off the coast of Kenya and "confirmed" the claim of a Kenyan teenager, Mwamaka Sharifu Lali ("Chinese Girl"), that she was descended from fifteenth-century Chinese sailors who probably swam to Lamu from a shipwreck in the archipelago.[5] The Chinese embassy in Nairobi gave Mwamaka a trip to her "ancestral homeland" in China, and offered her a scholarship to study medicine.

As an empire, China evolved a tribute system: a long tradition of exchanges with smaller nations in its sphere of influence. Visiting missions from the kingdom of Siam or Malacca would affirm the dominance of the emperor by ritual kowtowing. They would pay nominal tribute to him, and be rewarded with generous gifts and the right to trade.[6] These diplomatic gifts foreshadow the practices today. For most recipients, Chinese aid is institutionalized through a bureaucratic planning process. But "gifts" of aid packages are frequently announced along with other agreements during the visits of high-level Chinese dignitaries to developing countries, or the visits of those leaders to Beijing.

The pageantry of China's aid announcements may reflect these early diplomatic customs. But the content of Chinese aid and the way their aid is delivered also differ from the West, for at least four reasons. First, China's aid is still shaped by a *foreign policy framework* established in the 1950s. In particular, the principle of "non-interference in internal affairs" created a foreign policy straitjacket that for better or for worse still restrains aid policy.

Second, Chinese aid follows a distinctly different set of *core ideas about development*. As we shall see in this chapter, although China was for decades a revolutionary communist country, the economic development assumptions behind its aid were at first surprisingly similar to those backing aid from the West. This changed in the 1970s. The West began to doubt the notion that its experience could serve as a model, and embarked on a long road of continually rethinking and reinventing foreign aid. After the death of Mao Zedong in 1976, the defeat of his wife Jiang Qing's radical "Gang of Four," and the triumph of a more practical strategy at home, China's aid changed, but in ways that for the most part diverged sharply from the evolving notions of aid in the West.

Third, China is a developing country and an aid recipient itself. After 1978, China's aid and economic engagement with the developing world gradually began to *mirror the pattern* of the West, and particularly Japan's early commercial engagement with China. Today in Africa, China is repeating many of the practices and the kind of deals it forged with Japan and the West in its own initial turn to the market. It has swapped places.

Fourth, China's aid – like Japan's – is influenced by a regional pattern: the *developmental state*. Over time, foreign aid has become one tool in a range of economic instruments adeptly managed by China's state leaders to boost China's exports *and* its own development. Aid and other benefits are used not only to support the development of recipients, but to foster trade, help build competitive Chinese multinational corporations, and encourage the upgrading of China's own domestic firms.

Our view of China today is of an increasingly prosperous country, with a foreign reserve arsenal of some two trillion dollars. A global economic crisis is clawing a number of African countries back from the economic progress they made earlier in the decade. Should we be critical of China's claim that its aid should foster *mutual* benefit and its economic engagement with Africa be "win-win"? Shouldn't aid from such a powerhouse be mainly altruistic, "alms for the poor"?

The short answer to this is no. As a country with deep poverty still clustered outside the shining cities of Shanghai and Shenzhen, China would be irresponsible to set aside large amounts of funding for the sole benefit of other countries, many with higher income levels. Furthermore, the positioning of concessional finance as part of a package of engagement that is frankly about benefits for China as well as the recipient, creates a different set of expectations. It avoids the paternalism that has come to characterize aid from the West, an attitude that once provoked a bitter critique from Ugandan President Yoweri Museveni: "I have a real problem with this paternalistic arrangement of the so-called 'donor' and 'beggar' relationship."[7]

It also avoids the hypocrisy that inevitably accompanies aid when the aspect of mutual benefit is papered over. For example, the US Agency for International Development routinely justifies its budget requests to Congress by showing the high percentage of aid that comes back as benefits for America. At the same time, it tries to convince NGO critics that aid is really about reducing poverty. That said, China's aid needs to be evaluated on the same terms as it is given: does it foster *mutual* benefit?

In this chapter, we start by looking in the mirror: what was the West doing as it established foreign aid as a new instrument of foreign policy and economic engagement? What did *our* aid look like in the beginning? This provides the foil for what was then a very different model of aid, unfolding in China.

Aid from the West

Aid to developing countries became an institution as World War II was ending. In July 1944, a group of forty-four nations (including twenty-four from Latin America and the Caribbean, Africa, and Asia) met in the high-ceilinged, wood-paneled buildings of the Mount Washington Hotel in the New Hampshire resort of Bretton Woods to design a multilateral postwar financial architecture. Today, you can visit Bretton Woods and stay in the same room where British economist John Maynard Keynes lay awake at night, thinking about his plan to construct a system that would provide a lender of last resort, a kind of group insurance against another Great Depression (the International Monetary Fund) and a source of capital for reconstruction and development (the International Bank for Reconstruction and Development, or "World Bank").

European empires collapsed across Africa in the years after World War II. The Mau Mau insurgency struck at British interests in Kenya for most of the 1950s. The French faced rebellions in Algeria, Tunisia, Morocco, and Madagascar. In a 1960 speech to the apartheid South African parliament, British Prime Minister Harold Macmillan warned: "The wind of change is blowing through this continent." Belgium abruptly granted independence to the Congo in 1960; the Portuguese fought until 1974 to hang on to their colonies.

As the era of colonialism was beginning to give way to the eras of independence and the Cold War, the two Bretton Woods institutions, the World Bank and the International Monetary Fund, opened their doors in downtown Washington DC. Though the wealthy countries stacked decision-making to ensure that the more money a member country provided, the more votes it had, these new institutions were expressly constructed to foster trade, capital flows, growth, and economic development.

Bilateral aid was slower to emerge. In his 1949 inaugural address, US President Harry Truman framed the need to give assistance to the emerging nations as part of the battle between communism and democracy, a center-piece of his Cold War strategy. This aid would combine technical assistance and capital investment with the aim of increasing industrial activity and boosting production. "Greater production is the key to prosperity and peace,"

Truman said, "and the key to greater production is a wider and more vigorous application of modern scientific and technical knowledge."[8]

Professor Carl Eicher, an expert on foreign aid, once commented that in the 1950s a "big question about foreign aid" was "how to prove to rich countries that they would benefit from giving to the poor."[9] Truman tackled this by pointing out to a perhaps skeptical audience that: "All countries, including our own, will greatly benefit from a constructive program for the better use of the world's human and natural resources. Experience shows that our commerce with other countries expands as they progress industrially and economically."[10] Congress passed the Act for International Development in 1950, and the Mutual Security Act in 1952, establishing the forerunners of today's Agency for International Development. A decade later, Germany, France, the United Kingdom, Canada, and Japan had also established government agencies for aid.

In the 1950s and early 1960s, the West's ideas about aid were relatively simple. The experience of industrialized countries seemed to be a useful model. The rest of the world could modernize relatively quickly by building roads and installing electricity, importing Western technology, factory equipment, tractors, and seeds. Truman's 1949 "Point Four" speech reflected the experts' understanding: foreign aid should boost production and scientific knowledge, and fill local "gaps" of savings and foreign exchange.[11]

Walter W. Rostow, the era's most prominent development economist, charted five "stages of economic growth" in his 1960 book *The Stages of Economic Growth: A Non-Communist Manifesto*. Aid could accelerate progress in basic infrastructure, large-scale agriculture, and industry, enabling countries to reach "take-off" (Rostow's stage three). Delivering aid as loans was not seen as problematic: debt would be repaid with the future earnings from investments, much as Australia and the Americas had repaid the nineteenth-century European loans that built their railroads.

These ideas resonated across Africa. Even before colonialism wound down, Northern Rhodesia (Zambia) borrowed more than $40 million from the World Bank to build railroads and highways. Nigeria took out a loan of $80 million to build a hydropower dam on the Niger River at Kainji Island. In Liberia, where most farmers used small knives and machetes to harvest their grain, dodging burnt stumps and stepping over the small mounds where they had planted cassava and pumpkin, a government postage stamp offered a vision of progress: a long line of enormous combine harvesters moving in unison across a field of amber grain, silhouetted against a bright blue African sky.

If Cold War aid from the West was partly intended to forestall communist revolutions in poor countries, it seemed by the mid-1960s to be failing. Large-scale urban industrialization with Western technologies, mining, plantations, and tractors in rural areas added little employment. The focus on rapid growth, defended by President John F. Kennedy, who said "a rising tide lifts all boats," was widely critiqued as failing to "trickle down" to the poor. Revolutionary leaders and insurgencies continued to mount, and most of them (most noticeably in Vietnam) were camped in the countryside, drawing recruits from the poorest of the rural poor.

Marxist critics argued that aid fitted into a capitalist system that deliberately created inequality and made developing countries dependent on the West. The prosperity of the West (and Japan) was built through exploitation of the poor, they charged. Brazilian economist Theotonio dos Santos famously dismissed aid as merely "filling up the holes" that the West itself created.[12] But Marxist revolutions were not the only response. From Brazil to Nigeria, the inequality and insecurity generated by rapid growth helped foment military coups, and in the case of Nigeria, the Biafran civil war. And in Iran, where I hitchhiked with a friend in the autumn of 1977, writing home about the striking contrast between the medieval, mud-walled villages and the urban sophistication of Tehran, rapid change and insecurity helped bring Islamic fundamentalism to power.

The West responded by shifting the focus of aid. Funding for the green revolution in agriculture soared, partly in the hope that investing in rural areas might forestall a "red" revolution. In 1973, the US Congress passed the "New Directions" legislation, an act requiring the country's official aid to change emphasis from growth to poverty and basic human needs. The World Bank began to reorient its focus away from large-scale infrastructure and factories, and toward integrated rural development (IRD) programs: complicated attempts to simultaneously address basic needs and improve farm incomes. World Bank loans for IRD programs grew at an astonishing 50 percent *annually* between 1968 and 1979. The Bank committed $19 billion to IRD projects worldwide from 1976 to 1988.[13] Across Africa, Western donors adopted the IRD model, essentially taking responsibility for a province or a district, drawing lines across each country's geography in a faint echo of the carving up of Africa by the European colonial powers at the Berlin Conference of 1885.

At the same time, programs for more "appropriate" intermediate technology proliferated. The West stopped sending tractors and began to fund ox plows. They stopped building teaching hospitals in African universities and began to fund NGOs to deliver health care directly to the poor. In many African countries, NGOs eventually were managing 40 to 50 percent of health facilities.[14]

Not everyone favored this change. Roger Darling, a high-level USAID official, warned in a 1978 op-ed in the *Washington Post* that the "superficial" critique of " 'trickle down' development policy and its replacement with the 'human needs' strategy" was "a tragic shift from encouraging Third World productivity to merely providing welfare services." This is not going to solve poverty, he concluded: "it expands it." A year later, William Cotter, at the time head of the African–American Institute, and later president of Colby College, charged that the focus on basic needs dominated foreign aid to the extent that "projects intended to build the institutions or infrastructures of developing countries are now undertaken surreptitiously, if at all."[15]

Red Sun Rising

The Cold War also shaped foreign policy and aid in the People's Republic of China (PRC). For nearly four years after the defeat of Japan in World War II, a civil war continued to rage in China. In 1949, Mao Zedong and the communist People's Liberation Army pushed Chiang Kai-shek's People's Party (Kuomintang) and the government of the Republic of China (ROC) into retreat on the island of Taiwan. The two sides, PRC and ROC, faced each other in an undeclared truce across the Gulf of Taiwan, which after 1950 was patrolled by the US Seventh Fleet. Although Britain and the Nordic countries (Sweden, Finland, Norway, Denmark) recognized the new government in Beijing, the United States refused.

In 1950, North Korea invaded the South, and the United Nations Security Council authorized troops to help South Korean President Syngman Rhee push the Northern military back across the border. Chinese "volunteers" camped on the edge of the Yalu River on the border with North Korea moved into Korea to fight on the side of the North. The US imposed a total economic embargo on the PRC, an embargo that lasted more than twenty years. China's aid program thus began in an ad hoc fashion in 1950 with the transfer of grain, medicine, cotton, and other industrial materials to North Korea during the war. Support for socialist countries and Marxist independence movements marked the first years of China's aid, but China also sent aid to most of the other countries on its long borders (including non-socialist Nepal).[16]

China's suave premier Zhou Enlai introduced the "Five Principles of Peaceful Coexistence" during negotiations with India over the Tibet issue, in 1954:

1. mutual respect for sovereignty and territorial integrity
2. mutual non-aggression
3. non-interference in each other's internal affairs
4. equality and mutual benefit
5. peaceful coexistence

A year later, Zhou joined Indonesian President Achmed Sukarno, Indian Prime Minister Jawaharlal Nehru, Egyptian President Gamal Abdel Nasser, and several dozen new African and Asian leaders in the art deco hill town of Bandung, Indonesia, for the Afro-Asian People's Solidarity Conference. Representing half the world's population, surrounded by the spectacular volcanoes of Java's central highlands, they adopted the principles of peaceful coexistence as the foundation of the non-aligned movement. (This was also the moment when French demographer Alfred Sauvy's 1952 expression *tiers monde* or "third world" took root.)

More than half a century later, Chinese leaders still point to these principles as the bedrock of their foreign policy and their aid strategy. "Equality and mutual benefit" are reflected today in Chinese leaders' frequent insistence that aid is a partnership, not a one-way transfer of charity. An overriding concern with the "one-China policy" is reflected in the principle of state sovereignty ("non-interference in each other's internal affairs"). Diplomatic recognition of the Republic of China, still holding out in Taiwan, is seen as interference in an internal dispute. These long-standing principles and China's own experience of more than twenty years under a US economic embargo also help explain the Chinese resistance to calls by the West that they impose political conditions on their aid, or that they support economic sanctions. (Today, of course, non-interference is also convenient for business in places such as Zimbabwe or Sudan.)

From Mau Mau to Mao

Colonialism ended suddenly in Africa, violently in some places, such as Kenya, where the Mau Mau rebellion tried to force European rulers to step down. China sent modest amounts of covert funding, materials, and advisers to several independence movements. Some, such as Robert Mugabe's Zimbabwe African National Union (ZANU), received more. But for its first official aid project in sub-Saharan Africa, China built a cigarette and match factory just outside Conakry, the capital of Guinea.

Guinea was one of only fourteen sub-Saharan African countries to forge diplomatic ties with the People's Republic of China immediately after independence. The others either followed the lead of the United States and recognized the Republic of China in Taipei, or were too distracted by other issues to make a decision right away. Guinea's first president, Sékou Touré, had famously spurned French President De Gaulle's offer to join the other Francophone colonies in a semi-independence that retained a close association with France. In its February 16, 1959 issue, *Time* magazine reported what happened next:[7]

> Paris announced that all French functionaries would be withdrawn within two months. Touré's brash reply: Remove them in eight days. While French shopkeepers and businessmen stayed on, 350 officials and their families began moving out. French justice stopped. A ship heading for Guinea with a carload of rice went to the Ivory Coast instead. Radio Conakry temporarily went off the air. The Guineans charged that the departing French were taking everything – medical supplies, official records, air conditioners, even electric wiring.
>
> The governor's palace was being stripped when Guineans found that some of the furniture that was to be shipped to France actually belonged to Guinea. Thereupon a comic opera, two-way traffic began at the palace, with the French hauling things out and the Guineans hauling things in. When Touré and his willowy second wife (daughter of a French father and a Malinké mother) moved into the palace, they did not even have a telephone.

Eager to replace French interests in the bauxite-rich former colony, the United States and the Soviet Union both offered Sékou Touré aid. While

Touré skillfully played the two superpowers against each other, Beijing quietly made Guinea an offer of an interest-free loan of RMB 100 million (about $25 million) in 1960.[18] The agreement between the two countries stipulated that Chinese advisers would live in Guinea at a standard "not exceeding that of personnel of the same rank in the Republic of Guinea," a swipe aimed at both the Soviets and the Americans, whose personnel would not have dreamed of living like a local official in Africa.[19] When Sékou Touré visited Beijing, he was greeted like a hero. More than 200,000 people were mobilized in Tiananmen Square to welcome him.[20]

China's first official aid recipients in Africa reflected ideological interests. Along with Sékou Touré in Guinea, socialist leaders took power in Ghana (Kwame Nkrumah) and Mali (Modibo Keita) and both countries promptly received aid commitments from China. Yet as more countries won independence in the 1960s, it became clear that Beijing's goals in Africa were larger than simple support of socialist or revolutionary movements.

First, aid figured in the struggle to convince each new government to recognize Beijing as "China" instead of Taipei. With the help of the United States, Taipei was also actively courting Africa's newly independent countries in the 1960s. Second, ideological differences and concern about Soviet dominance had pushed Beijing to break from Moscow in the early 1960s. The new countries of Africa and the non-aligned world became even more important to Chinese diplomacy as the country tried to balance between Moscow and Washington in a bipolar world.

Western diplomats ignored China at first as they focused on the Soviet Union's activities in Africa. Then Chinese premier Zhou Enlai embarked on a very visible tour of ten independent African countries between December 1963 and February 1964. A wave of alarm rose across the West.[21] In Ghana, Zhou Enlai announced eight principles of Chinese foreign aid.[22] It would be based on equality, mutual benefit, and respect for the sovereignty of the host (the principles of peaceful coexistence). Loans would be non-conditional, interest-free, or low-interest, and easily rescheduled. Projects would use high-quality materials, have quick results, and boost self-reliance. Chinese experts would transfer their expertise "fully" and live at the standard of local counterparts. In the wake of the tour, China committed a total of nearly $120 million in aid to Congo-Brazzaville, Ghana, Kenya, Mali, and

Tanzania. Chinese diplomats gradually began to succeed in their courtship of more conservative countries such as Kenya and Nigeria.

While the West had an image of the future that aid ought to create, China was the first *developing* country to establish an aid program. And after 1949 China was also a socialist country, led by Mao Zedong, an ideological visionary whose goal of a permanent revolution put politics (and never economics) in command. As Chinese aid grew from ad hoc shipments of goods to a permanent feature of foreign policy, China's own development model lurched between a relatively moderate, pragmatic approach and a terrifying, punitive ideology propelled by Mao.

It was perhaps fortunate for Africa that China's first aid programs there were mainly established *after* the disaster of the Great Leap Forward (1958–60). A radical Maoist push to "take off" by establishing collective farms and backyard steel furnaces nearly overnight combined with several years of natural disaster to leave much of rural China denuded of trees and peasants starving. Some *twenty million* Chinese lost their lives in famine. Millions more died during the Cultural Revolution (1966–76). But in between these two extremes, a more pragmatic road prevailed. By and large, China's aid reflected this pragmatism.

After decades of civil war and Japanese occupation, Chinese leaders' first development concerns had been meeting the urgent needs of their exhausted population. At the same time, they wanted to lay the building blocks of a productive, modern socialist economy: "take agriculture as the foundation; industry as the leading edge."

Chinese delegations visiting Africa in the 1960s thought they saw a lot of similarities. Like China a decade earlier, Africa was emerging from "a long period of colonial plunder" and needed to produce food, clothing, and other daily necessities.[23] They recommended a mix of aid to meet "urgent and long-term needs," and offered a balance of technical training and modest turn-key projects in industry and agriculture that could be constructed quickly by Chinese experts and handed over, ready for their recipients to just "turn the key" and start production. They also began to send medical teams.

China's aid program in Guinea set the example. Between 1960 and 1969, the loan paid for the rapid construction of Guinea's first oil-pressing factory (peanut and palm kernel) and a bamboo processing center, funded a cigarette and match factory, built a series of paddy fields for irrigated rice, and a tea plantation. It also paid for two "prestige" projects requested by the Guineans: Conakry's "Freedom" cinema, and a 2,000-seat People's Palace and conference hall. The first thirty-four medical experts arrived in 1967, fanning out into four districts. By then, there were an estimated 3,000 Chinese aid workers in Guinea alone.[24]

"Dragon in the Bush"[25]

In the 1970s, strategic diplomacy remained the chief motivation behind China's aid: wresting diplomatic recognition away from Taiwan and countering the influence of both the West and, in particular, the Soviet Union. By 1973, the Soviet Union was giving aid to twenty African countries, with most of it concentrated on eight countries in strategic regions (the Horn of Africa, the Mediterranean). China spread its aid across thirty African countries, a policy it retains to this day. In all but the same eight Soviet allies above, China gave *more aid* than the USSR.[26] The rapid expansion of aid reflected China's success in winning over Africa's newly independent African countries. Between 1964 and 1971, when votes in the United Nations (organized skillfully by the permanent representative of Tanzania) finally gave Beijing back the seat occupied by Taiwan, China started aid programs in thirteen additional African countries.

The West was rethinking its aid program, moving from a narrow focus on production and infrastructure to direct support for rural development, basic needs, and poverty. Chinese aid operated in isolation from these trends. It continued to reflect China's domestic ideas about development: centrally planned interventions to boost production, health, and infrastructure. China funded state-owned factories in Africa, where skilled technicians from Shanghai's pre-war industries trained Africans to churn out substitutes for imports. Cotton textile mills dominated. Many African countries had been exporting raw cotton (Mali, Sudan, Congo-Brazzaville, Tanzania, Ghana). Chinese-built textile mills allowed them to produce the lengths of printed cloth favored by African women for their *lapas* (wrap-skirts). Medical teams of doctors and paramedics resembled the "bare-foot doctors" in rural China. Chinese construction teams built bridges, roads, power plants, and ports, and always a popular "prestige" project or two: a very visible "Friendship" conference hall, a modern government ministry building, or a stadium named in honor of a friendly president.

The Chinese stressed that their aid was primarily a tool for building self-reliant countries. The Chinese communists had been isolated as they battled Japan during World War II. In 1960 Moscow abruptly cancelled its aid to China and withdrew all technical assistants. This drummed home the message that developing countries such as China needed to rely primarily on themselves. Premier Zhou Enlai pointed this out in a 1964 discussion of Chinese aid: "It is not our intention to make them dependent on us," he explained. They need to "rely mainly on their own efforts."[27] This, said Zhou, will free them from the control of capitalism. And, he finished, this would be of immense help to China in its own effort to build an alternative to global capitalism's sticky embrace.

Learning from Daqing and Dazhai

In the mid-1960s, China's own development model started to veer sharply back to the permanent revolution favored by Mao. Signs of this could be seen in the growing emphasis on regional self-reliance rather than comparative advantage. It could be seen in a resurgence of disdain for economic analysis and the crackdown on private (instead of communal) income-generating activities, such as selling vegetables from a household garden or keeping a family pig. It was reflected in the glorification of "model" workers, industries, and agricultural brigades. And most of all it was symbolized by the boosting of two Chinese development models in a slogan that was repeated incessantly: "In industry, learn from Daqing; in agriculture, learn from Dazhai."

The massive Daqing oilfields lie in the bleak grasslands of northeast China where winter temperatures can plummet to 33 degrees below zero Fahrenheit (minus 36 degrees Celsius). Discovered in the 1950s, the oilfields were in their infancy when Soviet technicians packed their bags and headed back to Moscow. Forty thousand Chinese factory workers and engineers converged on Daqing in the dead of winter to prove that the Chinese could produce their own oil. Daqing produced the famous model worker Wang "Iron Man" Jinxi, a real man who embodied the "revolutionary spirit" of Daqing the way the myth of giant lumberjack Paul Bunyan symbolized the nineteenth-century opening of the frontier forests of North America.

As the *People's Daily* related the well-known tale in 2004,

> Jinxi and his drilling team let housing go and lived in tents, old cowsheds or shacks. Some dug underground shelters to sleep in. Equipment arrived by rail. Without waiting for the cranes or lorries, Wang and his team unloaded 60 tons of drilling equipment themselves. Using their shoulders, crowbars and home-made tools they hauled it across the plain to the oil drilling site. Water pipes for the drill had not been installed so they fetched thousands of gallons from a lake some distance away. Battling against the odds and driven by a common fervour, the men sank Daqing's first well.[28]

Tales of Daqing's fabled model worker were disseminated widely across China to emphasize the virtue of being "red" (an inspired communist) rather than simply "expert." (Today, Daqing exports "Iron Man" machinery, and Wang Jinxi's major legacy may be the selling of his image by China National Petroleum Corporation, which has registered the trademark in its major overseas markets.)

In northwest China's Shanxi province, Mao found a second model: Dazhai. A small production brigade of only eighty-five families, Dazhai was rapidly promoted as an outstanding example of discipline, sacrifice, cooperation, and self-reliance. On an eroded, drought-prone, barren plateau, the 160 able-bodied farmers of Dazhai followed their brigade leader Chen Yongui's call to "Reshape the mountains! Harness the rivers!" They built terraces, filled in gullies, and channeled streams for irrigation. They were said to have pooled their meager belongings, cooked in a communal kitchen, and eschewed the market.

An admiring article in the June 1977 newsletter of the British Society for Anglo-Chinese Understanding (SACU) informed readers: "If any place name is universally known in China today it is Dazhai. All over China, on walls, on posters, above arches, on river banks, a set of five characters proclaim: 'In Agriculture learn from Dazhai.' "[29] Poems celebrated Dazhai's "revolutionary" work spirit:

> Hammers, like battle drums, sound the charge;
> Like fire-crackers welcoming spring is the dynamite's blast,
> Bulldozers roll along with a rumble and roar;
> Spring has come early to these hills.

The farmers of Dazhai probably did work hard and creatively (like Daqing's Iron Man), catching the notice of local Communist Party officials. However, Chinese researchers who studied Dazhai after the fervor of Mao's Cultural Revolution died down found that much of the vaunted model was only possible because of extensive assistance from the government – assistance that would be impossible for other brigades to obtain.[30]

Mao and his supporters used the examples of Dazhai and Daqing again and again when they regained the upper hand in China in 1966, wrenching the country off the more moderate path it had followed since the disaster of the Great Leap Forward. The entire nation plunged into Mao's Great Proletarian Cultural Revolution. The feared teenage Red Guards rampaged through the houses of China's intelligentsia, destroying traditional art, collections of classical literature, and anything Western. The children of educated elites were sent "up to the mountains, down to the countryside" to be re-educated by the peasants. On rural communes and in factories, brutally long hours of work were capped by long evening struggle sessions, a kind of political group therapy that could turn violent at any moment for those with the wrong class background or attitude toward work.

The Cultural Revolution lasted for ten years, although it reached a peak between 1966 and 1969. China remained tightly controlled. Outsiders were allowed very little contact with ordinary Chinese, and few knew the tragedy of the period. The West was immersed in its own intense mobilization. Students were marching against their governments in the streets of Mexico City, Paris, and Washington DC. Mao's little red book, *Thoughts of Chairman Mao*, sold well in college bookstores (I bought a copy myself). How did this violent, painful period affect China's engagement in Africa?

Dazhai in Africa?

Zhou Enlai declared Africa "ripe for revolution" during his tour in 1964, and the Chinese gave material support and advice to guerrilla movements in the African bush. When I first went to Africa in 1983 to begin my research on China's aid, I wondered to what extent the Chinese themselves had tried to influence African countries to adopt their own model, either the radical socialism of the Maoist period, or the more pragmatic "Open Door" that was still relatively new. I found that the Chinese had named one of their rice stations Makali Commune, but made no effort to encourage communal production. In interview after interview, people told me that the Chinese working in their countries spent almost no effort trying to convince people to adopt their model.

One exception might have been in Benin. A successful rice project based on smallholder cultivation was recast into a centrally controlled state farm with "mutual aid teams" as in China.[31] But usually the Chinese were more pragmatic. Philip Snow reported that in 1964 Zhou Enlai advised Ghana's President Kwami Nkrumah to scale down his industrialization plans – they were "too ambitious." In Algeria, Zhou suggested that China was not a model to emulate, but a kind of "reference point."[32] Although during the Cultural Revolution Beijing sent politically mobilized Chinese to meddle in the internal conflicts of some of Africa's new states, this was later repudiated as one of the many mistakes of the "appalling catastrophe" of the Cultural Revolution. When it came to development assistance, the Chinese seem to have observed the principle of non-intervention; they did little lobbying for the Maoist model.

Many African leaders professed to admire China's rural example during the Maoist period. Or perhaps they were simply being canny. The Chinese gave relatively more aid to countries they believed to be fellow travelers on the socialist road: Tanzania, Guinea, and even Sierra Leone, whose President Siaka Stevens "posed," early on in his rule, "as an anti-capitalist," a masquerade he later abandoned.[33] The local *Daily Mail* ran a number of stories reporting calls by senior officials for the country to establish state farms. Siaka Stevens praised communal farming; the Minister of Finance called for a National Agricultural Brigade, which would be the "mobilising force," allowing small-scale farms to be joined in "collective farming units."[34]

Keeping up the socialist charade, after a visit to China, the Minister of Trade and Industry simply took Mao's name out of one popular Chinese slogan and substituted that of Siaka Stevens: "If we listen and practice the teachings of Dr. Stevens, we shall have a revolution of the Tachai [Dazhai] type here," he proclaimed.[35] A senior health education officer who accompanied the minister reported being "moved by the simple technology" people were using in China. He urged the Ministry of Health to follow the Chinese example by using traditional herbs to manufacture medicine locally, and biogas (methane) to provide electricity for rural homes.[36] Sierra Leone ultimately did none of these things. To find China's closest parallel in Africa, we need to look at Tanzania.

Tanzanian President Julius Nyerere visited China thirteen times. In 1967, inspired by Chinese moves toward collective farming and by his own ideas about African socialist traditions, Nyerere established a grand project of socialist cooperatives – *ujamaa* villages – modeled on China's experience. He also hoped that clustering Tanzania's scattered subsistence farmers in villages would enable the government to reach them more easily, transfer technology, and provide electricity and other services. "We are using hoes," Nyerere mused. "If two million farmers in Tanzania could jump from hoe to the oxen plough, it would be a revolution. It would double our living standard, triple our product. This is the kind of thing China is doing."[37]

In 1973, disappointed in the lack of enthusiasm displayed by farmers for the voluntary resettlement, Nyerere's officials began to forcibly move entire households into the *ujamaa* villages, tearing down or burning the huts of those who resisted. Six million people were ultimately relocated to *ujamaa* villages. Within two years agricultural production had plummeted, and food imports increased fivefold. The program was a disaster.[38]

The Maoist model had a different impact on China's aid, however, through the example set by Chinese aid workers and some of their choices. In Maoist China, as researcher Jonathan Unger reported: "the politically moral man or woman was supposed to remain behind to finish up work in the dark even if no one were around to notice it."[39] In their African projects, the Chinese tried to encourage Ministry of Agriculture technicians to disregard their fixed ideas about work they considered beneath them. Chinese experts jumped into the muddy rice paddies beside local farmers, and took turns scaring away birds, an activity normally done by children.

A local farmer told me how he was inspired to follow the example of the Chinese, who worked in the paddy fields by lantern late into the night. "You see the Chinese man there [in the fields] and you come." Once a visiting member of parliament came to consult a Chinese doctor and was surprised to find him scrubbing the floor of the office. While the World Bank recruited chiefs for its integrated agricultural development projects, the Chinese asked to work only with "peasant" farmers.[40] However, the mobilization spirit of the Cultural Revolution reached its zenith in China's most audacious achievement in Africa: the Tanzania–Zambia railway.

Tazara: The Tan-Zam Railway

Tanzania and Zambia may be China's oldest and closest friends in sub-Saharan Africa. Knit together by a long shared border, the two countries were each led for decades by charismatic African socialists who bequeathed them legacies of stability, peace, and broad-based poverty.

At the height of the chaos of the Cultural Revolution, China's premier Zhou Enlai offered to build Africa's longest railway, nearly 2000 kilometers, stretching from the copper mines of land-locked Zambia through Tanzania to the sea.[41] The enormous and costly railway project had been envisioned by Cecil Rhodes in the late nineteenth century, and briefly considered by the British colonialists half a decade later. In the lead up to independence, the man who would become Zambia's first president, Kenneth Kaunda, called again for the railway to be built; it was rejected as infeasible by a World Bank mission. Although a consortium of British and Canadian firms disagreed, they were unable to raise financing for the project. Germany also declined.

In 1967, Tanzania, Zambia, and China signed off on the project, to widespread skepticism. Construction began in 1970, finishing in 1975, two years ahead of schedule. This enormous railway line, with ten kilometers of tunnels and 300 bridges, still dwarfs any other infrastructure project to date in China's current wave of economic engagement in Africa. For decades afterwards the world knew of China's aid program through the Tan-Zam railway. Many were surprised to learn that China had done anything else in Africa.

In China, the railway project continues to represent the pinnacle of the kind of struggle, hardship, and "glorious achievement" pushed by Mao. The language of sacrifice parallels the tales of Daqing's Iron Man, or the energetic (if over-aided) agricultural brigade at Dazhai. In 2006, China's "Year of Africa," the Chinese media made sure that the history of the Tan-Zam railway was known in every Chinese home. A China Central Television (CCTV) show on Africa and China featured an interview with a veteran of the railway construction: "Sometimes we had to drink the water that we found in the elephants' footprints," he confided to the young interviewer. A journalist from China's official news agency *Xinhua* reported:

> Food was shipped from China, but the half-month voyage meant they were confined to eating dehydrated vegetables. Even soy sauce was a luxury. Sometimes, when supplies arrived, the wheat flour had gone moldy. Living in tents in the wilderness was dangerous too. They always had to check their shoes for snakes before putting them on in the morning. At night they could hear lions roaring outside.[42]

The enormous demands of the railway – with close to 16,000 Chinese technicians (at the peak), dozens of ministry bureaus, many shiploads of materials and equipment – added additional pressure to China's aid system. In 1972, Chinese teams were building close to 100 different turn-key aid projects around the world. China had committed aid to seven countries in Asia, six in the Middle East, three in Latin America, and twenty-nine in Africa by 1973. In a handful of countries where China had offered zero-interest loans to develop projects, the offer sat unused while leaders debated the costs and benefits of engaging more closely with the communist Chinese. But particularly in Africa, the storm of activity made the foreign aid work "more and more arduous," as a Chinese report admitted.[43]

Rethinking Aid

Aid was a surprisingly central focus for Beijing in these years. Between 1972 and 1977, the State Council sponsored five national conferences on foreign aid. The conclusions of the first conference rang with enthusiasm. The fourth conference in June 1975 came to a more sober conclusion: China's economic capacity was limited. The country should carry out the agreements it had already signed, but "control the amount of new agreements."[44] Largely due to Vietnam, which in those years soaked up 40 percent of China's entire aid budget, between 1967 and 1976 aid averaged around 5 *percent* of government expenditure.[45] The State Council decided that annual spending on aid should not be allowed to exceed a fixed percentage of the national budget. No conference was held in 1976, the year Mao died and China began to emerge from the decade-long nightmare of the Cultural Revolution.

In 1977, after a ritual denunciation of the crimes of the Gang of Four (Mao's wife and three of her revolutionary cronies) and the trouble they created for China's aid program, the fifth conference stressed that China should help its aid recipients "to rely on themselves" in developing their economies.[46] Despite (or perhaps because of) the interference of the Gang of Four, Chinese teams had completed 470 projects in developing countries over seven short years. In 1978, *seventy-four* countries were receiving aid from China, the largest group of them in Africa. By then, China had aid programs in more African countries than did the United States.

For a time in the 1970s, a more confident Third World seemed to be rising. Votes from African countries enabled communist China to finally be seated at the United Nations in 1971. The United States withdrew from Vietnam, and Ho Chi Minh's army marched into Saigon. The Arab embargo of 1973 pushed up the price of oil and demonstrated the muscle of OPEC, the Organization of Petroleum Exporting Countries. Developing countries were even able to muster enough support at the United Nations to pass a resolution calling for a radical "New International Economic Order" (NIEO). The NIEO declared that levels of aid should be raised and given without conditions. Wealthy countries should stop manipulating trade for their own benefit. They should not interfere if a developing country nationalized its own mineral wealth or expropriated foreign investments. All of this was non-binding but it had a lasting impact. The same demands continue to surface today in the critique of globalization.

In China, on the other hand, radicalism was being scaled down. The turmoil of the Cultural Revolution gradually quieted and China began to ratchet up its contacts with the outside world. In 1975, standing under the glowing red star that lit the ceiling of the Great Hall of the People, and making little eye contact with Mao, who sat with the other assembled delegates, Premier Zhou Enlai aimed an elegant silver bullet into Mao's radical ideas. Zhou's speech outlined a plan for "Four Modernizations." Building a modern China would require the country to end its self-imposed autarchy and extreme self-reliance. China would need to import technology from the advanced industrialized world, and pay for this with exports. Mao and Zhou both died in 1976. But Zhou's mission prevailed: China began to open up. And China's aid and engagement with Africa would undergo a dramatic transformation.

CHAPTER 2

Feeling the Stones: Deng Xiaoping's Experiments with Aid

In 1979, when militant Iranian students stormed the US embassy in Tehran taking fifty-three American diplomats hostage, I was living in Taiwan, immersed in intensive Mandarin classes. The American students in Taipei followed the unfolding events, tuning in to the BBC news on our shortwave radios. As the days ticked by for the hostages, the price of oil rose, peaking at the equivalent of $104 a barrel (in 2008 dollars). The world economy contracted sharply from the twin blows of high-priced oil and the decision by the US Federal Reserve to crush America's double-digit inflation by sharply raising interest rates. Demand for commodities dropped; import costs rose. And, one after another, poor countries went to the World Bank and the International Monetary Fund to ask for loans.

Thus began one of the most bitter and lengthiest debates the North and South have yet had over development strategy. In the North, the Bretton Woods economists pointed out that many countries had not managed their economies prudently. Jean Collin, Senegal's French-born Minister of Finance, admitted: "We carried out the First Plan by exhausting our reserves, and since 1965 we have been carrying out the Second Plan by exhausting our treasury."[1] With the treasury exhausted, they turned to international banks, who were only too happy to recycle the petrodollars sitting in the accounts of the oil-rich states. But the debate was also more ideological, about the proper role of the market and the state: the tide was turning sharply against the state.

In 1980, on the steamy coast of Nigeria, African heads of state met to deal with the growing economic crisis by endorsing the Lagos Plan of Action, a report that laid out a regional development strategy based on the principles of the 1974 UN New International Economic Order. The plan assumed that Africa's problems were primarily caused by an exploitative and unjust global economy. The World Bank countered this by commissioning a team headed by prominent development economist Elliot Berg to write *Accelerated Development in Sub-Saharan Africa: An Agenda for Action*. The Berg Report charged that mismanagement was at the root of Africa's underdevelopment: corruption, patronage, inefficient state-owned enterprises, excessive government controls, and borrowing to support subsidies and deficit spending. As we have seen, the World Bank's plan of action became known as *structural adjustment*.

The influential magazine *Foreign Affairs* singled out the Berg Report as one of the five most important books published on Africa over the first seventy-five years of the magazine's history. Its critique of the state-led development model and call for a more market-oriented strategy echoed the conservative revolution launched separately by British Prime Minister Margaret Thatcher and American President Ronald Reagan. Structural adjustment combined stabilization (bringing spending back in line with revenues, and imports back in line with export earnings) with market liberalization. While some form of stabilization has always been necessary for countries (or households) that overspend or run up excessive debt, the turn to the market was driven more by a paradigm shift in ideas.

Critics called the new ideas *neo*-liberalism. In the mid-1840s, the world's strongest industrial power, Britain, had been seized by a similar wave of enthusiasm for free ("liberal") markets. (*The Economist* magazine was founded then as a cheerleader for liberalism.) Pulling down tariffs and quotas on imports allowed Britain to import cheaper wheat from Russia and America, sugar from Cuba and Brazil, and beef from Argentina and New Zealand, paying at first with textiles from the factories in Manchester and later with a wide variety of industrial goods from what was then the world's workshop. The triumph of liberalism mixed with the advantages of being the world's foremost military and imperialist power propelled Britain's industrial revolution forward.

Neo-liberalism did not succeed in igniting similar industrial revolutions in the late twentieth century. The goal of structural adjustment was primarily about getting prices right, not getting production right. Countries were typically required to impose austerity policies (reduce deficits by cutting spending and limiting government wage increases) and liberalize markets (cutting import tariffs, eliminating price controls, and privatizing state-owned enterprises). Shock therapy involved doing all of this at once.

Structural adjustment loans often contained dozens of conditions that borrowers had to meet before they could receive installments of money. In theory, if a country in economic crisis took enough steps to liberalize markets, increase efficiency, and reduce the heavy hand of the state, it would regain access to credit from the World Bank, the IMF, and the rest of the global banks. Because the IMF's medicine was known to be bitter, governments would delay coming to the Fund for help until they were in a crisis with no other option. "Must we starve our children to pay our debts?" Tanzania's former President Nyerere famously asked.

China's turn to the market happened very differently. Cautious about external borrowing and in a region culturally inclined toward high savings rates, Chinese leaders were reluctant to borrow much as they slowly adjusted their own state-led economy. There was no shock therapy, no outside-driven conditionality, and the short, balding, round-faced man who became the face of China's transition – Deng Xiaoping – famously urged the country to forget ideological correctness and experiment, but carefully: *mozhe shitou guo he.* Find your way across the river, he said, but not like Mao, in a great leap. Keep your feet on the bottom and *cross by feeling the stones*.

Shorthand accounts of China's turn to the market portray 1978 as the watershed: before 1978, communism and isolation; afterwards, the market and the open door. Two key moments did mark the beginning and the end of 1978. In March, China announced an ambitious ten-year plan that focused on 120 key modernization projects, including thirty electric power stations, six trunk railroads, eight coal mines, ten new steel plants, five harbors, nine non-ferrous metal complexes, and ten new oil and gas fields. The requirements of meeting these goals, it is now clear, unlocked China's closed doors. In December 1978, at the famous third session of China's eleventh Communist Party Congress, the reformers won a mandate against the rearguard Maoists.

But in reality the transition was not so abrupt. When I first visited China in the summer of 1980, there was little outward sign of reform. Children playing in the parks were dressed in bright colors, but all the adults still wore the drab Mao suits of the past decades. The only glimpse of a private market I saw in a month of wandering around China was a single peasant farmer squatting beside an array of slightly shriveled vegetables laid out on a grubby piece of cloth on a sidewalk in a suburb of Shanghai.

Between 1978 and 1982, the country's reformers were intensely occupied with an ideological struggle. They had to persuade a nation that had barely survived the radicalism of the Maoists to embark on a new transition that seemed to threaten all that the People's Republic stood for. And they were not at all sure where China's aid program would fit in the campaign for the Four Modernizations. Prolonged high-level debates questioned the very idea of having an aid program in the face of China's own desperate needs.[2] This uncertainty about aid changed, not simply because Deng Xiaoping consolidated his power, but because of what China learned from Japan and the West.

An "Ideal Trading Partner"

Today we know China as an industrial powerhouse, the twenty-first-century inheritor of Britain's old label, the workshop of the world. But in the 1970s China was primarily an agrarian economy with immense reserves of natural resources – oil, coal, gold, copper – similar in structure to many African countries today. As China began to emerge from the Cultural Revolution and look outward, outside oil companies and mining firms began to eye China's natural resources with great interest.

Japan was earliest to enter the fabled China market. In 1973, worried about energy security and trying to diversify suppliers after the first oil price shocks, Japan began to import oil from China's Daqing fields where the "Iron Man" (Chapter 1) was still setting a bruising pace of work. Four years later, petroleum made up nearly half of Japanese imports from China.[3] In 1978, after seven years of arduous negotiations, the two countries signed a long-term trade agreement. Both would benefit. Japan offered to use low-interest yen loans to finance the export of $10 billion of its modern plant, industrial technology, and materials, and China agreed to pay by exporting the equivalent in crude oil and coal to Japan.[4]

Japan's arrangement followed an already well-entrenched pattern. In 1958, Japan gave its first concessional yen loan, to India: to develop iron ore mining in the beautiful coastal enclave of Goa, the former Portuguese colony south of Bombay.[5] The three-year credit financed Japanese technology exports, enabling a more advanced mining system to reach far beneath the surface, already at that time pockmarked by mines dug during the colonial period. Japanese equipment was still below Western standards, and concessional financing was designed to counter this by making it more attractive to recipients. India agreed to repay the loan over ten years by exporting two million tons of iron ore annually to Japan. As a specialist on Japan's aid, David Arase, pointed out: "The novel aspect of this so-called Goa formula in economic cooperation was that in exchange for assured access to important raw materials, Japan would provide the necessary equipment, technical training, and financing."[6]

Neither of the two parties worried much about environmental impact or social appraisal. Goa's mining belt would eventually provide 60 percent of India's iron ore exports. Today, the forests are destroyed, hills flattened, and farmers' fields smothered in silt. Yet as a 2003 study by Canada's International Development Research Centre pointed out: "Look beyond the fractured landscape, and you will see that jobs have been created, health and education standards have improved, and money spent locally has brought a measure of material wealth."[7]

These features of Japan's early foray into resource-backed concessional loans were repeated when Japan began engaging in China. China, as a Japanese analyst described it, found it "extremely convenient" to be able to import technology and expertise from Japan, while its "vast natural resources" made China an "ideal trading partner" for Japan.[8] There was no love lost between the two sides, particularly in China, where playing the "Japan card" is guaranteed to arouse an intense and sometimes frightening nationalism. But clearly both sides saw this as a "win-win" strategic partnership. By the end of 1978, Chinese officials had signed seventy-four contracts with Japan to finance turn-key projects that would form the backbone of China's modernization. *All would be repaid in oil.*

More than two decades later, as China faced the dual challenges of promoting its own, often lower-quality, equipment exports, and securing access to needed raw materials, Chinese officials drew on this early experience with Japan. It shaped Chinese perceptions of how relations between two countries at different levels of development might be beneficial to both. Three aspects that characterized the early pattern of this relationship would later be repeated in China's courtship of resource-rich countries in Africa: investment-for-resource swaps, "compensatory" trade, and media hype.

China needed to modernize its own resource base and infrastructure. It is not uncommon on the edge of a remote Chinese village to find an aged, rudimentary wooden structure built over a dark tunnel dug into the side of a mountain. Thousands of these backyard mines were promoted during Mao's push for self-reliance. China's post-Mao leaders were clear about the need to bring in advanced technology and move decisively away from these small-scale, highly inefficient, and dangerous mines. China's *Xinhua* news agency reported in 1980 that China planned to use foreign funds primarily "to boost production and exploit [its own] natural resources."[9]

China used Japan's interest in Daqing oil to build infrastructure for transport and energy, and export capacity. Japan cooperated, out of self-interest. The Ministry of International Trade and Industry (MITI) was the driving force behind Japan's development model. MITI pushed hard to ensure that Japan's first package of foreign aid loans (for which China paid "a peppercorn interest" of 3 percent) was mainly used to build railroads and ports to facilitate the export of China's oil and coal to Japan.[10] Once these were complete, the subsidized yen loans funded hydroelectric and thermal power plants, urban water supply, telecommunications and highways, and fertilizer plants. Japan also agreed to develop China's rich Liuzhuang mining area. Japanese firms prospered, and China's infrastructure expanded to support the demands of the growing economy.

The West followed Japan's lead. As early as 1978, the Los Angeles-based giant engineering corporation Fluor announced that it had signed a preliminary contract to construct an enormous copper mine in China's Jiangxi province. Bethlehem Steel, US Steel, and Germany's Thyssen Company negotiated large iron-ore mining projects. Within the next few years, state-owned China National Coal Development Corporation would sign a joint venture with Armand Hammer's Occidental Petroleum to open China's largest open-pit coal mine. China began selling Daqing oil to the US and Italy in 1979. Four years later, China held its first round of bidding for joint exploration of its offshore oil, awarding contracts to five oil companies from Canada, Britain, Australia, and Brazil. The "scramble for China" was on.

Compensatory trade, or *buchang maoyi*, a new form of barter, also characterized these deals.[11] Compensatory trade allowed companies without access to foreign exchange to import equipment and machinery, deferring payment until they could pay in kind with the goods thus produced. As a Chinese announcer commented: "the construction of an oilfield will be paid for with oil, construction of a coal mine will be paid for with coal, and construction of a factory will be paid for with the products of the factory."[12] A Japanese firm exported sewing machines to China and was paid with 300,000 pairs of pajamas. Beijing presented the Netherlands with a deal where the Dutch would undertake a major port renovation and be paid with exports of Chinese coal. Chinese companies signed more than 140 small and medium-sized contracts for countertrade in 1979 alone.[13] China was negotiating with Romania, Britain, France, Germany, the United States, and Japan to use large-scale compensatory trade arrangements to expand mining and to develop the off-shore petroleum resources that China's self-reliant Daqing technology was unable to exploit.

Finally, a familiar pattern of media attention accompanied the opening of China and opportunities for the West. As the fever of business interest in China rose higher, the media fed the frenzy, much as happened with China's first large deals in Africa in 2006 and 2007. Headlines predicted that Beijing's list of 120 Four Modernizations projects might require finance of $350 or even $600 billion by 1985 (more sober analysts put the figure at $35–50 billion). Western governments began framing attractive financing deals that could help their companies enter the door now being held open by Beijing. France was first in line, signing a somewhat murky, multibillion franc trade deal in late 1978.[14] In a televised interview in Beijing, United States Vice-President Walter Mondale promised Chinese audiences that he would ask Congress to provide $2 billion in preferential US Export Import Bank (Eximbank) trade credits over five years. Canada also pledged $2 billion. Belgium offered Beijing a long-term, interest-free loan.[15]

But like many of the media reports on Chinese deals in Africa today, many of these plump promises never materialized. By late 1981, for example, the US Eximbank had concluded only a single soft loan – for $28 million. Roger Sullivan, the president of the US–China Business Council, warned that the US was losing the $30 billion China market to other countries who could offer mixed credits.[16] "More than half of China's imports for power and chemical plants, telecommunications and transportation infrastructure are financed through tied aid," he claimed.

With their own businesses hungrily eyeing the opportunities on China's wish list of projects, Western governments also cobbled together packages combining loans with other assistance, hoping that China would bite. The US promised to finance the training of Chinese engineers in the United States and pay for American technical assistance for China's hydropower development. This did not guarantee that US companies would win contracts for China's major hydropower projects, but as *The Economist* noted, "it gives them an edge in the bidding."[17]

Others offered parallel aid projects that were intended to sweeten the deals on offer.[18] In 1988, on a brisk March day in Beijing, the Italian Foreign Minister cut the ribbon at a ceremony to open a first aid center donated by Italy. Three days later, in Tianjin, he signed an exchange of notes on an Italian loan to finance a large steel mill that would use Italian technology. France packaged a $221 million line of credit with a grant for a feasibility study for a large dam that they hoped could be built by a French firm. The Swedes were rewarded for their vigorous promotion of mixed credits with fifteen export deals. At a ceremony to sign contracts for Chinese orders of advanced Swedish equipment, Alf Svensson, the Swedish Development Aid Minister, admitted the utility of the practice. Sweden's mix of aid and loans helped the Chinese people, but "Sweden could also reap enterprise orders and create jobs."[19] (He might have said it was "win-win" for Sweden and China.)

By the mid-1980s, a Japanese newspaper glumly reported that European companies – assisted by a marked increase in government-backed soft loans – were out-competing Japanese companies in China, with new orders for industrial plants in a host of sectors (telephone systems, thermal power plants, industrial chemicals) "where Japan previously held sway."[20]

The West later tried to reform these practices in a voluntary system of restraint. We will hear more about this in subsequent chapters, but my point should be underlined here: China saw all of these tactics as *beneficial for China's development*. Japan and the West could use their modern technologies to exploit natural resources that Chinese technology could not yet unlock. China could pay for this investment later, with the resources that were uncovered. The subsidies and aid used by the West and Japan to wrap their naked hunger for China's markets meant that China was getting a discount on finance the country needed for its modernization.

China's leaders had a vision of a modern future, they held the reins of their own development tightly in their own hands, and they used the aid offered by the West and Japan to build a foundation that lifted 400 million people out of poverty. In 1978, it was not yet clear in Beijing how China could restructure its own aid program to make use of these lessons. That would change.

Crossing the River by Feeling the Stones

Deng Xiaoping's overall vision became accepted as policy in December 1978. China would embark on experiments aimed at transforming its command economy and would emphasize "mutually beneficial cooperation" with all countries (not just members of the socialist bloc). But what role would foreign aid play as China opened its doors? Not all of China's reformers were convinced that a modernizing China needed an aid program.

After the turbulence of Mao and his Great Leap Forward and Cultural Revolution, no major change would happen again in China without pro-longed study, discussion, and experimentation. China's leaders tasked a policy group to examine the lessons from the country's past experience with aid and make suggestions for the future. The group labored even as a border war broke out between China and its erstwhile ally and largest aid recipient, Vietnam, providing support to critics of aid. The diminutive Deng weighed in: foreign aid was the right thing to do in the past, he pointed out, it is the right thing to do now, and when China is developed, it will still be the right thing.[21]

In 1980, in Beijing's sweltering July heat, the policy group reported to the State Council, China's highest government body. Clearly, the level of aid and the number of large, costly projects initiated during the Cultural Revolution had far outpaced China's capacity. Zhou Enlai and Mao Zedong had embraced nineteen enormous "100 million RMB" projects – each worth about $50 million in the 1970s – during their terms in power. Delegates were shocked to hear that Mao's virtually complete disregard for economic costs and benefits had pushed China's aid (including military aid) to the astonishing height of an average 5 percent of government expenditure between 1967 and 1976. This would have to change.

Advocates of foreign aid made a strong case for the continued political importance of aid, but they faced two problems. Every turn-key aid project abroad was a sacrifice for a country that had fallen badly off track in its own modernization. Even worse, numerous projects had been handed over to African governments in good working order, only to founder and fail. This was a waste of China's scarce resources, and might put hard-earned political capital at risk.

Several months later, China's highest political bodies – the Central Committee of the Chinese Communist Party, and the State Council – issued a joint opinion on foreign aid. Deng's line won out. Foreign aid would remain a central part of China's foreign policy. China needed a peaceful and stable international environment in order to develop. Aid would be used to help China support anti-imperialism, anti-colonialism, and anti-hegemony (hegemony in this case being domination by the two superpowers, the Soviet Union and the United States). But aid would be set at more realistic levels. China's leaders put a moratorium on agreements for extravagant "100 million RMB" projects. And political imperatives at home required China to ensure that its limited aid funding also benefited China's modernization.

Aid and the Four Tigers

The experiments that evolved over the next decades involved many of the same strategies that China learned from Japan and the West. Others Beijing developed through trial and error. Together, they form strong evidence of the ways in which China used aid not only as a tool of foreign policy and a means to build political support abroad, but as a practical instrument to promote Chinese exports and help China's infant corporations expand overseas. Japan provided a ready model.

In the 1980s, Japan's rise fed the same kind of fascination and fear that many now feel with China. Former University of California, Berkeley professor Chalmers Johnson's publication of *MITI and the Japanese Miracle* in 1982 spotlighted the methodical way in which Japan's "developmental state" used its control over finance and other government tools as both carrots and sticks to propel its industrialization and exports forward. It soon became clear that despite the debt crisis and stagnation in most of the developing world, other parts of East Asia were also rising. The media dubbed Hong Kong, South Korea, Taiwan, and Singapore "Asia's Four Tigers." Growth rates of 8, 9, and even 10 percent a year were fueled by an export-led industrialization drive that scooped up customers in remote villages from the Andes to the Alps.

With Japan and the other parts of East Asia as models of the developmental state, China's government adopted similar goals. Economic cooperation (and aid) would help the country earn foreign exchange, not simply spend it. It would help Chinese companies move into new markets and new activities, and foster joint ventures between China's infant corporations and those in other developing countries. It would change by a careful mix of two things: China's experience as a recipient of aid, and its own experiments with reform at home: "crossing the river by feeling the stones."

Zhao Ziyang Goes to Africa

At the end of December 1982, Chinese premier Zhao Ziyang headed to Africa to "advance exploringly" (as his translator put it) "on the path of South–South cooperation." He visited eleven countries in a trip that lasted over four weeks. Zhao was greeted like a visiting rock star. Cheering throngs lined the streets of his motorcade. In Zimbabwe, five thousand people waiting at the airport to greet the Chinese leader stampeded onto the runway when security officials opened the gate an hour before Zhao was due to arrive. Five women were trampled to death, sixty-four people were injured and scores fainted in the crush.[22]

At a press conference in Dar es Salaam, the seaside capital of Tanzania, Zhao announced that henceforth four sets of principles – equality and mutual benefit; stress on practical results; diversity in form; and common progress – would guide the new China as it worked out its economic relations with other developing countries.[23] Although many of the details of Zhao's four principles echoed the eight principles of aid announced by Zhou Enlai in 1964, *Zhao did not actually mention the word "aid."* He emphasized instead that *cooperation* with African countries would *"take a variety of forms* ... undertaking construction projects, entering into cooperative production, and joint ventures."

Zhao explained that cooperation would build capacity and foster growth in China as well as in Africa, and that each side could complement the other. *Beijing Review*, China's authoritative English-language magazine, pointed out to foreigners that the four principles of cooperation were a significant change. Over time, China planned to switch the emphasis *away from aid*, and toward a variety of other forms of engagement that would "benefit both partners ... Economic co-operation between poor countries *cannot be sustained*," the magazine concluded soberly, "*if it is limited to one-way aid.*"[24]

Zhao's four-week trip was every bit as historic for Africa as Zhou Enlai's trip had been almost twenty years earlier, although it aroused much less alarm (or even interest) in the West. It sent a strong signal that *China wanted to remain engaged in Africa* as China's own adjustment was underway. In the 1980s, the demands of China's own modernization meant that ties with Europe, the United States, and Asia predominated for economic engagement, but *aid* policy clearly continued to favor Africa over other regions. As the dean of China–Africa studies at the University of Illinois, Professor George Yu, observed in 1988, "China's interest in and relations with Africa have persisted and expanded."[25]

As China's economy recovered from the initial jolt of adjustment, aid rose again. According to a study published by the Development Assistance Committee (DAC) of the OECD, in 1984 China was the eighth-largest bilateral donor in sub-Saharan Africa, with commitments very close to those made by Norway, and not far below Japan and the United Kingdom.[26] China would go on to direct an average of 57 percent of its foreign aid to Africa between 1986 and 1995.[27] Aid to Africa would increase, even as it dropped in other significant regions, such as Asia. This gave China a steady presence, credibility, and a strong foundation that Beijing would build on in the years after 1995. China's increased visibility in Africa today should be seen in this context: *China never left*, we just stopped looking.

At the start of the 1980s, China qualified as one of the world's twenty least developed countries. The country's annual per capita income of $208 placed it squarely between Mozambique and Burma. Ordinary people's dreams revolved around the "three major possessions": a bicycle, a wristwatch, and a sewing machine. It was highly unusual for a relatively poor country to even *have* an aid program (although India also offered aid to some of its neighbors in South Asia). China's Four Modernizations program required enormous resources at home, leaving little extra for aid. And two big challenges faced the Chinese: How could they improve the *performance and sustainability* of their overseas projects, avoiding the waste of precious resources? And how could they change their aid so that it also *served China's modernization*? Zhao Ziyang returned to Beijing and Chinese aid officials continued finding a way by "feeling the stones." The first step involved reforming the structure of the aid system (I will return to this in Chapter 4).

China also reformed its standard operating procedures for aid, adding more rigorous economic analysis to the feasibility studies they did before they actually agreed to do a project. In 1982, Liberia's government asked China to rehabilitate Barrake, a sugarcane plantation and factory near the remote coastal town of Buchanan. They expected a prompt and enthusiastic "yes!" Instead, the Chinese sent a fifty-man team to do a lengthy feasibility study. The team concluded that sugar production at Barrake would need an annual subsidy of $3.6 million. Liberia should look for a more profitable project.[28]

A third reform targeted weak local capacity. Brain drain, economic crisis, and "poaching" of staff by donor agencies robbed African governments of personnel with management and technical skills needed to run projects. The Chinese government had been giving scholarships for African students to study in China, but most project training had been done "on site." Now aid officials were authorized to send medium- and high-level African staff to China for six months to a year to develop management and technical skills, and the Chinese set up a fund for African human resource development to pay for these expenses. And, fourth, the Chinese expanded the existing system of countertrade (barter) to encompass their former aid projects. Let us look at how this worked.

Leather Swaps: Compensatory Trade in Africa

In 1984, China's Mali embassy arranged for a Chinese company to rescue a state-owned leather factory originally established as a Chinese aid project. The company provided *commercial* credit with deferred payment, allowing the factory to order spare parts and upgrade its production equipment.[29]

The Malian company paid them in kind by exporting cattle hides – something it had in abundance. China had used barter arrangements in trade with Africa as long ago as the 1960s, swapping Chinese goods for Africa's raw materials. But connecting countertrade to development projects was new. As with the new loans being made in China by Japan and the West, China's aid projects could use the products they produced to repay loans for working capital, spare parts, or even the original aid loan. This enabled aid recipients to avoid using scarce foreign exchange.

We can see the resemblance of these resource-credit swaps to arrangements used by China in Angola, Congo (DRC), and elsewhere in Africa in recent years. Widely thought to be new, these arrangements were already firmly in place in the late 1980s. As Taiwanese researcher Teh-chang Lin pointed out in 1993, the expanding practice of countertrade was transforming China into "a new and large buyer of primary products, one who is willing to supply *development goods and services in return for local products*. . . cotton from Egypt, rubber from Sri Lanka, coffee from Ghana, copper from Zambia, and so on."[30] Tanzania bought spare parts for Chinese projects by exporting cashew nuts. Sierra Leone exported coffee and cocoa to make some of its loan payments.

After the new millennium, as we will see in later chapters, Angola would use oil; Congo would use minerals; Senegal, peanut oil; and Ghana, cocoa, to repay *their* loans. This practice of interweaving aid and trade was alien to the foreign aid norms of the West. Oil companies and private banks have provided oil-producing countries with oil-backed loans for decades, but there was no tying of the loans to development purposes. This model of finance *used for development* and repaid with resources grew in part from China's earlier experience as the recipient of aid, particularly aid from Japan.

Being Responsible *to the End*

All of these reforms would help, but they would not be enough to sustain the benefits of projects – still a knotty challenge. Both China and the West experienced countless problems with their African projects collapsing post-handover. This worsened during the 1980s, when African countries spiraled down into the severe economic crisis brought on by a stormy global economy and their own mismanagement and policy decisions. The West decided to solve the problem by moving away from governments, using conditions on its aid to shrink the reach of the state, and emphasizing privatization or service delivery by NGOs. China took a different tack.

Throughout the lost decade of the 1980s and well into the 1990s, China focused the bulk of its aid on rehabilitating the dozens of former aid projects that had collapsed or were barely limping along, and developing ways to make their initial benefits sustainable. For every new project launched during this period, three were being consolidated (repaired, renovated, reconditioned). The first step in the consolidation policy was a decision in 1983 to send teams to Africa to survey former aid projects and determine their need for spare parts. In Tanzania the Chinese signed an agreement to renovate more than sixty former aid projects. Hydropower stations built earlier under Chinese aid, such as the 74-megawatt Bouenza project in the Congo, received complete overhauls. Upgrading and repairing completed projects was less visible, even less rewarding. Chinese officials complained mildly that it was more complicated than new construction, but they persisted. *Being responsible to the end* became a new slogan for aid.[31]

There was one major complication. China's approach to aid had been tightly bound by a strict interpretation of the hallowed foreign policy principle: *China would not interfere in other countries' internal affairs.* This created what one researcher called a "sovereignty trap."[32] Chinese experts could construct a project, they could train local people how to manage an irrigation system or produce textiles in a factory. But until this point they never involved themselves directly in management. This was seen as "interference in their host's internal affairs." Once the project was constructed and demonstrated to work, *they were supposed to go home.* And yet, on average, one out of every six turn-key projects needed a Chinese team to return after the project ended, to advise or conduct further training.

Release from the sovereignty trap would allow China to offer not just technical assistance but *management* assistance for their former aid projects. Because this was seen as a political issue, the decision had to come from the highest level: Premier Zhao Ziyang. He declared that offering management and technical cooperation for completed projects was *not* "interfering in internal affairs" but "*helping them to build self-reliance*" (another important principle).[33] The tide turned. Soon, Chinese teams implementing turn-key aid projects were *required* to propose the idea of long-term partnerships to the recipient country.

The idea of Chinese managers in state-owned enterprises was also viewed with distaste by some African leaders, such as Julius Nyerere, who believed it to be an infringement of sovereignty. (It was also resisted by those African officials who relied on being able to dole out jobs in state-owned factories as a key element in their patronage system.) Nonetheless, when Zhao brought up the idea in his 1982–3 African trip, some governments agreed to give it a try.

Sierra Leone was a test case. The Magbass sugar complex was completed in 1982 and became the first Chinese aid project in Africa to immediately hire Chinese experts as managers and pay them from the company's profits.[34] But it was Mali that became a laboratory for the Chinese to study and adjust the new practice. The state-owned sugar factory built by the Chinese, but handed over to the Malians a decade earlier, appointed Chinese experts as general manager and heads of all departments. The Chinese directly controlled personnel, finance, and materials. These changes raised output by almost 100 percent.[35] In 1989, *L'Essor*, a Malian newspaper, praised this "innovative cooperation policy" as "unmatched" in West Africa. The Malians asked for Chinese experts to run the rest of the five factories formerly set up by the Chinese aid program.

Having Chinese managers also helped China in its goal to consolidate its former aid projects. The five Malian factories paid the cost of the eighty-four Chinese experts and their airfare "saving us a lot of foreign exchange," the deputy director of China's Department of Foreign Aid commented in 1988. Some of the Malian factories began to earn foreign exchange through exports. They paid up-front for imported spare parts, new machinery from China, *and* began repaying the aid loans.

It is worth pausing here to emphasize the striking contrast between China's approach to aid in this period and that of most Western donors (Japan, interestingly, is more like China in this regard). For the West, once a project ends, it is turned over to the government, and donor involvement usually ends. In his 2006 book, *The White Man's Burden*, former World Bank researcher William Easterly criticized the donors' stubborn insistence that recipient governments take sole responsibility for former aid projects, believing that otherwise they would not be sustainable. "This intuition was once appealing," commented Easterly, "but the decades of evidence show that that dog won't hunt." Donors should "bite the bullet" and take permanent responsibility for maintenance and operating costs of some of their projects, he said.[36]

China's search for ways to consolidate their projects and ensure that new ones thrived was an effort to bite this bullet. But, ultimately, providing Chinese managers and providing new loan funding for rehabilitation was not enough to ensure sustainability. As a Chinese researcher pointed out in the case of Tanzania, China's management teams could not leave

> even more than ten years after the transfer of the enterprise, not because of the need to pass on the skills but due to the inability of the Tanzanian enterprises to survive and develop on their own. Chinese-built projects became a burden on the backs of the two governments. Once the Chinese side stopped "blood transfusion," the projects could not operate properly. Efficiency declined, machines became worn out, and finally the whole project became paralyzed.[37]

Chinese managers faced even more limitations in Sierra Leone. Problems with local corruption limited the Magbass factory's ability to cover its operating costs or repay the loan, as the Chinese had hoped. Local staff members regularly stole large quantities of the cane alcohol distilled at the plant.[38] Politicians expected "gifts" of 100 kg bags of sugar whenever they visited the factory. The government of Siaka Stevens fixed the factory's sale price for sugar at about a third of the retail price. (The Chinese told me that this ex-factory price was below their production costs.) The government then gave an exclusive contract to market the sugar to a well-connected local businessman, who pocketed the difference. In 1987, the Minister of Agriculture was fired in a corruption scandal linked to kickbacks from the sugar sales.

"We tell them to love and protect the factory," the Chinese manager at Magbass told me when I first visited the factory in 1988. The sugarcane was nearly ready for harvest, its white rippling plumes stretched to the purple hills on the nearby horizon. "This is their factory, their country's factory." Constrained by their new policy that would not allow a major aid investment like Magbass to simply be abandoned, the Chinese embassy made up shortfalls out of the aid budget. "This is not the Chinese way," the economic counselor told me later, at his office in Freetown. "We are guests. They shouldn't take advantage of us."

I also saw the frustrations of the Chinese team managing the non-profit Kpatawee rice seed multiplication farm in Liberia next door. In 1986, the Chinese general manager, Wan Yingquan, wrote to the Liberian Minister of Agriculture in politely expressed frustration: "There is a Chinese saying: 'The cleverest housewife cannot cook a meal without rice.' Honorable Minister, you may imagine how difficult it is to run an enterprise without money to pay the workers and buy necessary production means on time."[39]

Problems like those at Magbass and Kpatawee pushed the Chinese to begin to explore the links between aid and investment. China would never impose privatization as a condition for assistance. But privatization entered as one of a portfolio of ways to resuscitate failed projects, restoring them to life and (sometimes) health.

When no one was really looking, the groundwork for China's current engagement in Africa was being laid. In 1984, during my first visit to West Africa to research China's aid program, these experiments were already well underway. Chinese companies were bidding on aid projects offered by Germany and the World Bank. They were actively seeking consulting work. Beijing was sending missions to explore turning their old aid projects into commercial farms. They wanted to use aid to help foster joint ventures. Struck by what I was seeing, I wrote an article about China's new mix of cooperation and aid, and titled it: "Doing Well by Doing Good."[40] I noted how a Chinese foreign aid official repeated the new slogan on mutual benefit to me: "We are poor friends. And we are helping each other." This new kind of partnership was easier said than done, however, in the very difficult environment of places where I was living, such as Liberia and Sierra Leone. But there would be some successes, such as the partnership between the Lisk family and a company from China's Fujian province.

China, Melvin Lisk, and Okeky Agencies, Ltd.

In the late afternoon of a sweltering day in the December 2007 Harmattan season, my hired car – a battered, twenty-two-year-old Mazda – moved gingerly down a steep and deeply rutted mud street in Freetown. I had seen a small sign for the Okeky Agencies at the turnoff to this unpromising road. In the aftermath of the civil war and all its disruption, I was hoping to find someone around at Okeky's waterfront office, and I was not disappointed.

China's coastal province of Fujian established the Fujian–Africa Fishing Company in the early 1980s. They approached as many as forty African countries between 1981 and 1984 in a quest to negotiate fishing rights and develop joint ventures. As a trial effort to nurture joint ventures between Chinese companies and those in Sierra Leone, China set up a fund of about $10 million in 1985. The Fujian company finally found a partner in a local businessman, Melvin Lisk, who with his entrepreneurial wife Lillian ran Okeky Agencies, Ltd., a local broker. Lisk introduced the Chinese to Lillian, a Ghanaian woman he met when they were both students at Fourah Bay College in Freetown. They flew to China to meet the head company in Fujian province, and they signed the deal.

The first wave of Chinese joint ventures in Africa began in a small way in 1981, when two Chinese companies tentatively invested $660,000 in joint ventures worth about $3 million. By 1985, the Chinese government had signed off on twenty-seven small and medium Chinese investments in Africa totaling $24 million, with the Chinese holding more than half of the equity.[41] Uncertain about the local ways, the first Chinese companies to venture into African investments preferred arrangements where their local partners could take the responsibility for managing government relations and paying taxes and other fees. Okeky was part of this first wave.

I found Melvin Lisk in his office overlooking the calm waters of the harbor. During the ups and downs of the civil war in Sierra Leone, he told me, the Fujian company sold its shares to the China National Fisheries Company in Beijing. But the sixteen boats of the joint venture (all named simply Okfish, as in Okfish One, Okfish Two, etc.) continued to fish in the coastal waters of the Gulf of Guinea. The Chinese partners provided the vessels, and took 51 percent of the venture. Melvin and Lillian Lisk agreed to pay the licensing fees, royalties, local staff, and all the overhead. They built a refrigerated bonded warehouse and a repair shop, and retained 49 percent of the profits.

Each vessel carries fifteen men. The captain, engineer, boatswain, and first mate are still Chinese. Ten sailors are local. Fishing with industrial fleets like this raised new risks of over-fishing. They might also compete with the traditional fishermen in the shallower waters along the coast. To reduce these threats, each ship also includes a government observer from Sierra Leone Marine Resources, who radios in the latitudes and information on the catches, in the country's modest effort to monitor fishing in its territorial waters.

The venture has been profitable over the decades, but today times are hard, Lisk told me. Security is poor on the seas. The previous year, ten of the boats were hit by pirates. "They beat up the crew, took all their apparels and mobile phones, siphoned most of their fuel." I asked why, after almost two and a half decades, they were still using Chinese for the four top positions. He sighed. "A few years ago, I had two other vessels, all African crew, captains. But after four years I had to let them go. It never worked, the catch was always smaller, there was always some story or another. With the Chinese on board, you can run a boat efficiently."

Experiments like the one between Melvin Lisk and the Fujian fishing company confused observers. The union was sparked by a special fund arranged between the government of Sierra Leone and that of China. But was this *aid* that we would recognize in the West? Or was it just business? The Chinese were setting up a variety of funds they called "aid" and using them in novel ways. And as China's consolidation program brought many moribund projects back to life, the Chinese began to experiment more with the use of this kind of assistance as a catalyst for *investment*.

Aid as a Springboard for Investment

Investment overseas was a tricky area for a communist country at the start of its transition. Chinese leaders established trial guidelines for overseas joint ventures only in 1984. But linking aid to investment could potentially allow the Chinese to address three goals at once: a growing backlog of unpaid aid loans, consolidation of former aid projects, and experience (and maybe profits) for China's new corporations. Still cautious, moving pragmatically and "feeling the stones," the Chinese tried a number of experiments to explore how aid could feed into investment.

One strategy was for Chinese companies to "rescue" some of their former aid projects by leasing them – a form of soft privatization. Like a rental agreement, a lease turns over the property to an outside entrepreneur in exchange for the payment of a percentage, royalty, or rent of some kind. The entrepreneur does not own the property, but uses it like an owner. In 1987, the Chinese stepped into leasing on a trial basis, with the Mali sugar complex they were already managing, and the sugar refinery they had built in Togo.

Joint ventures were another strategy. While visiting Zaire in 1983, Zhao Ziyang proposed a debt-equity swap, where 10 percent of the more than $100 million in debts owed by Zaire could be transferred into Chinese shares in joint ventures. It took years, however, for socialist China and its partners in developing countries to work out the modalities of swaps like this. Jamaica was the first country to actually conclude a debt-equity swap with China. In 1987, Jamaica agreed to let the Shanghai No. 12 Cotton Mill take on the foreign aid debt of the Chinese-aided Polyester Cotton Textile Mill in return for 46 percent of the shares.

In 1991, after reviewing the experience with aid-related investment, Beijing allocated money for a special aid diversity fund to support additional experiments. The fund provide modest, medium-term loans (repayment in one to six years) at low interest, as seed capital for joint ventures in Africa, particularly for joint ventures that would help consolidate projects that had previously been funded under China's aid. Some African governments were offered soft loans to use (or on-lend to private firms) as local shares of a joint venture.

Aid-related joint ventures accelerated after this. China Complete Plant Import and Export Corporation (Complant), the company used by the Ministry to organize the implementation of aid projects, became part owner of a sugar company in Benin. Mali also used this strategy to partially privatize the Segou Textile Mill built by Chinese aid. The Chinese government sweetened the project with policy support and funding. China National Overseas Engineering Corporation (now known as COVEC) took on 80 percent of the shares; the Mali government kept 20 percent. The value of the shares was deducted from the foreign aid debt Mali owed to China. COVEC agreed to repay the factory's remaining debt and also contributed some of its own funding for rehabilitation.[42] The factory was still operating as of 2009.

We will hear more about aid-to-investment in agriculture and industry later in this book. Suffice it to say here that these swaps continued even after the millennium, when Tanzania negotiated a debt-equity swap with China Tianjin Import and Export Corporation for Chinese-built Ubungo Farm Implements on the outskirts of Dar es Salaam.

Building Business

Other ties between Chinese aid and Chinese business were also becoming more visible. In August 1979, the Chinese State Council passed laws that allowed some Chinese companies to seek business overseas.[43] In Nigeria and in Mali, two Chinese aid teams tentatively took on construction projects for profit that year. Chinese construction companies began to stick around after building an aid project, register as a local company, and bid on construction projects. Two years later, Chinese companies were earning hard currency with projects in nine African countries. The Chinese joined the World Bank in 1980 and the African Development Bank in 1985, which made them eligible to bid on projects financed by these banks. Chinese companies supplied labor for the Kigali–Ruhengiri road, funded by German aid in Rwanda, and bid on a World Bank-financed project in Rwanda. Their business was not limited to Africa, of course. In 1983, one of the Chinese engineering companies that built the Tanzania–Zambia Railway teamed up with a New York company, winning a bid to construct a hospital complex on the US-controlled South Pacific island of Saipan.[44]

In Africa, the construction business looked promising at the start of the 1980s. But after several years Africa's economic crisis had deepened, structural adjustment policy loans were on the rise, and the decline in infrastructure spending by other donors created difficulties for China's new overseas construction companies. Chinese leaders decided to follow the example of Japan and Europe, and combine aid with business more directly. The government would credit funds from the aid budget directly to a Chinese corporation, "supporting their efforts in contracting business outside of China."[45] Drawing on Chinese aid funds enabled Chinese companies to generate business, offering "a friendly project and a friendly price," as the Chinese economic counselor in The Gambia explained it to me in 1988, describing a winning bid to construct staff housing at a Gambian hospital. "We are interested in doing more work of this kind," a Chinese diplomat in Liberia said, as she handed me a glossy brochure describing the services Chinese companies could offer. "Please let others know." The Gambians hired a team of five Chinese to manage their 17,000 seat stadium (to "keep the lights guaranteed" as the Chinese explained). "It is a dormitory for athletes during matches," a Chinese commercial attaché told me. "When no match is scheduled, it is a hotel." He smiled. "It helps pay for the loan."

Chinese contractors also expanded their efforts to win projects financed by *other* donors. "African nations receive about $14 billion in assistance from foreign countries," *Xinhua* noted. "Chinese enterprises hope that they can make profits through contracting more projects involving this foreign aid."[46] And then there were new forms of Chinese aid that did not especially involve business, but rather were ways to stretch China's aid dollars, or decisions to add other programs modeled in part on what the West and Japan were doing. Tripartite cooperation was one of these new forms, and humanitarian aid another.

Tripartite Cooperation

One morning in early 1984 in a seaside neighborhood just outside Banjul, I watched nine Chinese experts from the China Building Material Company and a group of Gambians building a small factory that would later produce bricks. We were just down the street from the stretch of white beach where Swedish tourists strolled in their bathing suits past the modest Muslim market women squatting to wait for the morning fishing boats. China paid the airfare for the nine experts, The Gambia paid about $200 a month for each as living allowance, and the UN Capital Development Fund (UNCDF) paid the rest of the costs. China and the UN Family Planning Association created a similar arrangement to build a maternity clinic in The Gambia. Chinese aid officials liked these tripartite projects because they were low-cost, usually had quick results, and they stretched China's aid resources. "These projects have increased dramatically in recent years and it has become a new form of our foreign assistance," the Department of Foreign Aid noted in 1989.[47]

After joining the UN, China began making contributions to the United Nations development system in 1972. These contributions frequently became the seed capital for tripartite cooperation. In just two years, 1986–7, China was able to undertake forty-four small projects – twenty-three in Africa – with various United Nations agencies, on a tripartite basis.[48] A 1983 road project in Somalia co-financed with the African Development Bank and the World Bank, and discussions with the Canadian Agency for International Development on co-financing an agricultural project in Rwanda, demonstrated that China was at least open to tripartite cooperation with other donors. In Yemen, the Chinese joined with the Arab Fund to finance a gymnasium in Aden, and China State Construction Engineering Corporation carried out the work.

"We Are the World"

Aid-linked experiments like the ones described above blossomed like a hundred flowers around Africa and other parts of the developing world in the 1980s and early 1990s. But China's aid changed in other ways. For example, like other countries, they began to use the state-controlled Red Cross to channel some humanitarian aid in disaster situations. In 1981, the state-controlled Chinese Red Cross made a donation to Burma, for example. But it was the African famine of the mid-1980s that pushed the Chinese into a more visible role as a donor of humanitarian aid.

In the early 1980s, it stopped raining in stretches of the dry African Sahel and regions north of the equator. Drought and hunger spread from Ethiopia to Mauritania. Farmers sold their animals, ate their seeds, and then began to starve. Rural families started the slow, sad trek to towns where they might find food. NGOs in the West mobilized, and this time so did the Chinese Red Cross, making donations to the Central African Republic, Ethiopia, Senegal, and The Gambia in 1983, and Lesotho in 1984, when the rains also failed in southern Africa.

In 1985, the Chinese Red Cross raised nearly five million dollars from Chinese citizens for famine relief in Africa.[49] In July that year, Bob Geldof organized the first Live Aid concert – sixteen solid hours of music capped by the anthem "We Are the World." Beijing responded by organizing a Chinese Live Aid featuring jugglers and acrobats as well as contemporary Chinese music.[50] The Chinese Live Aid concert opened the door (but only a crack) to the growing world of citizen and civil society involvement in relief and development aid, a trend well underway in the West at that point. But two other developments in the 1980s would be far more influential in shaping the evolution of aid in China: the ratcheting up of diplomatic competition with Taiwan, and China's decision to join the World Trade Organization (WTO).

Checkbook Diplomacy

Largely because of American support for the exiled Republic of China's tenacious claim to be the "rightful" China, Beijing was excluded from membership of the United Nations and its Security Council for twenty-two years. Taipei sat in its place. Diplomatic recognition from African countries played a central role in the 1971 UN vote that gave China's seat to Beijing. But China's relations with African countries were not always smooth. Ghana, Burundi, and the Central African Republic (CAR) broke ties with China in the 1960s, recoiling in some cases from the radical activities of Chinese embassies during the Cultural Revolution. These ruptures accelerated again after 1989.

In Taiwan, a peaceful democratic transition was underway in the late 1980s. Flush with foreign reserves and encouraged by the worldwide opprobrium following China's violent suppression of the 1989 Tiananmen Square demonstrations, Taiwan began to reinvigorate its "checkbook" diplomacy. Box 2.1 tells the story. Liberia was first to make the switch, although Taiwan's dollars were ultimately unable to help President and commander-in-chief "Doctor" Samuel Kanyon Doe (he had received an honorary Ph.D. from a university in South Korea) stave off Charles Taylor's rebel forces. By the end of 1990, Guinea-Bissau and Lesotho had also reestablished relations with Taiwan. According to Chinese official sources, China's new aid commitments in 1990 rose by 68 percent, reflecting the diplomatic battles with Taiwan.[51]

Over the next two decades, nearly a dozen African countries were persuaded to officially "recognize" the Republic of China in Taiwan as "China." Beijing responded by invoking the "One China" policy. Any country establishing diplomatic ties with Taipei was agreeing with Taipei's position that the ROC was the only "China" (albeit with a government in exile on Taiwan). Like West Germany's Hallstein Doctrine after World War II, Beijing's One China policy required the breaking of ties with any country recognizing the ROC. The rivalry with Taiwan sparked a bidding

---

Box 2.1. Checkbook diplomacy

The Beijing–Taipei rivalry in Africa, 1989 to present

Countries that broke with Beijing to establish ties with Taipei	Countries that broke with Taipei to establish ties with Beijing
1989 Liberia*	1993 Liberia (second)
1990 Guinea-Bissau	1994 Lesotho (second)
1990 Lesotho*	1996 Niger (second)
1991 Central African Republic (second)*	1998 Central African Republic (third)
1992 Niger*	1998 Guinea-Bissau
1994 Burkina Faso*	1998 South Africa
1996 The Gambia*	2003 Liberia (third)
1996 Senegal*	2005 Senegal (second)
1997 Chad*	2006 Chad (second)
1997 Liberia (second)*	2008 Malawi
1997 Saõ Tomé and Principé	

---

*These countries had previously had relations with Taipei, and broken them to establish relations with Beijing, usually in the 1970s. *Swaziland is the only African country that has never established diplomatic relations with Beijing.*

---

war. Offers of aid (and, some alleged, cash payments) escalated on both sides. Liberia and the CAR switched between Taipei and Beijing twice (Box 2.1).[52]

The Chinese Ministry of Foreign Affairs responded energetically to Taiwan's diplomatic challenge. In July 1989, Foreign Minister Qian Qichen set off on an urgent trip to Botswana, Angola, Zimbabwe, Zambia, Mozambique, and Lesotho. In January 1991, he initiated a tradition of starting each new year by traveling to a group of selected African countries for high-level meetings. By 1995, Qian had visited thirty-six countries on these annual tours, and they have been repeated every January by his successors. Indeed, an African ambassador pointed to this in 2008 after a talk I had given to a group of African ambassadors in Washington: "China gives Africans more respect than they get from the West." I was struck by how many other ambassadors nodded vigorously in agreement.

Political competition with Taiwan had little effect on China's new business relations, however. In November 1989, almost two months after Liberia recognized Taipei and China broke off diplomatic relations (and just weeks before Charles Taylor invaded from the north, setting off years of civil war),

I spent an hour sipping green tea with the Chinese manager of the isolated, government-owned China Trade Center in the small Liberian town of Ganta. The pit-holed stretch of road in front of his shop was the last bit of paved road in that section of the country, and his shop was strategically placed. He planned to remain at his post despite the rupture of relations.

Down the road, China Heilongjiang Province International Economic and Technical Corporation reacted to the break in relations by closing the doors of the private Liberian hospital it was managing. Six months later, however, after unspecified "renovations," the eight doctors returned and the hospital resumed business. Even in Swaziland – which, alone among African countries, has never had diplomatic ties with Beijing – Chinese state-owned companies began to win contracts as early as 1991, a clear sign that the practicalities of business were taking priority over politics.[53]

The second factor was the faint drumbeat of globalization. On July 10, 1986, Beijing sent a formal request to Geneva to resume its status as a contracting party to the GATT, the General Agreement on Tariffs and Trade. (The GATT evolved into the World Trade Organization upon conclusion of the Uruguay Round of trade negotiations in 1994, while China and the other members, particularly the US, were still negotiating the terms of China's membership.) This would deeply affect China's aid and economic engagement in Africa in at least two ways.

First, the prospect of competing in a global market intensified the pressure on China's government to facilitate that competition. The aid reforms of the 1990s put a system in place to do just that. New institutions and instruments would enable the Chinese to weave their foreign aid together with other subsidies and special funds, constituting a formidable portfolio of developmental state tools, in the classic East Asian pattern first started by Japan. These tools, how they work, and some of the myths that have arisen around them, are the subject of the next four chapters.

Second, it affected China's vision of Africa as a market. By the late 1980s, the West and Japan were already seeing Africa as the "failed continent." British companies were pulling out of Africa. In 1990, London's *Financial Times* reported on a study of 139 British companies that had had investments in Africa: only forty-three remained engaged.[54] In Kenya, the number of Japanese firms fell from fifteen to only two. But Beijing's commercial attachés were carefully watching policy reforms across Africa and they saw something else: opportunity.

As early as 1988, officials from China's Department of Foreign Aid were pointing out that some African countries had "enlivened their markets," referring to Africa's own steps at trade liberalization.[55] China accounted for only 1 percent of Africa's imports, they noted. This should increase. Africa's population was poor, but it was growing. Market women in Ghana, Namibia, and Tanzania were already selling textiles, metal bowls, and small round tins of eucalyptus-scented Essential Balm stamped "Made in China." But these were only a hint of what China's government hoped would become demand for machinery, electronics, Chinese pharmaceuticals and other higher value-added technologies, an evolution Japan had experienced earlier. Aid would have to fit into this new emphasis on trade.

Let me conclude here by emphasizing these points: China's aid system and economic engagement today reflect what the Chinese learned from their experiments of the 1980s *and* from their own experience as a recipient of aid and the business that was linked to aid. The new tools brought the practice of economic cooperation for mutual benefit to an entirely new, intense level. As China's reforms deepened, aid would become even more about business; the Chinese would continue to "do well by doing good." In the new millennium, the push to "go global" would make use of all these lessons.

CHAPTER 3

Going Global: Foreign Aid in the Toolkit of a Rising China

On a piece of property owned by the Tanzanian Ministry of Defense, a small factory sits behind a sliding black gate marked "Tanzansino United Pharmaceuticals (T) Ltd." A stadium built by the Chinese towers in the background, glinting in the sunlight. China's old and new foreign aid meet here, in a flat and sandy neighborhood just outside of Dar es Salaam.

I visited Tanzansino with a member of its board of directors, Zhou Yong. Zhou is an old friend of Beijing University historian Li Baoping, a fluent Swahili speaker who is in turn good friends with Jamie Monson, chair of the history department at Minnesota's Carleton College, and an expert on the Tan-Zam Railway. Jamie introduced me to Li Baoping, who gave me an introduction to Zhou Yong. *Guanxi* ("connections") like this helped to open gates like Tanzansino's in Tanzania.

The factory was built as a Chinese aid project close to the end of the Maoist period.[1] It aimed to produce tropical vaccines and medicines, one of a handful of enterprises operated directly by the Tanzanian military. While Tanzania has been at peace for all of the years of its independence, Julius Nyerere maintained a relatively robust army. At one point, with the tacit support of all his neighbors, he marched the army across the border with Uganda to oust the brutal dictator Idi Amin after he had begun to threaten Tanzania.

Nyerere's army was successful in ridding Uganda of Idi Amin, who went into exile in Saudi Arabia. The factory, under Tanzanian management, was less successful. The Chinese were asked to return. In 1997, the embassy brokered a $3 million joint venture between New Technological Applications Center of northern China's Shanxi province and the Tanzanian Ministry of Defense. The factory limped along more or less until 2006, when Wang Lichen, the Chinese entrepreneur who started Holley Pharmaceuticals, saw an opportunity. One of Holley's specialties is artemisinin, an effective anti-malarial medicine derived from a Chinese shrub *Artemisia annua*, a variety of witch hazel. Holley was growing *Artemisia annua* in the purple mountains near Chongqing. Could the shrub also grow in Africa?

Wang Lichen is bullish on Africa: he is also the vice-chairman of the China–Africa Business Council. His company has distribution outlets in Tanzania, Kenya, Cameroon, Uganda, and Nigeria. China has targeted pharmaceuticals like his as a key technology export sector, one marked out for state support. Indeed, one of the promises made at the lavish November 2006 Forum on China–Africa Cooperation (FOCAC) Summit in Beijing was a grant of almost $38 million to supply artemisinin to the thirty malarial treatment centers China promised to construct across Africa.

Holley hired Zhou Yong, who had originally come to Tanzania in 1999 to run distribution and marketing for a Chinese pharmaceutical company, and made him the managing director of their Tanzania branch. They bought out the Shanxi company's shares, and applied for a Chinese loan to expand the joint venture. In 2006, Holley invested more than six million dollars in an *Artemisia annua* plantation in Tanzania.

Why did Holley set up in Tanzania, I asked Zhou Yong, as we drove out to see the factory under the blazing January sun. "The cost of importing medicine from China is high," Zhou Yong told me. "This creates an opportunity for us to produce locally. And the Tanzanian government gives a 15 percent preference for local products for its medical stores." I asked him what help he had gotten from the Chinese government. "They helped a lot in making contacts." He ticked off a few more points. "The Chinese government will buy our product to make donations to local hospitals and clinics. And the government has sent two medical teams, one in Zanzibar and one on the mainland. It's a good opportunity for us to introduce Chinese medicine."

The stadium towering above the factory shows another side of China's aid. In 2000, Tanzanian President Benjamin Mkapa, elected to succeed

Julius Nyerere when Nyerere stepped down, promised Tanzanians that he would build a state-of-the-art 60,000 seat stadium before leaving office in 2005. "The President made a commitment that he would like to leave Tanzanians a good stadium," Tanzania's Foreign Affairs Minister Jakaya Kikwete, who signed the agreement, told the BBC news.

But Mkapa found that it was not so easy to arrange to build the stadium. Tanzania was a Highly Indebted Poor Country (HIPC). Under the 1996 HIPC program, international donors were prepared to cancel some of Tanzania's mountain of debt to the World Bank and the IMF, but only if the government maintained a strict program of austere spending. To the Bretton Woods institutions, building a modern stadium in a poor country with an annual per capita income of $330 seemed a bit like the Romans building a new coliseum with the barbarians camped outside the city walls. It may have been a project with genuine local ownership. But was this really a good idea?

Mkapa pressed ahead. The Tanzanian government issued a tender for a very ambitious project, with an Olympic-size swimming pool, an athletes' village, and other amenities. In 2004, a French company, Vinci Construction Grands Projets, won the tender with a bid of $154 million. Under pressure from Washington, the Tanzanians reluctantly abandoned this more expensive option. Its cost "would have sown panic in the Bretton Woods institutions," a journalist noted.[2] They turned to the Chinese.

The stadium is "a *special* aid project," an official at the Chinese embassy acknowledged. Usually the Chinese government provides all the funding for projects like stadiums, but in this their grant of $20 million covered only half of the estimated cost; the Tanzanians would have to raise the rest. Beijing Construction Engineering Group got the contract. Mkapa (and the ruling party) got their stadium – a considerably simpler version. The International Monetary Fund continued to object, pointing out that the stadium's cost had not been included in the Public Expenditure Review, Tanzania's annual report card to its major donors. But President Mpaka "is very happy," a Tanzanian official said at the time, "because all of this is his work, the credit goes to him and I am confident that the stadium will be ready before the next elections."

The stadium, and the pharmaceutical factory sitting in its shadow, represented the political side of China's aid (the joint venture with the

Ministry of Defense, the stadium a politically important "prestige project"). But the factory is now in its third life: first as a traditional aid project, second as one of the joint ventures that rose in the consolidation experiments of the 1980s, and now part of the wave of Chinese companies *going global*. In Africa, there are many misconceptions about China's "going global" strategy. Some believe it is all about resources, others that it began as recently as 2002. Below, we will see how deep are the roots of this strategy, as well as how it works today.

Chinese leader Deng Xiaoping's cautious Open Door policies included "going out" as well as "bringing in." Chinese firms made their first tentative steps overseas in 1979. Through the 1980s, as we saw in the previous chapter, the government encouraged state-owned companies to bid on contracts, and form joint-ventures abroad. By the early 1990s, provinces like Fujian and Guangdong were actively promoting the overseas activities of their companies. Policymakers created additional tools and instruments to promote trade and investment overseas during the 1990s.[3]

As China entered the new millennium, its leaders' economic concerns continued to center on the United States, Europe, and Japan. Gaining access to the advanced technologies of these countries was a key reason why China applied to join the World Trade Organization. Those negotiations took nearly fifteen years, snagging frequently on details of China's pledge to liberalize its markets. During all that time, Beijing steadily prepared for WTO entry with its hallmark gradual reforms. Finally, in December 2001, China was admitted to the WTO. That year, China's tenth five-year plan marked the escalation of China's own globalization, "with Chinese characteristics." It formalized the directive for Chinese companies to "go global": *zou chuqu.*

Zou chuqu means, literally, "walk out." Walking out involved trade – finding *new markets* – as one step. But there was more. Chinese companies at the high end would be asked to establish *brand names* with global recognition (Lenovo in computers, Huawei in telecoms, Haier in home appliances). They would be encouraged to *invest overseas*, establish factories, buy property. Small and medium-sized companies would also be encouraged to go out, particularly those at the lower end, where moving offshore would aid China's domestic restructuring. Characteristically, the Chinese embrace of globalization, and the role aid would play in that embrace, would not look much like globalization viewed from the West.

Battle in Seattle

The establishment of the World Trade Organization (WTO) in 1995 marked a milestone in the march toward a global market. The WTO absorbed the GATT, the gradually negotiated set of rules established in 1947 to organize trade among the world's industrialized, capitalist economies. This new organization was also tasked with the incorporation of items on the "new" trade agenda – services, investment, and intellectual property rights – into the global trade regime. Yet almost as soon as the WTO began operations, the world's giddy rush toward globalization stumbled badly. Financial markets imploded across the developing world, a warning that would fail to avert the even more severe banking crisis that roiled the global economy in 2008.

The first post-WTO crisis began in Asia. Encouraged, and sometimes pressured, to remove restrictions on the free movement of capital ("open their capital accounts") before their regulatory systems were robust enough to regulate these flows, a number of Asian countries were ripe for disaster. It happened first in Thailand, where real estate troubles triggered capital flight, and ultimately a collapse of the Thai currency. Spooked, nearly $150 billion in foreign capital fled the Asia region in the course of a few months in the second half of 1997.

The economic crisis spread like a virus, with exchange rates tumbling across Asia. Former World Bank vice-president and Nobel laureate Joseph Stiglitz later charged that Washington – and the Bretton Woods institutions more generally – had badly bungled their response to the crisis, insisting on austerity and tighter monetary policy when the situation demanded exactly the opposite. The Chinese reacted with great sangfroid. They had not opened their own capital accounts, and they refused to exploit the crisis by devaluing their currency to grab market share from the more troubled countries. Beijing contributed one billion dollars to a temporary loan fund established by the IMF to assist Thailand. Nevertheless, there followed similar meltdowns, as Russia was forced to default on its external debt in 1998 and the Brazilian exchange rate collapsed that same year.

Then, in the spring of 1999, as Asia was still smarting from the wounds of its crisis, protests erupted into riots in Seattle, where the World Trade Organization was holding its annual ministerial meeting. Anarchists wearing black face masks smashed the windows of Starbucks and McDonalds. More thoughtful critics called on WTO members to reject the market fundamentalism that they said put the rights of corporations and private investors above those of workers, consumers, ordinary people, and the environment. These protests were a backlash against the power of a small group of countries (especially the United States) that had played a large role in shaping the global financial architecture and foreign aid to reflect *their* priorities and ideologies.

Rallies and marches began to take place outside meetings of the Geneva-based World Economic Forum, and each April at the meetings of the world's finance ministers at the Bretton Woods institutions in Washington DC. The September 2001 terrorist attacks in Manhattan that toppled the World Trade Center pushed the backlash against globalization off the front page. Yet the Bush administration's subsequent "war on terror" failed to recognize that the fallen twin towers were also symbolic of the fragility of the global financial architecture, something that became painfully apparent to the world with the financial turmoil that began in 2008.

In Africa, structural adjustment policies with their focus on growth, and demands for liberalization and privatization, continued to frame aid during the 1990s, even as aid officials and recipients alike grew increasingly weary of the failure of adjustment to foster economic recovery. Critics described the process as an elaborate charade: aid recipients pretending they would reform, and donors pretending to believe them. (China's promise to give aid "without conditions" showed how little the Chinese thought of all this.)

Even as structural adjustment continued to shape aid from the West, a renewed focus on poverty, governance, and concern about the cumulative debt and financial crisis that had plagued the developing countries since the 1980s gradually gained momentum. A coalition of NGOs called Jubilee 2000 built support for an agreement to cancel debt owed by the Highly Indebted Poor Countries (HIPCs). And in September 2000, almost 150 world leaders at the UN's Millennium Summit signed off on a symbolic commitment to eight Millennium Development Goals (MDGs) at the United Nations.

Pushed by Jeffrey Sachs, director of the Earth Institute at Columbia University, the MDGs marked a resurgence of optimism about aid.

In many ways, the eight goals were a triumph for NGOs and other critics of structural adjustment. The MDGs focused attention on *social* development: ending poverty and hunger, combating malaria, achieving gender equality and universal primary education. In Africa, donors increased their funding for social sector programs to 60 percent of the total.[4] But there was a cost. Funding for agriculture, which in the late 1980s received more than a quarter of total aid to Africa, fell to only 4 percent. Aid for manufacturing and infrastructure dropped to historic lows. The traditional donors left a vacuum, and who was there, ready to step in? The Chinese.

Deeper into Africa

China's rise as a donor *and* development model happened as many in Africa and elsewhere were growing weary with the old models of aid and global engagement. Chinese President Jiang Zemin attended the UN Millennial Summit in New York, but no doubt as he stood there with the other world leaders, he was thinking about another meeting that would take place in Beijing a month later: the launch of the new Forum on China–Africa Cooperation (FOCAC), in October 2000. Forty-four African countries sent their foreign ministers and those responsible for economic affairs to Beijing. Much like the FOCAC Summit held in Beijing in 2006, the first FOCAC meeting contained pledges that China would establish an array of new programs – debt relief, training programs, an investment fund – to move its economic cooperation with Africa forward.

In 2000, China was starting to harvest the fruits of nearly two decades of reform in its aid and economic relations with Africa. Buildings financed by China's aid or built by Chinese contractors had reshaped the skylines of dozens of African cities. In Ethiopia, Rwanda, and elsewhere, Chinese contractors who had originally arrived to carry out Chinese aid projects were now winning half or more of the construction contracts funded by other donors. Dar es Salaam alone had eight resident Chinese engineering companies, which had won more than 170 small and large contracts between 1990 and 1997.[5] A total of 42,393 Chinese engineers and skilled laborers were working in Africa in 2000.[6] China's Ministry of Commerce[7] approved fifty-seven Chinese investments in Africa that year, bringing the total number to just under 500. Two-way trade between China and Africa surpassed ten billion dollars. All this happened without much comment from the West.

As should be clear by now, Beijing's engagement with Africa involved a well-thought-out and long-term strategy, not the hasty, desperate scramble familiar from media headlines. This strategy addressed three central political and economic challenges. *First*, rapid growth was already outpacing China's ample natural resource base. In 1993, China became a net importer of oil. Logging had increased, and China was losing 500,000 hectares of forest every year, putting pressure on the watersheds. Africa's vast natural resources were a growing attraction. *Second* was a political challenge. Beijing needed to calm concerns that its rapid rise would preempt other developing countries' development prospects. It needed to establish China's reputation as a rising but "responsible" power.[8] And, as always, front and center among Chinese political concerns in Africa was Taiwan and its continuing campaign for diplomatic recognition. China's embrace of globalization created the *third* challenge. China would need to expand into new markets, manage the upgrading of its increasingly "mature" domestic industries, and build up its fledgling multinational corporations, those like Holley Pharmaceutical.

Beijing proceeded in three steps. First, a major aid reform in 1995 created new instruments to link aid, trade, and investment together. Second, after 2000, Chinese leaders took on a much higher profile stance as promoters of "common prosperity," creating regional organizations to support a series of programs that combined aid and economic cooperation. Third, parallel to joining the World Trade Organization, Beijing refined its portfolio of tools to aid its domestic restructuring by pushing its mature "sunset" industries offshore. A quiet decision to establish up to *fifty* special economic cooperation zones in other countries would become the most visible signal of this step.

Value for Money

China's 1995 aid reform, the *Indian Ocean Newsletter* commented, "marks the determination of the Beijing authorities to put an end to the era of pouring funds down drains and subsidizing flamboyant sports stadiums and presidential palaces. Now, the People's Republic of China wants value for its money."[9] In the 1990s, Beijing implemented a series of reforms that would shape China's aid program well into the new millennium. The reforms were sparked by lessons gleaned from the experiments of the 1980s, collected and discussed at a 1991 national conference on foreign aid. But they were also a product of public management reforms in China that went well beyond aid. They emphasized competition, efficiency, and "market-oriented" principles in the use of public money, including foreign aid.

Two organizational changes in the 1990s were especially key for the aid program. First, the trading companies and economic cooperation corporations owned by Chinese ministries were further separated from their parent ministries and pushed to operate as independent companies, responsible for their own profits and losses. These companies had been given limited independence to seek new business in the 1980s. But over the 1990s, their budgets would be progressively "hardened" and they could no longer count on regular transfers of budget support. Eventually, in the early 2000s, some of the large, state-owned enterprises would be closed down or merged, and almost all small and medium-sized firms would be privatized.

As we sat in his air-conditioned office in an otherwise eerily deserted building in Freetown, George Guo, managing director of the Magbass sugar complex, told me how these reforms affected his company, China Complete Plant Import and Export Corporation (Complant), previously owned by the Ministry of Commerce. "In 1993, Complant became an independent company," Guo said, "so we had to find commercial opportunities. We found that sugar was a good business, especially if it was a former aid project." Complant started by leasing one of China's former aid projects in Togo. "When we had success in Togo, we went to Madagascar. We changed from 'management cooperation,' where the local government is responsible, but the Chinese are asked to give continual help, to doing it on a purely commercial basis," he said.

In 1994, a second organizational change created three "policy banks" (China Development Bank, China Export Import Bank, and China Agricultural Development Bank). While other state-owned banks were asked to operate more on commercial principles, the three policy banks remained tools of the government, allowing Beijing to allocate preferential or targeted finance through a hybrid of planning and market means. China Eximbank and China Development Bank began to operate overseas.

The importance of policy banks like the Eximbank and China Development Bank in China's development model and its international economic relations cannot be emphasized too strongly. China, as I noted earlier, is in many ways a typical East Asian *developmental state*. It acts to accelerate development through the deliberate use of state policies. The central characteristic of a developmental state is its control over finance. This control need not be exclusive – but it must be important at the margin in order to influence the behavior of firms in directions determined by political leaders. In this regard, Beijing is following directly in the footsteps of the earlier Asian successes, Japan, Korea, and Taiwan, who all used development finance to "pick winners" in the globalization race.

In China, aid would become part of that process. The Chinese had learned a lot from being a *recipient* of aid, particularly aid from Japan. During the early 1990s, those lessons fed into the active debates on aid reform. In a rare glimpse into the thinking of China's leaders, we have a 1993 statement from Wu Yi, China's Minister of Foreign Economic Relations and Trade. China was reforming its aid program, "using as our reference the internationally practiced and effective ways of providing aid."[10]

The centerpiece of the reforms was the launch in 1995 of an entirely new system of concessional aid loans, offered through China's Eximbank. We will look at this more closely in the next chapter. But let me emphasize here that this 1995 reform marked the most dramatic formal change in China's aid program since its inception. In effect, China launched a new aid program.

Also in 1995, a clear mandate came down to the Ministry of Commerce from China's State Council: *combine aid to Africa, mutual cooperation, and trade together.*[11] The strategy was called the "Great (or 'Mega') Economic and Trade Strategy." The point was simple. Aid would be used to foster three kinds of initiatives, all growing out of the experiments of the 1980s and early 1990s.

Joint-venture investments in manufacturing and agriculture were first on the list. For example, Mauritius received a concessional line of credit of about six million dollars to support productive joint-venture projects.[12]

Assembly factories were a second target. Set up by Chinese companies in Africa, they would create demand for exports of Chinese machinery and parts, as well as fabric and other inputs. As the government put it in 1995: "Chinese trade corporations and manufacturing enterprises should be encouraged to invest in African countries with better investment climate to promote the export of our medium and small equipment, processing machinery, relevant technology, and labor service."[13] Vehicle assembly factories were set up with concessional loans in Côte d'Ivoire, Cameroon, and elsewhere. Finally, the government emphasized exploration and investment in mineral and forest resources. In 1996, long before the war in Darfur erupted, Sudan became the first country to receive Chinese aid to finance oil exploration, in a joint venture with China National Oil Corporation.[14]

The new aid program was deliberately shaped to assist Chinese firms to enter an unfamiliar region with daunting challenges. As Europe, the US, and especially Japan had long been doing, the Chinese now wanted to channel their aid money more directly as support for "mutually beneficial" business. But for countries in Africa long accustomed to the flexible, zero-interest terms of China's traditional aid, the announcement that China would now be offering more aid, albeit at a considerably higher cost, through its new Eximbank was at best a mixed blessing.

Entering Europe's Backyard

As the vacuum in Africa grew larger, with European and other wealthy countries de-investing and shifting aid funding out of infrastructure, industry, and agriculture, Chinese leaders saw vast opportunities for a new approach that would meet their own political and economic needs, as well as Africa's. Year after year, the Department of Foreign Aid reported that they were "pushing and supporting" (1992) or that they had "actively propelled" (1998) Chinese companies to do business overseas.[15] There were just two problems. More independent now, China's companies did not seem terribly interested in seeking business in Africa. They still saw Africa as Europe's backyard. Just as importantly, China's traditional partners in Africa were alarmed at the change in aid policy and unsure what it would mean for them.

The Chinese government had a lot of ideas for what Chinese companies should do: they should actually come to Africa and do intensive studies of local markets; the Ministry would help organize delegations. If exporting machinery, they should set up repair and maintenance shops to guarantee that customers' needs would be taken care of. If exporting Chinese medicine, companies should take care to translate directions in English and in French.

For their part, the Chinese government adopted a multifaceted approach to promote their new strategy and market it to African leaders. The state-owned Bank of China was directed to set up a branch office in Zambia in 1997, and China Construction Bank opened an office in Johannesburg in October 2000 to make it easier for Chinese companies to enter unfamiliar territory. Eximbank began offering preferential loans to construction firms in 1998 to boost their ability to win contracts overseas in the Middle East, South Asia, and Africa. This, explained a *People's Daily* story, will help them in a sector "which had long been monopolized by developed countries."[16] Eximbank followed this by opening overseas branches in Côte d'Ivoire and South Africa.

The State Council also directed China's state-owned companies to launch a number of trade, investment, and development centers across Africa. Each center was to be built and operated independently by an experienced Chinese company with extensive business interests in that country. The centers offered bonded warehouses for traders, referrals for legal assistance, travel and banking advice, and help with the complicated matters of customs clearance. In December 1995, Complant, newly independent from the Ministry, opened the first trade, investment, and development center in Guinea, China's first aid recipient. At least ten other centers followed.[17]

This was a potent symbol of the shift in priorities. The centers were constructed on a standard "build–operate–transfer" model. In Benin, for example, the Chinese government contributed a grant of RMB 17 million ($2.5 million) out of its aid budget to build the five-floor center, while Zhejiang Tianshi International Economic and Technical Cooperation Company did the design and construction. In a pattern that would become standard for the mix of aid and business, the Chinese company financed a share of the cost (about a quarter, in the Benin case) in return for the right to run the center for fifty years, after which it would be turned over to the host country.[18]

Additionally, the Ministry directed its municipal and provincial branches to organize delegations of "outstanding enterprises" to travel to Africa, exposing them to opportunities on the ground. A delegation from Yunnan province visited Djibouti in December 1995, and discussed setting up a tobacco farm, and a public–private partnership with the state-owned electricity utility. One of the Yunnan companies on this delegation later won a contract to manage Djibouti's Sheraton Hotel. These delegations increased after the millennium. In 2007, for example, Guangdong province organized a business seminar in Dar es Salaam, attended by 900 Chinese business people.

The new strategy was capped by a dramatic increase in visits by top leaders to Africa, where they explained and marketed the new program of aid and economic cooperation. Three Chinese vice-premiers fanned out to visit a total of *eighteen* African countries in 1995. Chinese premier Li Peng visited Morocco that year, and the following year President Jiang Zemin traveled to six African countries, the first time a Chinese president had ever visited Africa. Premier Li Peng followed this with a 1997 trip to six more African countries (Figure 3.1 maps the visits of top Chinese leaders since 1995). Li Peng emphasized to his worried hosts that "China's basic policy of providing aid to Africa has not changed [but]...China's policy has moved from aid donation to economic cooperation for mutual benefit."[19]

Zhu Rongji and the Tan-Zam Railway *Redux*

The challenge of explaining China's aid reforms may have been toughest with China's close allies, Tanzania and Zambia. Vice-premier Zhu Rongji, who had been purged several times in the Maoist era for his "rightist" views, was in charge of breaking the news about the shift in aid policy and how it might affect China's flagship project, the Tanzania–Zambia Railway. Zhu, a trained engineer who would become China's premier in 1998, was a complicated man. Alleged to be a direct descendant of the emperor who founded China's Ming Dynasty, he was known as China's "economic czar." Zhu pushed hard on issues such as China's WTO membership, global engagement, and domestic restructuring, but he was also intensely practical. Once, at a state banquet in Australia, he failed to reappear from a visit to the

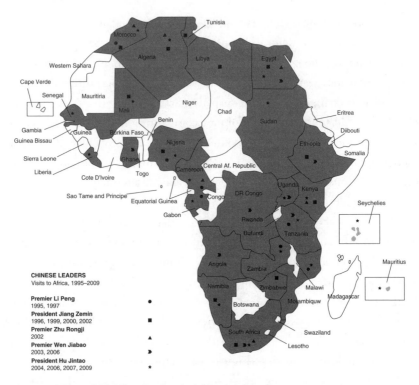

Fig. 3.1. Map of Chinese leaders' visits to Africa

lavatory. Security officials found him studying the mechanism inside the water-saving toilet, which he had disassembled. Given this, his attitude to the iconic railway is perhaps not so surprising.

The Tan-Zam Railway was a problem, and Zhu Rongji confronted it during his 1995 visit without a lot of sentiment. He knew the history: after the iconic railway was handed over in 1976, a group of Chinese experts remained behind to provide technical training, but the railway was operated by local staff. Losses mounted, and service deteriorated. In 1983, under the aid consolidation program, Tanzania and Zambia agreed to invite Chinese managers back. Two hundred and fifty Chinese were soon stationed across the different bureaus of the railway, in most of the top management positions. They raised the efficiency of the railway, paid their own expenses out of the revenues, and began to report operating profits. But China continued to provide new zero-interest loans for spare parts and rehabilitation, rescheduling payment when necessary.

In 1995, under pressure from other donors (some of whom were also financing Tazara), the railway was allowed to run on more commercial principles. This prompted concerns in Tanzania that socialist China would cease supporting the railway. But Zhu Rongji complimented the government on its "boldness" in making reforms.[20] Commercializing the railway should ensure better services, he said, and he promised a new aid loan. Noting that the railway was currently employing about 2,500 more workers than was necessary, Zhu commented briskly: "Laying off workers is not a good thing, but we will have no alternative of making *our railway* run efficiently other than doing what the reality dictates."[21]

Zhu's practical advice might have come from the local World Bank representative. The efforts to consolidate aid projects in the 1980s convinced the Chinese that aid for productive projects would only be sustainable if it involved Chinese companies more directly. By 1995, the Chinese attitude was not far from the famous Berg Report that blamed African governments for the problems plaguing the World Bank's projects in Africa.[22] But the solution was radically different. Structural adjustment programs were trying to use conditionality to create an enabling environment for the private sector in Africa. The Chinese also decided to use part of their aid to support private sector initiatives, *but* they did it by fostering cooperation directly between Chinese companies and those in the recipient countries. "Complant really started to expand into investment around the time of Zhu Rongji's visit to Africa," as the manager of China's Magbass sugar complex, George Guo, told me later. China's effort to promote exports to Africa, Europe's backyard, had another effect: a proliferation of Chinese traders in African markets.

"Koni ... Koni ... Koni"

In early 2008, the rains were late in northern Namibia. Between 2004 and 2008, as Swiss anthropologist Gregor Dobler reported, the number of Chinese shops in the border town of Oshikango quadrupled.[23] Rumors began to spread through villages near the Angolan border that the drought was God's punishment: Namibians had allowed the Chinese traders to open their shops on Sundays. In Dar es Salaam, Chinese traders were increasingly visible in the busy central market neighborhood of Kariakoo. Their small crowded shops sold traditional medicine, hair pieces, embroidered fabrics, and other Chinese goods. Some Chinese traders were even competing with the village women, squatting on the ground selling groundnuts and roast corn outside the fish market and the bus terminal, enticing customers with Swahili shouts of "Kranga ... kranga ... kranga! Koni ... koni ... koni!"[24]

In the 1990s, Chinese products and Chinese traders became a rapidly growing part of the landscape in African cities and rural towns. Many established larger, more formal shops to import Chinese vehicles, machinery, electronics, and equipment. Chinese companies were encouraged to sell and service small power tillers and other kinds of agricultural machinery first introduced through aid programs. In addition, with aid projects at one time or another in every country in Africa but Swaziland, and teams of Chinese laborers imported to work on these projects, some stayed behind. Drawing on *guanxi* (connections) to set up an import business was a fairly easy way to finance the first stage of plans that generally went far beyond a small market stall (or a patch of ground on which to sell groundnuts). This accelerated after emigration rules were somewhat relaxed in China in 1985. The pattern we see today of a Chinese presence in African markets is partly due to the success of government programs to push Chinese export businesses to expand into Africa, but there is no evidence that the Chinese government sends workers to Africa under a *plan* to have them remain behind as traders. These are individual decisions.

Packaging Soft Power

The process of preparing for WTO entry, the need for natural resources, and the goal of building and diversifying trade, meant that Beijing continued to be interested in Africa and other parts of the developing world for economic reasons. But, as the quiet ongoing diplomatic war with Taipei laid out in Chapter 1 made clear, China also needed to package itself as a *politically* attractive partner. In addition, as a rising power engaging overseas in foreign investment and resource extraction, Beijing wanted to make the case that China was not simply a newer version of Japan and the Western "imperialist powers." Beijing needed to make its aid and other forms of what Harvard professor Joseph Nye has called "soft power" much more visible. It needed to convince other developing countries that China's rise would be peaceful, and not zero-sum.[25]

Public framing of the growing ties with Africa as "win-win" took top priority. In 2000, as we saw above, the Chinese unveiled the Forum on China–Africa Cooperation. But the FOCAC model was soon echoed in the China–Caribbean Economic and Trade Cooperation Forum, and a similar forum linking China and Portuguese-speaking countries, both launched in 2003. The Forum on Cooperation between China and Arab States followed in 2004, and the China–Pacific Islands Economic Development Forum was set up in 2006. All of the new forums framed aid within a broad set of economic cooperation policies, and allowed for regular dialogue and high-level meetings. Each included promises of preferential funds for investment, tariff-free entry to China for many categories of goods, cancellation of debts, scholarships and training in China for officials from the region, and so on.

China's growing political engagement in Africa was clearly part of a broader strategy of engagement with the developing world more generally. In September 2005, Chinese President Hu Jintao reinforced this with a speech at the United Nations Summit on financing the Millennium Development Goals. China would step up to the plate, he said. Hu Jintao pledged to train 30,000 people and provide *ten billion dollars* in concessional finance and export credits to developing countries, over the next three years.[26]

Dragon Heads

"Going global" was partly about supporting sophisticated, high value-added, brand-name companies with their own intellectual property. It was also about nurturing "dragon heads" (national champions) to become globally competitive multinational firms. As part of the push, Eximbank and the National Development and Reform Commission (NDRC, China's state planning authority) began to provide lower-cost loans to Chinese companies to help them expand overseas.

The telecommunications firm Huawei received a $10 billion line of credit from China Development Bank to support its "going global" activities.[27] China National Oil Company landed a soft loan of $1.6 billion (repayable over ten years) for its investments in Nigeria. Several large construction firms like Beijing Construction Engineering Group (which built the US embassy in Beijing) received attractive lines of credit from China Eximbank. This helped them win bids to build dozens of overseas projects – casinos in

Las Vegas and the Bahamas, as well as the gleaming new stadium just outside of Dar es Salaam that we saw at the start of this chapter. China State Construction Engineering Corporation gained a $3 billion, five-year preferential line of credit in 2005, something that boosted its ability to win bids on contracts from Ethiopia to Botswana.

To foster the overseas investment, engineering contracts, and search for new markets that were all part of "going global," Beijing promised diplomatic support, export tax exemptions, help with risk assessments, easier emigration approvals, and insurance. They set up programs to give enterprises "with comparative advantages" interest rate rebates for loans taken out from China's domestic banks to finance working capital for overseas engineering contracts valued at $5 million and above.[28]

Investment responded to the incentives. Figures 3.2 and 3.3 show the growth over four short years in Chinese overseas investment in agriculture-related activities, mining, and manufacturing. They also show that this growth is not particularly steady. One reason may be *changes* in the incentives, put in place by the Chinese government to fine-tune investment decisions by firms. The State Council publishes regular catalogs listing overseas activities that are eligible (or not) for this support, and countries where investment would be encouraged (or not). For 2007, unsurprisingly, Beijing provided support for projects involving petroleum and a host of minerals, but also encouraged rubber and fuel oil plantations, cotton farms,

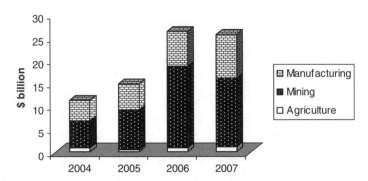

Fig. 3.2. Chinese outward FDI stocks: Manufacturing, mining, and agriculture

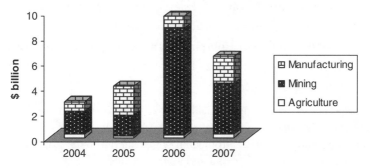

Fig. 3.3. Chinese outward FDI flows: Manufacturing, mining, and agriculture

Source: Chinese Ministry of Commerce.

and overseas factories for textiles, paper, farm machinery assembly, and medicines (like Holley Pharmaceuticals). At the same time, Sudan, Iran, and Nigeria were removed from the list of countries where Chinese companies could receive incentives for investment in oil, while Niger, Ecuador, and several new countries were added.[29] This move was widely perceived as political in nature, given China's image problems in Sudan. However, others believed it to be a practical response to an oversupply of Chinese companies in some countries, and a desire to encourage diversification.

About the same time that China's state ramped up encouragement for its winning firms to expand overseas, they also began encouraging the labor-intensive, less competitive "mature" industries (such as textiles and leather goods) to relocate to other countries. China's government acted to *anticipate* restructuring, not hold it back. They understood that forward momentum involves "creative destruction," the label given by the renowned economic historian Joseph Schumpeter to the forward march of innovation that brought the automobile, but left the makers of buggy whips high and dry. They also figured that markets for buggy whips lasted a bit longer in parts of the world where buggies (figuratively) were still being used.

Creative Destruction

For months in 2007 and 2008, the *Washington Post* that landed each day outside our door brought story after story focused on industrial pressures inside China, all with the same message: *China's outsourcing appeal diminishing*. Until prices fell in the global recession that began in late 2008, high fuel costs had tripled the price of transport across the Pacific. In the crowded areas of the Pearl River delta near Hong Kong, reported *The Economist* in January 2007,

> office rents are soaring, industrial land is in short supply and utility costs are climbing. Most significant of all are rocketing wages. In spite of the mass migration of workers from China's vast interior to the coast, pay for factory workers has been rising at double digit rates for several years.

A labor law that came into effect in January 2008 increased wage costs by another 10–15 percent. "Everyone should be aware," a member of Hong Kong's legislature commented, "that China has changed."

China's very success at creating new firms had led to problems of overcapacity. Fierce business competition drove margins razor-thin and made it hard for new businesses to get their foot in the door. A 2005 survey commissioned by the World Bank from Peking University economists Yang Yao and Yin He reported that of Chinese companies with plans to invest in Africa, more than 90 percent listed "markets" as the most important factor in their decision.[30] This helps explain why, like their US counterparts, most Chinese investors targeted Egypt, South Africa, and Nigeria, Africa's three most populous countries. The financial crisis that began in 2008 only intensified the pressure to look outward for new markets and lower-cost production sites.

Chinese leaders have also woken up to the environmental legacies of their headlong sprint through the early stages of industrialization: the infamous Beijing pollution and the poisoned rivers that snake through China's heartland. The five-year plan unveiled in 2006 emphasized a more environment-friendly growth path. This is also a factor in the growing interest Africa holds for some Chinese companies. In 2007, South Africa's deputy President Phumzile Mlambo-Ngcuka raised eyebrows in her country when she commented, "China needs to send some of its polluting industries elsewhere because it is choking on them," adding quickly that she believed South Africa had the capacity to manage emissions.[31]

In 2005, as Figure 3.3 demonstrated, China's outward investment in manufacturing *exceeded* that for mining. As Chinese industrialists start to put down roots in Africa, their path will in many cases have been smoothed by a Chinese state that is now encouraging the low end of Chinese industry to move overseas.

Beijing has continually adjusted the mix of incentives and costs to push forward restructuring. On the one hand, new incentives were put in place. In July 2006, for example, the Ministries of Finance and Commerce established a special fund Chinese textile companies could draw on to encourage more of them to move offshore.[32] On the other hand, costs were increased for those who stayed. For example, China has a system where firms that export can get rebates on the taxes they pay domestically. In 2007, this benefit and others were removed for companies in China exporting high emission (chemicals, smelting) and labor-intensive products (plastics, textiles).[33] While I was in China that summer, *China Daily* announced yet another change for the worse in the tax rules for low-tech exporting firms. "Tens of thousands of Hong Kong enterprises will have to give up their labor-intensive production, move out of familiar coastal bases," the newspaper concluded, "or upgrade their technology and product quality quickly."[34]

Two of the tools announced at the November 2006 FOCAC Summit – the China–Africa Development Fund, and support for the new overseas economic zones – are part of the restructuring plan. In 2007, the vice-governor of China Development Bank, Gao Jian, told *Caijing*, an independent Beijing magazine focused on finance and economics, that the China–Africa Development Fund was intended to help push Chinese companies to relocate their more mature factories offshore. "Chinese firms have faced overcapacity and upgraded their production methods in recent years, while Africa has a shortage of supply in consumer goods," Gao explained. "This should complement both economies," he added.[35]

Before we look at those two tools, let us put China's engagement in active restructuring into comparative perspective. The West gives very little assistance for manufacturing in Africa, the kind of medium-to-large factories that would create thousands of jobs. Between 2002 and 2007, World Bank loans for industry and trade combined came to less than 5 percent of all loans made to sub-Saharan Africa. The traditional donor countries allocated less than *1 percent* of their aid to industry.[36]

The World Bank's private equity arm, the International Finance Corporation, makes equity investments in African companies. But in the 1990s only about 10 percent of IFC investments went into manufacturing, while half financed projects in mining and oil. Although a broad swathe of IFC equity goes into African banks or equity funds, which might lend to manufacturers in their region, the IFC itself has averaged only around four manufacturing projects a year in Africa since 2000.[37]

What about the private sector in Europe and the US? Just like the official donor community, they have shied away from investing in African factories. European manufacturers started to wind down their factories when Africa's prolonged economic crisis began to bite into their profits. A third of British companies with manufacturing investments pulled out in the first decade of Africa's prolonged economic slump, including Leyland Trucks, Unilever (soaps, foods), Raleigh bicycles, and Boots and Wellcome (pharmaceuticals). By 1994, a mere sixty-five British companies still had equity investments in African manufacturing.[38] This pattern is only now slowly starting to reverse. US companies have been equally reluctant to invest in Africa, aside from the lucrative petroleum and mining sectors. Only 11 percent of US investment in Africa went into manufacturing between 1995 and 2007, and South Africa received nearly half of this.[39]

The United States government has tried in other ways to foster more investment in Africa. In 2000, the US launched AGOA, the Africa Growth and Opportunity Act. AGOA was intended to boost African exports to the US, but also to help boost US investment in the region. Three years after AGOA took effect, Stephen Hayes, president of the Corporate Council for Africa, told Congress: "As a tool for Americans to invest in Africa, AGOA has been an abysmal failure."[40] Susan Schwab, head of the office of the US Trade Representative, admitted to the annual AGOA Forum audience in 2008 that although investment by US companies was now higher, they were still heavily concentrated in natural resources.

And, of course, there is no official support in places like the United States for assisting industrial restructuring by helping "mature" industries relocate across the border or overseas. The relocation of these sunset industries follows a pattern known as the "international product life cycle," the name Harvard professor Raymond Vernon gave to a familiar trajectory. Over time, Vernon explained, the production of a product such as textiles, or radios, or computers will typically shift offshore to lower-cost locations. This happens in distinct (if stylized) phases. First, a country imports the product (unless it is something they invented). Second, they begin to produce it themselves for domestic use, using imported components: "knocked down" kits assembled locally. Third, they increase the "backward linkages" by producing some of the components locally. Fourth, they start to export it themselves, and, finally, facing pressure to restructure due to higher labor costs and/or pollution problems, they export the production process itself.

The inexorable workings of the international product cycle are highly political in wealthy countries. We call it "outsourcing" or "going offshore." During the 1992 American presidential election, candidate Ross Perot famously called it the "giant sucking sound" of jobs being pulled to Mexico by NAFTA, the proposed North American Free Trade Agreement. Communities and labor unions lobby hard to stop the product cycle from working its way through, to protect the mature industries (textiles, shoes, steel, electronics, automobiles) that are under pressure, to stop jobs from leaving for Mexico, and now China.

In 1994, the US Congress imposed a regulation (known as "PD 20") that prohibits the US Agency for International Development from funding any activity (such as helping a developing country attract US investment) if it was "reasonably likely" that it would lead to *any* jobs being lost in the US.[41] This ensures that aid from the US will not be used to help poor countries attract our sunset industries. China has no such restriction. They find aid and other tools, like the China–Africa Development Fund, useful precisely for this purpose.

China–Africa Development Fund

In May 2007, the China Development Bank launched the first phase of the China–Africa Development Fund (CADF), an equity fund that is expected over time to provide $5 billion in finance for ventures launched by Chinese firms. Three months later, in Beijing, I met with Gao Jian, vice-governor of the CDB and head of the fund, to ask him about his plans. We sat in a plush reception room, the perimeter lined with overstuffed velvet armchairs, the walls with delicately brushed Chinese paintings. An aide brought hot tea. Gao Jian sat beside me in the center of the room facing the door, his arms resting on either side of the chair. A small entourage of senior aides sat diagonally across from us.

Gao told me that the fund will encourage joint projects between state-owned or private Chinese firms, and African (or other nationality) companies. The fund will invest on commercial principles, he continued. "We're not seeking high profits from this fund, but just asking that we don't incur losses." He turned to look directly at me, and nodded slightly to emphasize the next point. "We regard Africa as entering already a new era. They have gotten rid of some of the problems: tribal problems, apartheid struggles. They are concentrating on economic development."

"This is not aid; it's a market-based fund," the fund's CEO Chi Jianxin commented later, explaining some of the thinking behind the fund. "The African market is very new and many companies are not familiar with it so they need to share the risk with other investors. Most Chinese companies don't have much experience in risk management." He pointed out that the China–Africa Development Fund would have a longer time horizon than most equity funds. "We think we will stay in a project for five to eight years, but if some need a bit longer we can do that."[42]

The fund planned to invest between $5 and $50 million for each project, in minority shareholdings. "We are interested in partnering with European countries," Gao Jian told me. "Many European countries have relationships with their ex-colonies. They may have developed a plan to invest in infrastructure, but they haven't raised the money. We can use these plans. We would like to join their efforts. We would like to have joint projects."

China Development Bank moved quickly to get the fund up and running. By the time the China–Africa Development Fund was launched in June 2007, the bank had already sent twenty teams to Africa to set up temporary offices, build relationships (as Gao described it), and scout out investment projects in agriculture, manufacturing, electricity, transportation, telecommunications, urban infrastructure, and resource exploration. The first few projects funded included a glass factory in Egypt, a gas-fired power plant in Ghana (a joint venture with a Ghanaian firm), and a chromium processing plant in Zimbabwe.

By my next visit more than a year later, the team running the fund had moved into posh new quarters in China's financial district. The CADF's board had approved funding for twenty projects worth about $2 billion by the end of 2008 and were evaluating more than one hundred other proposals.[43] At our meeting around a business-like rectangular table, Willie

Chao, the new fund manager, told me that his board had decided to allow the fund to invest in projects proposed by African entrepreneurs without any Chinese participation.

Although Africa equity funds have been launched by private firms in industrialized countries, the China–Africa Development Fund has no real counterpart in the efforts by governments of industrialized countries to foster economic development in Africa. During a trip to South Africa in 2008, French President Sarkozy announced that France would launch a 250 million euro ($368 million) investment fund for Africa. However, the French will purchase shares in other funds and not offer equity directly to companies. The US supports equity investment by American firms in Africa through the Overseas Private Investment Corporation (OPIC). But OPIC also provides no equity, only loans, political risk insurance, and other kinds of guarantees.[44] The British Commonwealth Development Corporation probably comes closest. It offers equity investment, but its total assets amount to $4 billion, and it has been around since the 1940s.

China's fund was criticized at first because participation was restricted to Chinese companies and their African joint-venture partners. But the Chinese listened, and decided to open the fund. At a dinner for a visiting delegation from the China–Africa Development Fund, China's ambassador to Liberia, Zhou Yuxiao, told Liberians that the fund's interest in Liberia might be a "turning point" in the two countries' economic relations. At the moment, ties were based mainly on aid, but foreign investment could be a shortcut to development. It's like "borrowing a boat to go to sea" instead of having to build it yourself. This worked well in China, he added.[45]

Tariff and Quota-Free Entry

At the Addis Ababa ministerial meeting of FOCAC in 2003, Chinese leader Wen Jiabao promised to give zero tariff treatment to an unspecified number of exports from Africa's least developed countries. The list of commodities and degree of local content stipulations ("rules of origin") were negotiated during 2004. The full list of 190 products was announced in each country in early 2005. At the Beijing Summit in November 2006, the Chinese pledged to increase the list to 440 commodities. This went into effect in July of 2007.

What impact is duty-free entry likely to have on Africa? The West has two similar programs. Europe's "Everything But Arms" (EBA) program generally allows duty-free and quota-free entry into the European Union for all goods from the least developed countries, except armaments. Entry for politically contentious crops – bananas, rice, and sugar – was to be phased in more gradually. The United States' Africa Growth and Opportunity Act allowed duty-free entry of most commodities, as long as countries were certified as having met a number of economic, political, and rule-of-origin conditions. Independent analyses of the Everything But Arms and AGOA programs have reported a range of effects for participating countries, from generally positive to somewhat disappointing.[46] The disappointments came mainly from the complex rules of origin that often limited duty-free access to products made from inputs that *also* came from the region. Under strict rules of origin, garments exported from Africa would generally have to be made using African cloth, buttons, zippers, even the lining for the pockets. Worse, for AGOA, the rules of origin were constantly changing, as Congress continued to modify the legislation. There were also problems on the supply side: it takes time to respond to new incentives, and potential entrepreneurs were not sure how long the incentives would remain in place.

China's program was said to cover almost all the exports from the least developed countries; however, a list of goods was not easy to obtain and this made it difficult to evaluate the potential development impact. China's Minister of Commerce Chen Deming commented that the program removed import tariffs on "farm products, stone materials, minerals, leather and hide, textiles, clothing, electric appliances and machinery and equipment," from thirty-one of Africa's least developed countries. He said that between 2006 and 2008 the program had transferred $680 million in tariff exemptions to the thirty-one countries.[47] This was quite a bit higher than estimates made by Adam Minson at the South African Institute of International Affairs, who obtained a list of products. Minson estimated that the economic value of the preferences was modest, only about $10 million per year, with the highest returns coming from things like sesame seeds, cocoa beans, leather and skins, copper, and octopus.[48] However, Minson's analysis relied on the value of export figures from previous years, and did not account for possible increases stimulated by the program.

As we saw above, Chinese companies have a set of separate incentives for agricultural and natural resource investments. Together, these incentives have stimulated new investment not only in copper (as in the Democratic Republic of the Congo) but in crops. Chinese entrepreneurs have begun to plant sesame seeds in Senegal to export duty free to China, for example. Minson also pointed out that although China was continuing to protect its cotton farmers by not allowing duty-free entry of raw cotton, cotton *products* from the least developed countries were being allowed in duty-free. If this were better publicized, Minson noted, it could "serve as an incentive to African producers to process raw materials locally before exporting them."[49]

Between 2006 and 2008, according to an analysis by Mark George, an expert at the Beijing office of the British Department for International Development, the value of exports from Africa to China increased by an average of 110 percent. Thirty-two countries in Africa showed an increase in earnings from exports to China, while exports from the remaining twenty had either decreased, or shown no change.[50] We can expect that the global financial crisis will roll back many of these increases, at least temporarily, reflecting the slump in Chinese import demand, and the related fall in prices of many African commodities.

Overseas Zones: Going Global in Groups

"Why did we develop so fast?" Li Qiangmin, China's ambassador to Zambia, said to me when I met him in the Zambian capital of Lusaka in 2008. "We had four special economic zones. *This is a shortcut for development.*" In 2006, China's Ministry of Commerce announced that overseas economic zones would become a key platform in the "going global" program. China would support its companies to establish *fifty* overseas economic zones in countries around the world.[51]

China's new overseas zones are similar (but not identical) to China's own model. In one of Deng Xiaoping's first major experiments, China set up Shenzhen and three other special economic zones in July 1979. These were intended to attract foreign investment by countries eager to enter China's markets or to move their own mature industries overseas (Hainan Island was added later as a fifth zone). In 1984, fourteen coastal cities carved out smaller areas as industrial and technological development zones, similar in concept but often targeting clusters of firms in different sectors. Over three decades, Chinese cities set up more than a hundred industrial and technology zones along the coast and eventually around the country.[52]

Export processing zones have at least as many critics as they do fans. Unions dislike them because they often operate with fewer labor restrictions and lower wages than the rest of the formal economy. They can be enclaves without any development connection to the rest of the country. Yet in places such as Ireland, China, Taiwan, Mauritius, and the Dominican Republic, special export zones are widely deemed responsible for a large chunk of each economy's initial industrialization success.

China's new overseas zones were *not* only about export processing, however. They could be for a range of activities, including services. Their one signal innovation was that they were to be *built and operated by Chinese enterprises* as profitable ventures. As the Chinese put it, the overseas zone model was company-centered and business-based. Companies would propose locations where they hoped to open a zone (or had already started one), put their own capital on the line, and compete with other Chinese companies for Beijing's support.

Although proposals for these zones would be *selected* purely on competitive market principles, the winning proposals would then be eligible for a range of supportive policies in classic East Asian "developmental state" fashion.[53] Companies could receive help with feasibility studies, land rents, and infrastructure. The Ministry of Commerce pledged to make up to $25 million in grants and up to $250 million in long-term loans available. Half of the expenses for Chinese enterprises moving into the zones could be reimbursed, and companies could get export tax rebates and easier access to foreign exchange in China's strict capital control system. In addition, the cachet of being selected as one of the sponsored zones might make policy banks such as the China Development Bank or China Eximbank look more favorably on companies' applications for finance or equity participation. And Chinese embassies would provide diplomatic support in negotiations with the host government over land, tax incentives, or work permits. The Ministry of Commerce even put a special team together to help push the Mauritius zone forward.

Why did Beijing select this unusual method of promoting Chinese investment overseas? The obvious answer, yet again, is that it fits with

China's own domestic experience – an experience they believed was a useful model. As in China, these zones would allow other developing countries to create a "protective bubble," a place where they could experiment with new approaches without having to change national-level policies. Moving production overseas also allowed the Chinese to ease some of their "trade frictions." But for China the overseas zones also provided a partial solution to two pressing domestic dilemmas.

First, more restructuring was clearly underway in China, and these zones provided an orderly way to transfer mature industries abroad rather than just letting them "creatively destruct." The focus of the zones was supposed to be on mature industries where China had excess production capacity (textiles, light industries, machinery, appliances, construction materials, pharmaceuticals, etc.). Each zone was supposed to include no more than three major industries, and ideally would present a cluster of related industries. In Pakistan, for example, the Haier-Ruba zone was specializing in home appliances; the Ethiopia zone would concentrate on textiles, leather goods, and building materials; and the Zambia zone at Chambishi on a cluster of metal processing factories, while its extension near the city of Lusaka would concentrate on electronics assembly.

Second, many of the industries that were unable to compete were small and medium-sized. MOFCOM promised to support the efforts of the winning companies to attract small and medium-sized companies into their zones. For Chinese companies unused to foreign investment, the zones provided a framework where much of the uncertainty and risk were mitigated. Fu Ziying, from China's Ministry of Commerce described the strategy succinctly in a speech at China's Financial Forum in 2007: "It is a way to support the Chinese companies to 'go global' in groups." This strategy "reduces anxieties" about foreign investment, and it can provide economies of scale, former Minister of Commerce Bo Xilai noted.[54]

As with all of China's major initiatives, there had been earlier experiments. Fujian Huaqiao Company built an industrial and trade zone in Cuba in 2000. In 2004, China Middle East Investment and Trade Promotion Center and Jebel Ali Free Trade Zone joined together to construct an enormous, $300 million trade center that could host 4,000 Chinese companies in the lively Arabian Gulf port city of Dubai. That same year, Tianjin Port Free Trade Zone Investment Company and the United States Pacific Development

Company began construction of a Chinese trade and industrial park in the South Carolina city of Greenville. By 2008, a dozen Chinese companies had set up production, logistics, and trade companies in the Greenville zone.

But the Chinese firm Haier, the world's fourth-largest appliance manufacturer, was a key pioneer. Haier built its first industrial complex outside of China in 1999: a 46-hectare industrial park in Camden, South Carolina, about 115 miles from Greenville where the Tianjin province project would later be located. Two years later, Haier and a Pakistani company, Panapak Electronics, constructed a joint industrial park near the Pakistani city of Lahore.

Haier's experience in Pakistan, knowledge of the local market, and familiarity with Pakistan's policy regime put Haier in a good position to win the first of China's officially sponsored overseas cooperation zones. In November 2006, Chinese President Hu Jintao dug a shovel into the Pakistani soil to launch construction of the zone, a joint effort by Haier and Ruba, a private Pakistani company.

Haier's proposal was one of eight selected in the first round of what the Ministry described as a "fair, just, and transparent" bidding system. The system worked as follows. First, the Ministry's branch offices were asked to promote the idea and the proposal guidelines among enterprises in their region, and help them to apply. In the first round held in 2006, more than sixty companies submitted detailed expressions of interest. About half of these were asked to submit formal proposals, documenting the market potential, the support offered by the host country, and its investment environment. The government's primary emphasis was on the likely profitability of the project, but the projects also needed to be given the green light by the Ministry of Foreign Affairs.

Twelve companies were invited to Beijing as finalists to appear before a panel of outside experts, and eight were finally selected. In the second round in 2007, the government raised the bar a little higher. More than fifty companies applied, twenty were allowed to submit formal proposals, and eleven companies had their proposals selected. At the end of 2007, China's Ministry of Commerce had signed off on *seven* official overseas economic zones in Africa (these are pictured in Figure 9.1, on p. 250).[55] "This is good for our own industrial upgrading," a Chinese analyst asserted. "We cannot always remain as 'the world's workshop' and stick to low-end manufacturing."[56]

The First Two African Winners

China's first two zones in sub-Saharan Africa were announced in Zambia and Mauritius, and both were sponsored by companies with substantial investments in each country. In Zambia, China Nonferrous Mining Group (operator of the copper mine where Zambians and Chinese have repeatedly clashed over labor and safety issues) began in 2003 to implement plans to develop a metallurgy industrial cluster on the large concession of land it held in Chambishi. The Zambian government was at the same time working out a legal framework for multi-facility economic zones (MFEZ). "So these two things came together," explained a Zambian government official. The Chinese company signed a letter of intent in December 2005.

China Nonferrous Mining Group aimed to develop a cluster of firms that would pull some of the industrial chain back to Africa by producing bars, wires, cables, and so on from raw copper, nickel, and other metals mined in Zambia and the region nearby. This would be Zambia's opportunity to finally add local value to the raw materials it had been exporting since British times. "The Chinese want to start manufacturing...in Zambia instead of just importing raw materials," Commerce and Trade Minister Felix Mutati told *Reuters* in 2007.

In Lusaka, I sat with Roy Kapembwa of the Zambian Development Authority in his new office across from a government complex built by the Chinese. Zambia's MFEZ regulations, he told me, required a minimum investment of $500,000 to be able to take advantage of government incentives, but there was no prohibition on Zambian firms or other foreign investors at Chambishi. He showed me the glossy, bilingual promotional materials produced by the Chinese for the zone.[57] The Chambishi zone promoters hoped to "bring in Zambian strategic investors with good performance and reputation." By 2011, they aimed to have forty Chinese companies and at least ten from other countries (hence the bilingual materials). And they added a "green" pledge: the operators of the Chambishi zone would apply to have its environmental management certified at the International Standards Organization's ISO 14000 global standard.

The proposal submitted by Shanxi province's Tianli Group for an economic zone in Mauritius was also one of eight selected in the first round. In June 2008 I visited Mauritius again. Although the farmers who had protested the terms of their removal from the land had by then agreed on a compensation package from the government and been resettled peacefully, some Mauritians continued to express worries.

"It is a voluntary colonization...a danger for our security," Anil Gayan, former Minister of Foreign Affairs and opposition member of parliament, had written in a January 2008 op-ed in a local paper, *L'Express*. "This is money from the People's Republic of China. The Chinese state, Beijing in fact, will decide the contours and the content of the project. What were their intentions, their strategic designs, when the Beijing authorities chose Mauritius?" he wondered, darkly.[58]

In fact, Beijing probably had little *strategic* interest in the Mauritius project, which had been initiated as a business proposal by the Tianli Group. And the content of the project was decided not in Beijing, but through negotiations with the Mauritius government. Later, Tianli hired a Shanghai firm, Wang Strategy Consultants, to create an overall design for the zone.

I met with an official from Tianli and two Mauritian officials at the government's Board of Investment in Port Louis. Before we started to discuss the project, the Mauritian officials played a promotional DVD prepared by the Shanghai firm. The ideas for the zone had changed radically over the past two years. They were very different from the Chambishi zone, and I was astounded at the new design.

Tianli had first envisioned an industrial hub producing for export, perhaps focused on textiles, along with a trade and distribution center for east and southern Africa to take advantage of the free port in Mauritius. But as the Tianli official, William Guo, told me, "We had a lot of meetings with the government here to find out what they wanted for the future of the country. The plan changed away from industry." The Chinese economic counselor stressed this point in a meeting I had with her later: "We are not doing the zone of twenty years ago. It is a *must* to do this in an environmentally friendly way. The company has realized this point. They are not going to be moving the polluting industries to Mauritius."

The promotional DVD showed a modern, airy city with boulevards of *filao* trees and garden apartments with views of the Indian Ocean. The zone (to be built using *feng-shui* design principles) would now be positioned as an "i-Park," emphasizing "intelligence, innovation, incubation, interaction."

There would still be some light industry, but Tianli was aiming to build something more like Dubai. They were now going out on a limb to attract higher value-added investors, along the lines of the vision Mauritius had for its service-oriented future.

Tianli hoped Chinese companies active in Africa would locate their regional headquarters in the zone. There would be a logistics center, two hotels, an international conference center, a state-of-the-art medical center, wholesale and retail shopping centers, an informatics tower, and a bilingual Chinese–English boarding school for the children of executives stationed in other parts of Africa. New employment, direct and indirect, would almost certainly expand beyond the several thousand in the original estimate, and many of them would be Chinese.

Tianli had wanted Mauritians to be able to invest in the zone, but the Mauritian government decided that the first phase at least should be only foreign investment. "We want these new jobs to be truly additional, from new companies," Finance Minister Rama Sithanen told me. "We want to avoid diverting Mauritian investors into the zone who would be investing anyways." In April 2008, Gao Jian visited Mauritius with a delegation from the China–Africa Development Fund. How did they like the plans, I asked. William Guo smiled broadly. "They *loved* it." The China–Africa Development Fund had decided to invest.

Jean-Noel Wong, a Mauritian partner at Kemp Chatteris Deloitte, chosen by Tianli to be its local consultants on the project, gave his overview of the project: "Mauritius was selected because we can be a platform between China and Africa. There is also the quality of the infrastructure, the good communication and telecoms facilities, and economic, political and social stability. If the project succeeds, as we think it will," Jean-Noel Wong added, "it will certainly have a snowball effect."[59]

Crossing the *Ocean* by Feeling the Stones

Bo Xilai, the former Minister of Commerce, described the "going global" policies as a new phase of Deng Xiaoping's familiar experimental strategy: "we are now crossing the *ocean* by feeling the stones." China's overseas economic zones and the $5 billion China–Africa Development Fund are attractive to many in Africa because they are a striking alternative to the aid business as usual. They represent China's twenty-first-century efforts to build on its own domestic experience. And they embed some of the lessons China learned in its aid and economic cooperation experiments of earlier decades.

These programs have some parallels in the West, but *not* on the gigantic scale envisioned by Beijing. They are particularly interesting in view of former Mozambican President Chissano's call for aid to be leveraged together with resources from the private sector, to promote domestic entrepreneurs in Africa. And they help explain the comment Roy Kapembwa of the Zambian Development Agency made to me, leaning across the large desk in his Lusaka office: "We are trying as much as possible to focus on China because they are ready. Where there are opportunities, they will take them. We need to move the country up the value chain."

Above all, these programs reflect the lessons of all the experiments since Mao died, the spirit of China's 1995 aid reforms, and the continued emphasis on aid as a lubricant for mutually beneficial cooperation. The $10 billion in preferential finance promised at the UN Summit in 2005 would target turn-key infrastructure projects but it would also be available, Hu said, for promoting cooperation between Chinese enterprises and those in developing countries. The Millennium Development Goals and China's own plan to "go global" came together in this pledge. It underlined the enormity of the resources available in China's coffers, and it was a wake-up call for the traditional donors. China, they could now see, was a player in the global system of aid and development finance. But, as we shall see in the next chapter, the mysterious new player with the large pot of money was not necessarily going to be playing by the traditional rules.

CHAPTER 4

Eastern Promises: An Aid System with Chinese Characteristics

News began to filter out late in 2007 that China was preparing to finance billions of dollars in roads, railways, and hospitals in the Democratic Republic of the Congo, allowing Congo to repay over time with mineral exports that Chinese companies would also develop. An editorial in the London-based *Financial Times* said: "Beijing has thrown down its most direct challenge yet to the west's architecture for assisting Africa's development."[1]

Headline-grabbing deals like the one in the Congo are layered onto China's *own* architecture of engagement with Africa. As in the West, the offices managing aid are separate from those that manage other forms of economic cooperation, even though aid might sometimes be part of a package of engagement. The Ministry of Commerce is at the center, issuing *grants* and *zero-interest loans*, and coordinating with China Eximbank on *concessional loans*. China has at least nine kinds of aid: medical teams, training and scholarships, humanitarian aid, youth volunteers, debt relief, budget support, turn-key or "complete plant" projects (infrastructure, factories), aid-in-kind, and technical assistance. Some of these are new, but others have been in place for a very long time.

The previous chapter outlined China's strategy for "going global" and its main instruments. This chapter introduces China's aid system, including its new youth volunteer program and other innovations. The level of detail on the history of the system and its component parts may be more than you want to know, particularly over the next few pages. But the introduction here of the key players is central to grasping how China works in Africa.

A Very Brief History

When China first began to give aid in the 1950s, there was no aid agency at all.[2] China's first dedicated office for aid, the Bureau (later, Commission) of Foreign Economic Relations, was set up in 1960, directly under the highest government body, the State Council.[3] The Commission took over the handling of material aid, turn-key projects (through China Complete Plant Import and Export Corporation, or Complant, a company that has already made several appearances in this book), and technical assistance. Decisions on new aid agreements would be made jointly by the Ministry of Foreign Affairs and the Commission of Foreign Economic Relations.

In 1970, in the face of the sharp increase in aid tasks described in Chapter 1, the Commission was upgraded to ministry status, becoming the Ministry of Foreign Economic Relations. At a major national foreign aid conference in March 1971, China's leaders announced that all provinces and major municipalities would set up offices of economic and technical cooperation to help carry out the increased work. Each central ministry – agriculture, railways, construction – and their branches in the provinces and municipalities also had economic and technical cooperation offices, as did large, state-owned companies like the Shanghai No. 12 Cotton Mill.[4]

In March 1982, in a government shuffle that consolidated a number of ministries, the Ministry of Foreign Economic Relations was merged with the Ministry of Trade to form the Ministry of Foreign Economic Relations and Trade. Within this larger ministry, aid was assigned to the new Department of Foreign Aid. The merger sent a clear signal that China expected to forge a closer relationship between aid and other forms of economic engagement.

As China began moving toward the market, bureaus of cooperation at provincial and municipal level were transformed into corporations. Likewise, the cooperation office of the Ministry of Railways became China Civil Engineering Construction Corporation; the office of the Ministry of Communications became China Road and Bridge Corporation, and so on. The latter two are now among China's largest overseas engineering firms.

This process was repeated at the provincial and municipal levels. For example, Jiangxi province set up China Jiangxi International Economic and Technical Cooperation Corporation. In keeping with the gradual move toward the market, these corporations were encouraged to develop a sense of themselves as *enterprises* with interests separate from their parent agencies. It was these firms that began to step out in the late 1970s, in an overseas "responsibility system." Once the China Jiangxi International Economic and Technical Cooperation Corporation fulfilled its assigned foreign aid construction project in Mali, for example, it had the freedom to seek out profitable opportunities. These companies could retain up to one million dollars of the extra foreign exchange they earned.[5]

To complete the history: the Ministry of Foreign Economic Relations and Trade became the Ministry of Foreign Trade and Economic Cooperation in 1993, and as of 2003, the Ministry of Commerce (for convenience, and because of the head-spinning name changes, I refer to the Ministry by this recent name throughout the book). Through all of these changes, there was always a central office in charge of the implementation of foreign aid. Today that office, the Department of Foreign Aid, is housed in China's Ministry of Commerce, but it fits into a network of other institutions that also have a role in aid.

China's Aid Institutions

The State Council (China's cabinet, headed by the Chinese premier and vice-premiers) still has an oversight role for aid (Figure 4.1). It approves the annual aid budget, any grants of cash above $1.5 million, all aid projects above 100 million RMB (about $12.5 million), aid to "politically sensitive countries" and any requests to exceed the annual plan for foreign aid.[6] The Ministry of Finance allocates donations to multilateral organizations: grants to United Nations agencies (such as UNICEF) or to the World Bank's International Development Association (IDA). The Ministry of Finance also manages the cancellation of foreign aid debt owed to China, and it signs off on the annual aid plans. But China's three central institutions involved in aid are the Ministry of Commerce, the Ministry of Foreign Affairs, and China Eximbank.

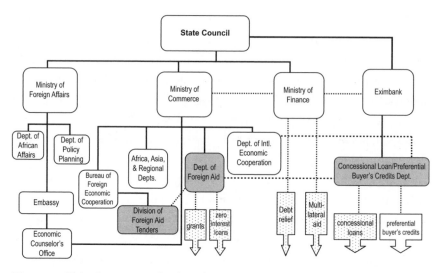

Fig. 4.1. China's system of aid and economic cooperation

Ministry of Commerce

Chang'An Avenue – the Avenue of Eternal Peace – was the main artery of imperial Beijing, a boulevard stretching from the city's east gate to the west gate, across Tiananmen Square. China's Ministry of Commerce occupies several large buildings around Beijing, but its headquarters on a long block of Chang'An Avenue west of the Forbidden City could hardly be more central. Several departments in the Ministry are important for foreign aid, but the center is the Department of Foreign Aid.

DEPARTMENT OF FOREIGN AID

As noted above, before 1982 the Department of Foreign Aid was a ministry, the Ministry of Foreign Economic Relations. Today, the Department is still the center of China's aid system as part of the Ministry of Commerce. It programs all the zero-interest loans and grants, drafts the aid budget and aid regulations, manages the Foreign Aid Joint Venture and Cooperation Fund (set up in 1998 to assist in the consolidation of earlier aid projects), and coordinates with China's Eximbank on concessional loans. But it is only one of a network of institutions with some responsibility for foreign aid, as Figure 4.1 indicates.

The Department of Foreign Aid is unbelievably small, with a staff of only about 100 (seventy professionals) in thirteen divisions.[7] A small cadre of about a dozen researchers focus on foreign aid, economic cooperation, and international development in the Ministry of Commerce's "think-tank," the Chinese Academy of International Trade and Economic Cooperation (CAITEC). This is a small fraction of the 1,612 staff in Britain's Department for International Development (DFID), or 2,200 in the US Agency for International Development (USAID). With the pledge to double aid in three years, they are now "phenomenally understaffed," as Adrian Davis, head of DFID's office in Beijing, said to me.

Unlike most aid agencies in the West, China's Department of Foreign Aid can call for help on Ministry of Commerce branches in all the provinces and the major municipalities. And, so far, the Department feels no need for specialist offices like "Women in Development" or "Governance and Democracy." When they need specialists to advise on agriculture, health, or education, they coordinate with the international cooperation offices in those ministries. The Ministry of Commerce takes the lead, however. When a British official asked the Ministry of Health's International Cooperation Department where China was building the hospitals and malaria centers promised in the 2006 Beijing Summit, they replied that they had no clue, they were waiting for the Ministry of Commerce to inform them.

The Department of Foreign Aid is also small because it has no overseas offices. Instead, the Chinese Economic and Commercial Counselor's office attached to China's embassy will designate one or more staff to oversee the aid program, trouble-shooting, monitoring, and checking up at their completion. These officials are not expected to be experts in development. In Mauritius, for example, the official in charge of oversight for aid was a young man from a provincial department of commerce who had scored well on the entry exams that regulate overseas positions for the Ministry. He had no previous experience abroad.

EXECUTIVE BUREAU OF FOREIGN ECONOMIC COOPERATION

In the old days of central planning, Complant was responsible for the implementation of most of China's turn-key aid projects. When central planning was phased out, and Complant was directed to become a real corporation, something needed to take its place. Gradually, a tender system evolved.

China learned about tender systems from the World Bank. The country's first tender systems were established to meet World Bank requirements for its foreign aid after China began to take out loans as a new member in the early 1980s.[8] A decade later, the Chinese began to set up a system of tenders and bidding for their aid projects. The Executive Bureau, part of the 2003 reorganization that produced the Ministry of Commerce, now handles these tenders, along with other practical steps for projects funded by grants and zero-interest loans (procurement, quality control, evaluation, training of Chinese staff). The Bureau also scrutinizes Chinese experts and technicians hired for aid projects for their skill level, and "political reliability."

DEPARTMENT OF INTERNATIONAL ECONOMIC COOPERATION

Not to be confused with the Executive Bureau above, this department manages some areas of support for Chinese companies seeking business overseas, including offshore resource development, investment, labor services, international contracting, and overseas economic zones.[9] They coordinate with the China Eximbank on decisions for preferential export buyer's credits (for example, the $2 billion in preferential credits promised for Africa for 2006–9) and manage other subsidy programs for international engagement that are not part of the foreign aid budget.

Ministry of Foreign Affairs

Ministry of Foreign Affairs diplomats on the ground are the "front line" in advising the leadership in Beijing on the quantity of foreign aid for a particular African country. As a Chinese diplomat explained it, "we have to coordinate with the Ministry of Commerce because they have China's commercial interests in mind, but they also have to take our views into account because foreign aid is for policy objectives, not to make money." African governments see this political interest clearly. As one African official explained to me, unlike other foreign experts, the Chinese "are a *political* mission."

The Ministry of Foreign Affairs drafts the annual plan for aid together with the Department for Aid in the Ministry of Commerce. It also signs off on any changes in the aid plan, and decisions on cash aid, along with the Ministries of Commerce and Finance. Yet the division of labor between the Ministry of Foreign Affairs and the Ministry of Commerce is an uneasy one when it comes to foreign aid. The politely veiled statement above masks what a high-ranking UN official called "the war between MOFCOM [the Ministry of Commerce] and the Ministry of Foreign Affairs" over the control of aid.

"The Ministry of Foreign Affairs has no clout," Bonnie Glaser, an American analyst with the Washington-based Center for Strategic International Studies (CSIS) said, "and that creates problems for them, but MOFCOM is very reluctant to give up the power in its hands."[10] A Beijing-based Chinese insider told me flatly that in most of the large projects now being financed in Africa, "Foreign Affairs is irrelevant." An adviser told a World Bank meeting where we shared a panel that when it comes to large deals like the mineral investments in the Congo, "The Ministry of Foreign Affairs *used* to be part of the approval process, but now they don't even get invited. They don't have a seat at the table."

It is clear that a power struggle of some kind is going on, but to say that the Ministry of Foreign Affairs is irrelevant is putting it a bit strongly. In one area at least, the MOFA clearly had some clout. At least eight African countries have received foreign aid since 2000 specifically for their ministries of foreign affairs, usually for a new ministry building, a trend in Chinese aid that could be rivaling the well-known building of stadiums.[11] This investment may not have lowered poverty, but it would certainly bring a warm glow to the hearts of the African diplomatic corps, a key constituency in the ongoing tug-of-war with Taiwan.

China Eximbank

China Eximbank definitely *does* have a seat at the table. We saw briefly in Chapter 3 how the Eximbank was established in 1994 as one of China's three "policy banks." As other Chinese banks were being gradually commercialized, this decision allowed Eximbank and the other two policy banks to operate primarily as tools of the government. Japan and Korea provided the models for China's Eximbank. According to an Eximbank official, the bank is expected to operate on a break-even basis: not making a profit, but not requiring regular subsidies. Since just before the millennium, the Eximbank has been at the center of China's strategy of "going global."

In 2005, as Eximbank was in the midst of a major expansion, Li Ruogu was appointed its president. Li, at the time deputy-governor of China's central bank, was an outspoken graduate of Princeton University's Woodrow Wilson School with a law degree from the prestigious Peking University. In 2004, he told the *Financial Times* that bashing China over its currency exchange rate policies was wrong; the US should focus more on its lack of industrial competitiveness. "China's custom is that we never blame others for our own problems. For the past 26 years, we never put pressure or problems onto the world. The US has the reverse attitude – whenever they have a problem, they blame others." Li's comments were later reprinted by China's official news agency, *Xinhua*, suggesting support for Li's outspokenness.

About 60 percent of Eximbank's portfolio consists of export seller's credits (Figure 4.2). These are large, preferential loans for *Chinese* companies operating abroad.[12] A growing share of Eximbank's portfolio goes to export *buyer's credits*, issued to *importers* of Chinese goods or services (in targeted sectors), allowing them to pay the bank back over time. Export buyer's

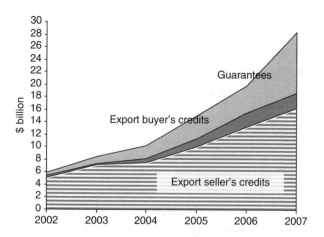

Fig. 4.2. China Eximbank (annual disbursements)

Note: Totals do not include concessional loans.

Source: China Eximbank, *Annual Reports* (2003–2008).

credits began on a relatively modest scale in 2000, and were only rolled out for buyers in Africa in 2005. They are usually issued at competitive commercial interest rates that parallel the rate set for China's government bonds.[13] And, as we have seen, since 1995 China Eximbank has operated China's relatively new program of concessional foreign aid loans.[14]

By 2007, China Eximbank had become by far the world's largest export credit agency, as Figure 4.3 makes clear.

Eximbank's overseas offices reflect China's regional interests. Asian business is handled directly from Beijing. Eximbank has a field office in Russia, and two Africa field offices. One, in a chic neighborhood in Paris, covers the Francophone African countries (an earlier Abidjan-based office moved here when war broke out in Côte d'Ivoire). The southern Africa office, with a staff

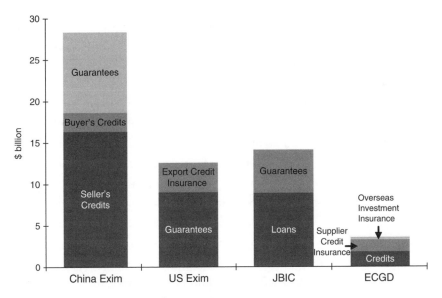

Fig. 4.3. Major export credit agencies, 2007

Notes: Figures modeled after Todd Moss and Sarah Rose, "China Exim Bank and Africa: New Lending, New Challenges," Center for Global Development, CGD Notes, November 2006. Data for China is 2007 disbursement; US for 2007 authorization, Japan for FY 2007 commitments, and UK for 2007/8 issuances.

Sources: 2007 Annual Report of the Export-Import Bank of China, 2007 Annual Report of the Export-Import Bank of the United States. Japan Bank for International Cooperation Annual Report 2008, and 2007–8 Annual Review and Resource Account of the Export Credits Guarantee Department (UK).

of four, is in a suburb of Johannesburg. Field office staff travel frequently to check up on Eximbank's projects, scout out opportunities, meet with Chinese companies and hear their project ideas, and cultivate relationships with African governments. But for important negotiations Eximbank always sends a team from Beijing.

China Eximbank's Concessional Loans

Eximbank's concessional loans are the only part of their operations that can be called foreign aid. The subsidy for the interest rate on concessional aid loans comes directly from the Chinese government's foreign aid budget (Eximbank issues bonds to finance the principle). Eximbank coordinates with the Department of Foreign Aid on these loans, as suggested by Figure 4.1. And in a nod to the language of official development aid, the concessional loans are specifically issued *to promote economic development and improve living standards in developing countries*. China also asks countries who wish to qualify for a concessional loan to grant some kind of preferential treatment to the project: tax-free repatriation of the payments on the loan; relief on import tariffs for inputs; lower income tax.

At one stroke, the system of concessional aid loans created in 1995 created a large new pool of foreign aid funds without requiring much additional outlay from the budget. The program started slowly, even experimentally. Eximbank approved an average of only fourteen concessional loans per year between 1995 and 2004. The number then doubled (Figure 4.4).

Zhao Ziyang's historic trip to Africa in 1982–3 emphasized that China's Africa engagement would henceforth be expected to benefit both sides. Tying the foreign aid funds to Chinese goods and services was intended to ensure that aid would benefit China, as it benefited the recipient (albeit in a relatively restricted way, limiting its choice of products and services). The government also made it clear that, unlike the zero interest loans, there would be no cancellation of these loans or easy rescheduling. Once the interest rate and terms were negotiated and signed, they were expected to be firm.[15] Finally, the concessional loan program was, like China's other aid, at least partly political in nature. As an annual report pointed out, the program was "catering to the need of China's economic diplomacy."[16]

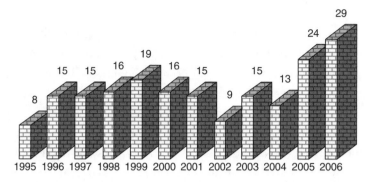

Fig. 4.4.   Annual number of Eximbank concessional loans approved

Source: Almanac/China Commerce Yearbook (various years).

The Development Bank That Doesn't Give Aid

In May 2008, a crowd gathered in Nairobi, Kenya, to watch Yang Zeyun ("Mark Yang") dig a shovel into the ground of a bare field that was scheduled to become the China Development Bank-financed Great Wall Apartment complex. But as Yang, managing director of the Chinese company Erdemann Property Limited, the project developer, explained, the Great Wall Apartments project was not aid: they were using market principles. The 528 low-cost apartments would each be sold for about $50,000 to Kenyans of moderate income, who could finance their purchase through fifteen-year mortgages from CDB's partner, the Development Bank of Kenya.[7]

China Development Bank does *not* give official development aid, but rather provides non-concessional development finance. Like Eximbank, it raises a large share of its funding through the issue of bonds overseas and in China. As a policy bank, CDB provided loans to other levels of the Chinese government, or state-owned companies such as China Three Gorges Development Corporation, to finance investments in domestic infrastructure. CDB prioritized projects that China's other banks were less inclined to fund: in the mountains near Tibet, or in the far western region, for example. Based on total assets, the CDB is more than *five times larger* than the Eximbank.

Very few of CDB's loans have been made overseas: only 1–3 percent between 2005 and 2007, but this appears to be changing.[18] CDB has moved into Africa gradually. By the end of March 2007, the bank had financed only thirty projects in Africa, for a total of about $1 billion.[19] But, as a policy bank, CDB has also supported China's "going global" policy through the policy loans it extends to China's "dragon head" national champions. In 2006, for example, one of CDB's clients, the major Chinese telecommunications equipment firm ZTE, was able to work with CDB and the Beijing office of a major New York-based law firm, White and Case, to develop a competitive package worth $1.5 billion aimed at winning a major tender for Ethiopia's millennium telecoms expansion project.[20]

CDB also established the China–Africa Development Fund introduced in Chapter 3; this is its equity investment arm for Africa. Although there is some rivalry between the two, the CDB has sometimes joined with China Eximbank to finance major projects.[21] And the two banks sometimes work with the same clients. In March 2009, for example, CDB extended a $15 billion financing package to support ZTE's overseas business, a sum nearly matched in May 2009 by Eximbank, which concluded a line of credit worth $10 billion with the giant firm.[22] CDB was commercialized in mid-2008, the first of the three policy banks to go public.

The institutions above comprise the main actors involved in China's aid and economic cooperation in Africa. Anywhere between twelve and twenty other ministries and agencies have some kind of role in foreign aid,[23] making China's system sound like a recipe for chaos. Chinese scholar Ai Ping described the aid bureaucracy as it existed in 1999 as "fragmented."[24] The different offices responsible for aid in the different ministries rarely met. They reported vertically, but had no horizontal links. They were insulated from the public, and even from other departments in their own ministry. Yet the multiplicity of institutions is similar to the United States, which provides foreign aid via at least twenty-six different government departments, agencies, and offices. The Agency for International Development is the central aid agency for the US, but it only oversees 45 percent of US foreign aid.[25] France has a similarly complex structure of aid-related offices.

To alleviate the fragmentation problem, the Ministry of Commerce established task forces that bring all the agencies involved in foreign aid together periodically. China also has a number of specific networks across different topic areas: end-of-project inspections or evaluation, emergency humanitarian aid, debt relief, human resources and training, Forum on China–Africa Cooperation, and Eximbank concessional loans.[26] These networks are necessary because of the wide variety of aid activities undertaken by the Chinese *beyond* turn-key projects and technical assistance. We turn to these next.

Acupuncture at King Harmon Road

In the late afternoon of a hot December day, I stopped by King Harmon Road Hospital in Freetown, Sierra Leone. The team of Chinese doctors just getting off their shift at the hospital all came from Hunan Province, gathered from different government hospitals and university teaching centers by the provincial government and convinced to come to Africa. "It's a deep experience," one of them told me. "The people are very poor." One doctor specialized in acupuncture, another in traditional Chinese medicine, but the rest have familiar specialties: endocrinology, ophthalmology, pediatrics, gynecology. The Hunan doctors lived together in a house not far from a group of Chinese agricultural specialists. They planned to be there for two years, joining the nearly 1,000 Chinese medical workers in Africa in early 2008.

China's medical aid began in April 1963 when a team of doctors landed in newly independent Algeria at the end of the war with France. More than sixty-five developing countries and territories have hosted Chinese medical teams since then. Some 20,000 medical personnel have served abroad under the rotating medical team program. In 2007, forty-eight Chinese medical teams, each with an average of twenty-five doctors and nurses (sometimes spread among more than one hospital or medical center), were working in forty-seven countries worldwide, and in thirty-seven African countries. Madagascar, for example, had thirty Chinese medical specialists posted to four different hospitals.[27]

The Ministry of Health is in charge of the medical teams and the medical experts are paid by the Ministry of Health. Teams are organized by provincial-level branches of the Ministry of Health. Most provinces are "twinned" with particular countries (Appendix 5). Medical teams get up to six months of training in foreign languages, international relations, and area studies before they leave. The work unit in China continues to provide the doctor's salary to his or her family, while expenses, airfare and a stipend are covered by the local government, which also provides housing and pays for the Chinese medicines used by the team. In the poorest countries, such as Mali or the Central African Republic, China will cover the airfare and provide the medicines as a grant.

A very senior doctor sent to West Africa might earn around $800 a month, a Chinese official estimated in 2007, compared with the diplomatic staff down the road, who would be earning around $2,000 a month, often topped up with an extra "hardship" stipend. After a home leave, some doctors return. Zhong Liangting, team leader for the Madagascar mission, had served in three previous teams. But such zeal is increasingly rare, as an official at the Ministry of Commerce told me. "It is becoming a problem for the Ministry of Health to find doctors who will agree to go because they can earn more through *hong bao* [traditional red envelopes used for "gifts" of money] payments from their patients in China."

Some Chinese doctors will stay on, or return to establish commercial clinics in Africa. In Mozambique, I spoke with Jiang Yongsheng, a Chinese doctor who came to Maputo in 1991 on a foreign aid medical team, settled in Maputo and became the personal physician of two Mozambican presidents. But many of the Chinese clinics sprouting up in towns and villages across Africa are opened by people with no connection to the medical teams.

The ratcheting up of aid from China announced at the Forum on China–Africa Cooperation Beijing Summit in November 2006 also included building twenty-seven hospitals in Africa (some general, some specialist) and providing medical equipment for an additional three hospitals. The Chinese also pledged to build thirty anti-malaria centers which would be equipped with diagnosis and treatment equipment. Each country receiving a center was to be assisted by two Chinese experts, who were dispatched to train African medical workers in the use of the Chinese herbal drug. An initial supply of artemisinin would be provided gratis.

There seemed to be no relationship between the old-style medical health teams and the new malaria centers. But there was every indication that the new centers were a business-oriented response to reforms of China's medical aid announced in 1999 by the Chinese Ministry of Health.[28] The Ministry said it would develop a short-list of high-quality suppliers of domestic medicine and equipment (companies like the firm Holley Pharmaceuticals which we met in Tanzania), and use this list for future aid work. Furthermore, services that were formerly free (such as medical teams) would gradually be changed into jointly run hospitals, pharmaceutical factories, and other kinds of "mutually beneficial cooperation."[29] The goal of the reforms, as China's news agency *Xinhua* noted, was ultimately to promote the export of China's pharmaceutical products and medical services. With the new anti-malaria centers and the popularity of artemisinin across Africa, this goal appeared now to be within reach.

Learning from China

Around 500 years before the Christian era began, the ancient Chinese sage Confucius said: "If you plan for a year, plant a seed. If for a hundred years, teach the people. When you sow a seed, you will reap a single harvest. When you teach the people, you will reap a hundred harvests." Since 2000, the Chinese government has accelerated the training component of its foreign aid, focusing in part on transferring information about China's own experience with urbanization, economic growth, and poverty alleviation. By 2007, the Ministry of Commerce reported that, over the years, China had held 2,500 short and medium-term training courses in twenty different fields (management, economics, agriculture, health, justice, education, etc.) with more than 80,000 people participating.

At the United Nations meeting on the Millennium Development Goals in 2005, Chinese President Hu Jintao promised to offer training to more than 30,000 people from developing countries between 2006 and 2009. Pledges at the November 2006 Forum on China–Africa Cooperation made it clear that half of these would be from Africa: 5,000 every year for three years. The new training programs included courses ranging from economics and trade, telecommunications, security, health, water pollution technology and sewage treatment, agriculture, and financial management. While sowing seeds and reaping harvests may be among the expectations, the harvests reaped are likely to be more positive public relations for China.

In my travels across Africa between 2007 and 2009, I frequently ran into people who volunteered to me that they had been on training courses in

China. Rhoda Toronka, the CEO of an African Chamber of Commerce, Industry and Agriculture, went to Beijing for three weeks on a training course for African chambers of commerce. "The course was pretty in-depth," she told me. "We learned about international relations, how China opened up, how to do business in China, how to exchange ideas. We studied their legal system, we learned how *we* can open up. You go to China, you see China..." She paused, and then said, "We can learn from them."

Foreign-aid-based training is organized by the Ministry of Commerce, which puts out requests for proposals from different ministries and government units. China's International Poverty Reduction Center won a Ministry tender to organize training programs for African officials in charge of their national development agencies. As part of their training, the African officials, one or two per country, were flown to the beautiful region of Guilin in southwest China. They might easily have been distracted by the craggy mountain scenery, immortalized in countless misty Chinese paintings, and the fragrant osmanthus trees, giving off the scent of ripe peaches and apricots along the Li River. But their goal was practical: to see first-hand China's new village-based participatory development strategies in Menghua Village.

Kawusu Kebbah, head of the government's donor coordination office in one African country, attended one of the poverty reduction workshops in China. As we sat in his office overlooking a wall guarded with rolls of barbed wire, he told me about his field trip to the village:

> We saw how in China, they might have a national poverty strategy but projects, activities are decided by the villages. In our next Poverty Reduction Strategy Program (PRSP), we will try to incorporate some of this. Our PRSP was national. We went around the country, held a lot of focus groups, heard about their priorities. We came back to the capital, we ranked the priorities for the whole country. But the different districts and chiefdoms really have different priorities. Malaria might be more of an issue in some spots, in others it might be water.
>
> In those three weeks in China I learned that they have borrowed lots of things, but they adapt them. They don't just copy everything they see from other nations that are doing well. They adapt. Now I see this in my work here. The World Bank thinks PRSP is a good thing, so we adopt it. [He laughed.] The Burundi PRSP and ours are practically the same. What we have been doing since the war is looking at Tanzania, Ghana, Burundi. We just adopt it. As though it is "one size fits all."

Scholarships for university study in China have also been an important component of China's assistance and the projection of China's "soft power." During the late colonial period, China hosted students from Kenya, Uganda, Malawi, and other colonies struggling for independence. Beijing University professor Li Baoping estimated in 2006 that more than 18,000 African students have received Chinese government scholarships to study in China.[30] Between 1983 and 1986, when China's aid budget was tight, they decided to quadruple the number of African students granted scholarships per year from 400 to 1,600, a clear sign that Beijing sees study in China as a cost-effective way to implement some of its goals for Africa.[31]

The Ministry of Education handles scholarships for students from developing countries doing degree courses in China. Students can study technical subjects: agronomy, medicine, engineering, or science. But they have also studied Chinese history, literature, and philosophy.[32] At the November 2006 Beijing Summit, China pledged to double scholarships for African students (then at 2,000 per year) to 4,000. Beijing pays the costs of tuition, airfares (for the poorest countries), and housing, and gives students a small stipend – the same level a Chinese student can expect. African governments routinely top up the stipend, although Sierra Leonean students, who were getting only $66 extra per month from their government, complained sadly that their increment was the smallest of all the foreign students in China.[33]

By contrast, many Western donors have shifted away from university scholarships. My university has a branch of the Hubert H. Humphrey program for mid-career professionals from developing countries. We also host Fulbright students, but even combined, both programs are relatively tiny. In academic year 2006–7, the US government provided university scholarships for a total of only 3,450 foreign students, all told. In 1990, USAID programs funded 9,128 university students, but only 1,212 in 2000.[34]

Humanitarian Aid: After Disaster

Small sums of money and material aid have been a part of Chinese responses to disaster for decades, as we saw in Chapter 2. China has given bilateral earthquake relief to Algeria and Iran, mud avalanche relief to the Philippines, tents, mosquito nets, and blankets to Iraq and Somalia, and even donated $5 million after the Katrina hurricane disaster in the United States. Countries where the Chinese have no diplomatic ties have sometimes received shipments of food or blankets in a crisis. But this was almost always done on a bilateral basis (disaster relief and humanitarian aid are not usually part of the budget for external assistance, but come from other sources). A Chinese diplomat explained this Chinese attitude to me: "A few years ago, I was deputy director of the Southern Africa region at the Ministry of Foreign Affairs. There was a food crisis. The World Food Program (WFP) came to China to ask for donations. I said to them: our food aid has already reached southern Africa. If we can move more quickly than the WFP, why do it multilaterally?"

Today, China's humanitarian aid has greatly increased, consistent with Beijing's relatively new desire to project itself as a "responsible major power."[35] It is also increasingly being channeled multilaterally, as in Zimbabwe's 2009 drought, when the Chinese made a $5 million cash donation to support WFP operations. This new multilateralism began during the 2004 Indian Ocean tsunami. At first, China reacted unilaterally, as its foreign emergency response mechanism swung into motion. Wang Hanjiang, head of the Department of Foreign Aid, met quickly with his counterpart in the Ministry of Foreign Affairs to map out the first steps in China's response. After getting approval from the State Council, they called in the Foreign Affairs Office of the Chinese Ministry of National Defense, and the Ministry of Civil Affairs, which carried out the tasks.[36]

The Chinese were proud that a planeload of supplies from China was the first foreign aid to arrive in Sri Lanka, flown directly from a Beijing factory only two days after the disaster. Chinese medical teams and engineers were posted to a number of countries struck by the tidal wave. But then China publicly pledged more than $60 million, and channeled almost a third of this through the UN – a first. (Some in the region speculated that China's historic response was partly done to outgun Taiwan, which had pledged $50 million for the recovery effort.) Private citizens in China donated more than $61 million through the Chinese Red Cross and the China Charity Federation.[37] With the disaster of the Pakistan earthquake following the tsunami, China's official bilateral humanitarian aid for 2005 ultimately totaled nearly $128 million, with NGOs and Chinese companies raising an almost equal amount.[38]

China's "Peace Corps"

Sun Yingtao, Liu Wei, and Zhu Yuchen are the face of China's newest "soft power" aid program: a Chinese youth volunteer corps.[39] An agriculture student from Hebei Province, Sun Yingtao was posted to the southern Ethiopian village of Asossa where he worked with the Ethiopian Department of Rural Development, teaching vegetable cultivation to subsistence farmers and displaced refugees. Liu Wei worked at an Ethiopian ministry teaching secretarial skills. In the Youth League Training School classroom in Laos, where Shanghai resident Zhu Yuchen went to teach computer skills, half of the computers were out of order.

Chinese teachers have worked in African schools and universities for decades (more than 523 in at least thirty-five countries). The Chinese Language Council has sent more than 2,800 volunteers overseas to teach Mandarin.[40] But the youth volunteer program is the first effort to send Chinese youth to assist in various development fields abroad. It sprang from a domestic volunteer program, "Go West" (i.e. to China's underdeveloped frontier regions), organized in 1996 by the Central Committee of the Chinese Communist Youth League, primarily out of concern about rising levels of unemployment and the potential for instability among young graduates who were no longer guaranteed jobs after finishing university.

In 2002, the Communist Youth League sent the first batch of youth volunteers overseas, to Laos and Burma. The Ministry of Commerce took over funding and coordination of the program in 2005, launching trial operations in eight countries, including sending twelve young Chinese volunteers to Ethiopia. Chinese President Hu Jintao announced at the November 2006 FOCAC Summit in Beijing that China would send 300 youth volunteers to Africa between 2006 and 2009.

The first set of volunteers for Africa passed through three months of tests and hurdles before being chosen out of tens of thousands of applicants. They were posted for relatively short six-month stints (the traditional youth volunteer programs, for example the US Peace Corps, or Japanese Overseas Cooperation, have a standard two-year commitment). The Chinese Youth Volunteers Association arranged only two weeks of training in local languages and customs. The Ministry of Commerce paid for their travel costs, health and accident insurance, and provided a monthly allowance of $200.

Only volunteers working for state-owned enterprises were selected, for a host of reasons. As a former volunteer said to me, this gave the organizers more confidence that they would be getting people who would be "politically reliable." State-owned enterprises could also be asked to continue to pay the volunteers' salaries while they were abroad, and to give them back their jobs on their return; private companies could not be compelled to do this.

In early 2007, the Seychelles became the second African country to receive volunteers. Ten volunteers (their ages ranged from twenty-three to thirty-nine) were selected from more than 1,000 applicants: five doctors, two nurses, two music teachers, and a teacher of Chinese. A year later, China had sent more than a hundred youth volunteers to five African countries (Ethiopia, Zimbabwe, Seychelles, Tunisia, and Mauritius), assisting in a number of fields, including agriculture, biogas technology, medicine, physical education training, and Chinese language and music.

Why have you come to Africa, a visiting reporter asked Liu Wei. "We are a new generation that benefited from China's economic reform," she responded, much as an idealistic American Peace Corps volunteer might have done. "We care about the world," she said. Some are motivated by personal goals. Zhu Yuchen applied to be a volunteer to experience the "toughening" her parents gained when they were sent down to the countryside during Mao's Cultural Revolution. Sun Yingtao wanted "to know the real Africa and do something good." This people-to-people program contrasts sharply with the main face of China's aid to date – state-owned construction companies with compounds of taciturn workers living behind a fence – but it is also, so far, extremely small. The United States Peace Corps, by contrast, has over 8,000 volunteers working in seventy-four countries.

Does China Give "Cash Aid"?

Aid for budget support is a growing trend in the West, where donors have begun to believe that a relatively well-governed country should be able to make its own decisions about how to use foreign assistance. Although the Chinese are aware of this trend, they are not following it. They rarely give cash aid in any significant amount.[41] Small amounts are sometimes provided as a rapid response to emergencies or disasters, in keeping with a growing trend among other donors.[42] Even for these small amounts, there is a tight chain of accountability. The Ministry of Foreign Affairs, Ministry of Commerce, and Ministry of Finance have to jointly approve cash aid of less than $1.5 million; anything over $1.5 million has to be approved by all three and by the State Council itself.[43] In some cases, observers have mistaken announcements of *grant* aid (donations, or "free aid") as implying a cash transfer, but this is usually not the case. China's many aid grants are almost always delivered in kind, as exports of Chinese goods and services. One way to tell the difference: a normal grant-in-kind will be announced with a value in Chinese currency (RMB yuan). A cash grant will normally be announced with a value in US dollars.

The exception to China's general policy of avoiding cash aid comes in the diplomatic battles with Taiwan. The conventional wisdom on China's diplomatic arm-wrestling with Taipei today is that "the game is over" for Taiwan. But meetings of high level Chinese and African government officials still routinely feature rhetorical statements that the African country supports the One China policy, a sure sign that it continues to be salient for the Chinese. As a Beijing-based Chinese scholar said to me, "It's really the aid recipients that have the power. African and South Pacific countries still have a priceless bargaining chip: Taiwan."

In 2007, a court order in the vibrant democracy of Costa Rica forced the Costa Rican government to publish the actual diplomatic agreement underpinning its decision to break diplomatic ties with Taiwan and establish them with Beijing.[44] Included in the agreement was a pledge of a grant of $30 million *in cash* that would be delivered over two years, along with another $100 million grant in the usual form of Chinese turn-key projects.[45] Although the Costa Rican government did not initially publish the agreement, it is notable that the cash aid was written into a formal diplomatic agreement, and not wired into someone's private bank account. An attempt by Taiwan to restore diplomatic ties with Papua New Guinea ended in scandal when two ethnic Chinese "brokers" pocketed $30 million wired to their account by Taiwan's Ministry of Foreign Affairs. This affair shed some light into the workings of "checkbook diplomacy."[46] In November 2008, the newly elected President of Taiwan, Ma Ying-Jeoh, pledged to put an end to the costly diplomatic wars with Beijing.[47]

Aside from whatever cash component might be involved in the diplomatic struggles over Taiwan, Africa has had at least four modest cases of

Chinese budget support. Landlocked Central African Republic (CAR) is one of these. A history of coups and countercoups (some quelled by French troops), decades of misrule under the self-proclaimed Emperor Bokassa I, and a steady decline in life expectancy mark most of the decades since independence. In 2003, the government fell to yet another coup. François Bozizé, the new leader, found that donors' doors were mostly shut – the foreign aid community wanted to see elections, governance reforms, concrete progress on macroeconomic management. The exception was China, which agreed to provide emergency budget support to pay civil servants' salaries.

The story circulated through cyberspace after a journalist remarked that "Beijing stepped in, bankrolling the entire civil service," speculating that the move was, somehow, related to the oil riches next door in Chad.[48] (As I note below, it was probably more likely due to Chinese concerns about CAR's continued flirtations with Taiwan.) The story might have ended there, another example of China's disdain for good governance, except for this postscript. Eventually, the CAR did hold acceptable elections.[49] But assistance was *still* slow to arrive. The UN sent a special appeal to the international community to send emergency financial assistance to pay salaries (or "bankroll" the civil service as the Chinese had earlier done) in order to stem the strikes and unrest that had so often brought down previous governments. There are "no personnel available to distribute food, medicines and school materials, improve the broken down health and education infrastructure, or deploy the forces of law and order," the UN representative warned. If assistance did not come quickly, he said, "no good governance reforms would take place."

A year after the elections, most donors had still not provided any aid. According to one observer, they were now waiting for the International Monetary Fund to sign off on the CAR's economic management.[50] A year later, as Bozizé was getting ready to leave for the 2006 Beijing Forum on China–Africa Co-operation, he had to cancel his trip. Rebel forces had captured the city of Birao. The point here is not that the Chinese were beneficent when the other donors were not, but that the international community was united in the goal of better governance. As the UN noted, there were legitimate reasons to provide aid to pay civil servants. There were also reasons to wait. Neither decision was clear-cut.

China also provided modest cash budget support to Liberia, Guinea Bissau, the Seychelles, and Zimbabwe. In 2004, at the end of Liberia's civil war, China provided $3 million to cover 100 days of operations for the power-sharing transitional government, and $1.5 million in 2006 for budgetary support to the administration of President Ellen Johns on Sirleaf.[51] Just after its 2005 elections, Guinea Bissau, also a fragile state recovering from civil war, received a cash transfer of about $4 million to help it pay public workers' salaries.[52] The Seychelles received $1.5 million for balance-of-payments support in 2007, and in 2009 Zimbabwe received $5 million in cash, also to help pay salaries.[53]

Cash transfers are highly unusual for China's normal aid, as I noted above. Costa Rica and most of the African countries above feature among the group that has switched back and forth between Taipei and Beijing. Economic crisis and fragile states are omnipresent in Africa, but reports of Chinese budget support are not. I suspect that it may require Taiwan waiting in the wings to call forth actual cash from the keepers of the coffers in China.

Dumping Debt

Finally, debt relief also qualifies as official development assistance (ODA). Across most of Africa, debt from all sources began to accumulate unpaid in the 1980s, multiplying with penalties, interest, and the rollover of principle through the 1990s until several dozen poor countries were effectively bankrupt. After successful pressure by NGOs and the Jubilee 2000 campaign, as I noted in Chapter 2, the World Bank, IMF, and the "Paris Club" of official bilateral donors finally launched the HIPC (Highly Indebted Poor Countries) debt reduction program in 1996. Ten years later, this program had reduced debt significantly for thirty-three out of the forty-one eligible countries; most were in Africa. The HIPC program promised steep reductions in the stock of unpayable loans, but only after countries successfully followed a complicated steeplechase with hurdles that could take years to jump. This was supposed to provide incentives for good macroeconomic management and ensure that the resources saved would be used for poverty reduction. The extent to which this has worked is still hotly debated.

China did not participate in the HIPC program. Like Tokyo, which initially took the position that canceling (rather than rescheduling) debt provided the wrong incentives, Beijing was slow to accept the position that debt owed to China should be canceled outright. At first, when many of its aid loans started to come due in the early 1980s, China rescheduled them, sometimes just for a year or two. Repayments for the Tan-Zam railway were put off for ten years. Payments in Ghana and Niger were stretched out over twenty years instead of fifteen. Other countries simply did not pay, but the Chinese kept careful track of each debt, for each loan, for each project. Then, after the West and the multilateral lenders had begun to finally cancel debt for the most highly indebted poor countries, Chinese leaders belatedly launched a series of debt cancellation pledges that would affect Africa.

The first pledge, announced in 2000 at the first FOCAC Summit in Beijing, deliberately paralleled the HIPC language. China would reduce or cancel 10 billion RMB yuan of debt (about $1.2 billion) owed by the HIPCs and least developed countries in Africa. The second promise, made in New York in 2005, was a bit more specific. China would cancel "or forgive in other ways all the *overdue parts as of the end of 2004* of the interest-free and low-interest governmental loans owed by all the HIPCs having diplomatic relations with China."

This 2004 move extended debt cancellation to the small number of HIPCs outside of Africa. It emphasized the importance of political ties, and it specified that only the overdue portions of loans would be canceled. In 2006 at the Beijing FOCAC Summit in November, Chinese leaders made a third pledge, which paralleled the New York pledge for the eligible countries, but specified that debt canceled would be "all the interest-free government loans *that matured at the end of 2005*," i.e. those that had reached the end of their twenty-year repayment period. And in 2008 Chinese leaders made a fourth pledge: to cancel all outstanding interest-free loans for the least developed countries that had matured before the end of 2008. These rolling loan cancellations are likely to continue.

Most of China's public pledges were consciously couched as debt relief for "highly indebted" and "least developed" countries. This does not mean, however, that China followed all the rules of the HIPC debt relief regime negotiated in Washington and Paris. Chinese debt cancellation was non-conditional. They did not require governments to prove their ability to manage their economies or to develop strategies to use the canceled debt for poverty reduction. This meant that China canceled debt for at least six countries that qualified for the HIPC initiative because of their high levels of debt and poverty (Comoros, Côte d'Ivoire, Eritrea, Somalia, Sudan, and Togo), but which had failed to follow the steps of the World Bank/IMF dance, and so were stuck in what the HIPC program called the "pre-decision point," the purgatory of high debt, but no relief.

How did the debt cancellation work? The Ministry of Finance set up a committee involving MOFCOM, the People's Bank of China (China's central bank), Eximbank, and the China Development Bank.[54] "The country has to apply to have the debt cancelled," a Chinese official told me. "It doesn't just happen. The Chinese government will see how the money was used. They will consider this thoughtfully. They will refuse applications from some whose economy is doing well. They don't need debt relief."

Countries with the most pressing problems were handled first. The Ministry of Commerce sent a delegation to discuss the debt with the Chinese embassy in the country and the local Ministry of Finance. Figures on overdue debts were carefully compared and reconciled, loan by loan. A Chinese professor who advised the Ministry told me: "These zero-interest loans were rescheduled so many times, the countries couldn't even find the agreements anymore!" Debts were written off for each individual loan. The pledges focused specifically on the overdue, interest-free foreign aid loans (not on other debt – export credits, for example). Ultimately, 376 separate "mature debts" would be written off.

However, there has been almost no cancellation of the Eximbank concessional loans, which were only disbursed for the first time in 1997. In 2000, these early loans were still in their grace periods, with countries paying only the interest. Later, as principal payments started to come due, some of the earliest concessional loans were restructured or rescheduled. One of these loans was given to a cement plant in Zimbabwe.

The Sino-Zimbabwe Cement Plant, a joint venture between China Building Material Industrial Corporation for Foreign Economic and Technical Cooperation (one of the foreign aid companies previously owned by China's Ministry of Construction) and Zimbabwe's state-owned Industrial Development Corporation sits in the sun-baked, red-earth area of Gweru District, smack in the center of Zimbabwe. The cement venture received one of the first concessional loans from China Eximbank.[55] In 2006 both loans were restructured, and the interest rates reduced to 2 percent. But repayment began on time, using foreign exchange earned from exports of the cement and held in an escrow account, a pattern we will see again.

Many myths have arisen around China's debt cancellation program. The New York-based Council on Foreign Relations wrote that China had canceled $10 billion in debt, more than triple the actual amount.[56] (In June 2008, Premier Wen Jiabao announced that China had canceled a total of 24.7 billion yuan, or about $3.6 billion.[57]) Others have written that China typically cancels debt for political leverage, or for countries with which it has close political and economic ties. The Zimbabwe story above should cast some doubt on this.

One factor *is* political: as with other aid, China has only canceled debt in those countries that stick to the One China policy. In Africa, that meant no debt was canceled for the three HIPC countries (Burkina Faso, São Tomé and Príncipe, and The Gambia) that switched recognition to Taipei during the 1990s. But in general the range of countries with debt canceled since 2000 is a bit beyond what one could call "close friends": forty-nine countries worldwide, thirty-two in Africa. The list leaves out some with longstanding ties (Egypt, Mauritius, Zimbabwe, Pakistan) and includes others where ties are modest at best (Liberia, Togo, Somalia, Burundi). But politics may have influenced the decision to cancel at least some debt for at least six African countries that were above the poverty line for HIPC (Angola, Cape Verde, Djibouti, Equatorial Guinea, Kenya, and Lesotho).

This chapter has given a broad overview of the changing elements of China's aid program. But how does it all work? And how does aid fit into China's overall economic embrace of Africa? To answer some of these questions, the next chapter takes a close look at aid, economic engagement, and their overlap. Much (but not all) of the story focuses on one country: Sierra Leone. Small, war-torn, resource-rich, and with bad neighbors, Sierra Leone presents many of the problems that have made African development such a challenge. But it is also surprisingly typical of the way China has worked in countries across the continent, and indeed around the world.

CHAPTER 5

Orient Express: How Does Chinese Aid and Engagement Work?

It is 1984, late one morning in the dry Harmattan season. I have just arrived at Goma, the site of a Chinese aid project, a dam that will eventually power a modest, 4-megawatt hydropower station in the remote hilly rainforest of Sierra Leone. The trip took hours, first to the village of Panguma, squeezed into the back of a pickup truck transporting villagers and their market purchases over a narrow, pitted dirt road shaded overhead by the interlaced branches of trees. Goma is further, down a temporary road that relies for bridges on large logs laid across the region's many streams. We are not far from the border with Liberia. Graham Greene might have passed near here in *Journey Without Maps*, the memoir of a trek he made from the border of Sierra Leone through Liberia in the uneasy period before World War II.

The site is a buzz of activity, with more than 600 local villagers and 105 Chinese, including three cooks. After a long day at the project site, the Chinese workers spend several hours laboring in their vegetable patch to ensure they can eat familiar food and earn a bit of pocket money. A section of the hill near the Chinese workers' camp is fenced off with a lattice of sticks. Later that day, after their shift ends, I watch more than a dozen Chinese men hoeing terraced patches of spring onions, squatting to fix green beans tied to a stake, weeding a patch of pumpkins. Near the communal kitchen, several men line up in front of a small scale, carrying yokes with twin baskets full of vegetables that will be weighed and credited to their account.

Eighty miles away at the Bambuna waterfall, a small group of Italian engineers watch over the beginning stage of the construction of a dam, a project that will hit numerous snags and fail to be completed before the start of the civil war. The project is highly mechanized, providing little local employment. Every two weeks, the Italians have a shipment of food air-freighted from Rome. An agriculture project funded by the US Agency for International Development spent project funds to construct a small suburban neighborhood of spacious ranch-style houses for their foreign advisers, complete with a cul-de-sac and streetlights. It would not have looked out of place in Ohio. Chinese agronomists and engineers slept in bunks in a building that would later be used for storing rice seed.

Years later, in Tanzania, an official reminisces to me about his visit to the Tan-Zam railway site in 1970. The Chinese workers were living in extremely simple conditions, he tells me, shaking his head to emphasize just how simple it was. He contrasts this with the Swedes, who, he says, built a hydroelectric dam at Kidatu and stayed in a beach hotel 150 miles away. They took helicopters to the building site. Decades later, little has changed in the way all of these actors actually work in Africa. Some of the contrasts are still stark.

The Chinese have gone to a great deal of effort to position themselves as an alternative to the aid business as usual, particularly in Africa. "How can you reduce poverty, but live in a five-star hotel?" a Chinese scholar asked me rhetorically during a meeting in Beijing. Western critics might easily retort: "How can you finance a presidential palace for Sudan and call it foreign aid?" There *are* differences, even in areas as basic as terminology. "We are not very comfortable with the word 'donor'," a researcher in the Chinese Academy of Social Sciences told me in Beijing. "The recipient's hand is always below the donor's hand." But in other ways, surprisingly, it seems the Chinese are a lot more like the traditional donors than either side is willing to admit.

Beijing versus Paris

As part of the pledge to meet the eight Millennium Development Goals, the traditional donor community promised in 2000 to reform the aid architecture (Goal Eight). The details of the pledge were worked out in a series of meetings organized by the Development Assistance Committee of the OECD. In 2005, in Paris, donors and aid recipients came together, signing the Paris Declaration on Aid Effectiveness, which promised a new system of mutual accountability based on ownership, alignment, transparency, harmonization, and results. Partner countries (aid recipients) were supposed to set the agenda (ownership). Donors were supposed to align their programs with their partner's agenda, and work through local governments rather than setting up independent projects (alignment). They promised to share information in order to avoid the overlap that commonly happens (transparency), and do more "pooling" of resources, and budget support (harmonization), so that recipient governments would have more control. Needless to say, all of this has been a rather big challenge for the traditional donors.

The Chinese sent a delegation to the Paris meeting. They signed the pledge. But by all accounts, they were thinking of their own role as a recipient of aid, not their role as a donor. Their own program of aid, and the way it is knit into economic engagement, present two big challenges to the global aid regime.

First, the Chinese challenge assumptions about the *content* of aid. Infrastructure is central to their funding program, much as it used to be for donors like the World Bank. Between 1946 and 1961, 75 percent of World Bank loans financed transportation and electricity projects, but this focus changed before most African countries were even independent.[1] For a host of reasons, Western aid for infrastructure fell far behind funding for the social sectors (Japan was an exception to this trend).

Senegal's President Abdoulaye Wade noted that "China has helped African nations build infrastructure projects in record time," referring to the Chinese penchant for quick results.[2] Pointing out that Senegalese laws require Chinese companies to partner with Senegalese firms in order to win contracts, he commended them for "transferring technology, training, and know-how to Senegal." At the millennium, Europe promised $15 billion for African infrastructure, he noted, but eight years later they had not fulfilled this promise. "The Chinese are ready to take up the task, more rapidly, and at less cost."

The ramping up of Chinese funding for infrastructure was noticed by other donors, who were pushed to respond. At a workshop I attended at the Center for Global Development in Washington DC, an adviser to Liberian

President Ellen Johnson-Sirleaf told us how China's prompt agreement to Liberia's request for road reconstruction was noted by other donors. "Suddenly roads became a priority sector in Liberia," he chuckled. A South African diplomat noted that a month after China's monumental Forum on China–Africa Cooperation (FOCAC) Summit in November 2006, European Union representatives began talking to their African counterparts about infrastructure. This was "a direct result of Chinese engagement," he concluded.[3]

Second, China's approach to the *implementation* of aid is different. In the Paris Declaration, the West promised to emphasize host-country "ownership" and to align its aid with partner country agendas. Donors pledged to build capacity rather than relying on foreign experts. But ownership does not fit well with donors' continued reliance on conditionality – the promise that we will help you, if you first do x, y, and z. And the rhetoric of partnership sits uneasily beside the reality that aid experts sent from the West may cost upward of $300,000 per year, and live like pashas in comfortable homes, often circled by walls topped with shards of glass. In Mozambique, donors hired 3,500 technical experts (usually foreign), paying out $350 million each year, a sum equal to the salaries of 400,000 local people.[4] Several of these experts are friends of mine, some are former students. They do great work, I am sure, but they also cost *a lot*.

Hiring locally can create other problems. In a poor country, the attractiveness of a well-paid job in the local office of an NGO or aid agency is obvious; even better is a chance to work overseas for that agency. But "poaching" staff from governments can deplete local capacity. The Chinese use a lot of their own people (and I will discuss the drawbacks of this below). But their way of doing things usually leaves government officials in government.

China has also been reluctant to coordinate or "harmonize" its aid with aid from other donors. For decades, traditional donors have coalesced in clubs like the Development Assistance Committee of the OECD, and the Consultative Group (CG) of donors led by the World Bank in most low-income countries. For many borrowing countries, the traditional donors were an effective aid cartel, imposing a hegemony of ideas about aid practice and the content of aid programs.

Conditionality was a key instrument for this. During the long terrible years of the debt and economic crisis that began for many African countries in the late 1970s, donors agreed to support each other in imposing conditions on aid. These began as narrowly economic, but expanded as countries' creditworthiness collapsed. By the late 1980s, World Bank loans had an average of sixty different conditions and benchmarks.[5] But as Senegal's President Wade noted, China was not so demanding. "China's approach to our needs is simply better adapted than the slow and sometimes patronizing approach" of Europe.[6]

Harmonization in the Paris Declaration was meant to address another problem: donor fragmentation – the fact that some countries might have dozens of donors, and even more non-governmental organizations (NGOs), each calling for regular meetings and quarterly reports. This means that Tanzania, for example, produces 2,400 quarterly reports for its donors every year.[7] Harmonization involved donors agreeing to one donor taking the lead in a sector, instead of multiple donors all doing their own independent projects. But this required meetings, the sharing of information, and greater transparency, all areas where China has been reluctant to change.

That said, the Chinese are less elusive in the international aid arena these days than they were several decades ago. Although there is still a general hesitation about joining donor gatherings like the Consultative Groups, when invited by an African government (and sometimes even when invited by other donors), the Chinese will usually attend. They do not like to present themselves as donors, of course. That is an initial problem. But even more than this, I suspect, they do not want to be under the leadership of the World Bank. On this issue, China's ambassador to Pretoria, Zhong Jianhua, said: "The World Bank always wants countries to join them and to follow their process. But is the record of the World Bank in African countries so good?"[8]

In this chapter, we see how China's aid and economic engagement works in Africa. Some of the Paris Declaration issues will arise: ownership, alignment, results, and so on. We will look at capacity building, conditionality, the use of Chinese labor, and sustainability. We start in Sierra Leone, where China's approach was very typical, even if Sierra Leone's civil war was not.

An Oriental Big Power

For more than a decade, Sierra Leone was engulfed in civil war, mainly in the east, the "blood diamonds" region. Child soldiers, high on a mix of cocaine and gun powder, were told to murder their parents. Fathers who tried to protect their children were forced to choose which of their arms would be chopped off. Freetown swelled with a million refugees, others fled north to Guinea. After many abortive attempts at peace, the war finally ended in January 2002, and an uneasy peace descended on the country.

The Chinese had joined Britain in sending military assistance to the government of President Ahmad Tejan during the war. They were mildly engaged with the other donors. Chinese representatives joined the World Bank-led donor consortium, the CG.[9] They attended a meeting in London arranged to coordinate donor efforts, and the embassy sometimes sent its top political officers (but not the economic team) to CG meetings in Freetown, where they said little but were at least at the table.

Even before the war had formally ended, the Chinese put aid teams together to renovate some of their earlier projects. They began discussions on a joint project with the UN's Food and Agriculture Organization (FAO). With encouragement from the embassy, Chinese firms arrived to lease some state-owned companies: the Bintumani Hotel, and the Magbass sugar complex, the latter one of China's former aid projects. "They not only showed interest in investment in Sierra Leone after the war, but they did during the war and before," former President Kabbah told the BBC news. How did this work?

"Our company leader came here in 2000," explained Dong Wen, the general manager of the Bintumani Hotel. We sat in her office at the hotel's hilltop location overlooking Lumley Beach where the UN military mission still occupied the only other large beach hotel, the Mammy Yoko. Dong Wen's company, Global Trading, is a subsidiary of Beijing Urban Construction Group, the main contractor for the famous "Bird's Nest" stadium built for the 2008 Beijing Olympics. Global Trading contracted a twenty-five-year lease with the government of Sierra Leone to rebuild and operate the Bintumani in August 2000, before the war had formally ended. "The Bintumani was in ruins," a former government official remembered. "Local people were using it for a toilet. It required a huge investment." After spending $10 million to renovate the hotel, Global Trading opened the Bintumani for business in January 2003.

"Why a hotel?" I asked. "In China, many big companies own their own hotels, we have two or three small hotels, but this is our only big hotel," Dong Wen told me. When I expressed surprise at the choice, she laughed. "I was surprised too! It's very far from China, it's not easy for us, for the Chinese staff. At that time we wanted to help Africa. And our boss had a good relationship with the president, Kabbah. In 2000 they had just finished the war, and," she shrugged, "we invested." With the renovation of Bintumani under its belt, Global Trading began to bid on other construction contracts.

An agreement signed in May 2001 wiped away all the Chinese debt that had gone into default by 1999. I asked the Chinese ambassador how they managed the process of debt cancellation and whether they imposed any conditions. "There is no negotiation," he said, shaking his head. "They have no capacity to pay back."

Other formal aid agreements were soon signed. They followed China's standard system for the grants and zero-interest loans controlled by the Ministry of Commerce (Eximbank's concessional loans are discussed below). First, the two sides signed an overarching Agreement on Economic and Technical Cooperation. These agreements spell out the amount of aid pledged, whether it will be offered as a grant or a zero-interest loan (or both), and the repayment terms of the loan.[10] With the pledge of aid in place, the two countries then collaborate to identify areas of need where the grant and/or line of credit can be used. Between 2001 and 2007, China and Sierra Leone signed at least eight separate agreements like this, each involving a grant, zero-interest loan, or a combination.

China's first aid initiatives after the war brought in shipments of food and goods for refugee relief. But they also focused on rehabilitating China's past aid projects. Two monumental projects in Freetown, the stadium and the Youyi ["Friendship"] Ministry Building, received total overhauls financed through grants. The Youyi Building was re-covered with gleaming new white tiles. On a sunny day it made a blindingly bright landmark in its suburban location. A 2006 editorial in the local *Concord Times* expressed appreciation for this form of reconstruction aid: "The Chinese helped build

Youyi Building and the National Stadium for us, but regrettably we could not maintain them. The stadium and Youyi Building had almost turned an eyesore save for the intervention of those who built the structures to renovate them."

Two aid projects negotiated in 2005 included a new stadium in Bo District, and a new Foreign Ministry office complex at Hill Station. An official in Sierra Leone's Ministry of Foreign Affairs beamed when he showed me the elaborate book containing the architectural drawings for their new complex, clearly a diplomatic success. The case might even be made that its construction freed up government resources to be spent on more developmental tasks. Sierra Leone's Ministry of Foreign Affairs was in a dismal building, with its entrance up a dark narrow staircase past a collection of trash deposited by the Harmattan winds blowing down Free-town's narrow streets. But a *stadium* in the upcountry town of Bo?

When I met with Chinese ambassador Cheng Wenju in the embassy's formal reception room, with chilly air-conditioning and a helpful cup of hot green tea, I asked him: Was this really the best use of funds for an extremely poor country? He sighed and closed his eyes briefly. "From our point of view, it is not necessary to build another stadium in Bo. No African country has two [Chinese-built] stadiums. The infrastructure in this country is bad. They need other things. But, they insisted. So, finally we respected their choice." He paused for a moment to sip his tea, and then continued. An election had just taken place. "The new government could ask us to stop it. But I don't think they will change their mind. Bo is an SLPP [Sierra Leone People's Party, the party that lost the election] strong-hold, so there is an issue of national unity. It would be a national issue to stop the stadium now."

Stadiums are of course popular with the people as well as their govern-ments. Although they don't meet *our* definition of what a poor country "should" do with pledges of aid, it was a project with genuine ownership. Alhaji Momodu Koroma, former Minister of Foreign Affairs, had been part of the negotiations, and he smiled when I asked him about the Bo stadium. "Ah, the Chinese really kicked against that," he recalled. "But remember, football is quite popular here. And we have thousands of youth, you can't absorb them all into vocational schools. You need to think of innovative ways to absorb their energy."

Fighting in the civil war burned villages to the ground, but largely spared the town of Bo. Now best described as shabby, the streets of Bo wind out from a jaunty central tower with a long-broken clock. There are still hints of the charm that long ago gave the town the nickname "Sweet Bo." Just before Christmas in 2007, I walked from my Bo hotel to the site of the stadium. After waiting more than two years for the Sierra Leone government to clear the area, the Chinese embassy arranged for a local Chinese firm to do the job. The vast expanse stood empty in the pink-grey twilight. Bo's tropical forest had already shot out green vines along the edges of the clearing, creeping across the red soil. Three months after my visit, the Chinese construction company that had beaten sixteen other companies in a tender arranged in Beijing arrived and immediately got to work.[11]

"Why does China, an oriental big power, come thousands of miles to develop relations with Sierra Leone?" China's ambassador Cheng Wenju asked rhetorically.[12] Stung by claims that China was only in Africa to grab natural resources, he announced that, "Till now, China has not mined even one carat diamond, or rutile, or any other mineral product in Sierra Leone." But, he said, "Both Chinese and Sierra Leonean friends feel regret for . . . not having introduced more Chinese companies to invest in Sierra Leone."

The Chinese also launched a number of other aid initiatives: the health team I discussed in Chapter 4, schools and a hospital, several agricultural projects (see Chapters 9 and 10), but aid was not central to their engagement. In Freetown, the former deputy Minister of Finance told me:

> The Chinese ambassador was the most active of all the ambassadors. He kept insisting that aid is not what the country needs, but commercial ties. The ambassador and the economic counselor are always looking for commercial potentials, and they look to see how they can work with the government to realize it. The other donors might do a good job at their big projects – microfinance or livelihood programs. It lasts for three years, then everybody sits down and waits until another program comes in. The program does not last beyond those three years. So we are standing still.

When I asked former Minister of Foreign Affairs Alhaji Momodu Koroma to compare China with his country's other donors, he said:

> There is a difference, and it is huge. What they want to help you with, is what you have identified as your need. With Britain, America, *they*

identify your needs. They say: "Look, we think there is a need *here*." The German President visited. They promised €12.5 million [$17.5 million] for assistance. President Kabbah said we will use this for rural electrification. But a few months later, GTZ [the German aid agency] said it would be used for their human security project.

In his eyes, there was still some way to go before the traditional donors really trusted Sierra Leone's country ownership (perhaps for good reason).

China Eximbank, Huawei, and Sierratel

The traditional donors have raised concerns about China's practice of combining aid with business, something we will return to later in this chapter. This mix of aid and commerce is demonstrated well by China Eximbank's first concessional loan aid project in Sierra Leone, launched by Huawei, one of China's top telecoms companies. Huawei developed several projects with Sierratel, the state-owned telecommunications company. One of these, financed through Chinese foreign aid, involved extending the wireless telephone system operated by Sierratel. There were no bids for this project. "Huawei proposed it to Sierratel," the Chinese ambassador told me. Here is how the process worked.

Huawei negotiated and signed a preliminary contract for the project with Sierratel in July 2006, pending financing. Five months later, Sierra Leone's Ministry of Finance and China's Ministry of Commerce signed a framework agreement, which provided the general terms for taking and repaying a Chinese renminbi concessional loan of about $16.6 million.[13] (The framework agreement, concessional terms of the loan (2 percent interest, twenty years repayment), and the fact that it was made in Chinese currency, establish that it was considered foreign aid by the Chinese.) The final loan agreement was signed in April 2007, with China Eximbank. "It is one kind of aid," China's ambassador confirmed to me later that year, adding "this is the first time Sierra Leone has used a concessional loan from the Eximbank."

According to China's Ministry of Commerce, only well-qualified, highly capable companies (like Huawei) with "rich experience in opening the markets in developing countries" and using "leading edge technology" are eligible to propose projects for Eximbank concessional loans.[14] The Huawei experience shows the fruit of the Department of Foreign Aid's efforts early in the 1990s to "push" and "support" Chinese companies to find business overseas.[15] The system is similar to the request-based aid system developed decades ago in Japan.

Learning from Japan's Request-Based System

In its first decades, Japan's aid system largely depended on Japanese companies, who frequently identified projects themselves and proposed them to the host government, "which would then 'request' that the Japanese government fund them."[16] The system helped Japan expand exports, and its focus on raw materials like cotton or timber, energy, industry, and mining was designed for mutual benefit.

This process reduced the costs of aid delivery, but it also entailed risks. Firms became representatives of the Japanese government in the field. They identified projects and later implemented them. Yet having companies identify the project and then arrange the funding without a transparent, competitive process was problematic. A report by a major Japanese newspaper on the Japanese practice as it stood two decades ago quoted a politician:

> Aid money is like spy money. The Diet [Parliament] doesn't decide how much goes to which country, and the people are not told how it is being used. Moreover, it keeps growing and growing. As far as being the goose that lays the golden egg in financing political payoffs, it is super high grade.[17]

A major scandal over Japanese aid corruption in the Philippines shed light on the potential for abuses in request-based systems. When former President Ferdinand Marcos fled the country in 1986, his personal papers were seized by the US government, and handed over to Congress. They revealed that for more than a decade, about 10–15 percent of Japan's Overseas Economic Cooperation Fund loans in the Philippines had been "systematically kicked back to Marcos and his cronies by more than 50 Japanese aid contractors through a system of bid rigging, contract fraud, and illegal payments."[18] Competitive bidding with transparent tenders is intended to ensure that a project's costs are realistic and fair. Yet the Marcos scandal revealed that corruption could still thrive even within what seemed to be a transparent and competitive bidding process, by using bid rigging and other forms of insider collusion. Although the Japanese public was outraged, the scandal failed to lead to substantive reforms of Japan's system. These risks are clearly also present in China's system of request-based aid. We will return to this in Chapter 11.

The Eximbank Cycle

The Huawei project above demonstrates one of the features of China's aid and engagement: the Chinese usually finance their own companies *directly* to carry out projects. Unlike the World Bank, for example, they do not usually issue aid funds into accounts controlled by the host government. As a Chinese analyst explained, China Eximbank wants "to guarantee the economic benefits *and* the safe return of loans."[9] There are exceptions. For creditworthy governments like Botswana or Mauritius, with good economic environments and low risk, the Eximbank can issue the loan directly to the borrowing government. These institutions would then collect repayment, and service the debt to Eximbank. For less creditworthy governments, such as Sudan or Angola, the Eximbank disburses the loan directly to a Chinese enterprise or joint venture, believing this can better guarantee its productive use, and thus repayment.

A diagram from the China Eximbank describes a typical cycle for concessional loan projects (Figure 5.1). For the Huawei project, it would have worked like this. Huawei suggested the project. Sierra Leone's Ministry of Finance applied for the loan. Eximbank did a preliminary appraisal and approved going ahead. Sierra Leone's Ministry of Finance signed a framework agreement on the terms of the loan with China's Ministry of Commerce (because it is foreign aid financing, the Ministry of Commerce is involved), and a concessional loan agreement with the Eximbank (Steps 1–4). Huawei does the work or exports the goods, and asks for payment from Sierratel, the state-owned telephone company (Step 5). Sierratel signs off on the request, and sends it on to Sierra Leone's Ministry of Finance (Step 6), which then asks China Eximbank to disburse payment to Huawei (Steps 7 and 8), and accepts responsibility for repaying the loan (Step 9). For all the problems that request-based systems pose for transparency and integrity, they at least reduce problems of embezzlement in the borrowing country. As Sierra Leone's former Minister of Foreign Affairs Alhaji Koroma said to

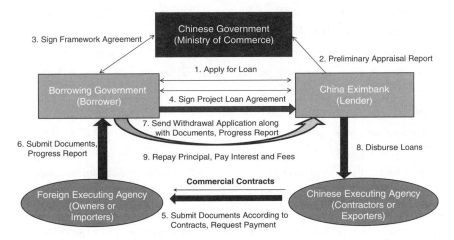

Fig. 5.1. China Eximbank concessional loan cycle

Source: China Eximbank website. Translation by Zu Yiming and author.

me as we sat in the lounge of my hotel in Freetown, the Atlantic Ocean crashing against the rocks below: "They give aid, grants, loans, but you never see that money."

From Aid to Profit: CNEEC Consolidates Goma

Quite a bit of China's engagement in Sierra Leone was about consolidating former aid projects, often by trying to turn them into businesses, as we saw in Chapter 2. China National Electric Equipment Corporation's return to the Goma hydropower plant, the project I visited two decades ago, conformed to this pattern.

In most parts of Sierra Leone, and particularly in Freetown, electricity shortages continued to be a persistent problem long after the war had ended. Part of the problem, as former President Kabbah pointed out, was "vandalism and frequent criminal sabotage of electricity installations by unpatriotic people," who were stealing the copper, cutting and stripping the wires. "These acts have...made the job of providing electricity to our homes and workplaces very difficult," he complained.[20] But decrepit installations were also at fault.

China National Electric Equipment Corporation (CNEEC) returned to Dodo Chiefdom after the war to repair and expand the 4-megawatt Goma hydropower plant. Their work at Goma ensured that power continued to flow in a part of the country that, by coincidence, had been a rebel stronghold. "Sixty percent of the people in Sierra Leone have never slept in a house with electricity," a citizen told the BBC news in 2005. "Out of the twelve districts we have in Sierra Leone, only two have electricity, Bo and Kenema."

Unlike Huawei's telecoms project, CNEEC's repairs were *not* financed by foreign aid. CNEEC expanded the Dodo hydropower plant under a short-term financing arrangement whereby Sierra Leone would repay them by selling the power. But many people in Sierra Leone believed that CNEEC took on the modest three million dollar hydropower project with a view to positioning itself for a larger project: a proposed 100-megawatt dam at Bikongor Falls near the border with Liberia. An official at Bo-Kenema Power Services alluded to this when we met in his office not far from the Bo clock tower. His utility company still owed CNEEC $600,000. "They came for the money, but we don't have it. At one stage it was Chairman Mao," he told me philosophically, shaking his head. "Suddenly, the Chinese have trillions."

The Chinese company's interest in Bikongor was longstanding, and the Sierra Leone government had long desired the project, too. A UN report assumed in 2003 that the company would be developing the Bikongor project, after CNEEC produced a pre-feasibility study.[21] China's government understood Sierra Leone's desire for Bikongor, Ambassador Cheng Wenju declared in a 2006 speech. Referring to China's own difficulties in overcoming electricity shortages, and the potential of Bikongor, he said: "China is willing to lend a hand." However, he continued, the project was costly and would take a long time to construct. China "would like to hold discussions with the Sierra Leonean side and other cooperative partners with the aim to find a practical and feasible solution to launch this significant project as early as possible."[22]

Called to a meeting on Bikongor, the World Bank and the African Development Bank declined to partner with Sierra Leone and CNEEC in providing a financial guarantee to the project. Bikongor could sell power to neighboring Liberia at market rates, as well as provide power in Sierra

Leone, the project's backers argued. But the two international banks worried about management problems for a state-owned enterprise, and Sierra Leone's ability to repay upfront financing, given its status as a Highly Indebted Poor Country (HIPC) with strict limits on its debt-carrying capacity. CNEEC then approached the China Development Bank, which sent a team to examine the project to see if potential existed for a resource-backed guarantee.

As we saw in Chapter 2, in the late 1970s China learned how resources could be used to leverage investment and loans from Japan and the West as the wealthy world rushed to profit from China's initial opening-up. Infrastructure was a key part of China's "Four Modernizations." Beijing's strategic planners remained in control of this courtship. They swapped Chinese coal and oil for the modern technology, railways, underground transport, and ports built by companies from Japan and the West. China needed to develop ample energy supplies, so the Chinese opened their mountains and rivers to mining companies and engineering firms for hydropower and mineral extraction. Today, resource-backed guarantees have become an important vehicle for expanding Chinese engagement in Africa, even if the number of projects financed like this is still small. How do these work?

China's Resource-Backed Infrastructure Loans

Sierra Leone's experience is typical, both in the Chinese conviction that Sierra Leone probably had untapped capacity to invest in resource-backed infrastructure, the lack of transparency around the process, and the concerns all of this raised for many people. Just before the November 2006 Beijing Summit, for example, the government of Sierra Leone signed a memorandum of understanding with Henan Province Institute of Geological Surveys to survey the entire country for mineral deposits. Two more agreements with Henan followed in 2007; details of these were never made public. Sierra Leone's former president told his parliament that Henan would develop a comprehensive database that could be used to attract investors, banks, and other lending institutions.[23] Staff at Sierra Leone's Department of Geological Survey explained to me that the two agreements aimed to further explore the feasibility of developing resources as collateral for Chinese loans that could potentially pay for very large infrastructure projects.

The government hoped that this might make the Bikongor project a reality.[24] Others in Sierra Leone were more concerned. Jonathan Dambo from the ruling Sierra Leone People's Party colorfully castigated his own government for signing what seemed to him an "obnoxious...eighteenth-century agreement...that would merely have sapped nectar from this country."[25] With the terms remaining secret, it was hard to determine how much nectar was actually involved.

Around the same time that Henan was exploring the feasibility of resource-backed infrastructure projects in Sierra Leone, word trickled out that China Eximbank was negotiating a similar arrangement in the Democratic Republic of Congo. The package ultimately approved by the Congolese parliament in May 2008 was massive.[26] China Eximbank agreed to finance more than $6 billion in infrastructure, using just a single copper and cobalt mining joint venture as guarantee. Mining would not begin before 2010 at the earliest, after two years of environmental and other feasibility studies conducted by independent third parties. But as Paul Fortin, the Canadian CEO of Congo's state-owned mining company Gécamines, commented: "Congo doesn't have to wait for its infrastructure until it has the money. Building starts immediately with the natural resources as guarantee. Except in oil-rich states, I know of no other deal quite like this."[27] The Chinese approach side-steps all the conditionality and just gets right to the point, he said. You want infrastructure built? You have resources to guarantee a loan? We have a deal.

After talking to the Eximbank in China and its partners in Africa about these resource-backed infrastructure loans, I set up a round of meetings in Washington. I wanted to know why the Bretton Woods twins generally have a dim view of resource-backed loans. In a meeting at the IMF in the chill of early winter, far away from the tropical heat of the countries we were discussing, an Africa specialist told me, "No one else is lining up to provide funding for development in the Democratic Republic of Congo. A country like the DRC needs infrastructure. It can't attract much donor aid. Given these limitations, the Chinese are filling a huge gap. But it all depends on the terms."

Resource-backed loans mortgage future revenues and they reduce a country's flexibility to use those future revenues. If the infrastructure being built is clearly linked to the government's priorities, the revenues pass through the budget, and a neutral third party supervises bidding and construction, these loans *can* be positive. "But there are big governance risks," another Bretton Woods economist warned. "The same companies are involved in extracting and exporting the resource *and* building the infrastructure. There are no international tenders. Who will ensure that the country gets value for its money? We've seen commodity booms before. In the past, Zambia *double* mortgaged its copper. Are the Africans going to be able to work this to their advantage?"

The terms of the Angola agreement required three or four Chinese companies to bid on each contract, although the process is not very transparent. An independent third party inspects each project.[28] The price for the oil that finances the loan is not fixed in advance, but valued at market price prevailing on the day it is sold. Likewise, the DRC arrangement "is a great deal," a cheerful mining specialist at the World Bank told me, sitting behind a desk buried in stacks of paper. "We ought to get off our high horse and work better with the Chinese."

But one of the difficulties for the World Bank and the IMF is that, by convention, they are *privileged creditors*. Loans made by the World Bank (IBRD), for example, are supposed to be paid before all other loans. Each IBRD loan usually contains a "negative pledge" clause that "prohibits the establishment of a priority for other debts over the debt due to IBRD."[29] All Paris Club creditors are supposed to respect the privileged creditor status of the Bretton Woods institutions. But China is not a member of the Paris Club.

There is no international rule or law on the privileged creditor status. It appears nowhere in the Articles of Agreement establishing these institutions; it is merely a convention. Resource-backed loans complicate this arrangement. It is much simpler (at least as viewed from Washington) if all revenues go into the budget, and then are used to repay debts in order of priority. If a significant share of revenues is held outside the budget and used to repay the very large Chinese debt *first*, this could shake the foundations of the system of privileged creditors.[30]

Sierra Leone is a small country; Angola and the DRC are very large, but the same patterns of aid, economic cooperation, investment, and finance were playing out in many of the developing countries where China has diplomatic relations, much as they played out in China when Japan and the

West first came calling in the 1970s and 1980s. Aid connected to business in many ways, but in most Chinese *aid* packages *construction contracts* were a far more common element than the search for natural resources. China's aid projects typically have small profit margins for Chinese companies, only 1 to 2 percent, by some estimates, compared with 10 to 15 percent for commercial projects.[31] But they help generate new business. A Chinese company operating in Gabon reported: "we received six more construction projects in Gabon after we finished the Gabon Senate Plaza [an aid project]. We also received five from Lahore, Pakistan, and one from Istanbul, Turkey, after the Pakistan South Port [aid] project came to an end."[32]

In Sierra Leone, no one raised concerns about Chinese workers (although, as we shall see below, this has been an issue elsewhere). A World Bank official told me during my visit. "We want to see the Chinese come in and increase competition on contracts. There is a high premium on European contractors. On that scene, it is very good to have them." As I was leaving Sierra Leone, a Chinese company, the China Railway Seventh Group (which was not established locally), won two large World Bank contracts for road rehabilitation.

We have now seen some of the key features of China's approach compared with the other donors: the focus on infrastructure, the mix of aid and other forms of economic engagement, the deference to "ownership" (defined as African *government* ownership), the refusal to accept poverty as a reason to go slow in developing debt-financed infrastructure, the relative ease of the debt cancellation process, the search for creative ways to link Chinese interests in "going global" (Huawei, for example) with local interests in improving infrastructure. The next few sections address the fact and fiction of China's model in four areas that get a lot of press: conditionality, tied aid, the use of Chinese labor, and capacity building.

Aid Without Strings?

The idea that China gives aid "without strings" or conditions has become one of the key "facts" about Chinese aid. Conditions imposed on aid can include economic policies or governance reforms. They can also be quite specific in their details. Not surprisingly, conditionality-based aid is widely disliked by African leaders. Former Mozambican President Joaquim Chissano charged that donors frequently form "a common front in an unbalanced power relationship that may have dire consequences to the recipient country."[33] A Ugandan official was more charitable: "The fact that a country gives you aid makes them think they have a license to tell you how to run your affairs. These conditions are probably well-intentioned, but they are humiliating."[34]

It is not difficult to get African government officials to expound on the contrast between China's approach and the detailed and intrusive conditions often considered necessary by international donors. As the former Sierra Leone government minister Dr. Sesay told me, the Chinese will simply build a school, a hospital, and then supply a team of doctors to run it. "The World Bank will say: 'you must not have so many teachers on your payroll. You must employ some expatriate staff. You must cut down on your wages.' The Chinese will not do this. They will not say 'You must do this, do that, do this!'"

Here, I focus on economic conditionality (Chapter 11 delves into conditionality on governance and corruption). Are the Chinese breaking down the Washington Consensus that countries should implement certain kinds of economic policies (budget discipline, trade liberalization, and so on) before receiving aid? Do they really refrain from imposing economic conditions?

Decades of controversy over the Washington Consensus have raised many doubts about whether the economic conditions that often accompany aid are always good for development; this remains a heated area of debate. But whether they hurt or help may almost be beside the point. As former World Bank economist William Easterly and others have shown, countries frequently ignored most of the conditions, while donors continued to lend, making it very hard to tease out what the development impact of conditionality actually was.[35] In the face of these critiques, Britain and Norway decided to eliminate economic policy conditions on their aid.

China never has imposed economic conditions.[36] When I asked the Chinese ambassador to Sierra Leone whether China had put any conditions on the concessional loan he helped negotiate for the Huawei project, he replied: "This project should be profitable if it is run well. All of the telecoms projects here are profitable. I have talked to them many times. They must guarantee the profits. They should compete with other companies. Sierratel is indigenous, they have some advantages. But the problem is the management and the large number of staff. They have to feed them, even though efficiency is in question. For us, this is an experiment to see how to revitalize this parastatal [state-owned company]. I hope they will grasp this golden opportunity. But we have no conditions on this loan," he concluded, smiling. "Just good advice."

The fact that China does not attach explicit conditions to its *aid* does not mean that Chinese financiers and investors have no preconditions before they invest or provide finance for *commercial* projects. As we saw in the case of Tianli's zone in Mauritius, described in the prologue, investment projects can be marked by tough and prolonged bargaining over rates of taxation, royalties, the price of land, the number of residence permits that will be allowed, and so on. In Zimbabwe, China National Aero-Technology Import and Export Corporation (CATIC) agreed to a public–private partnership with the Zimbabwe government to build new coal-fired power plants. But CATIC required that Zimbabwe raise electricity tariffs to cost-effective levels as a pre-condition for its investment.[37] Most governments see business conditions such as these as part of the negotiation process, far different from the more intrusive conditions that require the government to privatize its enterprises, cut its payroll, or hold elections before it receives aid.

Non-interference in internal affairs is China's "brand" as a donor. But there is one exception, of course: Beijing has always insisted that partner countries observe the One China policy. If countries grant diplomatic ties to Taiwan, Beijing suspends diplomatic relations, and with it economic aid. (Business can continue as usual, however. Chinese companies had eleven engineering contracts in Malawi the year before China and Malawi first formed diplomatic ties.)

The importance Beijing places on the One China policy lay behind a much-reported but widely misunderstood incident where China was widely believed to have meddled in Zambia's 2006 presidential elections.[38] Here is the story as it has often been told. The opposition candidate, Michael "King Cobra" Sata, was concerned about Chinese labor practices and the growing presence of Chinese traders. He brought the governing party's cozy relationship with Beijing into the election as a rallying issue. The Chinese ambassador threatened that Beijing would break off relations with Zambia if Sata was elected. "Hardly a model of non-interference," one analysis concluded.[39]

Is this really what happened? Many journalists failed to mention that in addition to Sata's promise that he would chase bogus Chinese "infestors" out of the country if elected, Sata *promised to recognize Taiwan*. During the campaign, Sata visited Malawi (which still recognized Taiwan at that point) and allegedly accepted contributions to his campaign from Taiwanese businessmen. At Lusaka airport, on his return from Malawi, Sata announced that Taiwan was "a sovereign state" and should be recognized, adding that Hong Kong was also really an independent country.

The Chinese ambassador in Lusaka took the unusual step of holding a press conference to condemn what he called "these irresponsible remarks" and express the Chinese government's concern. He also warned that Chinese companies were holding back on investment out of fears raised by Sata's vitriolic campaign. But the thrust of his remarks was on the sovereignty issue. Officials from Sata's campaign, he said, had shown him a copy of a memorandum of understanding Sata had signed with Taiwanese officials in Malawi, promising that Sata would restore diplomatic ties with Taiwan, should he be elected. Sata needed to understand that Taiwan and Hong Kong were "part of China" and *not* independent states. He accused *Sata* of meddling in the internal affairs of *China* by signing agreements with Taiwanese officials and advocating Taiwanese independence.

The rest of the world saw this unusual scene as *China* intervening in the Zambian election (which Michael Sata ultimately lost). In the first version, the character that should be played by Taiwan is entirely off stage. Knowing that there is another way to interpret this story does not change the facts. The Chinese ambassador *did* warn publicly that China would reconsider its relations with Zambia should "King Cobra" win the election. But it does put a different spin on the reasons why this happened, and what it might mean for the future of China's policy of non-interference in the internal affairs of other countries.

Tied Aid?

I often hear it said that China insists on tied aid, when other donors have abandoned this practice. If only the latter was true. Tied aid requires recipients to use goods and services from the donor country. Studies routinely calculate that tying aid reduces its effectiveness by some 10 to 30 percent.[40]

Tied aid tends to bias donors to support projects with high import content instead of local inputs. It could seduce recipients into opting for development investments that are low on their priority list. It diverts trade. If the donor is a relatively high-cost country, it means that each dollar of aid will go for pricier, and not necessarily better, goods and services.

As recently as 2001, according to figures published by the Development Assistance Committee of the OECD, Italy's official development aid was 92 percent tied, and Canada's, 68 percent. Led by the UK's Department for International Development, OECD members have made much progress in reducing tied aid for procurement (food aid and technical assistance are not included in these measures; they are still largely tied). Yet it has been quite difficult to move the lower-income donor countries away from the politically comfortable practice of ensuring that aid funds are spent back home. In 2007, for example, 50 percent of procurement aid from Portugal and Greece was still tied to their own goods and services.

In the United States, congressional restrictions made it very difficult to unite aid, until very recently. For many years, the US Agency for International Development's website boasted that US foreign assistance generated over $10 billion in exports of US goods and services, supporting about 200,000 US jobs. "US assistance programs help create demand for US products and services," the website explained. "To ignore the developing world is to risk losing a niche in the most important markets of tomorrow."[41]

Clearly, as it ratchets up its engagement in Africa, China is following in the footprints left by the wealthy countries. The Ministry of Commerce's grants and zero-interest loans are tied to Chinese companies and goods (although projects can get permission to buy equipment locally or order it from third countries when they consider it necessary). Foreign aid project tenders are posted publicly, but companies eligible to bid on them must be on a list of pre-qualified Chinese firms.[42] China Eximbank's concessional aid guidelines state that the exporter or contractor should be a Chinese company, and that inputs for Eximbank-financed concessional aid projects should be procured from China. Officially, however, aid through Eximbank is only tied at a level of 50 percent.[43]

In Angola, 70 percent of an oil-backed infrastructure credit offered by China Eximbank was reserved for Chinese companies. This was widely, but mistakenly, reported to be Eximbank's policy on "tied aid" (as we will see below, the Eximbank credit in Angola was not, in fact, aid, and the reservation of 30 percent for local firms was *Angola's* policy, a condition they had written into the Eximbank framework agreement.[44] Congo was able to make a similar demand in the negotiations for their multibillion Eximbank package: 10 to 12 percent of the work was to be subcontracted to Congolese companies.[45]

Demands like these can be a welcome stimulus for local business, although each step in subcontracting reduces the value of a loan, since typically each level takes a cut for administrative overheads. Former UN workers Clare Lockhart and Ashraf Ghani report how this happened in a UN housing materials project in the remote Bamiyan district of Afghanistan.[46] A UN agency in Geneva took 20 percent of the $30 million project for overheads, subcontracting the project to an NGO based in Brussels. The NGO took 20 percent, and subcontracted to an Afghan NGO, which took its 20 percent, and so on, in five layers of contracts (a local company was finally paid to do the work). A Chinese company in Angola estimated that similar layers of subcontracting reduced the value of the work done by the loan by some 40 percent.[47]

Furthermore, in weak states with big infrastructure contracts, subcontracting mandates risk heightening corruption: a free-for-all in a spurt of contracts for unqualified local companies headed by people with political connections. At the conference where I first met him, my research assistant Tang Xiaoyang reported a joke he heard circulating around the Chinese contractors in Angola:

> Three companies bid on a construction tender. An Angolan minister opens the bids. A Chinese company offers to do the work for $3 million: $1 million for labor, $1 million for equipment, $1 million profit. A European company says it can do the job for $6 million: $2 million for labor, $2 million for equipment, $2 million for profit, but the quality will be better. An Angolan contractor bids $9 million: "$3 million for you, $3 million for me, and $3 million for the Chinese company to do the work."

A joke exaggerates, but sometimes it hits close to the bone. In theory, mandating that a percentage of loan-funded business go to local companies is good for development. In practice, it might create further challenges.

"Hordes of Experts"

We also read, over and over, that the Chinese rarely employ locals in their projects. Chinese projects *do* routinely use more of their own nationals as staff and skilled technicians than projects carried out by companies from any other country. They often set up self-contained compounds and live apart from local people. Yet the idea that the Chinese always bring over planeloads of their own workers and do not employ Africans is wrong.

Let us look more closely at the reality of Chinese practices in this area. The Chinese "insist on sending hordes of their own laborers" in their projects, *Time* magazine noted in 1968.[48] Construction of the famous Tan-Zam Railway employed some 16,000 skilled Chinese at its peak (but many tens of thousands of Africans).[49] In the Fouta Djallon highlands of Central Guinea, where three of West Africa's mightiest rivers, the Niger, the Senegal, and The Gambia, have their headwaters, 200 Chinese engineers and technicians labored for two and a half years beside 470 Guineans to build the 3-megawatt Kinkon dam on the Kokolou River. In 1980, a rice project in The Gambia had forty-five Chinese technicians, while a similar World Bank project hired only three expatriates.

Policies encouraging Chinese labor exports as a way to earn foreign exchange have been around for nearly three decades. In 1987, the *New York Times* broke a front-page story that China State Farm Agribusiness Corporation planned to supply Chinese peasants as contract labor for American farms under the Department of Immigration's temporary farm worker program.[50] (The New York Chinatown entrepreneurs in charge of the program explained that these Chinese farmers would "be professionals, not just anyone who is jobless off the street." Dolores Huerta, a co-founder of the United Farm Workers, called the plan "outrageous.")

In 2007, according to Chinese statistics, 743,000 Chinese were officially working overseas under labor contracts (the category includes experts and technicians).[51] While 70 percent were sent to work in Asia (including Hong Kong), 114,000 Chinese were working in Africa, including North Africa.[52] Additional labor contractors might work under the radar, smuggling people into Europe or America. But in Africa all the workers visibly employed on construction projects done by state-owned companies and other large firms like Huawei will be accounted for in these numbers.

Algeria and Sudan hosted more new Chinese workers in 2007 than any other African countries, although the number in Angola was also significant (Figure 5.2). These figures do not count the people who arrive independently as traders, stay on after a contract finishes, or come through the extended family and business networks that have traditionally marked the Chinese diaspora. South Africa, with at least 100,000 Chinese, is a prime destination.[53] A range of estimates suggest that anywhere from 300,000 to 750,000 people from mainland China have come to work in Africa since the 1990s, some settling more or less permanently. Any frequent visitor to Africa will notice that there are definitely more Chinese on the streets, in the towns, than in previous decades. A former student of mine from Japan working for the UN in West Africa reports to me that he is called "Chinaman!" wherever he goes. African children in some towns are beginning to call *all* pale-skinned foreigners "Chinese! Chinese!"[54] Yet there are also more Koreans, Malaysians, Taiwanese, and so on seeking business in Africa. This makes it hard to know the truth about numbers.

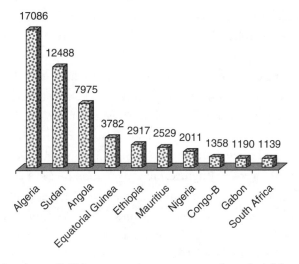

Fig. 5.2. Number of Chinese workers sent to selected African countries in 2007

Source: *China Commerce Yearbook* (2008).

Africans have fiercely criticized the Chinese practice of shipping in varying amounts of Chinese labor to work on projects, and a robust mythology has developed around this issue. The reality is that the ratio of Chinese workers to locals varies enormously, depending on how long a Chinese company has been working in a country, how easy it is to find skilled workers locally, and the local government's policies on work permits. In Sudan, where Chinese companies have been working in the oil industry for over a decade, 93 percent of workers in China's oil operations were said to be Sudanese.[55] Research by Tang Xiaoyang in Angola and the Democratic Republic of Congo showed that Chinese companies resident for five years had halved their ratio of Chinese employees compared with newly arrived Chinese firms.[56]

Pascal Hamuli, the Tanzanian project manager for a Chinese aid project constructing village water systems, told me that his project employed about fifty Chinese engineers and technical staff, and about 500 local workers. This parallels what South Africa's Center for Chinese Studies found in Tanzania. Chinese companies (most resident for some years) employed Tanzanians at a ratio of eight or nine for every Chinese. In Angola, just emerging from civil war, with a shortage of skilled manpower, the relationship was on average almost the opposite.[57] They noted that many of the construction projects in Angola were implemented by Chinese state-owned companies, with political pressure for rapid construction (in this case, before scheduled elections).

Why do some companies continue to bring in Chinese workers, who cost much more and also require expensive airline tickets? The shortage of local skills and pressure to complete a job quickly, as in Angola, is one answer. Ease of communication is another issue, but there are others. "Chinese people can stand very hard work," Lui Ping, the general manager of China National Overseas Engineering Corporation in Zambia told a British reporter. He employed fifteen Zambians for every Chinese, but said there is "a cultural difference. Chinese people work until they finish and then rest. Here they are like the British, they work according to a plan. They have tea breaks and a lot of days off. For our construction company that means it costs a lot more."[58]

Liu Yulin, the Chinese economic counselor in Tanzania, gave me his view of why there were not many Chinese workers in Tanzania: "Tanzania doesn't want to give work permits. And it's more expensive now to bring people from China. Some don't want to come. It costs a thousand dollars a month for a Chinese worker now. This is ten or twenty times what it costs for local salaries. Localization is the only way."[59]

Ultimately, as this suggests, African governments are the ones in control of the issue of Chinese labor in their countries. African governments have increasingly sought to ensure that the employment and economic stimulus effect of Chinese loans spill over to their nationals. Angola requires *all* employers to have at least 70 percent Angolan staff. The DRC insisted that at least 80 percent of the workers in China's multibillion dollar infrastructure and mining venture must be Congolese. At the same time, although governments are well aware of local demands for employment, they also gain political capital from commissioning projects that are completed rapidly, particularly before an election.

Before we leave this issue, let us keep in mind the other side of aid and foreign labor: the export of expertise from the West. Former Dutch Minister for Development Cooperation Evelyn Herfkens estimated that the traditional donors were employing more than 100,000 expatriate technical assistants in their African aid projects at an annual cost of some $5 billion.[60] The high salaries most Western aid workers enjoy are a source of some bitterness for local people. "Chinese interventions are not tied to a lot of experts who get half or three-quarters of whatever aid is coming to the country," an official in the president's office told me in Sierra Leone. In Liberia, a newspaper editorial praised the Chinese for sending a team of doctors to staff the local hospital, instead of "scores of relief workers who make triple digits in salaries for 'working in dangerous zones'."[61] It is worth keeping these thoughts in mind when looking at China's use of its own experts in projects overseas.

Capacity Building

For both the Chinese and the traditional donors, the use of skilled and expensive expatriates is a response to perceptions (and often the reality) of low levels of capacity in many African countries. Capacity building is a nut the traditional donors have yet to crack. An analysis I did more than a decade ago for the now defunct Washington DC think-tank, the Overseas

Development Council, pointed out many reasons for this, among them donors' failure to invest in higher education, and a tendency for donors to set up project implementation units outside of government and dismantle them at the end of a project.[62] Donors realize that their technical assistance is a "systematic, destructive force that is undermining the development of capacity," as a former World Bank vice-president, Edward (Kim) Jaycox, once charged. All these problems still characterize aid. Technical assistance currently gobbles up a quarter to a half of all aid, by some measures.[63] One could be forgiven for wondering if the donors (or the governments they assist) really have an incentive to build capacity.

What about the Chinese? Under the 2006 FOCAC pledges, the Chinese promised to provide short-term training to 15,000 Africans over three years, as I noted in Chapter 4. These short-term training courses in poverty reduction, new leather technologies, and a host of other areas are not linked to specific projects and will do little to build capacity. As part of its pledge to help with the Millennium Development Goals, Chinese premier Wen Jiabao announced in September 2008 that over the next five years China would train 1,500 principals and teachers for the schools it was building in Africa, and 1,000 doctors, nurses, and managers for the health sector in the thirty African countries receiving new hospitals from China.[64] Depending on the extent of training involved, this could have a more significant impact.

However, vocational training in Africa is a new thrust of China's aid-financed construction. In Ethiopia, a large training and vocational education center financed by Chinese aid and jointly operated by the two countries opened in early 2009. The school will eventually enroll 3,000 students, with courses to be taught by Chinese and Ethiopian teachers in construction skills, architecture, engineering, electronics, electrical engineering, computers, textiles, and apparel – all areas of interest to the several hundred Chinese companies now operating in Ethiopia.[65] China also built and operates a vocational training center in Uganda, and the Chinese are building two centers in Angola.

In addition, the pledge to provide university scholarship programs for 4,000 Africans between 2006 and 2009 to earn degrees in China *will* help build capacity, at the higher levels important for sustainable improvements. (At the MDG Summit in 2008, Premier Wen Jiabao pledged *another* 10,000 university scholarships for developing countries over the next five years.)

Africans with degrees from Chinese universities may be less marketable overseas, and thus less likely to participate in the brain drain to the wealthy countries, at least for a while.

What about capacity building during project implementation? Chinese aid teams are directed to follow five clear steps to gradually transfer their skills and technology to local counterparts.[66] Even if all five steps are followed and skills transferred, this might not ensure that skilled people remain with a project. As a Chinese economic officer in Liberia pointed out to me, "Local people are trained and then they are free to switch or be switched to another job." These jobs might be with an aid agency. Skilled Kenyans, for example, were paid five times more to work for international aid agencies than in the civil service.[67]

The pace set by China's "Orient Express" brand of rapid implementation also frequently clashed with the need for local counterparts to learn on the job. Chinese team leaders became impatient. Local counterparts sometimes complained that the Chinese were forging ahead, not including them in decision-making, and even working at night, a practice that the local counterparts were not eager to follow. But the project files I dug into, in my quest to learn how Chinese aid worked, recorded letter after letter from Chinese team leaders pleading for local counterparts and failing to get them. In Liberia, for example, a team leader wrote that his team would be leaving in nine months, and they were still waiting for counterparts to arrive. "I hereby want to repeat that I ardently wish all our Liberian Deputies to take their posts as soon as possible ... so that they can run the project by themselves after our leaving."[68]

In Sierra Leone, a local newspaper recalled how the Chinese constructing the massive Youyi ministerial building "asked for Sierra Leone counterparts in every one of the sections, to understudy them and to be *au fait* with the equipment."[69] However, the government failed to supply counterparts until *three weeks* before the Chinese left. Stadium officials in Sierra Leone could not find the blueprints and blamed the Chinese, who, they were sure, had packed them off to China. By contrast, the Gambian government quickly assigned counterparts on Chinese construction projects "from the word 'go'," as one official told me. Gambian officials who had worked with the Chinese on a stadium project showed me the blueprints and electrical diagrams for the buildings. (That made me wonder what *really* happened in Sierra Leone. Did the Chinese take the blueprints back, or were they stuck in a back room somewhere, under dusty piles of forgotten files?)

The more sustainable solution to the capacity dilemma may come out of the marriage of Chinese *companies'* needs and their own practical strategies for meeting those needs. Chinese firms are setting up training institutes in Africa to address local skills shortages they have identified for their own projects and business plans. China's major telecoms company Huawei has established training centers in Angola, South Africa, Nigeria, Egypt, Tunisia, and Kenya to train Africans in skills needed to operate and maintain wireless telephones and broadband internet systems. As Bo Xue, Huawei's manager for sub-Saharan Africa explained, Huawei had to import expertise from China or Europe, but this was high-cost and provided only a short-term solution: "The sustainable long-term solution [is] to invest in training local people."[70] Huawei's rival ZTE joined together with Ethiopian Telecommunications Corporation to set up a joint communications institute to train 3,000 Ethiopian telecoms engineers, as part of a larger project.[71] As African countries move to embrace the information superhighway, they will increasingly be relying on local Chinese-trained technicians, a capacity building solution pushed by profit, not altruism, but perhaps all the more sustainable because of that.

Furthermore, some private Chinese companies are building African capacity in manufacturing, a subject we will return to in Chapters 7 and 8. In May 2009, as we walked past a row of Nigerians hard at work in a local plastics factory, the official accompanying me, Andrew Udeh, told me that they had been using technical experts from China for more than six years. "The Chinese transfer their technology. They will monitor it. They will supervise it. If you wish, they will manage it for some years before transferring it over," he told me. "Their presence in Nigeria is empowering Nigerians," he added, "particularly the Ibos, who believe in manufacturing."

China is different from the traditional donors in how it does aid. The political relationship is very important everywhere and not simply in strategic countries. This fosters a lot of genuine concern with government ownership, even if the government wants a new stadium or a presidential residence. There is very little paternalism, and no conditionality on aid (aside from the One China policy). Grants and zero-interest loans primarily finance diplomatic investments: politically friendly projects that are sometimes also useful for development (stadiums, ministry buildings, irrigation systems, hospitals and schools, bridges and roads). Concessional loans usually finance projects with potential for a clear economic return (telecoms, energy, public utilities). The Chinese continue to return to repair and rehabilitate former projects, sometimes because of their political importance, sometimes because they might now turn into a business venture. They work rapidly, using a lot of skilled Chinese workers, but they usually employ many more Africans. China's aid experts still live simply and you will not find them in five-star hotels. But they are unlikely to align their aid with aid from the other donors, or to join efforts at aid harmonization, particularly, it seems, if led by the World Bank.

On the other hand, there are similarities. Like other donors, the Chinese have not yet figured out how to build capacity or really transfer their skills. Their aid is still largely tied, as it was for most of the traditional donors until recently. The Chinese have learned much from other donors, particularly Japan, and their model of how aid connects to business. We can see this most clearly from the active search for ways to finance construction in poor countries with a lot of needs and business potential, but without much current revenue in their budgets. As we shall see in Chapter 6, China's natural resource-backed development loans are not concessional enough to qualify as aid, but they do offer a way for some of the wealth generated by resource-rich but impoverished countries to be channeled into roads, clinics, and other infrastructure. Chinese companies are also proposing public–private partnerships, the kind promoted by the World Bank: build, operate, and transfer (BOT) schemes that would have Chinese partners constructing economic assets such as toll bridges and roads or power plants.

This overview of how China's aid and economic engagement works leaves much unanswered. More details on impact will emerge in Chapters 7 through 11, which focus on agriculture, industry, and governance. But a central question, much misunderstood, remains to be addressed: how much aid does China actually give? I turn to this in the next chapter, which dips into the murky and secret depths of China's official aid program, and provides answers.

CHAPTER 6

Apples and Lychees: How Much Aid Does China Give?

Maputo, the faded colonial capital of Mozambique, sits along one of Africa's most beautiful coastlines, where white sand beaches line the southern curve of the continent nearly all the way to Cape Town. In 2007, when Chinese President Hu Jintao visited, Mozambicans stood beneath the flowering red acacias and the pale blue jacaranda that line Maputo's broad avenues and cheered his motorcade. Hu Jintao signed agreements for debt cancellation and a new loan package. Mozambique would receive aid worth more than $200 million, including a new stadium and a large agricultural center.[1] One agreement *not* signed was a long discussed Eximbank loan for the controversial $2.3 billion Mpanda Nkua ("the scream of the passing water") hydropower dam on the Zambezi River.

On the other side of Africa along the rough Atlantic coast, Angola's government had finally ended a decades-long civil war in 2002. Over the next few years, Angolans negotiated three credits from China Eximbank, a total of $4.5 billion. All were used to pay for infrastructure, and all were guaranteed by Angola's oil revenues. The interest rates on these loans were widely (and, it turns out, erroneously) reported as 1.5 percent or even 0.75 percent. This *looked* like aid, but was it?

In 2006, the Nigerian government and China Railway Construction Corporation (CCRC) signed an $8.3 billion contract to rebuild the 2,733 km colonial-era railway between the coastal city of Lagos and the capital of northern Nigeria, Kano. CRCC's motto is "Cut Paths through Mountains and Build Bridges across Rivers." The corporation was formed through the mergers of several state-owned railway companies. Two of these, the Railway Engineering Corps (formerly owned by the Chinese army) and China Civil Engineering Construction Corporation (the former foreign aid office of Beijing's Ministry of Railways), cut their teeth in Africa in the 1970s building China's biggest foreign aid project, the Tan-Zam Railway. The new Nigeria contract would be China's largest overseas project for 2006.[2] But was it aid?

I first learned about the Nigeria project in an op-ed in the *New York Times*, which told readers that the Chinese had offered $9 billion in "aid" to modernize Nigeria's decrepit railway network.[3] On hearing this, the op-ed continued, a World Bank official – in town to negotiate a private sector-led cleanup of the mismanaged railway in return for a meager $5 million loan – packed his bags and went home. The "aid" figure touted in the *New York Times* was mind-boggling, an enormous sum. But it was also completely wrong.

Between 2007 and 2009, negotiations for a genuinely massive project that *would* be financed entirely by China Eximbank emerged out of the war-ravaged Democratic Republic of Congo, the former Zaire. China Railway Engineering Corporation (CREC, a rival of the companies working in Nigeria), along with the Chinese hydropower company Sinohydro and China Eximbank, concluded an astounding package deal. Eximbank would provide a loan of $6 billion, in two installments, to finance infrastructure. Sinohydro would be paid by these loans to build power plants and repair Congo's water supply across the country. It would also build thirty-two hospitals, 145 health centers, two hydroelectric dams, two large universities, two vocational training centers, and thousands of low-cost houses. CREC, the publicly listed Fortune Global 500 company that built Shanghai's high-speed Maglev airport train, would renovate Congo's colonial-era railway lines and build thousands of kilometers of roads.

As I noted in the previous chapter, the infrastructure agreement proposed by the two construction companies was backed by Congo's rich resources. CREC and Sinohydro would establish a joint venture with Gécamines, Congo's state-owned mining company, to reopen a disused copper and cobalt mine owned by a Belgian company and develop two new mining concessions. These investments, about $3.25 billion, would be financed by the two firms in a mix of shareholder credits and bank loans. The revenues from the mines would then be used over fifteen years to repay the initial loans.

The package deeply worried the West. The IMF raised alarms about the macroeconomic impact of the enormous project. A reporter who traveled to the Congo for the BBC TV program *Newsnight* said the deal seemed unfair to the Congolese.[4] On hearing this, Paul Fortin, the Canadian-born director of Gécamines, a lawyer and the man who spent months negotiating the deal with the Chinese, pointed to the ruins of the Belgian mine and replied: "Rubbish. Without the Chinese, all this will just be scenery."

Congolese ministers called the deal a "vast Marshall Plan" for the war-torn country as their parliament debated, then hesitantly approved, the package in May 2008. But the original Marshall Plan was 89 percent pure grant aid.[5] From this perspective, the large Chinese loans did not much resemble the Marshall Plan. "Would the European development aid community tolerate us operating like the Chinese?" a European diplomat sniffed. He assumed the deal was "aid." Was it?

These brief vignettes give a headlines-only tour of some of the more striking examples of China's recent injections of development finance into Africa. They are typical of the kinds of projects that prompted *The Economist* to declare that China has "concentrated its aid" in countries like Angola, the Democratic Republic of Congo, Equatorial Guinea, Nigeria, and Sudan.[6] We will return to all of these later in this chapter, but let me say at the outset that most of these examples are *not* "aid" in China's accounting, and they would also not qualify as official development assistance (ODA) according to the criteria of the traditional donors.

The Chinese aid program is frequently portrayed as enormous and secretive. It is true that China has proposed very large loan packages in a small number of African countries (as well as smaller packages in nearly every other country), but most of what is on offer is not official development assistance, as this is defined by the traditional donors. Transparency about aid figures remains low, but it is not impossible to find information. To dig into all of this more deeply, we have to look at the technical aspects of what is and is not "aid." If this is not your cup of tea, I invite you to move on to the next chapter now. For those of you who are keen to know more about this, bear with me.

In the prologue to this book, I described how, decades ago, the traditional donors in the OECD set up a Development Assistance Committee (DAC) based in Paris, and tasked it to define "official development assistance" in a manner that would allow for reliable international comparisons.[7] They agreed that official development assistance (or ODA) would be defined as funds and technical assistance, given on strictly limited concessional terms, primarily to promote economic development and welfare, in developing countries that fell below a threshold income level.

Grants qualify automatically, but loans need to have below-market interest rates, with long grace periods (before payment of the principle begins) and long repayment periods. Combined, the terms of an ODA loan must make the total cost of the loan (over time) at least 25 percent lower than a loan made on commercial terms.[8] This reduction in the cost of the loan is called the "grant element" of the loan.

The DAC also tracks official loans in a second category called "other official flows" or OOF. This is money that comes from governments, but does not qualify as ODA. It would include loans with a grant element of less than 25 percent, or it could be (and I quote the OECD here) "official bilateral transactions, whatever their grant element, that are primarily export facilitating in purpose. *This category includes by definition export credits.*"[9] It also includes government funds that support private investment in developing countries. This point is worth repeating: none of the OOF loans qualify as official foreign aid, no matter how cheaply they are given.

China's lack of transparency on aid is slowly changing. In 2008, Chinese premier Wen Jiabao announced at a high-level meeting on the Millennium Development Goals that China had disbursed a total of $30 billion in aid to all developing countries since 1950, of which about $13 billion was in the form of grants. He also announced that China had budgeted around $346 million in grants and $102 million in zero-interest loans for Africa at the end of 2007. In a similar, almost offhand manner, we learned that China's aid to Africa from 1956 to 2006 amounted to just under $6 billion.[10] Aside from these unusual revelations, most information about official aid is still considered a state secret, although this is changing.

Why is China so secretive about aid? The specifics on foreign aid are sensitive, in part due to the ongoing diplomatic battles with Taiwan. In addition, Beijing professor Li Anshan speculated that Chinese culture played a part – it is considered "improper or even immoral" to call attention to your assistance. Also, he suggested, many people within China believe that China itself is poor and should probably not be giving funds to other countries.

This latter concern is echoed in a critique posted by a Chinese citizen in an online website. Writing in 2003 under the title "China's Foreign Aid Should be Public Knowledge," Du Daobin spoke of his surprise at learning from overseas media that China had given $2.4 billion to North Korea and canceled $950 million in African debt.[11] "Thanks to the overseas media," Du said, "taxpayers in China have learned for the first time that a considerable proportion of their tax dollars is not benefiting China or its people...As a citizen, I would ask the decision-makers in Beijing to explain the reasoning and wisdom of such assistance...There are so many people in China who are in dire need, yet why are we giving away 30 billion yuan? Are we back in the colonial days when Chinese people were considered less worthy of help than foreigners?...Don't we citizens have the right to know how much is given away and what for?"

There are chinks in the bamboo screen that hides China's aid figures from their citizens and from the rest of us.[12] One thing is clear: China's reluctance to publish aid statistics does not mean, as some believe, that China does not *know* how much aid it gives. Rather, aid is part of a tightly controlled government reporting system. Each year the Department of Foreign Aid assembles the main foreign assistance budget and sends it up through the Ministry of Commerce to the Ministry of Finance, which collects the rest of the aid budgets from other ministries. This budget includes the cost of the Department's turn-key projects, military goods, grants-in-kind, expenses for training programs in China and technical assistance overseas, foreign-aided joint ventures and cooperation projects, and the youth volunteer program.[13]

The aggregate budget figures for external assistance expenditures are published annually in the *China Statistical Yearbook* (Figure 6.1). But the Chinese do not use the same categories used by the OECD. For example, the Chinese have used some of their foreign aid money to support joint ventures between Chinese firms and firms in developing countries. China includes military aid in its expenditures for general foreign aid. These would probably not qualify as ODA as the OECD has defined it.[14]

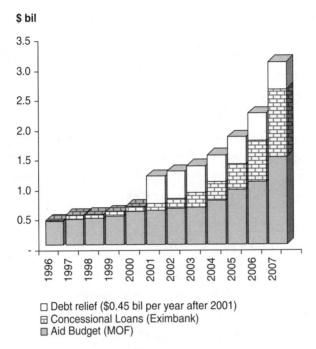

\$ bil

□ Debt relief (\$0.45 bil per year after 2001)
⊞ Concessional Loans (Eximbank)
▨ Aid Budget (MOF)

Fig. 6.1. Chinese official aid* 1996–2007

*Author's estimates.

Note: See Appendix 6 for figures and assumptions.

Sources: *China Statistical Yearbook*; China Eximbank *Annual Reports*; author's research.

The figures reported in the *China Statistical Yearbook* include grants and zero-interest loans. However, since the Eximbank raises the capital on its concessional loans from the market, the Ministry of Finance only includes in the budget what it pays Eximbank for the interest rate subsidy. For example, if Eximbank gave out \$100 million in a concessional loan with an interest rate of 2 percent, and the central bank lending rate was 6 percent, the annual subsidy would be 4 percent, or only \$4 million. So a \$100 million concessional aid loan given in 2009 "costs" the foreign aid budget only \$4 million that year. This makes it hard to compare China's officially reported aid expenditures with the ODA figures reported by the traditional donors to the DAC, where the rules require the entire face value of concessional loans to count as official development assistance, just as if they were grants.

Premier Wen Jiabao's 2008 announcement on aid was a sign of greater transparency. We can expect this to increase. In 2007, Wang Shichun, the director of the Department of Foreign Aid, said that China would become more transparent about its aid process, cooperate more, "and draw on international aid expertise to improve its own work."[5] The Chinese commissioned a team of Beijing scholars to study the OECD–DAC's system of aid statistics. This has enabled the Ministry of Commerce to calculate China's aid totals using the same DAC methodology employed by the traditional donors, in preparation for greater transparency in the future. It is quite likely that China will follow in the footsteps of other non-OECD donors, such as Taiwan and South Korea, and publish these figures. But until they do, we will have to estimate them.

Estimating China's Africa Aid

China committed approximately $1.4 billion in official development aid to Africa (including debt relief) in 2007, according to my estimates. This should reach almost $2.5 billion by 2009. I have stitched this figure together out of bits of facts released over time, including China's official budget for its traditional external aid, and several Eximbank reports on the value of its concessional loans. This is how I did it.

Chinese aid needs to be divided into three areas: Ministry of Finance external assistance expenditure, China Eximbank concessional loans, and debt relief. I started with China's Ministry of Finance official figures for external assistance expenditures, as published in the *China Statistical Yearbook*.[16] This makes up the bottom part of each column in Figure 6.1 (the figures on which these tables are based can be found in Appendix 6). The Eximbank concessional loan figures are more difficult to obtain. China Eximbank published the annual value of its concessional foreign aid loans in its annual reports only until 2001, so I begin with these figures. The annual report for 2005 mentioned that between 2001 and 2005 concessional lending grew at an annual rate of 35 percent.[17] Using this growth rate brings China's annual concessional loans to around $0.425 billion in 2005. I assume the growth rate almost doubled thereafter, as China expanded concessional loans in the second half of the decade.[18]

To truly compare "apples with apples" we need to add debt relief to China's aid, since this is reported as aid by the traditional donors (the Chinese do not count it as aid). Here we actually have good, firm figures from the Chinese. Between 2001 and June 2008, as I noted in the previous chapter, they wrote off $3.6 billion in debt owed by a variety of mostly low-income countries.[19] Averaged over the period 2001 to 2008 adds about $450 million to each year of aid, which I add to the top of the columns in Figure 6.1, for those years. This would make China's official development aid in 2007 (including debt relief) approximately $3 billion.

This gives us a set of estimates for Chinese aid worldwide, but what percentage of this aid went to Africa? And how fast is it likely to grow? We need to take each of the three areas for aid separately, beginning with the Ministry of Finance figures. Between 1986 and 1995, annual reviews of China's engagement with Africa written by Chinese officials reported a varying percentage of Chinese aid going to Africa, from a low of 37 percent to a high of 75 percent, with no clear trend.[20] In 2003, Minister of Foreign Affairs Li Zhaoxing told a group of African officials that aid to Africa between 2000 and 2003 absorbed an average of 44 percent of China's total aid.[21] Chinese officials have told me that less than a third of China's aid is now allocated to Africa. They have also said that China's aid in 2006 was around $300 million. Thirty percent of the Ministry of Finance official foreign assistance expenditures for 2006 would be $309 million, which is consistent with what I was told. The figure for China's foreign aid concessional loans from the Eximbank assumes that 50 percent of Eximbank's concessional loans go to Africa.[22] Finally, we also know that the Chinese canceled $3 billion in debt for Africa between 2001 and 2008, with more promised, an average of $375 per year in debt relief (80 percent of China's debt relief goes to Africa). So far we are on fairly firm ground, anchored by official published budget figures and Chinese sources.

The growth rate of China's aid presents yet another challenge. We know that between 2006 and 2009 China's aid to Africa was scheduled to double (the Chinese have never clarified which areas of aid they are counting here, but my discussions with Chinese officials lead me to conclude that they were speaking about aid from the Ministry of Finance's budget for external assistance, not the concessional loans or debt relief). Chinese officials have told me that their aid budget for Africa will double to around $600 million in 2009. I have used that estimate here. It is quite possible, however, that China will exceed its pledge. This has been the pattern for most of China's pledges: promise less, deliver more. Again, this is in sharp contrast to the traditional donors. At their 2005 Gleneagles Summit, members of the wealthy G-8 pledged to double aid to Africa by 2010, a pledge most of them will not actually meet.

My estimates for growth rates for China Eximbank's concessional loans are based on the November 2006 pledge to commit $3 billion in concessional loans to Africa between 2007 and 2009. Figure 6.2 assumes this pledge will be realized and allocates the $3 billion across the three years. Finally, I assume that debt cancellation will continue at the same rate, at least through 2009. That final amount tops each column in Figure 6.2.

We can double-check my estimates against some of the official figures that emerge from the curtain of secrecy from time to time. For example, at a June 2008 United Nations meeting on financing the Millennium Development Goals, Chinese premier Wen Jiabao announced that Beijing had extended $451 million in grants and zero-interest loans to Africa in 2007.[23] My estimate (Figure 6.2) was $440 million, based on 30 percent of the MOF official figures for external assistance for 2007. These are very close.

Likewise, officials at China Eximbank occasionally provide glimpses into their concessional loan program. Eximbank officials told the World Bank

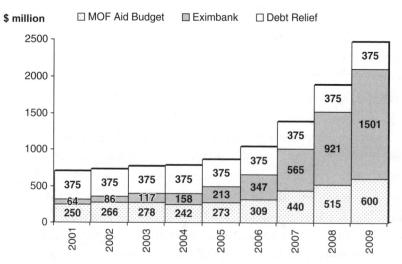

Fig. 6.2. China's annual African aid*

*Author's estimates.

Sources: Author's research.

that by the end of 2005 they had funded fifty-five concessional loan projects in Africa, worth a total of $800 million.[24] In April 2007, a Chinese official said that the Eximbank had by then financed a total of eighty-seven concessional loan projects in Africa, worth about $1.5 billion.[25] My estimates for China Eximbank's accumulated totals for concessional loans in Africa are presented in Figure 6.3 (it simply sums the annual figures for concessional loans from Figure 6.2). The estimate I have made of an accumulated total of $803 million for Africa in 2005 matches the $800 million figure almost perfectly. My estimate of accumulated commitments of concessional loans of $1.7 million at the end of 2007 also fits well with the April 2007 figure of $1.5 million. This suggests that the assumptions I am using for these estimates are quite close to the actual figures. The relatively small size of Eximbank's concessional loan program was also confirmed when they opened their books to gain a global credit rating. Standard and Poor's reported that concessional loans at the end of 2005 represented only 3 percent of Eximbank's assets (about $1.16 billion).[26]

How does China's aid compare with the traditional donors? As noted above, Africa probably received ODA commitments of about $1.4 billion

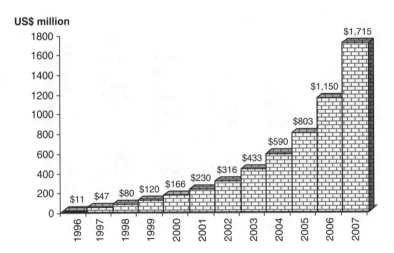

Fig. 6.3. Eximbank accumulated concessional loans to Africa* ($ million)

*Author's estimates for 2002–2007.

Source: Eximbank *Annual Reports* (for figures 1996–2001), Eximbank (2007) and author's estimates based on Eximbank's reported average growth rate for concessional loans 2001–2005.

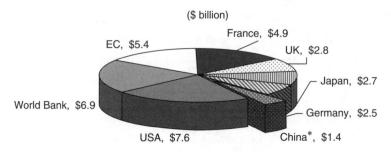

Fig. 6.4. Major Donors, ODA commitments to Africa, 2007

*China figure is author's estimate.

Note: All figures include North Africa.

Sources: OECD/DAC statistics; World Bank *Annual Reports*.

from China in 2007. In contrast, the United States committed $7.6 billion in ODA to Africa in 2007, including debt relief, with other traditional donors committing lesser amounts (Figure 6.4). Although Chinese aid is on track to double by 2009, as promised by Chinese leaders, it is likely to still be relatively small compared with the traditional donors (Figure 6.5).

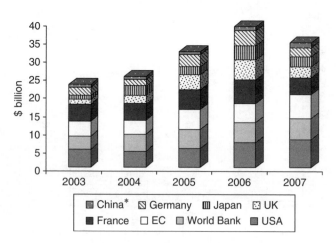

Fig. 6.5. ODA commitments to Africa, 2003–2007

*China figure is author's estimate.

Note: All figures include North Africa.

Sources: OECD/DAC statistics; World Bank *Annual Reports*.

One is Aid, the Other is Not

The aid figures I have estimated are far smaller than the figures reported as "aid" in the media and even by other researchers. There are several reasons, in addition to the secrecy of the basic figures, why those who write on this subject miscalculate the figures on Chinese aid. First, the China Eximbank offers two kinds of below-market credits. Only one of these truly qualifies as aid. Let us look at this a bit more closely, because these two instruments are often confused.

At the November 2006 Forum on China–Africa Cooperation Summit in Beijing, the Chinese announced that they would offer $2 billion in preferential export buyer's credits and $3 billion in concessional loans. Only the $3 billion is considered "aid" both by the Chinese and by the definitions set out by the OECD, which, as noted above, do not include export credits as official development assistance, no matter how concessional the terms. Both have fixed interest rates (usually about 2 or 3 percent). Both use "framework agreements" that set down the terms of the loans. And in both cases the Chinese government gives Eximbank a direct subsidy to enable the fixed interest rate to be reduced several percentage points below the market. For this reason, China's Ministry of Finance needs to sign off on preferential export credits and concessional loans. As an official at Eximbank described it, "The Chinese government bears the risk of these, not the Eximbank." Finally, there is considerable mystery about both of these. Concessional loans are apparently not included in the figures published in the Eximbank's annual reports, and although preferential buyer's credits probably are included with the published totals for buyer's credits, there is no indication of the proportion that are issued at highly preferential rates.

There are also several key differences. Preferential buyer's credits are always issued in dollars (or another foreign currency). They are usually larger than the concessional aid loans ($200 million or $500 million credit lines are not unusual), and have a maximum maturity of fifteen years. All of the loan must be used to finance the purchase of Chinese goods or services, and the buyer must put up at least 15 percent of the cost as a down payment. The framework agreement containing the terms of the loan is signed by the Eximbank itself and the borrower. The credit will finance only up to 85 percent of the total project cost. The Ministry of Commerce subsidizes the interest rate of preferential buyer's credits out of special funds established for this purpose, and Eximbank coordinates with the Ministry's Department of International Economic Cooperation on these credits. There is nothing specifying that the export needs to be in support of *development*.

On the other hand, concessional foreign aid loans are always issued in Chinese renminbi (RMB) with a minimum loan size of RMB 20 million (around three million dollars). Grace periods are usually five years, with maturity in twenty years. At least 50 percent of the loan must be used for the purchase of Chinese goods and services (this was reduced from an earlier level of 70 percent, showing that the Chinese are aware of the global effort to reduce tied aid). The framework agreement giving the terms of the loan is always inter-governmental, signed by a representative of the Ministry of Commerce, not Eximbank. The Department of Foreign Aid is in charge of these loans. As the Eximbank explained it: "The terms of the concessional loans are not in our control. This is a framework agreement between the governments, we just obey the terms. The Department of Foreign Aid does the negotiations. They represent the government. Our bank just does the financing. MOFCOM (the Ministry of Commerce) will give us several projects and we can select among them. As long as there is enough in the concessional loan fund and the projects are well-designed, we will finance as many as we can." The recipient's Ministry of Finance signs for the borrowing government.

Package Financing Mode

A further reason for confusion is the "package financing mode" used by the Ministry of Commerce and the Eximbank. This mixed credit mode should be familiar from Chapter 2, where we saw it used by Japan and the Europeans *in China* decades ago. In 2004, an Eximbank official commented that his bank was now "forming mixed credits by combining concessional loans, seller's and buyer's credits in support of large overseas engineering projects, particularly in developing countries."[27]

An early example of this was the financing for a 2001 contract won by China Harbour Engineering Company for the Gwadar Port Project in Pakistan. The $248 million project was financed from the Chinese side by a package: grants of $49 million, an interest-free loan for $31 million, an

Eximbank concessional renminbi loan worth approximately $58 million, and a market-rate export buyer's credit of $60 million.[28] Aid comprised about 70 percent of the package. In 2006, China Eximbank reported that it had signed agreements offering package financing with Congo-Brazzaville, Ethiopia, Equatorial Guinea, Nigeria, and Mauritania, and was negotiating packages with Ghana, Namibia, and Eritrea, suggesting that the mixed credits were popular in Africa.[29] Yet as an official at the Eximbank told me: "Mixed loans are not easy to do. At least two departments need to coordinate. It is complicated. And governments in less developed countries prefer the concessional loans. We would like to mix the loans, but the fact is, it is not very welcome."

As they evolved, mixed credits employed less aid, and more market rate finance, as an example from Ghana demonstrates. In 2007, the Chinese Eximbank committed to finance Ghana's multimillion dollar Bui hydropower project on the Black Volta River. Like so many African countries, Ghana is plagued by power cuts and leaders viewed hydroelectric dams on the country's rivers as a solution that would reduce dependence on foreign energy, while also providing a renewable source of power. This particular dam, however, would flood a large portion of the Bui National Park, home of Ghana's last remaining rare hippos and lions, require resettlement of people living near the park, and suffer all the problems of silting and poor performance during droughts that can plague hydropower. We will return to these environmental problems in Chapter 11. My question here is: was this aid?

The Eximbank's package combined an export buyer's credit of $292 million at a commercial interest rate with a concessional loan for $270 million at 2 percent.[30] Both loans were backed by Ghana's cocoa exports, and would be repaid from a dedicated escrow account into which Ghana would deposit an agreed amount of its cocoa export revenues. The second loan would have qualified as official development assistance, but not the first.

The Ghana example brings up yet another reason why so many of China Eximbank's projects in Africa are mistakenly thought to be "aid." Many reporting on this issue are simply not familiar with the financing terms used for export credits and international loans. Like other export credit agencies, China Eximbank offers its export buyers credits at "competitive" rates, based either on the Organization for Economic Cooperation and Development's posted monthly Commercial Interest Reference Rate (CIRR), plus a margin (for example, CIRR plus 0.75 percent), or on the London Inter-Bank Offered Rate, plus a margin (LIBOR plus 1.25 percent, for example).[31] Between 2004 and 2008, LIBOR varied between a low of 1.2 percent and a high of 5.6 percent. In order for China Eximbank to help its own companies get business, it makes the rates as attractive as possible, often through using internal cross-subsidies, i.e. charging some borrowers higher rates and others lower ones so that its portfolio remains profitable overall. China Development Bank operates in a similar manner. All of Eximbank's export buyer's credits are at rates better than countries like Ghana could get from an ordinary commercial bank. But this is true of all loans offered by export credit agencies, otherwise there would be no real reason for them to exist.

Let us look again at some of the projects outlined at the beginning of this chapter. The oil-backed loans in Angola also turned out to be made at commercial rates (we will hear more about these in Chapter 11). The first loan of $2 billion was issued at LIBOR plus 1.5 percent, the second at LIBOR plus 1.25 percent. Projects financed out of each loan could be repaid over seventeen years. These rates for Angola's oil-backed Eximbank loans were described as "deeply concessional" by one study.[32] But in fact, as Simon Scott, head of statistics for the OECD's Development Assistance Committee, confirmed, any loan with a LIBOR rate is, by definition, at a market rate of interest. It is *"not concessional at all."*[33]

The financing terms for the enormous, natural resource-backed infra-structure package negotiated for the Democratic Republic of the Congo were almost entirely commercial. The loan for the mining investment was agreed at 6.1 percent (a fixed rate), while the loan for infrastructure would be given at LIBOR plus 1 percent (still a commercial rate).[34] The entire package contained only a single zero-interest foreign aid loan: $50 million for Congo's state-owned mining company Gécamines, to be delivered in the form of equipment.

Chinese finance for the Nigerian Lagos–Kano railway project, described in the *New York Times* as "$9 billion" in "aid," is another example of a mixed credit. China Eximbank actually offered Nigeria two lines of credit: $2 billion at a commercial rate, (contingent on Nigeria providing the right for Chinese companies to develop several oil blocks) and a preferential buyer's credit of $500 million at 3 percent interest.[35] Former Nigerian Minister of Finance Dr. Shansuddeen Usman reported that the grant element of the mixed credit was only 21 percent, below anyone's measure of foreign aid.[36] After Nigeria's 2007 elections brought a new economic team into Abuja, the railway project was put on hold amid falling oil revenues and accusations of inflated costs.

Big Mistakes

Finally, there are simple mistakes that sometimes turn out to be big ones. An Associated Press story reported China's premier as saying that China had given Africa "more than $44 billion in aid" since beginning its aid program. This figure was subsequently included in an important World Bank report, which seems to have influenced the analyses of other journalists.[37] But what China's premier *actually* said was *RMB* 44 billion ($5.7 billion).[38] The *Christian Science Monitor* claimed that China's aid to Africa in 2006 alone was "three times the total development aid given by rich countries."[39] But African aid from rich countries was about $30 billion in 2006. And, as we have seen, China gave at most only a small fraction of that.

The way in which the Chinese program their aid, and even the way they normally count contributes to some of these mistakes. While the West counts in units of a thousand, hundred thousand, million, and so on, the Chinese commonly use ten thousand (*wan*) as a basic unit for large numbers. We have no such unit in the West, and I have seen Chinese translators struggle to convert Chinese figures announced in units of ten thousand into Western figures in units of a million or hundred thousand. On another note, Chinese aid loans are very often given as a line of credit good for three to five years, as I noted in Chapter 5. These packages are generally announced during state visits. In February 2009, for example, Chinese President Hu Jintao visited Mauritius and promised a grant, an interest-free loan, and a preferential export buyer's credit.[40] His visit to Namibia resulted in a similar package.[41]

These lines of credit and promises of grant aid are then disbursed for projects that are negotiated over time. Each round of negotiations or even a formal expression of interest, is capped by separate memoranda of understanding (MOU). When a decision is made, each project has a separate loan agreement. Sometimes researchers or reporters add all of these together: the initial line of credit, mention of a project in an MOU, and the final loan agreement.[42]

Furthermore, the signing of an MOU is a weak commitment at best; often the initial Chinese MOU for a project is only two pages long.[43] One cannot assume that funds have actually been committed. For example, the $2.3 billion Mpanda Nkua dam project in Mozambique has been repeatedly included in estimates of Chinese loan commitments to Africa since 2006, although as of mid-2009, no agreement had yet been reached. In fact, Mozambique eventually awarded the Mpanda Nkua contract to a Brazilian firm, Camargo Corrêa. The $1.0 billion dollar-plus Kafue Lower Gorge hydropower project in Zambia, described in several recent studies as "being developed" by the Chinese company Sinohydro, was stalled at the MOU stage, Zambian officials told me. In August 2008, the Kafue Lower project was re-opened for competitive bidding in a process assisted by the World Bank's International Finance Corporation.[44]

Sometimes errors multiply as they travel across the internet, where it can require real detective work to track down the origin of some stories. In 2004, *The Economist* reported an erroneous figure of $1.8 billion for China's "development aid" for Africa in 2002.[45] This was repeated in a *Boston Globe* article, which became the source for an article in *Current History* that said the 2002 figure of $1.8 billion was the "last" time "official statistics" on Chinese aid to Africa were released.[46] The *Current History* article was subsequently cited by researchers at the World Bank, who repeated soberly that "The last officially reported flows are for 2002. For that year, China's government reported that it provided $1.8 billion in economic support to all of Africa."[47] An International Monetary Fund study cited the World Bank report as its source for the same figure.[48] Apparently, no one checked to see if there had actually been any official statistics reported by China in 2002 or at any point before or since for its annual aid to Africa (there were not).

The $1.8 billion figure circulated for African aid was nearly three times higher than the amount the Chinese actually provided in their official 2002 budget for external assistance for *all* developing countries (Figure 6.1). Where had *The Economist* come up with the figure of $1.8 billion? I had a hunch, and so I checked the statistics published every year by the Chinese Ministry of Commerce for the turnover (revenues) for "economic cooperation" in Africa.[49] Sure enough, the figure was $1.8 billion in 2002. But "economic cooperation" is not aid. This figure includes *all* the work done by Chinese contractors in Africa, whether the contract is paid by the World Bank, the Africa Development Bank (ADB), an African government, other companies that hire Chinese engineering firms, or the Chinese government itself. Chinese companies win about a quarter of all major World Bank construction contracts in Africa, and a half of those funded by the ADB.[50] It would be like reporting US aid to Africa as the revenues earned across the continent by the giant US contracting firms – Bechtel Corporation, Fluor, or Kellogg, Brown and Root (KBR) – or Swedish aid as the turnover of the Swedish company Skanska. "Urban myths" like this are accepted as facts by all too many who are looking at China in Africa.

Is China Bigger than the World Bank?

"China to Surpass World Bank as Top Lender to Africa." The Bloomberg news service broke a story with this headline in late 2006, saying that China had lent $8.1 billion to Angola, Mozambique, and Nigeria alone that year, while the World Bank had committed $2.3 billion for the whole of Africa.[51] This would make Chinese loans more than *three and a half times* larger than loans from the World Bank. The journalists cited "World Bank figures" for their data on Chinese loans, which made it sound authoritative, except that the World Bank actually had no figures on Chinese loans (and in truth, as I later learned, the World Bank was as much in the dark as everyone else). The journalists were also wrong on the magnitude of World Bank commitments to Africa in 2006, which were $5.4 billion, not $2.3.[52] But they were right on one thing: China probably did surpass the World Bank in lending to Africa in 2006, but only by a tiny amount, as we shall see.

Comparing loans from "the World Bank" and from "China" (mainly China Eximbank) is a lot like comparing apples and lychees. They do not offer the same kind of fruit. The World Bank's loans in most African countries are zero-interest, with repayment over thirty-five to forty years (this is called IDA terms).[53] Most of the Chinese Eximbank loans, and the growing number of China Development Bank loans and supplier's credits from Chinese companies, are at market rates, and usually need to be repaid in ten to twenty years. (A smaller difficulty comes in because China and the

World Bank view different groups of countries as "Africa." The Chinese include North Africa in their regional figures, while the World Bank only includes sub-Saharan Africa. I have adjusted the World Bank figures to include North Africa.)

Let us try to compare these apples and lychees (as a colleague of mine once said, one can do some fruitful comparisons with apples and oranges).[54] Figure 6.6 gives official figures for amounts committed worldwide by the World Bank and China Eximbank in 2007. This gives us a rough indication of the size of resources that would be available for Africa. While the World Bank's portfolio consists almost entirely of actual loans, around a third of the Eximbank's commitments consisted of guarantees (these would usually be guarantees for supplier finance, so in that sense it is appropriate to count them as Chinese loans). Concessional lending probably made up 3 percent of Eximbank's portfolio, but almost 50 percent of the World Bank's lending. Eximbank's mission is export promotion, and the bulk of its lending goes for

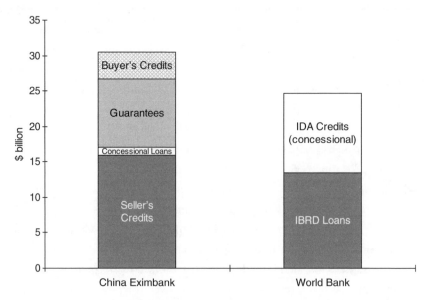

Fig. 6.6. China Eximbank and the World Bank financial commitments, 2007

Sources: China Eximbank *Annual Report* (2008); World Bank *Annual Report* (2008); and author's estimates for Eximbank concessional loans.

medium and long-term trade financing, part of a system that helped China's exports reach $1.4 trillion in 2008.

Now let us move from this total portfolio to loans extended to Africa. The World Bank is quite transparent about this: sub-Saharan Africa comprised 20 percent of its loan commitments in 2007. It is much harder to pin down the facts on China Eximbank's loans, but we do have several pieces of the puzzle. China Eximbank had approved an accumulated $6.5 billion in export credits (non-concessional) for 260 projects in thirty-six African countries by the end of 2005, and more than 280 African loans for $11.6 billion at the end of 2006. This suggests that Eximbank approved close to $5.1 billion in finance for Africa in 2006 (not including the concessional loans).[55] Separately, in June 2007, at a meeting on project financing for Africa, Eximbank president Li Ruogu announced that loans to Africa made up 20 percent of Eximbank's "business volume,"[56] (interesting, exactly the same as the World Bank). Twenty percent of Eximbank's total business volume for 2006 ($25.7 billion) would be exactly $5.1 billion, which suggests that my estimated parameters are right on target.

Figure 6.7 uses these parameters to give estimates of China Eximbank's Africa loan commitments between 2005 and 2007.[57] This figure shows that loans from China Eximbank are actually very close to the commitments

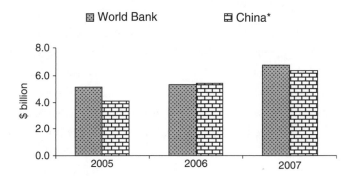

Fig. 6.7. World Bank and China Eximbank Africa commitments

*Author's estimate.

Note: World Bank figures include North Africa.

Sources: World Bank *Annual Reports* and author's research.

made by the World Bank in Africa; they are nowhere near three and a half times larger. In the three-year period 2005–2007, the World Bank committed $17.4 billion, while by my estimates China Eximbank likely committed close to $16 billion.

One last point on this comparison: we know that China Eximbank is not China's only financier in Africa. As Chapter 4 pointed out, China Development Bank has increased its loans to Africa, but as noted there, these have been at relatively modest levels, totaling about $1 billion as of March 2007.[58]

Both China Eximbank and the World Bank have announced plans to scale up finance in Africa. In 2007, as I noted in the prologue, China Eximbank president Li Ruogu commented that his bank planned to commit $20 billion to African projects over the next three years, a figure that fits perfectly with the trend line I have outlined above. A spokesman for China's Ministry of Foreign Affairs told reporters: "The World Bank shouldn't be the only bank providing loans to Africa. No individual organization can monopolize relationships with African countries."[59] But again, when comparing these two large financiers, keep in mind that most of China Eximbank's finance would not qualify as aid, while most of the World Bank's finance in Africa does. We need to keep this in mind: we are *comparing apples and lychees*. We will return to this at the end of this chapter, when we consider the impact of Chinese loans on African debt.

Comparing Apples and Apples

China Eximbank finances Chinese foreign investment in Africa, Chinese contractors seeking business, Chinese exporters of machinery and equipment. Most of this is not aid, and the Chinese make no claim that it is. If we are going to have an accurate picture of Chinese aid in Africa, we need to compare apples with apples: aid with aid. Likewise, to grasp the whole picture, we would need to compare Chinese finance with the *totals* for finance coming from the traditional donors and their banks. Figure 4.3 provided a glimpse of the size of China's export credits in 2007 compared with a few other large exporters. Official government export credits for Africa in recent years have sometimes been large, but they have a high degree of variability. Germany reported official export credit commitments of $3.5 billion in 2005, for example, but less than $100 million in 2007.[60]

Second, we need to look at other flows from private banks and export credit into Africa. Banks from the wealthy countries sent a total of $15.5 billion to Africa in 2007, mainly from the United States, Germany, and the UK.[61] Figure 6.8 shows commitments for official development assistance, official export credits and other official flows, and private bank loans and non-bank export credits. Here we have a more realistic scale of engagement from the traditional donor countries (and the EU) compared with China. It confirms that China is a formidable financier for Africa, even without including estimates for loans extended by China Development Bank. On a bilateral basis, China comes third behind the US and Germany. It shows why observers began to worry about the scale of Chinese finance, and the impact it might have on a region emerging from a decades-long debt crisis, but it also shows that China is not alone here: private loans from other countries have also increased.

Finally, Figure 6.9 puts some of this in perspective by comparing the scale of African engagement by China, the US, and Europe. Clearly, European ties with Africa continue to be enormously important. Africa remains "Europe's back door." The Chinese remain very aware of this,

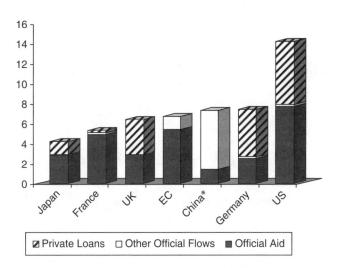

Fig. 6.8. Total financial flows to Africa, 2007 ($ billion)

Note: *Estimate. Figures are commitments.

Sources: OECD.Stat; author's research.

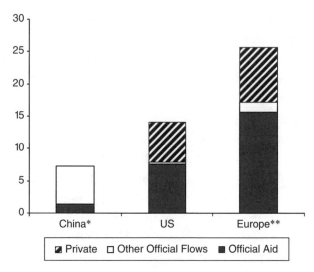

Fig. 6.9. China, US, Europe: Total financial flows to Africa, 2007 ($ billion)

Notes: *Estimate; **Europe includes commitments by the European Commission, Germany, France, and the UK only.

Sources: OECD.Stat; author's research.

even as they continue to pry open that door and help push their companies through.

Will Chinese Loans Create a New Debt Crisis?

Headlines such as "China loans create 'new wave of Africa debt'" accompanied many of the first round of stories on China's ramped-up export credits in Africa.[62] In 2006 the IMF quietly began to warn several countries, Sudan for example, that they were risking promised debt relief from the West by taking out new loans from China.[63] The US Treasury Department released a study highlighting the "free rider" problem.[64] As Timothy Adams, former Treasury undersecretary for international affairs, told the *Wall Street Journal*: "There are some aggressive countries out there that are ramping up their export-credit agencies and looking to take advantage of countries with lightened balance sheets. We want to send a strong signal that those kinds of behaviors will be frowned upon."[65] When he was President of the European Union in 2007, Portugal's secretary of state João Cravinho warned: "Europe has tried to end Africa's debt in the past and will not do the same with Chinese debt . . . We hope China takes that into account."[66]

The lack of transparency on Chinese lending fueled reasonable fears that the high figures mentioned in the media were creating a veritable Everest of debt that would be impossible to service. Many in the traditional donor countries also grumbled that Chinese lenders were taking advantage of the space opened up by debt relief paid for by wealthier countries, hence the "free riding." (Others point out that freeing countries of old debt *should* allow them to borrow again.)

The evidence on new debt in Africa's poorest countries is not robust, and that on new debt from *all* the non-traditional lenders (Russia, India, Korea, and Brazil, for example) is particularly poor. The available information suggests that Chinese loans closely fit a country's ability to repay.[67] The larger, less concessional loans are offered to countries such as Angola, Congo, Nigeria, and Sudan, all with rich deposits of natural resources that can serve as collateral. Smaller, poorer countries (Togo, Mali, Rwanda, Burundi) tend to receive grants and zero-interest loans. Exceptions are the poorer countries where loans have been offered for profitable *projects* (like a wireless network), or where collateral exists (cocoa export revenues in Ghana; sesame seeds in Ethiopia) that can serve as a guarantee of repayment.

There is every indication that the Chinese do not intend to write off the Eximbank and China Development Bank loans they are now making. "We have good bookkeeping. At the end of the day, we want our money back," a Chinese researcher told me. The president of the World Bank, Robert Zoellick, told a press conference, "at least from the statistics that I have seen, China has paid attention to debt sustainability and has certainly a strong willingness to discuss this issue, because they want to get paid back too."[68]

In November 2008, as the financial crisis was spreading to Africa, I met with China Eximbank president Li Ruoguo in the Eximbank's gleaming new offices. The year before, Li Ruogu had published an article, "A Proper Understanding of Debt Sustainability of Developing Countries," in a major Chinese journal.[69] Listening to him, it struck me once again how differently the Chinese see the task of development and how their experiences at home have shaped their views. Li argued that his bank does consider debt sustainability, but he emphasized that what they really look at is *development* sustainability.[70] I asked him to expand on this concept. "The IMF does not understand this idea of *dynamic* sustainability," he told me. "Their debt sustainability framework is overly static. Take Angola, for example. Before China's engagement with Angola, their credit rating was D, 'highly risky'. Now the rating has been upgraded to C or better. Germany, Japan, Denmark are rushing in to provide loans to Angola."

"A barrel underground is of no use for development," Li said, glancing over at the window that framed the Beijing skyline, where skyscrapers towered above the old *hutong* neighborhoods. "Our framework allows countries to do development first, instead of waiting a long time and paying year by year. It's a fantastic resource." Li Ruogu also told me that he believed the IMF and World Bank were wrong to rate an entire country as "debt-distressed" rather than looking at individual projects. The two Bretton Woods institutions can sanction an HIPC (Highly Indebted Poor Country) if it takes out anything but a highly concessional loan. "But if a *project* is commercially viable, then why should it need a subsidized concessional loan?" Li said.

Even resource-poor countries whose balance sheets may not look good sometimes have untapped capacity to service a future debt, if borrowing goes for productive projects (electricity, telecoms, or an export-oriented investment as in the DRC). Eximbank figures this future capacity into its lending decisions when deciding how much debt a country can sustain; currently, the World Bank and the IMF do not.[71] "The Fund struggles with this," a high-ranking IMF official admitted to me. "Debt sustainability analysis is not a tool for a particular loan. It doesn't give a minister the ability to decide between loans." "We have a different style than the World Bank," a senior official at China Development Bank said. "We look at a package of projects. It's easier to do, more efficient, the whole package can be financially attractive even if some parts of it are not. In China, we followed this model: a loan from one window, equity investment from another."

Chinese financing in one of Africa's poorest countries, Ethiopia, may be a test case for debt sustainability. In 2006, Ethiopia, an HIPC, signed a $500 million master loan with China Eximbank to finance at least thirteen infrastructure and production projects, including a cement factory.[72] The loan was secured by Ethiopia's exports to China (in 2006, the value of Ethiopia's sesame seed exports to China came to nearly $110 million).[73] If the sesame crop were to falter, Ethiopia could have trouble financing payments on this loan.

In 2007, as I noted in Chapter 4, China's major telecoms firm ZTE offered a competitive supplier's credit (at LIBOR plus 1 percent, over ten years) as part of a complicated package that enabled ZTE to win a competitive $1.5 billion tender to supply equipment and construction services to Ethiopian Telecommunications Corporation's $2.4 billion Millennium Project.[74] The Millennium Project will bring fixed line and wireless service to a country with one of the lowest telephone densities in the world. Telecoms is a highly profitable activity in Ethiopia, under a government monopoly. But subscribers pay their bills in Ethiopian *birr*, which cannot be used outside of the country. Ethiopia will need to repay ZTE using its scarce foreign currency. One rumor making the rounds of Addis Ababa claimed that ZTE would be first in line for equity shares in a private–public partnership with the Ethiopian Telecommunications Corporation. If so, the debt-equity swap envisioned would follow in the footsteps of similar deals worked out in the 1990s with Chinese debt.

A study by Helmut Reisen and Sokhna Ndoye at the OECD pointed out that in Angola and Sudan Chinese investment and the higher prices stimulated by China's demand for raw materials considerably *improved* debt-distress indicators in both countries.[75] Yet in 2008, as the global economic crisis began, global commodity prices fell sharply. In Beijing I asked Li Ruogu whether this had changed his views on extending credit for the proposed multibillion dollar package in the Democratic Republic of the Congo, for example. He waved away the question: "We have increased our reserves to cover risks. And we did our feasibility analysis for the DRC using a projection of the average price over the last forty years. The price of resources fluctuates, but *resources are limited*. They will go up in the long run."

China's aid and economic engagement in Africa is still marked by a lack of transparency, which fuels rumors. Newspapers could accept as credible a story that the Chinese pledged $6 billion in aid just to woo Malawi away from Taiwan.[76] They could print stories that China was giving $9 billion in aid for just one project in Nigeria, or that Chinese aid in Africa was three times higher than aid from the traditional donors.

China's official aid is much smaller than generally believed. At the same time, China Eximbank's export credits (which can also finance joint-venture investments) are much larger than those available from the governments of the traditional donors. If the Eximbank's plans to provide $20 billion in export credits to Africa between 2007 and 2009 reach fruition, China Eximbank alone will have committed nearly $32 billion to finance Chinese trade and investment in Africa between 1995 and 2009, or $36 billion if we include my estimates for concessional foreign aid loans.[77] These are very large sums. Even so, it is easy to overstate the scale of China's Africa engagement vis-à-vis the West, as Figure 6.9 points out.

Furthermore, some of China Eximbank's large loans have been signed but stalled for years, as in Nigeria. A number of large hydropower projects assumed to be underway in places such as Mozambique, Zambia, Guinea, and Gabon have not gone beyond expressions of interest. Even large agreements that appear to be quite firm, as in the Democratic Republic of the Congo, will take place slowly, in several phases, each with separate financing commitments. The global financial crisis is certain to affect new loan commitments as well. The accelerated pace since the November 2006 Beijing Summit is not likely to be sustained. The Chinese will not withdraw from Africa, but they will certainly pause, and assess how they are doing in crossing the *ocean*, to Africa, by feeling the stones.

Many other concerns have been raised about the Chinese government's mode of operating in Africa. Is China using aid mainly to get access to natural resources such as oil? Does China make corruption worse? Are the Chinese propping up dictators (Sudan) and hampering opportunities for democratic transitions (Zimbabwe)? These are significant questions, central to our understanding of China's engagement in Africa. We will return to them in Chapter 11, after we have had a chance to see Chinese aid and engagement at work in the fields of industry and agriculture. This enables us to begin to evaluate the Chinese proposition that their aid and economic engagement is part of a system of *mutual benefit*: good for China, but also good for Africa.

CHAPTER 7

Flying Geese, Crouching Tiger: China's Changing Role in African Industrialization

The conventional wisdom about China's impact on Africa's weak manufacturing sector is overwhelmingly pessimistic. In one cartoon image, a crouching tiger reaches across the globe to Africa, talons stretched out over a set of cowering factories. "China has destroyed the fledgling plastics industry in Nigeria," an American journalist writes.[1] "Scarcely any Chinese manufacturing firms have set up plants employing local workers," an article in the *China Economic Quarterly* asserts.[2] "There is no evidence," a South African scholar concludes, "that Chinese firms will begin to use sub-Saharan Africa as a manufacturing base."[3] South African unions blame a tsunami of Chinese clothing imports for the loss of 67,000 jobs in their textile industry, while a Nigerian scholar accuses the Chinese of deliberately following a "*policy* of deindustrialization" in his country.[4]

A closer look suggests that these grim visions may not capture the full reality of China's role in African manufacturing. Umar Sani Marshal, a Nigerian industrialist, said that his northern city of Kano was being rejuvenated by growing Chinese investment in plastics manufacturing: "Most of the plastic goods that are going to the market were imported before, but now when you look at it, the Chinese are discovering that they can have raw material at a cheap rate, they can have a good environment, they can have cheap labor," he said. "The highest number of private employers in Kano are the Chinese and they have been expanding day by day."[5]

Kenyan political scientist Michael Chege argued that the flood of Chinese imports had not crushed Kenya's manufacturing sector, which was growing at rates as high as 7 percent through 2007.[6] The impact of competition with Chinese textile exports *has* been severe for African fabric factories. Africa's apparel export industry was also badly hit by a wave of competition from Chinese garments. But at least until the global financial crisis hit in 2008, there was a silver lining in the rebound of some African garment exporters (Lesotho, Mauritius, Kenya). And in some regions, in some sectors, contacts between Chinese and African entrepreneurs have helped to catalyze an industrial transition.

By the turn of the millennium, mainland Chinese companies had already sunk their money into 230 different manufacturing projects across Africa.[7] This investment was highly uneven, with Africa's more developed countries – South Africa, Nigeria, Kenya, and Mauritius – accounting for the bulk. But, as we have seen, the Chinese government has ratcheted up its policy of encouraging Chinese companies to move into manufacturing in Africa. The message has gotten out. In 2005, a survey of 150 Chinese firms with overseas investment projects found that Africa accounted for nearly 20 percent of the projects; almost half of those (twenty-three projects) were in manufacturing.[8] Some of China's largest industrial firms are setting up plants in Africa. At the same time, small factories owned by new Chinese investors are multiplying.

Peng Yijun, a forty-eight-year-old entrepreneur from Baoding, is one of these new investors.[9] In 2000, Peng developed a vegetable farm in Kenya and found a rich reward in the combination of fertile soil, a favorable climate, and high prices in local markets. He scouted out other opportunities, and in 2003 he returned to Baoding, bought an entire candle factory, and shipped the whole lot to Kenya. Within three years, Peng was producing 700–800 tons of candles annually, supplying half of the market in his region. He went back to Baoding in 2006 to buy machinery for a second factory, this time to process farm products.

At the large end of the scale, we find firms like Hisense, one of China's top electronics companies. Hisense is familiar to Australian audiences, where as a marketing ploy the company purchased naming rights to

Melbourne's premier indoor arena. (The *Vodafone* signs were removed and replaced with *Hisense* just before the start of the Beijing Olympics.) Hisense began exporting televisions to South Africa in 1993, after sanctions had been lifted. In 1997, they made "an aggressive decision" (in their words) to purchase a Johannesburg factory owned by the Korean electronics company Daewoo, which was downsizing after being hit hard by the 1997 Asian crisis. Hisense began assembling televisions and DVD players in South Africa. By 2008, their South Africa factory was exporting to more than ten countries in the southern Africa region. That year, Hisense began construct-ing a $19 million industrial park to double the size of its television business and to add refrigerators and washing machines. They expected to create 1,100 new jobs.[10]

An increase in manufacturing is not part of the Millennium Development Goals. The early stages of industrialization are almost universally dirty. Machinery is frequently unsafe and accidents occur. Employers try to push the work week beyond forty hours, the better to profit from their fixed costs, and workers resist. Factory work is repetitive and dull, disruptive to fam-ilies, and a wrenching transition for people who have grown up in a rural village. Gone now from England, Blake's "dark satanic mills" will live on in urban areas of the third and fourth worlds.

And yet for most countries the transformation from low to higher income occurs when entrepreneurs embark on a sustained period of industrial transition. Manufacturing – more than microfinance – will be a central route out of poverty for most countries. That is why it is so important to discern whether engagement with China will catalyze or crush manufac-turing in Africa. We consider this question in this chapter and the next. This chapter provides the setting, and the surprisingly deep history of China's extensive but troubled involvement in African factories. The next chapter dives into the crux of the issue: will China's engagement wipe out Africa's young factory sector, or finally allow it to reach a take-off?

Challenges and Opportunities

China's prowess at manufacturing needs little introduction. Africa's feeble performance is equally well known. Between 1990 and 2005, manufacturing grew by almost 12 percent annually in China, slowing down only when the global financial crisis hit in 2008. The majority of Chinese exports are now high-tech. In contrast, after a wrenching period of industrial decline that lasted until 1994, sub-Saharan Africa ended the same period with an average manufacturing growth rate of just over 1.5 percent. Almost no change at all occurred in industrial structure or movement up the value chain.

There are many explanations for the poor performance of manufacturing in Africa, all still fiercely debated. Any comparison with China first has to recognize that it has been an industrialized country far longer than most parts of Africa. Shanghai was already deeply industrialized in the 1930s, and the Soviet-inspired socialist drive for heavy industry under Mao built on that foundation. By the 1960s, manufacturing already made up 30 percent of the value of China's economy, compared with half that amount, on average, across Africa.[11]

After 1970 Africa's industrial development largely stagnated, while China's was surging ahead. Some blame the World Bank and IMF structural adjustment policies and trade liberalization for wholesale de-industrialization in Africa. Others point out that even during the 1970s, before the adjustment era, a third of the countries in Africa were already seeing big declines in manufacturing.[12] Whatever the cause, with very few exceptions (Kenya being one), the handful of African countries that had moved beyond basic food processing and textiles into higher-tech sectors such as machinery and transport equipment suffered a setback after 1970.

Government policies certainly played a key role, including poorly implemented import substitution policies, badly maintained infrastructure, weak education sectors, and few engineers, or few with enough technical skills to adapt imported technologies or develop them further.[13] In the 1960s and 1970s, out of chauvinistic nationalism, socialist convictions, or simple fear of a challenge to elite power, some governments pushed down the minority economic groups that might have spearheaded industrial transitions. This was the case for the many Indians who settled in East Africa under the British, and who were scapegoated as "alien capitalists" by some governments after independence. In Uganda, for example, the dictator Idi Amin expelled some 80,000 Ugandan Indians, including many who had started manufacturing firms. Tanzania nationalized many Indian businesses. Kenyan leaders decided to allow their Indian firms to spearhead industrialization, with significantly more successful results.

The Chinese believe that their industrialization and open door to foreign investment are partly responsible for their remarkable reduction in poverty. But many Africans see only the downside of competition from foreign investment, and not its possible catalytic effect.[14] At a panel on China and Africa at the World Social Forum in Nairobi in January 2007 a Tanzanian critic charged that Chinese foreign investment was a crouching tiger: "First, Europe and America took over our big businesses. Now China is driving our small and medium entrepreneurs to bankruptcy," he said. "You don't even contribute to employment because you bring in your own labor."[15] One of the speakers, Cui Jianjun, secretary-general of the China NGO Network, gave an emotional defense: "We Chinese had to make the same hard decision on whether to accept foreign investment many, many years ago," he said. "You have to make the right decision or you will lose, lose, lose. You have to decide right, or you will remain poor, poor, poor."

Flying Geese as Industrial Catalysts

It helps to have someone more experienced leading the way. For foreign investment to contribute to an industrial transformation, as it did in China, it needs to foster what economist Albert O. Hirschman called "backward and forward linkages": a textile industry creates demand for ginning, spinning, and weaving, and can supply a garment industry, which can create its own demand backward for buttons and designers, and so on. Contacts with foreign firms can create these linkages and catalyze local industrialization through many channels. African traders who buy goods directly from foreign factories can pick up ideas. Foreign buyers can provide exporters with feedback and models. But foreign investment may work best at spinning off waves of innovation.

This happens in at least four ways.[16] First, if the level of technology is not too advanced, a foreign-owned factory can serve as a role model. People can see it and decide *yes, we can do this too*. Second, skills can "spill over" from foreign firms when their local employees leave, taking skills they learned on the job to other companies, or starting their own firms. Third, foreign companies might subcontract some parts of their work to local firms, and help them to meet the standards demanded. (This is more likely when the local firm is started by someone trained by the foreign firm – someone they trust to know the ropes.) Finally, competition in local markets can push local companies to invest in new technologies, improving quality – *if* it does not drive them out of business first.

The ability of spillovers to catalyze industrialization is affected by the local skill levels and the technology gap. A factory producing leather shoes or garments will be more likely to have spillovers than one producing silicon chips, for example. Spillovers tend to happen more where clusters of firms of the same type gather, since proximity speeds the mobility of labor and ideas. Spillovers will be more likely when the foreign firm is further away from its home base, as transport costs and convenience will give it an incentive to source more inputs locally.

In most of Africa, all of these factors have mattered little, since foreign investment in manufacturing has been so weak, as I elaborate below. Across the board, African firms have been isolated from their counterparts on the next rung up the technology ladder, and this has impeded the transfer of ideas and learning from the outside. The coming of Chinese firms, far from their homeland, using lower-level technologies and with a tendency to cluster, could change this. But export industries can also be ghettos of restricted labor rights, full of foreign investors walled off from contact with domestic firms, contributing little to a sustainable transition. If this were to happen with the growing number of Chinese industrialists, it would be an enormous loss for the African countries that host them.

We have seen Asian firms spark a sustained industrial transition elsewhere in the world. Japanese investment in the Thai automobile parts sector helped Thailand overtake the United States as the world's main producer of one-ton pickup trucks.[17] An even faster transition happened in Bangladesh with Korean garment firms rapidly being outnumbered by companies started by their former Bangladeshi employees.[18] By 2005, the Bangladesh garment export industry was employing 2.5 million people.[19]

In Chapter 3, I discussed the international product cycle, where, over time, production shifts from the place where a product was first invented to lower-cost locations. In Japan, they call this cycle the "flying geese," after the V formation where the lead goose eventually drops back and a new goose takes the lead.[20] Japanese aid for industrial development in Southeast Asia was used to foster this "flying geese" pattern of restructuring.[21] When I lived in Thailand in the late 1970s, the local textile industry there was in transition.

A decade earlier, Japanese companies owned most of the textile industry; a decade later, most were owned by Thai firms.[22] By then, about a third of the 211 industrial firms owned by the major Thai conglomerates were joint ventures with foreign firms, mainly Japanese.[23] China, as we shall see below, is following in Japan's footsteps in this. But today's state-sponsored engagement in manufacturing also fits into a long-established pattern of China's aid to African industry.

Marlboro Man

China's first aid project in Africa was a factory that allowed Guinea to manufacture cigarettes out of its own tobacco, as we saw in Chapter 1. In keeping with mainstream development ideas, China's initial wave of aid in the 1960s and 1970s focused on light industry: factories to allow countries to process their own natural resources and substitute for imports.[24]

There was not a lot of variety. Cigarette factories processing local tobacco were popular. In addition to the Guinea project, China built cigarette (and match) factories in Benin, Mali, Somalia, and Tanzania. Africa also had a comparative advantage in cotton production, and the Chinese built at least eight major cotton spinning and weaving factories in Africa. Several countries received tanneries and shoe factories (Mali, Tanzania). Chinese aid projects in agro-processing (rice mills, maize flour, groundnut oil, palm oil, tea) were common.

Sugar factories (usually with a plantation attached, as in Magbass) were also in demand. China built eight large sugar complexes in this first wave of aid. Teams of Chinese also put their stamp on an assortment of other kinds of factories: building materials (bricks, stone crushing), machine tools, and three that made vaccines or pharmaceuticals. Not surprisingly, Mali, Guinea, and Tanzania, where Mao felt a kinship with the socialist leaders, were the most favored in this early period. In Mali alone, China built factories for sugar, pharmaceuticals, tea, textiles, cigarettes and matches, tannery and leather processing, and a large rice mill.

We already know what happened to these factories built decades ago. In keeping with both Chinese and African expectations of the era, they were all state-owned enterprises. Without exception, they declined when the Chinese left. Politicians used them as convenient sources of patronage, and employees felt free to pilfer materials.

The Maoist preference for aid via monumental factories lasted less than a decade beyond Mao's death in 1976. A number of large factory projects promised to various countries proceeded to completion in the 1980s, among them the Anie sugar complex in Togo; Cimerwa, Rwanda's first cement plant; the Mulungushi textile factory in Zambia; and an ice factory and fish market in Uganda. A handful of new aid-funded factories were launched in the 1980s in places like Mozambique (textiles, shoes) and Zimbabwe (textiles), which came to independence later than the rest of Africa. Sometimes new joint ventures could make use of old aid projects. In Uganda, a new Chinese–Ugandan joint venture in fishing on Lake Victoria was able to make use of the ice factory in Kampala funded earlier by a soft loan from China. But under the pragmatic Deng Xiaoping, China's industrial aid in the 1980s focused more on consolidating or rehabilitating the earlier factories.

Much of this was political. The Chinese were reluctant to see these large and visible fruits of their aid slowly decaying. But they also believed that with Chinese management the factories could actually be profitable. Most African governments resisted selling off their state assets until the 1990s, but leasing them was sometimes a different matter. By the late 1980s, as we have seen, Chinese companies were managing or leasing sugar factories built by Chinese aid in Mali, Sierra Leone, Benin, Togo, and Madagascar. Other state-owned companies returned to pick up the pieces at textile and cement factories.

But the Chinese were already looking ahead toward their future industrial engagement with Africa. Reporting on a conference on international economic cooperation held on the banks of the Yangtze River in Wuhan in October 1985, researcher Xue Hong from the Chinese Academy of International Trade and Economic Cooperation gave a concise analysis of the international product cycle and how it was going to shape China's own outward investment in the future. Many developing countries, he said, were asking China to "invest and set up factories in their countries."[25] But China was still investing very little overseas. To most Chinese, only a few years into the turn to the market, the idea of China having its own multinational corporations or being a foreign investor was outlandish, even heretical.

Weren't multinational corporations part of the system of exploitation used by the West?

Xue then outlined what he saw as an inevitable trend. China would "digest, absorb, and remold" advanced technologies from abroad. Then, over time, China would transfer its production of "mature" products to developing countries that were just beginning to move into those products. "Surely they will have the desire of importing our 'second-level-transferred' technology," Xue said. He added, using the term that would become widely known more than a decade later, "going out" will help China sustain its policy of "bringing in" investment by improving the balance of foreign exchange.

Knowing that policymakers were already thinking along these lines in 1985 helps us see why two of the new aid tools developed in the 1990s (an aid fund for equity joint ventures operated by the Ministry of Commerce and the concessional loan fund established by the China Eximbank in 1995) were used to re-enter the industrial sector. Both of these funds were originally geared toward productive joint ventures, particularly those that would meet three objectives. They should be small and medium-sized production projects producing for local needs and supported by local resources; boost demand for Chinese equipment and machinery; and involve "mature" technologies – those China was already outgrowing.[26]

Between 1992 and 2002 at least ninety-three joint ventures received loans from the joint-venture and cooperation fund worldwide.[27] Many were based on projects established earlier as aid. Some we saw in Chapter 2: the Mali tea factory and textile mill, the Togo sugar mill, for instance. Aid loans helped them upgrade some of the old machinery. Frequently, as one of the experiments of this period, the unpaid debt incurred to build the factories was swapped for equity shares. In Tanzania, I visited the China–Tanzania Friendship (Urafiki) Textile Factory in 2008 to see the outcome of one industrial project where the Chinese tried to transform aid into mutual benefit.

Friendship Textile Factory's Rocky Road

On the outskirts of Dar es Salaam, behind a long wall that stretches the length of a couple of city blocks, a factory compound houses the multiple buildings of Urafiki, the Friendship Textile Factory. In 1969, a reporter for the *Black Panther* newspaper traveled to Tanzania and wrote admiringly about the factory that China had built during the chaos of the Cultural Revolution. "The essential thing," he decided, was that China had left Tanzanians to manage the factory "themselves and consequently they are learning from their own mistakes." If this had been a traditional foreign investment project, he went on, the managers would all be white, and the locals would provide only their "cheap labor and raw materials."[28]

Eventually, however, the mistakes were too much for the Tanzanian government. In 1984 they asked the Chinese to return to rehabilitate and run the factory. In the mid-1990s, when Beijing introduced the new system of foreign aid and concessional loans for joint ventures, Friendship Textile mill seemed a good candidate for a trial run.

"We got the order from the government to go here in a joint venture in 1997," Huang Lilan, the managing director of the factory, told me as we sat in her office overlooking the dozen or so buildings of the complex. "I myself have been here now for seven years." Her ambitious textile company is owned by the municipality of Changzhou, which sits on the south bank of the Yangtze River, in Jiangsu province. They took on 51 percent of the textile mill. "Our city is famous for its textile industry," she smiled tightly, before telling me, "We do not get a lot of help from the Chinese government. They provide loans, but we pay interest on them."

A few days earlier I had met by chance with a young Chinese man who used to work at Friendship and now worked for another Chinese company. "Manufacturing is not a good option in Tanzania," he told me. "The electricity supply is not regular and sometimes it isn't the right phase, which breaks the machines. And the water supply is awful. But the most terrible thing is industrial relations," he said.

The factory has twenty-four Chinese supervisors, and anywhere from 1,000 to 1,600 Tanzanians, who range from senior staff to temporary workers. The new Chinese managers agreed to keep 800 of the former workers – union members who had been employed by Friendship for years. These became permanent workers, and another 800 were hired on temporary contracts. "We wanted to introduce a system of eight hours plus four hours overtime, with extra pay and other benefits, so that we could have two shifts a day, like in China," the young man told me. "This took two years to arrange, and then after eighteen months, the unions began to lobby against the system. The permanent workers don't want to work overtime, but the temporary workers always want more hours, especially the young ones."

Now, he said, the factory is effectively bankrupt. He knew that a similar Chinese effort to revive the aid-funded Mulungushi textile factory in Zambia had failed the previous year. "Now the Chinese government is more focused on economic results," the young man said. "They will give you help, but not forever." He finished by telling me he was relieved to be away from the factory: "I was tortured by the problems. Corruption, for example. It's something like breakfast here, very popular."

"Friendship is working well," an official at the Chinese embassy told me, referring to the factory's output. But then he admitted that the Chinese government continues to support the factory with subsidized loans. "Friendship loses $500,000 annually," he said, shaking his head. "If we weren't there, it would die."

The factory is barely managing financially, Huang admitted as we sat in her office, decorated with faded pictures of Changzhou on the walls. "We were expecting to pay the capital back on the loan, but now we have lost hope. Our main problem is the high cost of everything: raw materials, ink, and labor." They still export to Malawi, Mozambique, and Kenya, she said, but not much – only about 4 percent.

The factory itself is old but spacious, clean, and well lit, with bright bands of colored fabric moving through the machinery, guided by Tanzanian workers who keep their eyes on the rapid transit of the cloth. Huge red and white banners – "Profit is a Result of Increased Effort" – hang from high beams at the top of the cavernous buildings. Huang told me what had happened recently with the new salary levels set by the government for labor-intensive industries like Friendship. "Three months ago, the Ministry of Labor suddenly announced that the minimum salary for textile workers would rise on January 1 from about $41 per month to $140." She sat back in her chair. "With fringe benefits, that would be $184 per month!"

To Western eyes, these figures all seem abysmally low, and indeed the US State Department estimates the minimum wage in Tanzania to lie below the level that could provide a family with a decent standard of living. But when the government announced the new wage rates, the Confederation of Tanzanian Industries (CTI) argued that raising wages in a struggling labor-intensive sector would be ruinous. In the 1990s, when Tanzania started to liberalize its economy, the country had fourteen textile mills. Only four survived. The Confederation presented the government with comparative research on wage levels for textile workers in other low-income countries. In Kenya, the minimum wage was $79 a month; in Nigeria, $45; Madagascar, $28; Vietnam, $44; and so on.[29]

This debate on wages is a familiar one in most countries on the brink of industrial transition. Poverty reduction would happen, the Confederation argued, not by sharply raising wages for existing factory workers but through labor-intensive industrialization, attracting rural migrant workers with wage rates higher than the informal sector, but still affordable for industries facing global competition. This is also the World Bank's position, as they try to persuade countries to liberalize "rigid" labor regulations. On the other hand, the unions argue that keeping wages low traps countries in a "race to the bottom," and makes it impossible for the working class to have enough buying power to create effective demand for the industrial products they produce. The CTI won out in this round. "The government ended up deciding not to do it," Huang told me, "out of fear that the textile factories would all have to close."

"In China," Huang had said as we finished our interview, "government policy is very good for the investor. Labor is very cheap, it is very comfortable. Here, it is very poor. Every day we have electricity problems, water problems. The workers do not have much education and they do not work hard. We have been here eleven years. We have brought a lot of companies here to try to get them to invest, but none of them have."

In a reception room at the end of the tour, the factory's production statistics are collected in a series of colorful charts that track the annual productivity per worker, the consumption of inputs like fuel and electricity per unit of output, and total sales, which seem to be strong (in 2006 sales literally moved off the chart). The statistics all seem to be going in the right direction. But what strikes me most is a section of the room labeled "the future." A series of artist's drawings sketch an attractive vision of "Friendship Mall" with a pagoda-like roof. Chinese and Tanzanians stroll along the garden walkway carrying shopping bags. An outdoor food court is anchored by the golden arches of a McDonalds on one end, and the white-bearded face of Colonel Sanders and KFC on the other. The factory is not really visible in these drawings. And it makes me wonder about the future of China's textile manufacturing in Dar es Salaam.

Cars, Calf, and Cows

The Friendship textile mill is the struggling face of China's earlier aid system, a relic of 1969, still on life support from the Chinese government forty years later. But in the 1990s, using the Ministry of Commerce's new joint-venture and cooperation fund and the concessional loans from the Eximbank described in Chapter 4, China began to increase aid for industrial ventures, financing (among other projects) a new cement plant, and a woolen knitting factory in Zimbabwe, a bedding factory in Botswana, an ice-making factory in Cameroon, a copper-processing factory in Zambia, and a pharmaceutical factory in Kenya. Two aid-funded factories were reportedly set up in Sudan to produce medical gauze and embroidery, and the Chinese gave aid to establish at least four tractor and farm machinery assembly joint ventures in an assortment of countries. In Ghana, Chinese aid funded ventures in cocoa processing (Calf International Cocoa) and fish nets and rope (Ghana Shandong Netting Company).

Information on these projects is scarce and fragmented. In my travels in Sierra Leone, for example, I was surprised to find the Okeky Agency still chugging along in its 1985 arrangement with a Chinese fishing company, Magbass still producing sugar, and the Chinese-built hydropower station still producing electricity. People I asked in Freetown were not always aware of what was happening in the hinterlands of their own country. We do know, however, that some of the Eximbank concessional loan projects launched in the first round of the new aid system set up in 1995 failed, mainly because politics entered into the decisions on aid.

In Côte d'Ivoire in 1997 the Chinese embassy (responding to the call from above for more joint ventures) played a large role in bringing together two Chinese companies and a local firm as a partner in a joint venture to set up an automobile assembly plant in Abidjan. The Eximbank gave the project a concessional aid loan. But the Chinese companies assumed that because this was an aid project it was "political," and they did not need to consider the economics closely. As a Chinese researcher who investigated the project concluded, they ignored their own responsibility for appraisal, "thinking that the government would fix any problems that arose."[30] None of the joint-venture partners apparently noticed that import duties on finished automobiles and on components were the same: 29 percent. No one noticed that competition was already fierce in the automobile market, which was relatively small. And the cost of water, local labor, and electricity were all higher in Côte d'Ivoire than in China, giving the new company no cost advantage at all.

The Calf Cocoa International cocoa processing factory in Ghana was also overtly political.[31] In 1998, Ghana received one of the early Eximbank concessional lines of credit for RMB 150 million ($18.1 million). The Rawlings government used the loan to fund Ghanaian participation in three private joint ventures with Chinese investors: a gold mine, a fishing net and ropes factory, and the Calf Cocoa project. The Calf Cocoa project, built near the Tema industrial estate, was a joint venture between China International Cooperation Company for Agriculture, Livestock and Fisheries (CALF) which held 55 percent, and Caridem Development Company (45 percent). And here the politics become pretty clear: Caridem was the money-making arm of an NGO, the 31st December Women's Movement, and this NGO was headed by President Jerry Rawlings' wife Nana, and linked to the women's wing of his political party.

The trouble may have begun when Rawlings stepped down as president in a smooth transition, after declining to run in the election of 2000. By 2002 the $6.9 million factory was complete and the equipment installed. But Ghana's Minister of Finance refused to authorize the Eximbank to release the last tranche of money ($1.8 m), saying it was not convinced that Caridem could repay the loan. The project was widely viewed as a vehicle to help finance election expenses for Rawlings' party. The factory still sits idle.[32]

A third example comes from Namibia. The Northern Tannery project in Ondangwa was planned between 1997 and 2000, around the same time as the projects in Ghana. Namibia's Minister of Trade and Industry decided to use a concessional line of credit offered by China's Eximbank in 1997 to construct a tannery in the north of the country, where unemployment was high and raw hides and skins were said to be plentiful and often tossed away.[33] The idea of a state-sponsored tannery in the north had been incubating at least since 1994, in a government led by SWAPO, the liberation movement turned political party. It was clearly a development project "owned" by the Namibian government.

The Eximbank credit financed the construction, machinery, equipment, and technical assistance – about $6 million – all arranged through the Shanghai Corporation for Foreign Economic and Technological Cooperation, the former foreign aid office of the Shanghai municipality. A Chinese construction company resident in Namibia built the factory, but the Chinese wisely did not invest in the project. Instead, local businesses were pressed by SWAPO to join together and invest in the factory to help the government create economic development and jobs. Rather reluctantly, twenty-five businessmen scraped together a total of a little over $140,000 as their equity contribution, only about 10 percent of the amount needed.

Like some of the other aid-funded factories, the tannery was plagued with difficulties. The idea that the north was teaming with surplus skins, tossed into rubbish heaps, turned out to be wrong. Opened in 2002, the factory, which could process 10,000 hides a month, had difficulty securing supplies. The general manager, Alfred Andreas, told a reporter that they struggled to process 8,000 to 15,000 hides annually. "We only get a few hides during the festive season when people are having their traditional weddings," Andreas said. The factory closed its doors late in 2006, with Namibians pointing fingers at each other.

Social scientists say that the plural of "anecdote" is not "data." Until researchers *do* have data, we will not know how the other aid-funded industrial projects fared. However, I suspect that the problems I have highlighted here are not at all unique. Chinese companies in the 1990s (when most of the new industrial aid projects were funded) were very unfamiliar with African political economy. State-owned themselves for the most part, they may not have been sufficiently skeptical about the ability of an African government to uphold its side of a joint venture. Ignorance was blended with insouciance: confident that the Chinese state would cover them for projects perceived as primarily political, some companies (such as in the Côte d'Ivoire case) failed to practice even the most basic level of due diligence.

Just before the new millennium, the China Eximbank and the Ministry of Commerce reviewed their experience with the new aid instruments established in the 1990s (Chapter 4). The Eximbank's concessional loan program by then had funded sixty projects in thirty-one countries worldwide, for a total of about $470 million.[34] Only a portion of these were in manufacturing. Although the Eximbank was a policy arm of the Chinese government, its management grew increasingly concerned about the poor results of many projects and the burgeoning debt that would be difficult to recover.

After the millennium, those who were still running the former aid projects, now transformed into investments, found it harder to get concessional loans to keep them afloat. The Chinese management of the Ubongo farm implement factory, a former aid project in Tanzania, applied for a loan from the Eximbank, but were turned down. When the troubled but politically important Friendship factory applied for a new loan from Eximbank in 2000, they had to wait until 2003 for it to be approved.[35] The new instruments developed for economic cooperation (overseas trade and investment zones and the China–Africa Development Fund) sprang from the conviction that in Africa sustainable investments had their best chance of survival when Chinese companies themselves took the lead, did their own feasibility studies, and risked their own capital. Of course companies run by ethnic Chinese had been doing just this for decades in Africa.

Asian Tigers and African Factories

We have now seen China's longstanding involvement in African industrialization, and how Beijing experimented with new instruments of aid and economic engagement in the changed environment of the 1990s reforms. But while all this was happening, Chinese entrepreneurs from Taiwan and Hong Kong were way ahead, moving into Africa with little direct assistance from their governments. Some were reacting to higher labor costs and new environmental regulations at home. Others were seeking production locations that would enable them to beat US and European quotas on textile and garment exports imposed on the East Asian tigers early in their export-led push. Many Hong Kong industrialists were concerned about a 1983 agreement between China and the UK that would return the colony to China at the expiration of a 100-year lease in 1997. They rushed to diversify their investments and find alternative passports that might provide some insurance for their families.

Taiwan's industrialists took advantage of incentives offered by a fellow pariah government in South Africa (under apartheid) to set up more than 300 factories.[36] Others moved into neighboring Lesotho. Some came to the Indian Ocean island of Mauritius, encouraged by their personal contacts among the many ethnic Chinese who lived there. In Mauritius they helped catalyze an industrial boom.

Emerging from colonialism in the late 1960s, Mauritians heard about export processing zones (EPZs) then being established in Taiwan, and decided the idea might work for them. More than 90 percent of the early capital invested in their successful zones came from Hong Kong. Joint ventures appealed to the local Franco-Mauritian capitalists, whose wealth was based in the sugar industry, and to Sino-Mauritians (3 percent of the population) and others who had accumulated wealth through trade. By the late 1990s, about 60 percent of the capital invested in the zones was Mauritian. The flying geese were transferring over; the model worked.

In multiple trips to Mauritius, I learned that most local investors had been joint-venture partners or employees of Hong Kong EPZ firms. Mauritians gained experience in international marketing, learned how to obtain the latest technologies and how to manage large-scale industrial production. They "felt confident enough to start their own EPZ enterprises," as a local analyst explained.[37] By the turn of the century, economist Dani Rodrik was calling Mauritius a "superstar" for its rapid growth and industrial transformation, improved equity, and robust democracy. Others simply spoke of the "Mauritius miracle."

Mauritius is a classic example of a cluster of ethnic Chinese companies acting as catalysts through investment. We go to Nigeria for another example. In the 1980s, a cluster of African traders from an entrepreneurial town in the east of Nigeria began to travel to Asia, bringing back Asian information, technology, and expertise to help them in their move into manufacturing. The result was another industrial transition in a town once known as "the Japan of Africa."

"Original and Taiwan"

The town of Nnewi, Nigeria, has personality, something very clear on my first visit back in 1991. The road into Nnewi from the regional metropolis of

Onitsha is lined with billboards advertising products made in Nnewi factories. In the center of the busy town, Nnewi's famous motorcycle-riding women, babies strapped to their backs, rumble past the traders arriving from all over West Africa to bargain at the hundreds of chaotic stalls of Nkwo, one of the region's biggest vehicle parts markets. Counterfeits, originals, made-in-Nigeria, made-in-Germany: if you need a spare part you can probably find it. Down the dusty lanes on the outskirts of town are several dozen factories, a vibrant but embattled cluster of firms making vehicle parts for the Nigerian market and the region beyond. In his novel *Anthills of the Savannah*, Nigerian author Chinua Achebe has his main character disguise himself as an itinerant trader, squatting beside the road calling out: *"Na small motor part him I de sell. Original and Taiwan."* The industrial history of Nnewi is intertwined with Taiwan, Hong Kong, and, more recently, China.

The Igbo people of Nnewi have specialized in transport since the early colonial period. By the 1930s, they were running bus services and managing extended spare parts distribution networks radiating out from the Nkwo market to all of Nigeria's major towns. Nnewi's first Asian contacts were with Japan. Taiwan came to dominate the supply of motor vehicle spare parts in the 1970s. Taiwanese traders flocked to Nnewi to take orders for generic copies of Mercedes, Peugeot, Toyota, and other "original" vehicle parts. They returned home, had the parts reproduced, and exported them back to Nnewi.

But the Nnewi traders did not simply sit back and wait for the traders from Asia. As early as the 1950s, some were making their own journeys to place their orders. Over time, a few leaders began building their own name brands. And in the early 1980s they started building factories. One of the first traders to venture into manufacturing told me, "For eight years I imported these things and saw how simple they were to make. So I decided to start manufacturing them."[38] By 2006 a quarter of the Nnewi firms were exporting to regional markets, advertising their brand name goods across West Africa.[39]

Automotive parts are a typical "first stage" product in industrialization. Many Nnewi manufacturers started out by purchasing used machinery and equipment from an Asian factory that was upgrading its own product lines. A manufacturer of oil filters bought the entire Singapore factory that used to supply his trading business and had it shipped to Nigeria. By the mid-1990s, many of the Asian producers were themselves relocating to China, and the focus of Nnewi trading shifted to China as well.

In the rainy season of 1994, I met Chief Godson Onwumere, the owner of PMS Electrical, a thin man, light on his feet, with dark glasses and a polished look as though he had stepped off the set of a Nollywood (Nigeria's Hollywood) film. Onwumere had partnered with Ming Kee, a Hong Kong factory, to produce molded plastic electrical parts. He sent his brother and brother-in-law to China to be trained in Ming Kee's Shenzhen factory. Ming Kee located machinery for him and provided technicians and assistance to get the production process up and running. This process of getting Chinese technical partners was repeated by other Nnewi industrialists. I met two of them during my visit to southeastern Nigeria in May 2009.

One of the Nnewi industrialists with Chinese technical partners was Innocent Chukwuma, a "swashbuckling businessman" in the words of one Nigerian newspaper. Younger brother of Gabriel Chukwuma, one of Nnewi's early auto parts industrialists, Innocent Chukwuma started a trading company in 1986 to sell Honda motorcycle parts, and later entire motorcycles. He realized at some point that the shipping costs of bringing in new motorcycles would be greatly reduced (and the tariff lower) if he brought them in disassembled and put them together in Nigeria. In the late 1990s, he built a motorcycle assembly factory in Nnewi.

In 2002, the government of the neighboring state of Enugu put its broken-down Eastern Plastics factory up for sale, and Chukwuma decided to buy it. He went back to China, and with the help of his business partners there, he picked out machinery, hired a handful of skilled engineers, and started producing plastic motorcycle parts for his assembly factory. Renamed Innoson Technical and Industrial Company, the Enugu factory had grown into one of the largest plastics manufacturers in Nigeria, with nearly a thousand employees. As Chukwuma showed me around the plant, I watched hundreds of Nigerian workers producing six major product lines, now including melamine tableware, roof ceiling panels, and dozens of injection molding plastic products. What about competition with Chinese imports, I asked. "Our prices are cheaper than imports from China and the quality is better," Chukwuma told me. "We get most of our raw materials locally, from a petrochemical plant in Port Harcourt. We supply Kano, Lagos, all of Nigeria and even neighboring countries."

But Chukwuma wanted to go beyond plastics. Foreigners can come to Nigeria and in a few years, build big businesses and send millions of dollars home, Chukwuma pointed out. "Why can't we Nigerians who own the country and understand its business secrets perform better?"[40] In 2007, he began a new venture in Nnewi: a factory to assemble mini-vans and mini-trucks, with inputs from China's Wuling Auto, one of China's top ten auto manufacturers.[41]

Chukwuma faced multiple challenges. An "epileptic" electricity supply and poor roads were two problems. But Nnewi is not far from Nigeria's volatile Delta region, and the security situation was deteriorating, with armed robbery on the roads and an epidemic of kidnapping. Chukwuma had arranged for two police armed with AK-47s to accompany me when I visited Nnewi. We passed through at least a dozen security roadblocks in a trip that should have taken an hour and a half. In 2007, two Chinese engineers and a Nigerian staff member were kidnapped from Innoson's Nnewi factory site and held for ransom (the kidnappers had targeted Chukwuma himself, but he was not there that day). Two of the victims were rescued, but one of the Chinese engineers was never found. Work on the automotive factory was suspended for some time, but had recently resumed.

In Nnewi, I met Andrew Dibal, a tall, soft-spoken man from northern Nigeria who spoke fluent Chinese and served as the interpreter for the Chinese experts who had returned to get Innoson's factory up and running. The Nigerian government had sent him to China to do a master's degree in agricultural economics and management at a university in Zhejiang, one of China's most vibrant business regions. Now he worked for Innoson.

Down an unpaved road in another part of Nnewi I met Chika Emenike, whose Kotek Industrial Company was producing motorcycle brake pads with Chinese technical partners. Emenike was also constructing two new factories to produce bottled water and packaged noodle soups. He had employed a Nigerian professor from the nearby polytechnic as a consultant, and was waiting for visas for Chinese experts who were coming to install the machinery, a condition of the one-year guarantee offered by the exporter. The new factories were joint ventures with his Chinese partners, whom he had known for more than ten years. "We did the research together. We found out these businesses are very good," Emenike said.

Chukwuma's latest investment is also a joint venture. With two Nigerian partners and a Chinese company from Wuxi, he is building a factory to produce tires. The enormous plant, still under construction, stretches across four large plots in Enugu's industrial estate. His Chinese partners are long-time business associates, and in fact Chukwuma also owns 51 percent of a profitable tire factory in China with them.

Chinese companies are a catalyzing presence in Nigeria's automotive spare parts clusters. Chinese firms provide technical assistance to Nigerian industrialists and some Chinese companies are beginning to invest in automotive parts manufacturing there. In Tanzania, eight Chinese companies had registered with the Tanzania Investment Commission as vehicle assemblers or component manufacturers.[42] In December 2007, I spoke with one of them, Zhu Jinfeng, who is also the chairman of the Chinese Business Chamber of Tanzania. His motorcycle assembly operation employs thirty-three Tanzanians and five Chinese technical staff, in a joint venture with a Tanzanian partner, and when we spoke he was building a second factory to manufacture custom truck bodies. Significant Chinese assembly investments in Africa include a joint venture between Dongfeng and Nissan in Angola, and one between the Chinese auto company Geely International and a consortium in Uganda.[43] At the same time, however, three-quarters of the Nnewi autoparts factories reported that the impact of cheaper imports from Asia was "very severe" on their business.[44]

This is the crux of the matter. On the upside, if ventures like those described here take root and grow, and *particularly if they are competitive enough to export*, even if only to other countries in the region, there is a chance they could catalyze clusters of component manufacturers. Clusters like this already exist in South Africa. More than 350 firms manufacture vehicle parts, supplying components to the local assembly industry and exporting, even to America. The Chinese have not yet invested in South Africa's auto parts industry, but they are surely keeping an eye on India, which has been one step ahead. Tata, India's top vehicle company, bought a major assembly operation from Nissan in South Africa in 2006, and two years later was exploring assembly ventures in Senegal and the DRC.

On the downside, Chinese exports already provide intense competition for auto parts manufacturers in Africa. African firms' fate rests on the degree to which their own governments establish a more conducive environment for business. Policies, reliable electricity, good roads, security, well-organized ports are all very important. Chinese loans for infrastructure should be helpful here, if strategically employed. The mix of carrots and sticks employed by the Chinese state to shape the future of its automotive companies' engagement in Africa will also matter. China's automotive components industry is clearly targeted for "going global," but is far from "mature" enough to be pushed offshore, unlike the Chinese leather industry, as we shall see next. And in the leather industry, Chinese aid is already helping create a synergy between a resource many African countries have in abundance – skins and hides – and the needs of an industry Beijing clearly hopes will go global and stay there.

CHAPTER 8

Asian Tsunami: How a Tidal Wave Can also Be a Catalyst

In a nondescript neighborhood in the northern Nigerian city of Kano, the strong smell of a traditional leather tannery greets visitors before the tannery is actually in sight. Tanning animal skins involves a chemical process. They must be soaked, pickled, treated with tannin, dried, all the hair and remaining flesh removed, rubbed, and then washed. Traditional tanners work with a pungent combination of urine, salt, lime, tree bark, animal brains, and feces. In Kano skins soak in a succession of large pits for days, even weeks. The foul smell clings to the skin of the tanners themselves. It lingers in my memory even today, and it helps explain why in Japan and India, tanning was long restricted to low-caste populations.

The modern chemicals used are more efficient but more likely to pollute water supplies. Tanneries in many places are still often redolent of decaying animal flesh. Yet Africa has enormous untapped resources for leather. Fifteen percent of the world's cattle and 25 percent of its sheep and goats live and die in Africa, but the continent supplies less than 2 percent of the global leather trade.

This could change. Since 2005, Beijing and prosperous local municipalities have progressively tightened the structure of taxes, tariffs, prohibitions, and incentives to force restructuring in the Chinese leather industry.[1] Twenty years ago, under similar pressure from their governments, leather factories from Taiwan and South Korea began to relocate to China. Many clustered in Wenzhou, in eastern China's Zhejiang province, home to almost 4,000 shoemaking companies, each employing an average of a hundred Chinese workers. But now a similar exodus is beginning in Wenzhou. Some are moving to Vietnam, others to India. And some are coming to Africa.

Leather Goes Global

One of Wenzhou's most prominent private companies, Hazan Shoes, invested $6 million in 2004 to set up a factory in Nigeria. In Lagos, I met with Eva Yang and Jack Hong, Hazan's young management team. They were planning to expand into a new factory on the Lekki peninsula, in one of China's overseas special economic zones. "Right now we are only doing the final assembly stage here, but our boss wants to set up a shoe production cluster, to bring the entire value chain here to Nigeria," Eva told me. Hazan's website explained that the company was following the three steps in Beijing's call to "go global": "First we have advanced into the international market, then we have implemented international marketing with our own brand. Finally, we set up processing factories in foreign countries."[2]

African policy reforms intended to foster local industrialization are also clearly part of the calculation for Chinese companies looking to go global. In 2004, Nigeria made it more difficult to import finished shoes. Jack and Eva cited this shift as one of the factors that drove Hazan to begin assembly operations in Nigeria. A Beijing-based company, Huiding Leather, made two trips to Kenya to explore setting up a factory closer to their supply of skins and hides.[3] They found that higher electricity and water charges in Kenya would push their production costs at least 10 percent above those of their Beijing factory. But by moving to Kenya they would also avoid having to pay Kenya's new 40 percent export tariff on unprocessed hides.

Finished leather, ready to turn into jackets or handbags, is worth five times the value of a "wet blue" semi-processed hide. As part of the series of training seminars promised to Africa, China funded capacity building in the leather industry with several month-long training courses at the China Leather and Footwear Industry Research Institute in Beijing.[4] Technicians from at least eight African countries with significant indigenous leather industries participated. They studied the chemistry of tanning and had field visits to local tanneries. They also practiced with new cutting-edge Chinese machinery, and learned about more environmentally friendly techniques: leather processing methods that use less chromium and other toxic chemicals, and vegetable dyes.

Moving the leather industry offshore will be a challenge for weak environmental institutions in many countries, as the case of a Chinese tannery in Uganda suggests.[5] In September 2006, Sun Jun, operator of a foam mattress factory employing forty-one people in Uganda's capital, Kampala, opened a new $1.5 million tannery in the industrial town of Jinja, where the white Nile begins its journey out of Lake Victoria.

Over the next six months, Skyfat Tannery processed and exported sixty containers of wet blue hides worth $4 million. But then the national water and sanitation company that had constructed sewer lines to the new factory served notice that their systems could no longer handle the effluent. Skyfat would have to treat its own factory wastes. In November 2007, the Jinja authorities ordered Skyfat and a neighboring tannery to close down for three weeks to alleviate the stench. The situation grew worse over the next few months until Uganda's National Environmental Management Authority (NEMA) stepped in and sealed the access of both tanneries to the municipal sewage lines. Nearly 250 people were thrown out of work. In May 2008, Skyfat finally submitted plans to NEMA for approval of a $173,000 effluent treatment plant. Skyfat's environmental officer, Chris Isingoma, blamed the Uganda Investment Authority for approving the investment without spelling out clear expectations for pollution abatement.

Pollution, effluents – the dark and dirty side of the leather sector hangs like its stench over its economic promise. At the same time, the move by Chinese companies into production in Africa has the potential to catalyze a flying geese model in leather. If this happens, it is likely to happen first in Ethiopia. Ethiopia's experience provides some early insights into what may follow across the Sahelian leather belt of Africa.

Chinese imports captured more than 80 percent of Ethiopia's local shoe market following trade liberalization.[6] Ethiopian researcher Tegegne Gebre-Egziabher wanted to know: did local shoe manufacturers cope with this onslaught by taking the "low road" (cutting their own margins, dropping into the informal sector to avoid taxes, going out of business) or would they take the "high road" (upgrading their processes, buying new machinery, improving quality)? In 2006 he surveyed a sample of ninety-six local firms in the Ethiopian shoe industry to find out.

Gebre-Egziabher did not include the country's thirteen large and more capitalized shoe factories – 34 percent of the sector output – in his survey, so we do not know how they were able to respond to competition from China. But the picture differs strikingly between microenterprises and the small and medium-sized firms. Many of the sixty-six microenterprises in the survey were part-time, and had been making shoes by hand or with obsolete machines. They were hit hard, with 30 percent reporting some form of bankruptcy, 45 percent downsizing. Small and medium enterprises (SMEs) also suffered significant adjustments, with 36 percent losing assets and money, and 20 percent downsizing. But at the same time the SMEs were much more likely than the micro firms to respond to competition by upgrading (Figure 8.1).

This tale, fortunately, has a coda. After several years of adjustment, 82 percent of the firms Gebre-Egziabher spoke to told him that they were now competitive against Chinese imports. Moreover, the leather sector in Ethiopia was booming. Despite ranking tenth in the world for livestock production, Ethiopia only earned $90 million from its leather exports in 2006–7. But the government of Meles Zenawi was pushing through new incentives and policies intended to make Ethiopia the leather center of Africa.

Six new tanneries opened in 2008, and sixteen new footwear and leather goods factories were under construction.[7] A Chinese company, Sino African

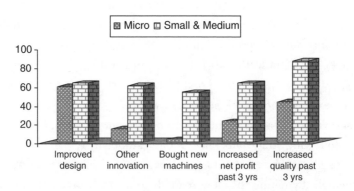

Fig. 8.1. Ethiopian shoe firms: Responses to Chinese competition, by size (%)

Source: Gebre-Egziabher (2007).

some learned to speak local languages and became citizens. Eugenia Chang, with textile factories in South Africa and Lesotho, won a seat in the South African parliament.

In the 1990s, many African countries had some kind of textile industry, but few were exporting. These import-substitution factories were hit by a wave of competition after governments liberalized the textile trade, usually as part of the conditions attached by the World Bank and the IMF in exchange for loans. Even countries such as Nigeria that did *not* liberalize textile imports found themselves swimming in smuggled goods. By 1994 Nigeria's textile industry was "an emaciated mirror image of its former self."[11] Textile production in cotton-producing countries such as Malawi, Tanzania, Zimbabwe, Kenya, and elsewhere plummeted. Chinese imports were part of this scenario, but a small part. As Figure 8.2 shows, Chinese exports had not yet begun their dramatic surge into Africa.

Surprisingly, garment imports from *America*, the second-hand clothing called *mivumba* in Uganda, *salaula* in Zambia, seriously bruised the infant clothing industries in Africa. The dated blouses and old jeans that you gave to your local charity are as likely as not to end up pressed into bales, packed into a container, and sold wholesale to African market women. The United States is one of the biggest exporters of used clothing to Africa, something

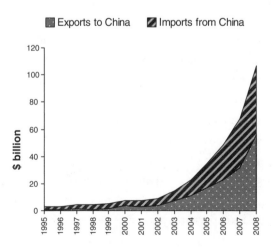

Fig. 8.2. Africa's trade with China

Source: Chinese Ministry of Commerce.

that should not surprise anyone who has wondered where on earth a rural Kenyan teenager obtained his Che Guevara t-shirt.

What has the overall impact of Chinese aid and state-sponsored engagement been in the textile industry? Anecdotal evidence punctuates much of this discussion, and in an extended process of global restructuring, the jury is still out on what will happen even over the medium term. On the one hand, there has been extensive Chinese aid and investment in the textile sector. Between 1979 and 2000 Chinese companies invested in at least fifty-eight textile manufacturing projects in Africa.[12] They bought majority shares in at least four of the massive textile complexes (such as Friendship) originally financed by the Chinese aid program.[13] Other Chinese companies formed joint ventures to buy newly privatized textile mills in Niger, Guinea, Uganda, and elsewhere.[14] Between 2000 and 2006 Chinese aid financed upgrading for at least six of these joint-venture textile factories as they struggled to become competitive.[15] China's COMATEX textile factory in Mali still employs nearly 1,500 workers. In 2003, Tianli Industrial Group built a new spinning mill to take advantage of incentives offered by Mauritius for backward integration in its textile industry. They expanded the mill in 2007 with a loan from China Eximbank.

The impact of Chinese *competition* as opposed to investment is another story. To see what is actually happening, first we need to distinguish between the impact on African textile companies producing mainly traditional African "wax" print fabrics and those that produce a variety of garments for export markets abroad. Chinese copies of African fabrics badly battered producers of African printed cloth across the continent, including most of the Chinese-aided ventures and those bought by Chinese companies in the past decade. Some have been knocked out altogether. In Zambia, as we have seen, the closing of China's Mulungushi factory provided a powerful symbol of this, although rumors that Mulungushi will re-open crop up periodically in the Zambian media.

Ironically, the strength of the Zambian currency, the kwacha, boosted by the higher prices for copper exports (due in part to Chinese demand), contributed to the influx of cheaper imports and the higher prices of Zambian textiles in export markets. But factories in other countries were also hit. Enitex, the Chinese joint venture in Niger, laid off most of its workers in 2007. Between 2004 and 2008 seventeen Nigerian fabric factories closed, six of which employed more than a thousand workers each.[16]

Export-oriented garment industries tell a different story. By 2005, only six sub-Saharan African countries had developed significant apparel export industries: Kenya, Lesotho, Madagascar, Mauritius, South Africa, and Swaziland. All suffered in 2005 with the ending of the Multi-Fibre Arrangement quotas and the rise of competition from China.[17] Temporary safeguards imposed in the United States and Europe allowed all except South Africa to stabilize in 2006; some began to recover (Figure 8.3).[18] "The Mauritian clothing industry has effectively weathered the onslaught of Chinese competition," a Mauritian economist wrote in 2009.[19] In Madagascar, where French, Asian, and Mauritian companies had established factories, output from the textile industry stagnated for two years, but then jumped up by almost 30 percent in 2007.[20] In Kenya, due in part to a large domestic market, garment manufacturing continued a steady expansion.[21]

Then we have South Africa, which falls somewhere in between. A modest exporter, it also has a large domestic market, like Nigeria. Both export and domestic markets have faced bruising competition. Estimates of jobs lost in the textile and apparel industry between 2003 and 2006 ranged from 12,000 to 67,000.[22] South African unions, a key constituency of the ruling African National Congress Party, lobbied hard for quota protection against Chinese textile and apparel imports. As British researcher Ian Taylor has noted,

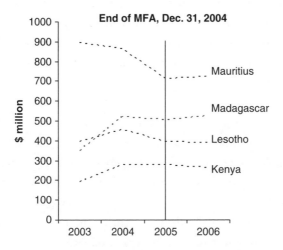

Fig. 8.3. Impact of end of MFA on major African clothing exporters

Source: Otexta (US) and Eurostat (EU) in Cling et al. (2007), p. 8.

unions in southern Africa took the position that they could not compete with Chinese exports "because of government subsidies, an artificially weak currency, and the absence of independent trade unions in China, which depressed working conditions and kept costs down."[23] But, said Taylor, pointing to lower labor productivity, poor infrastructure, and costs of doing business in Africa that were 20 to 40 percent above other low income regions, "the reality is somewhat different."

Some South African economists took issue with the attack on Chinese imports as the cause of the industry's difficulties. "The blame game is becoming tiresome," commented Phil Alves, an economist at the South African Institute for International Affairs, "not least because much of it is based on misperceptions."[24] Even when protected by tariffs of 30 to 40 percent, the textile industry in South Africa had been declining for at least fifteen years, he told the South African *Business Day*. "A more balanced view would have to acknowledge that South African producers have not invested enough in capacity, technology and management, the rand has been strong, labor is less productive in South Africa, and other internal costs are high." Others pointed out that the declines had taken place mainly in the export industries, which would not be helped much by import quotas.

South Africa negotiated a two-year voluntary export restraint program with China, involving quotas on thirty-one categories of textile and apparel export products. With South Africa their most important export market in Africa, the Chinese offered a grant of RMB 250 million ($31 million) for skill-building in the South African textile industry. They offered to promote joint ventures and provide preferential loans to help South African firms modernize their textile industry.[25]

South African follow-up on the Chinese offers was "poor," Sanusha Naidu, a South African researcher, noted. Nervous about corruption, the Chinese asked the South African government to recommend a training institute that would be able to use the Chinese funds for capacity building in the textile industry. But the South Africans decided to distribute the funding among a variety of vocational training programs. "None of the money is being spent on the development of the textile industry," Naidu found.[26] An analysis by experts at the Trade Law Centre of Southern Africa found little evidence that the local industry had used the breathing space to push forward determined restructuring. There had been no recovery of

South Africa's own exports, they reported.[27] The quotas might even have done long-term damage by pushing importers to find equally competitive suppliers in Vietnam, Bangladesh, and Malaysia.

"Why can't South African producers make the same product for a competitive price?" David Mtshalii, a South African market stall owner asked. "The Chinese have to pay for transport, pay duties and pay taxes to get the product here, and still it is cheaper. It is bad for the people working in the textile factories, but they have to move on or become more competitive."[28] South Africa's textile exports continued to decline, and the government waited until November 2008, a month before the Chinese quotas ended, to launch an action plan to recapitalize and upgrade the clothing and textile sector.[29]

China had its own experience with restructuring. In the late 1980s the Chinese began preparing for the competition that they expected would hit when China joined the WTO. Some textile factories were still using looms made before World War II. The government masterminded a large-scale reform. They pushed consolidation, financed research and development, and brought in foreign technology. Between 2000 and 2005 Chinese textile companies spent $18.8 billion bringing in state-of-the-art machinery.[30]

Restructuring was "painful," China's ambassador to South Africa told an interviewer. "We had to close down the small scale and technologically outdated factories. We had to channel redundant textile workers to other trades through training. It was a difficult and enormous job. But it has paid off."[31] African countries, he suggested, could learn from this experience. Lessons from China featured prominently in a series of textile industry capacity building workshops the Chinese offered to African officials.

For China, the textile and clothing industry has been a useful stage on the road to development – a stage that is continually evolving. Recently the textile industry has begun to move offshore. Under the "going global" policies, the Chinese government offered incentives for Chinese companies investing in spinning, weaving, and garment production overseas.[32] But is the export-oriented textile sector a good route into industrialization *for Africa*?

We in the West think we know what labor-intensive manufacturing in relatively low-cost countries looks like: sweatshops with low wages, abusive conditions, no unions or labor protections, footloose factories in a desperate race to the bottom. Some countries and some factories do reflect this caricature, but it is not the picture everywhere. Lesotho has done well by promoting itself as a socially responsible production site. (Rock star Bono visited in 2006 to call attention to Lesotho's more progressive policies.) In Madagascar, researchers found that the export-oriented textile industries were *more* unionized and had *better* social benefits than ordinary industries.[33]

That said, those African countries that decided to join the global textile industry picked a sector that holds no guarantees except that the ride will be bumpy. Chinese competition is already being amplified by competition from Vietnam, India, Bangladesh, and others. To succeed requires nimble responses by government. In Lesotho, industrialists have the personal cell phone number of the Minister of Industry on their speed dial. "If a container gets delayed at the border post, they call him," a researcher told the South African paper *Business Day*.[34] It also requires skilled entrepreneurs with good knowledge of foreign markets, steady electricity and water supply, and, quite likely, some form of preferential entry into wealthy markets.

Ethnic Chinese have been central to the development of this industry in Mauritius, Lesotho, and Swaziland, and important in Madagascar and parts of South Africa. As a former adviser to the Lesotho textile industry told me, some of the ethnic Chinese who operated textile factories in Lesotho arrived in southern Africa from Taiwan and Hong Kong with their families, as small children. They are citizens of African countries, less likely to pack up their factories and disappear overnight. "Most of them stayed in Lesotho when times were bloody tough – the end of the MFA, the massive appreciation in the value of the South African rand – they stayed."[35] Some of the current wave of mainland Chinese entrepreneurs will themselves settle in Africa. Will they be drivers of change?

Drivers of Change?

In 2007 the UN's annual report on world investment stated flatly: "in sub-Saharan Africa, no significant manufacturing FDI [foreign direct investment] took place."[36] Yet as the authors were writing that report, Chinese companies were actively exploring manufacturing opportunities across Africa. They were grabbing the carrots extended by their own developmental state, which used all the instruments (including foreign aid) at its disposal, and they were responding to signals put in place by some African governments.

Growing Chinese interest in African manufacturing acts as a counter-weight to the more obvious interest in trade and natural resources. The two are not unrelated. The Chinese government *wants* exports of Chinese machinery and equipment to overtake cheap consumer goods in the export mix, moving up the value chain.[37] As we saw in Chapter 3, it *wants* mature industries to move offshore. Setting up factories that process African raw materials *in Africa* is part of this strategy.

We looked at the auto parts, leather, and textile industries above. But Chinese companies are moving into other sectors too. Remember Melvin Lisk, owner of the Okeky Fishing Agency in Sierra Leone? In 2007, Lisk, his Ghanaian wife, his Chinese-speaking son, and their joint-venture part-ner China International Fisheries Corporation invested $5 million in a tilapia and ocean fish processing factory in Ghana. When I asked him why they did this in Ghana instead of Sierra Leone, Lisk told me simply: "the market is much larger."

Assembly of household appliances is a common entry point for local import substitution manufacturing. We saw earlier the large-scale invest-ments by the Chinese company Hisense in South Africa. China's appliance manufacturer Haier, which lost out on a $1.28 billion bid to buy the US company Maytag in 2005, surpassed Whirlpool the following year to become the largest refrigerator maker in the world. Haier joined with the venerable West African–Greek firm Paterson Zochonis in a joint venture in Lagos, Nigeria, to assemble ozone-friendly refrigerators.[38] In Ethiopia, one of China's leaders in telecoms, ZTE, announced a joint venture in mobile phone assembly with local firm Janora Technology.[39] As noted in Chapter 3, both countries were chosen to host China's new overseas trade and economic cooperation zones.

In a reflection of the search for herbs that was part of the mission of Chinese admiral Zheng He's fifteenth-century voyage to Africa, Chinese companies are investing in pharmaceuticals.[40] Holley's pharmaceutical fac-tory in Tanzania and Sichuan Guangda Pharma in Nigeria will both produce the anti-malaria drug artemisinin. Shanghai Pharmaceutical planned an artemisinin factory in Madagascar, home of *Catharanthus roseus*, the rosy periwinkle that proved to be an important source of alkaloids critical to some modern cancer treatments. Three other Chinese companies had already invested in the pharmaceutical industry in Madagascar. A Chinese company from Anhui province entered into a $4 million joint venture with a Ghanaian company, Danpong, to produce antibiotics, anti-retroviral and anti-malarial drugs for export in the region.

Another important trend is the backstream diversification being done by some Chinese construction companies in Africa. Factories are being built to produce cement, bricks, glass, steel rods, and other building materials, instead of importing them.[41] The China–Africa Development Fund took a 40 percent share in a plate glass project in Ethiopia as one of its first equity investments, following this by investing in a $60 million cement plant. A Chinese company and a Kenyan firm agreed to establish a $130 million solar panel factory in Nairobi. Four Chinese companies concluded joint-venture agreements for a cluster of building material factories with Sisay Tesfaye, an Ethiopian manufacturer. "There is a lot that I am planning," the young entrepreneur (who has a degree in business administration) told an Ethiopian newspaper, "not just for profit, but also for the mental satisfaction I get when I see my country's image changing."[42]

Catalyzing Local Industry

Will Chinese manufacturing investment help change the image of Africa? And will continued Chinese investment help change the image of *China* in Africa? The answer to this depends critically on two things: whether or not Chinese (and ethnic Chinese) investment catalyzes *local* industry, and whether or not Chinese companies employ *local* workers in Chinese factories.

The first question gets at the heart of what Chinese investment might mean for a sustainable industrial transition in Africa. My research in Mauritius and Nigeria showed multiple cases of spillovers from ethnic Chinese manufacturing to African investors through joint ventures and the demonstration effect. In both countries the local people who learned from the Chinese were already entrepreneurs for the most part (traders, in the Nigerian case; traders and sugar exporters in the Mauritius case). As development economist Peter Bauer pointed out in the 1950s, traders are more likely to be the source of entrepreneurial energy that could spark an industrial take-off than other social groups. But are there other cases? So far, there has been very little research on this key issue.

A 2005 World Bank survey included some data on fifteen Chinese manufacturing firms in four African countries (Ghana, Senegal, Tanzania, and South Africa).[43] These are small numbers on which to make any sweeping conclusions. But the researchers found that these Chinese companies tended to build up new factories rather than buy existing companies. The factory investments were relatively recent; *half* had been set up only in the previous three years. Perhaps as a reflection of their relative newness, the Chinese companies were less integrated with local businesses than other African firms. They were about half as likely to purchase raw materials locally as companies owned by indigenous Africans (but slightly more likely than Indian companies).

In Tanzania, however, I found that a third of the Chinese manufacturing investments approved by the Tanzania Investment Commission involved joint ventures with Tanzanians, who, on average, held 31 percent of the shares.[44] Zhu Jinfeng, the chairman of the Chinese Business Chamber of Tanzania, told me, "Most Chinese companies here have local partners. They help with the market and getting things done."

It was also the case that entering Tanzania as industrial investors allowed Chinese entrepreneurs to obtain coveted work permits for up to five Chinese staff. Officials at the Tanzania Investment Commission said that they had no way of actually following up on these applications. They told me that they suspected that some who had applied were not really manufacturers, but importers. The Chinese factories I visited in Tanzania were in fact actual production sites, although I also met several Chinese entrepreneurs who admitted to me that they had been given permission to enter as manufacturers, but were still "looking for the right opportunity." Swiss anthropologist Gregor Dobler found that several Chinese traders in the Namibian town where he was doing research had imported old machinery and set up pseudo-factories simply to obtain work permits for themselves and their employees to operate as traders.[45] A similar situation may have been happening in Sierra Leone.

Before I visited Sierra Leone in 2007, I had read in the *Financial Times* about a Chinese industrial zone there, with factories producing mattresses, roofing tiles, and hair lotions.[46] After the civil war ended, a Chinese firm, Henan Guoji, came to the ruined country seeking investment opportunities. Primarily a construction firm, Henan Guoji offered to renovate the National Workshop, a complex built by the British to maintain a railway that no longer existed, and turn it into an industrial and trade zone. "The National Workshop was trashed. It was a refugee camp during the war," Joe Kallon, the former Deputy Minister of Finance told me. For its share of the joint venture, the government contributed the land, the structures, and some tax concessions. Dr. Kadi Sesay, the Minister of Trade and Industry, approved the plan. She told Sierra Leone's cabinet there was no revenue from the workshop at all at present. "Whatever we get from Guoji is additional."

After telling me this, Kallon sat back in his chair and looked out the window where a group of young men were kicking a soccer ball in the rutted street. The zone had come in for criticism during the 2007 elections. Henan Guoji was accused of using the cover of manufacturing to import goods duty-free as inputs, but then selling them. "This deal may look bad now because of the tax concessions, but it looked great after the war," he said. "Guoji put a team together immediately. They paid for all the rehabilitation of the National Workshop. The Chinese came in when nobody wanted to touch us with a barge pole." In my visit to the site, I saw warehouses and service centers. Several buildings housed machinery that was lying idle, although some simple assembly operations were in place, providing modest employment, but little value-added. Henan Guoji had tried to attract Chinese manufacturers to invest in the zone, I was told, but had not found much interest.

Stories like this offer a warning for anyone tempted to simply accept government approvals of Chinese foreign investment proposals as robust evidence that a boom in manufacturing is about to take place. They also emphasize how important it is to do systematic field research before drawing conclusions. But they also indicate that much is in transition, in often changing environments. Today, in many countries, construction and trade are more profitable than manufacturing. But if electricity supplies can be guaranteed, if they can import inputs without facing major obstructions at the ports, Chinese companies will be open to moving into manufacturing, as they are now doing in parts of Nigeria, Mauritius, Lesotho, Kenya, and elsewhere.

What impact will this have on indigenous manufacturing capacity in Africa? We have seen how Nigerian entrepreneurs learned from ethnic Chinese manufacturers. Case studies in Lesotho and Kenya shed a little more light on spillovers. In Lesotho there were almost no spillovers from ethnic Chinese firms to Basotho entrepreneurs. A 2004 study found that 61 percent of supervisors in the Chinese factories in Lesotho were Basotho, developing skills that might serve them well in venturing into business on their own.[47] But, as of 2008, there was only one indigenous Basotho entrepreneur in Lesotho's entire textile industry. "Running a factory is a complicated thing," Lesotho textile expert Mark Bennett told me. "It is unreasonable to think that within such a short space of time – eight years in the case of Lesotho – local entrepreneurs could have been created."[48] The Nnewi traders in Nigeria were *already* entrepreneurs, and it still took several decades of exposure to Asian factories before the first of them ventured into manufacturing himself.

By contrast, Kenyan researcher Joseph Onjala found spin-offs starting to happen in his study of China's economic engagement in Kenya.[49] Some former employees trained by export processing zone (EPZ) firms had left to start up small garment factories using the experience they had gained. But, even more interestingly, some Kenyan factories employed foreigners, and some of the *foreign* employees had left EPZ firms to set up joint ventures with local investors. If this trend were to spread, the impact on African manufacturing might be significant in the medium term.

Chinese Workers in African Factories

The Tanzanian critic we met briefly in the previous chapter burst out in a passionate critique aimed at Chinese activists on a panel at the 2007 World Social Forum: "You don't even contribute to employment because you bring in your own labor!"[50] We have already looked at this issue with regard to construction projects in Chapter 5, but here we focus on manufacturing. Some manufacturers in Africa (not only Chinese) do import Chinese workers. The temptation to do this is strong, where governments and local unions allow it. On average, workers in Africa have lower output per day than workers in China, Vietnam, or in other Asian countries (Figure 8.4).[51] They may also be more costly. In South Africa, labor costs per unit of production

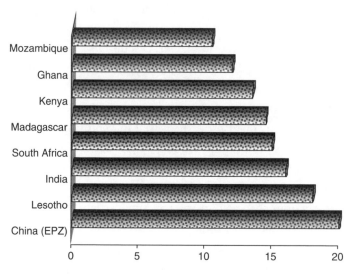

Fig. 8.4. Factory-floor productivity: Men's casual shirts, per machine operator, per day (average, 2001)

Source: Cadot and Nasir (2001).

in the garment industry were more than double those in China's Shenzhen export region, higher than Brazil and Malaysia, and nearly at the level prevailing in Poland.[52]

The young Chinese man who had worked at the Friendship factory in Tanzania gave me a spontaneous example of local labor productivity compared with China: "Here, the weaving machines are old style, but on this same machine in China one woman can operate 32 machines at once. This is easy, it's common. But here, a man operates eight machines at the same time, and this is the maximum, excellent, he will get his picture on the wall!" Likewise, ethnic Chinese factory owners in Lesotho had similar complaints: "Workers aren't motivated... workers aren't skilled enough... there are a lot of things that workers can't do – the learning curve is very slow."[53] (Local workers blamed poor training and supervision, difficulties in communication, and a hostile work climate for their lack of effort.)

For these reasons (and not for their low cost, as importing labor generally requires a firm to offer salaries higher than in China, plus airfare), some Chinese firms bring in overseas workers to set the pace for a particular task, or to operate specialized machines. In 2005, a World Bank survey of a small sample of Chinese companies in Africa found that exporting companies (presumably factories) employed a workforce that averaged 20 percent Asian and 80 percent African.[54] *Xinhua* reported that 90 percent of the employees in Hisense's factories in South Africa were local; presumably 10 percent were Chinese.[55] But except for Mauritius, where the Central Statistics Office regularly reports on expatriate employment, there is little hard data on this practice.

So what do we see for Mauritius? In recent years, up to 15 percent of the workforce in exporting factories (with Chinese, Hong Kong, and Mauritian owners) has been Chinese (Figure 8.5).[56] In a 2005 visit to Floreal Textiles, I watched two young Chinese women in a room full of Mauritians putting the final touches to sweaters being knit for the British chain Marks and Spencer. Each of the Chinese workers was assigned to a specialized job that could have been a bottleneck in the production process. The evidence suggests that Chinese textile factories *and* those owned by others are likely to employ a small core of Chinese labor, if allowed, but the vast majority of workers across the industry are likely to be African. Is this a trade-off that Africans are willing to make?

What does the future hold? One development to watch will be the outcome of the Chinese government's push to establish overseas economic cooperation zones as one platform for Chinese economic engagement with Africa. As we saw in Chapter 3, seven of these zones had been approved for

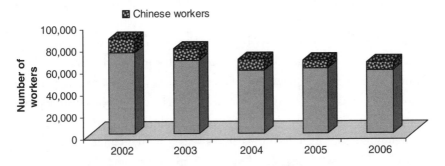

Fig. 8.5. Chinese workers/all workers, Mauritian export industries

Source: Mauritius, Central Statistics Office.

Africa by the end of 2007: in Zambia (Chambishi), Nigeria (two zones, one in Lekki, near Lagos, the other in Ogun state), Mauritius (Tianli), Egypt (Suez), Algeria (Jiangling) and Ethiopia (Orient). Some of the Chinese enterprises sponsoring these zones ran active ad campaigns, in English, to stimulate interest by non-Chinese investors. These clusters could help – *if* they are well linked to local entrepreneurs and the rest of the local economy. As Oxford economists Paul Collier and Anthony Venables have argued, clusters like these can catalyze productivity upgrades and provide a well-trodden path that African countries could follow to diversify into more competitive manufacturing.[57]

The challenges presented by investment in Africa are still manifold. Even before the global financial crisis spread to Africa, the International Finance Corporation, the equity arm of the World Bank, commented that its investments in Nigeria and South Africa had a success rate of less than 50 percent.[58] Roads, telecommunications, and electricity generation are still enormous problems for African factories. Energy, transport, water, and security costs make up only 13 percent of the bottom line for textiles in China, but 33 percent in Kenya.[59] Truckers are paid $3,937 a month in Germany, and $160 in Zambia, but it still costs far more to send a container from Lusaka to Lesotho than it does from Berlin to Barcelona. Poor governance, corruption, continued political instability – these continue to be problems for manufacturing, and development more broadly.

Yet, for most of the wealthy world, manufacturing proved to be important on the road toward progress, and ultimately prosperity. Across most of Asia, countries have followed this path, with similar results. For most of sub-Saharan Africa, the industrial revolution still lies in the future. A prolonged economic crisis and poor policies led many Western companies to withdraw from African manufacturing. With few exceptions, they have yet to come back. The World Bank provides little assistance for African manufacturers. Factories do not have much appeal for bilateral donors. This leaves the Chinese almost alone in their growing involvement in this sector, an involvement that now reaches far beyond the dozens of factories established during an earlier era of foreign aid, and includes the factories set up by the Chinese diaspora in Mauritius, Lesotho, Madagascar, Nigeria, South Africa, and elsewhere.

The impact of the steep rise in Chinese imports on Africa's fragile factories is very real, but, unlike a real tsunami, this wave has not swept away everything in its path. In Nigeria, Chinese and Nigerian manufacturers are competing effectively against Chinese imports in the plastics industry. A host of Ethiopian shoe producers improved their skills and technology after weathering competition from Chinese imports. Kenyan firms have handled the competition well, even in the garment industry.

In 2008, Africans imported more than $50 billion worth of Chinese goods. Many were inexpensive consumer goods that could be produced in the region: shoes, handbags, garments, household appliances. As we have seen, a growing number of Chinese companies are starting to do just this. Chinese economic zones being established in Ethiopia, Mauritius, and Nigeria are targeting regional and domestic markets, not just exports to Europe and America. Perhaps, with appropriate policies, a new era of import substitution will arise – a more strategic import substitution that also promotes exports, as in Asia's own early industrialization, avoiding the overvalued exchange rates and mistaken protections of the first era, but learning from Asia's giants, the flying geese that are now touching down in flocks across Africa.

CHAPTER 9

Exporting Green Revolution: From Aid to Agribusiness

Early one morning in December 2007, I waited in the dark with a crowd of people near the waterfront bus station in Freetown, the capital of Sierra Leone. We were standing just down the street from the charred shell of the City Hotel. In the late 1940s you might have glimpsed the novelist Graham Greene there, sitting in the basement bar nursing a pink gin. Eventually the bus to Kenema arrived out of the shadows and we boarded. The bus was comfortable – one of a fleet of refurbished blue Mercedes buses imported from Brazil – but the journey was long, dusty, and bumpy, on a road in various stages of renovation and decay. Other vehicles were scarce, but we passed a battered truck with the slogan "Pekin Big Man" brightly painted above the windshield.

Kenema is the major town in eastern Sierra Leone, the "blood diamonds" area, where the brutal civil war swept in and out of the terrorized villages. Before I left, Alhaji Jah, an elder in the Sierra Leone People's Party, told me that he did not think I would find much at Lambayama, the site of one of China's early aid projects. Thirty years ago, on the edge of Kenema, the Chinese had dammed the Lambayama stream and constructed a 56 hectare rice station, one of ten across the country. But Kenema was in the center of the conflict zone. The Lambayama station was unlikely to have survived.

When I arrived at Lambayama late that afternoon, I was understandably surprised to see peaceful fields of irrigated rice stretching out on both sides of the road to the distant line of trees on the horizon. Water gurgled down the irrigation canals. Lamin Saffa, the local district agricultural officer, a polite, quiet man, walked me around the station. Two of his young children tagged along. "We have more than 150 farmers in our association," he told me. "We are still doing two crops a year. The dam works fine, but because the farmers don't maintain the canals well, we can't irrigate all the land in the dry season. But none of it has been abandoned. It is all being used."

Surely, I said, during the war this area went to weeds? "No," he replied. "During the war there was a camp for displaced people here. People came here from the villages, where the fighting was worse. When Kenema was cut off from supplies, the people relied for their survival on the rice here at Lambayama."

We stopped to speak with Lamin Sesay, a Kenema mason who has rented a quarter-acre plot from the station since 1995. He told me that with fertilizer he can harvest 15 bushels of rice from his plot; without, he would be lucky to harvest half that. "We don't use fertilizer at all now," Saffa said. "We have no budget for supplies." As we walked back to his office, Saffa told me: "I do appreciate this kind of technical assistance much better than giving money to politicians for projects that never come. Just imagine, this area was developed long ago, and we are still benefiting."

Sierra Leone imports 85 percent of its grain, one of the highest levels in Africa. Next door, Liberia imports 75 percent. The people in both countries eat rice as their staple food. And in both countries rice is highly political. On one of my visits to Sierra Leone, I picked up a newspaper with this screaming headline: "Rice, Rice, Rice, Everywhere, Yet Not a Single Grain to See to Buy. There Will NEVER be an End to our Rice 'WAHALA' [troubles] in This Country!"

"Rice is our priority," Dr. Sama Monde, the former Minister of Agriculture in Sierra Leone told me in December 2007, as we sat in the office of the consulting firm he and some other out-of-work politicians had recently founded. "We had rice-related wars in 1919, 1954, even the regional crisis started with the 1979 rice riots in Liberia. Until we solve the rice problem, we can never be sure that the troubles will end." We talked about the civil war, and he began to paint a picture of his youth in the Kono district, a land "flowing with milk and honey" (and rice), an area now pockmarked with bulldozed pits. During the war rebels forced their captives to dig for diamonds here, at gunpoint.

His reverie ended with a phone call relaying a rumor that a student protest march in a village near the mining area in Kono had turned violent. So many young men, so few jobs. He sighed as he hung up the phone. "I want to move beyond these small-scale rice demonstrations. We are looking to China now, not as a donor, but an alliance of engagement. They say it is for mutual benefit. I believe they can do it. They come through as being very sincere. It is we that have to put our house in order," he said. "We have to figure out what to request from them that will be tangible and benefit our population."

Challenges and Opportunities

China feeds 20 percent of the world's population on only about 8 percent of the world's arable land, growing about 95 percent of what it consumes. Half the cultivated land is irrigated, some in fields used since the reign of ancient emperors. Yields are normally at least triple those in Africa. Policymakers believe that China's agricultural technology, seeds, and expertise can be a central part of the "win-win" pattern of engagement in Africa.

But there is more. China's commitments in order to gain WTO membership, required a gradual reduction in tariffs, exposing rural farmers to global economic competition. "Many Chinese officials and farmers thought of investing in Africa when they were considering ways to cope with the challenges brought about by the WTO entry," a 2002 *Xinhua* article reported. Development has consumed farms located near towns and urban areas. Chinese planners see overseas farms as a way to relocate displaced Chinese peasants and provide long-term, offshore "insurance" for China's own food security.

Just as energy is a national security issue for China, so too is grain. The Chinese have watched Western countries use food as a political weapon to pressure the former Soviet Union, Iraq, and other countries.[1] They do not want to be vulnerable to similar pressures. Beijing has set the "red line" for its own food security at 120 million hectares, just enough to ensure 95 percent self-sufficiency in grain. In 2006, with about 122 million hectares of arable land remaining, policymakers warned that the country was approaching a danger point.[2] Fifteen million Chinese farmers were expected to lose their land between 2006 and 2011.[3] "Land grabs" by unscrupulous developers exacerbate rural tensions: mass disturbances, many over land, rose eightfold between 1995 and 2005.[4] The Chinese leadership monitors the pulse of rural discontent closely, always remembering that Mao's revolution came out of the rural areas before it swept across the cities.

Halfway across the world, Africa has been a net food importer since 1973. Most of the poor live in the rural areas, many as subsistence farmers using "slash and burn" cultivation methods. With very little irrigation and irregular rainfall, rural Africans experience chronic food insecurity. Agriculture needs to be done more intensively, with better water control. There is untapped potential for irrigation. The island of Madagascar, where farmers of Malay–Indonesian origin began to migrate around AD 200, today boasts Africa's highest rate of irrigation on cultivated land: 31 percent, often in labor-intensive terraced hillsides that resemble those across the foothills of Indonesia.[5] The massive Gezira scheme started by the British a century ago between the White and the Blue Nile gives Sudan the second-highest proportion of irrigated land in sub-Saharan Africa: 11 percent. At the other extreme, we find the Democratic Republic of Congo (0.1 percent) and Ethiopia (3 percent), where drought and poor governance regularly invoke tragic famines. All too frequently, we see on our televisions the mute, suffering faces of mothers watching their children slowly starve.

Once again, in trying to interpret Chinese practices, we need to take note of changing patterns in Western aid. Despite the visibly obvious failures of food security in Africa (and possibly because of frustrations engendered by those failures), funding for agriculture in aid agencies like the World Bank slid from 23 percent of loans in the early 1980s to only 5 percent just before the millennium.[6] It has only recently begun to increase. An internal study conducted by the World Bank found that agriculture projects were more expensive to prepare and implement, riskier and generally more contentious than other kinds of projects.[7] Some donors, such as the United States, channeled funding into food aid. The trend toward policy lending discouraged donor support for the nuts and bolts of long-term capacity building. American agricultural economist Carl Eicher contended that pressure from non-governmental organizations (NGOs) for a range of "people-centered" rural activities actually took funding away from the donor–government partnerships required to support agriculture.[8] Donors now have no shared consensus about what foreign aid can do to assist development in rural Africa, Eicher lamented. Enter China, which *has* developed a clear strategy for engagement in rural Africa, shaped by the sometimes bitter lessons of four decades of its own experience with agricultural aid.[9]

During the Cultural Revolution, radical Maoists sent Chinese youths and intellectuals "up to the mountains, down to the countryside" to serve the people. Today, Chinese leaders want their farmers and companies to go "down to the African countryside" to serve China's strategic interests. Some longstanding practices continue. Under the consolidation effort, Beijing has sent agricultural teams to many countries to breathe life back into former projects such as Lambayama. China's South–South Cooperation program, a joint undertaking with the UN Food and Agriculture Organization, is active in several African countries. Training continues at an accelerated scale. Between 2003 and 2008 more than 4,000 Africans traveled to China for agriculture-related courses lasting from three weeks to three months.[10] Beijing is also merging business and aid in the establishment of fourteen new agro-technical demonstration stations across Africa.[11] Chinese leaders see Africa as a huge potential market for hybrid seed and other Chinese biotechnology, a training ground for Chinese multinationals aiming to challenge the rich world's leaders: Bayer, Monsanto, and Syngenta, part of the overall "going global" strategy. This chapter and the next explore these issues.

China's Traditional Aid

Agriculture has been a feature of China's aid since the mid-1950s when the Ministry of Agriculture established a foreign aid office. Since 1960, over forty-four African countries have hosted Chinese agricultural aid projects, and nearly 20 percent of China's "turn-key" aid projects in Africa involved agriculture, a total of more than ninety farms.[12] A Cornell University graduate student told me that every year at his Beijing-based alma mater, China Agricultural University, more than ten professors will go to Africa for two years. "They don't really want to go," he admitted. "Two years is too long. But the Ministry of Agriculture will give a quota of ten, and the university will select them."[13] And off they go. More than 10,000 technical experts from China have served in Africa.

China's engagement in African agriculture has been highly political. In the early years, China helped construct the kind of large, state-owned farms that symbolized socialist modernity: Tanzania's Mbarali State Farm consisted of 3,200 hectares developed for irrigated rice, a dairy farm and poultry operation, and its own hydropower station.[14] But China's approach shifted when agricultural aid became a point of battle with Taiwan.

Launched in 1961, Taiwan's "Operation Vanguard" emphasized small and medium-scale rice and vegetable cultivation. Close to its peak in 1968, Operation Vanguard was fielding 1,239 Taiwanese agricultural experts in twenty-seven countries, many in Africa.[15] As Taipei began to lose the battle for diplomatic recognition, Beijing promised to take over the projects abandoned by Taiwan. This reshaped China's agricultural aid, as projects became smaller, more focused on demonstration and extension and less on production by the state.

By 1985, the Chinese had outpaced Taiwan, with agricultural projects in thirty-four countries (twenty-five in Africa) covering 48,000 hectares of farmland.[16] As late as 1997, competition with Taiwan remained salient: "Food issues threaten the stability of a state," two Chinese researchers commented. "Thus some African state leaders are eager to gain immediate success and this provides opportunities for the 'money diplomacy' of Taiwan. *We expand China's political influence when we strengthen agricultural aid for Africa.*" But, they cautioned, "The political effects will be realized through economic impact."[17]

Achieving sustainable economic impact was often a problem, however. Technically, China proved that African savannahs and swamps could be transformed into rich green reminders of Asia. The bright fields of green shoots ripening to fat heads of grain made a compelling demonstration. In my research in Africa in the 1980s, I saw Ministry of Agriculture files on Chinese projects stuffed with letters from people asking for assistance from the Chinese. One farmer told me: "If people see us working there and working well, they will copy. It is a pride to me that they do come and look at my own swamp." But, like the World Bank, which by its own count had a dismal failure rate of 50 percent for its rural development projects in Africa, the Chinese could not ensure that any of this would last after they left.[18]

Rice yields in sub-Saharan Africa typically decrease several years after development, an FAO report concluded, because farmers do not practice good management. This happened at China's Mbarali rice project in Tanzania, where yields fell from 8.2 to 4.0 metric tons per hectare between 1980 and 1989.[19] A well-managed Chinese field should have "three colors in one day" *san yen, yi tian*: gold in the morning with the ripe heads of grain; black at noon, when the field has been harvested, plowed, and prepared, and green in the evening with the transplanted seedlings. In China, a single crop of irrigated rice requires an average of 150 labor days per hectare, while African rainfed millet needs only fifty labor days, and rainfed upland rice seventy-nine labor days. The Chinese also use high levels of fertilizer and pesticides to increase yields.

Interestingly, the more closely practices in West Africa resembled "best practice" in China, the more profitable they were.[20] But farmers often refused to follow Chinese practices. If farmers weeded properly, they could expect to almost double their rice yields. Yet, as a West African official complained, farmers "are careless about weeding. Their promising time for the weeding is always tomorrow which will never come."[21]

Farmers in China level their rice paddies to create a uniform depth of water for the rice seedlings. A typical Chinese rice paddy looks like a lake, with only the green shoots sticking up above the water. "When the Chinese were here, they didn't want to see any land above water," a field assistant told me. But people complained that this was "too difficult. When the Chinese left, those people who were still here decided it was level enough." Farmers typically left humps of land sticking up above the water; seedlings planted here would wither and die. African farmers were simply not used to the demands of the Chinese system. Switching from crops that require fifty or seventy-nine days of labor to one that requires almost three times that amount will not happen easily in the labor-scarce environments still common in much of rural Africa.

A lot also depended on the capacity and attitude of the local government. In Sierra Leone a meeting on the Chinese stations chaired by Sierra Leone's chief agriculturalist expressed "regret" for the way the Ministry was managing the ten farms in 1979, only two years after the departure of the Chinese: "these farms are currently flourishing with weeds."[22] But in The Gambia, where I once spent many pleasant weeks interviewing farmers living along the broad banks of the Gambia River and its tributaries, most were still growing what they called "*Chinese faro* [rice]." And they were getting more effective assistance from what was then a democratically elected government with a rural base of support. But The Gambia was somewhat of an exception, I later learned.

Doing Well by Doing Good?

"We've assisted African agriculture quite a lot, but haven't gotten much return," a Chinese economic officer stationed in Africa admitted to me in 1988. Yet while many of the traditional donors were withdrawing from agriculture, hoping that liberalization and "the market" would foster development, the Chinese stayed engaged. In 1986, Beijing announced the preparation of another seventy agricultural aid projects for Africa, many of them efforts to consolidate or repair earlier projects.[23]

At the same time, China's aid reforms in agriculture emphasized multiple experiments. Business was an early concern. As we know, in the 1980s the Chinese decided to change the economic and technical cooperation offices of Chinese ministries (formerly responsible for carrying out aid under the state plan) into corporations. In 1984, Sierra Leone became the first African country to host one of the new corporations formed from the economic and technical cooperation offices of Chinese ministries. China Agricon (China Agriculture, Livestock, Animal Husbandry, Fisheries and Engineering Service Cooperation Corporation), a company formed in 1983 and owned by China's Ministry of Agriculture, set up a combined office–residence near Lumley beach on the outskirts of Freetown.

I met with the enthusiastic Lei Shilian, China Agricon's director, in 1988. Among other pieces of business, they had prepared a feasibility study for a curious project: to reactivate the Rolako station, one of the ten constructed by Chinese aid, for a local businessman with high-level connections to Sierra Leone's former president.[24] But Sierra Leone's politics proved a problem for the new Chinese entrepreneurs. China Agricon found other business in Rwanda, Uganda, Madagascar, and Libya developing fish ponds and paddy fields, often under contract to other donors.[25]

Another early experiment involved a loan fund set up in 1985 to promote joint ventures between China's new corporations and African companies.[26]

In a 1988 interview, the Chinese ambassador in Sierra Leone told me that he had suggested to Sierra Leone's Minister of Agriculture that they use part of the new loan to jointly reactivate some of the Chinese rice stations as profitable ventures. A Chinese team visited five of the stations, including Lambayama, but decided against the investment. A joint venture in oil palm in eastern Sierra Leone between China Agricon and Choithrams, a local Indian-owned trading firm, was more successful.

These experiments showed that agriculture could potentially generate good business. Furthermore, by the mid-1990s it was clear that China's traditional agriculture projects were not sustainable in Africa without continued Chinese support. "Almost all of them without exception have gone through the odd cycle of 'quick starting, quick results, and quick decline'," a Chinese researcher noted after visiting a group of projects in the late 1990s.[27] Yet there was the Taiwan issue. African countries *wanted* agricultural aid. Taiwan was good at agriculture. The diplomatic struggle with Taiwan meant that China would have to continue aid to agriculture, as two Chinese researchers argued, "to meet the needs of our diplomatic work."[28] But aid for agriculture would have to also guarantee economic profits for China, create jobs in Africa, and help resolve African food supply problems, i.e. it would need to be *of mutual benefit*.

Structural adjustment provided an opening. Chinese companies could fit into many of the gaps created by structural adjustment and the reluctant withdrawal of the African state. As a wave of privatizations occurred in the 1990s, Chinese companies took advantage of the fire-sales to set up joint ventures and take up long-term leases on their old projects. Mpoli Farm in Mauritania, the Sikasso tea plantation and factory and the Segou sugar refinery in Mali, and Koba farm in Guinea all made the transition from aid to business. This held more potential for "consolidation" than simply returning year after year to repair and renovate. It was a new way to sustain the political and economic benefits of aid.

After the millennium, Chinese interest in African investment quickened. In the lead up to the historic 2006 Beijing Summit of the Forum on China–Africa Cooperation (FOCAC), China's National Development and Reform Commission commissioned a team of forty domestic and international experts to collaborate for six months on a roadmap for China's investment in Africa. Chinese leaders assembled the tools of the socialist development state – finance and tax incentives – to support the roadmap. China would "encourage and support competitive, large agricultural enterprises, including private ones, to invest in Africa."[29] Beijing also expanded the list of commodities from the poorest countries given duty-free entry into China from 190 to 440. This encouraged some Chinese investment: an entrepreneur who decided to grow sesame in Senegal to export to China, as we saw earlier.[30] As part of the pageantry surrounding the November 2006 Forum on China–Africa Cooperation Summit, Chinese President Hu Jintao made a pledge of 100 agricultural experts and ten agricultural demonstration centers for Africa.

Just after the summit ended, a Chinese official explained to the *International Business Daily* that China's interest in energy and mineral projects in Africa was "likely to trigger some negative reactions."[31] China could use agricultural aid to help smooth the way. This could be a way to "combine 'getting' and 'giving'," he said.

In view of all the emphasis on business, I was surprised when I saw the list of pledges made at the summit. China's plan to construct ten agricultural demonstration centers seemed a throwback to projects of the past decades, the same projects that were handed over and then began to flourish with weeds. But as I learned more about these centers, it became clear that they were not conventional at all: they married aid to China's global business ambitions.

This brief sketch gives the background, but it raises many questions. How successful were these experiments? How did they work? How might the Chinese find profit in aiding African agriculture? Were Chinese farmers now likely to move in droves to Africa, as some media reports suggested? It was hard to get answers to these questions in my meetings in Beijing. I had to journey back to rural Africa to piece together the full story.

Wang Yibin and South–South Cooperation

Early on a Saturday morning in December 2007, I sat at a table in the hostel of a Chinese-built stadium in Freetown, listening to Wang Yibin, chief of mission for the Chinese team on the South–South Cooperation project of the UN Food and Agriculture Organization (FAO). The outdoor cafeteria of the stadium was empty save for the bottles strewn about after what had clearly been a lively Friday evening. Looking up from where we sat, I could see a few Chinese and several Africans coming out to stretch on the long balcony of the hostel, regarding us with some curiosity.

I barely made the meeting. Neither Wang nor I had realized that on the last Saturday of each month the national government holds a popular city-wide clean-up in Freetown. For several hours no traffic is supposed to move. All buses, taxis, and private vehicles are grounded. In the absence of a functioning public sanitation service, the residents of the crowded city turn out to sweep the streets and clean the gutters of their neighborhoods. I finally found a battered taxi that agreed to take me, and we sped down the deserted streets. A soldier with a gun slung across his shoulder stopped us at Congo Cross, but then waved us on after peering intently into the car.

Wang Yibin was one of 500 Chinese experts posted to Nigeria under the South–South program in 2004. As Chapter 2 noted, China's experiments in "tripartite" cooperation began in the late 1970s, usually with UN agencies of various kinds. In 1996, China began tripartite cooperation with the FAO. This trial effort joined with the FAO's South–South Cooperation program after the millennium. The South–South program matches up developing countries who offer to work with counterparts in other countries on food security. The two partner countries and the FAO contribute to the costs. The program had some curious partnerships: China assisted Bangladesh, for example, but Bangladeshi experts were assisting The Gambia.

I had first read about Wang Yibin, the deputy director of the Department of Agriculture in Zhong Xiang, a city in Hubei province, in a newsletter published by the Nigeria program. He had won praise for his enthusiasm and creativity. Posted first to Nigeria's Edo state, he built a demonstration fish farm and a fish hatchery for the chief of his district. Wang was then dispatched to build a large fish pond as a demonstration on the land of former Nigerian President Olusegun Obasanjo. Pleased with Wang's work, Obasanjo asked him to remain in Nigeria, but he declined, and headed home to Hubei. A number of people in his group returned to Nigeria after their contracts ended, however. "Nigeria has money, oil," Wang explained. "Why did you decide to come to Sierra Leone?" I asked him. "To help the African people," Wang replied. "I was also poor when I was a child. People need food. Also," he added, "I am a Chinese government officer. If the Chinese government asks me to come, I must go."

Wang was full of energy as he explained the South–South program to me that morning. "In China the population is very high but we can feed our people. Now we are hoping that this country can develop fast. Our team here has done a lot of work. We have rice, vegetables, fish ponds. We each have a counterpart. When we went to Makali [station and training center] we found it had been abandoned because of the war. The Chinese government spent a lot of money to build that station. I sent a team to Makali, to do some repairs of the hydroelectric power station, fix the dam. We are shipping a container of hybrid rice seed there. I want to make that farm good! But it must be little by little. China used to be like this: no money, no food. In 40 years, we solved it, but not in one or two years. That's impossible."

"Everything can grow here," he continued, his gaze sweeping up to the green distant hills where clouds were gathering. "But they need dams to save the water, they need to use irrigation to grow crops. In China, during Mao's time, we built a lot of dams. We just did it. But it is very hard here because people say, 'the land belongs to me. I want money!' But if you don't have a dam, you can't save the water. They should cooperate more! The first thing is to change the minds of some people. But foreign aid can't do that. Some people want food, but they don't want to work. I tried to get people to work for money, to help build the dam, the fish ponds, but very few were interested. They want everything for free. This is not good. They want the president to give them food. In China, Chairman Mao changed our people's mind. He said: we will just do it by ourselves, we will work hard."

Wang reminded me of an enthusiastic Maoist Peace Corps volunteer. He embodied the spirit of the Maoist-era heros: the Iron Man of Daqing or the hard-working villagers of Dazhai, but with a twist. Like so many pioneering Chinese today, he thought of the potential for profit in what looked to him to be the empty lands of Africa. "I invited two companies I know to come here, but they wouldn't come," Wang told me. "The poor roads, lack of electricity – they were not interested. I thought about doing something here myself, in Moyamba, but it takes four or five hours to get there, only 75 miles, and there is no electricity. In China, we have power 24 hours a day. To process things, you just switch it on. Our Chinese farmers were concerned about this situation." We will see later that Wang's view of the vast emptiness of African land was far from the reality: local communities jealously guarded their rights to every square kilometer.

From Weeds to Seeds

As part of the policy of consolidation, Beijing sent a team of Chinese experts from Hubei province to Sierra Leone in 1988 to rehabilitate some of the rice stations built during the 1970s. Their company, Wuhan Municipal Foreign Cooperation Corporation (like Complant, a former foreign aid office), was *still* working there when I visited almost twenty years later. Their experience reflects the emphasis on consolidation that marked China's aid, starting in the 1980s, but it may also be a harbinger of the shift from aid that relies purely on long-term transfers to aid that is used to jump-start more sustainable business relationships.

On a sunny morning late in December 2007, I arrived unannounced at the gate of the combined office and residence of the Chinese team at the Ministry of Agriculture demonstration farm just outside Freetown. Two of the Wuhan team members, Yin Lixin and Sun Jun, met me cordially. By 1988, Yin told me, the rice stations China had built in Sierra Leone were "wasted." These projects were intended to produce lush green reflections of China's own rice fields, and be visible symbols of "friendship." Having them "flourishing with weeds" was a problem.

Wuhan is the largest city in Hubei, a major center for irrigated rice. Between 1988 and 1993 teams from Wuhan rebuilt three of the ten stations (Lumley, Makali, and Lambayama), constructed a small hydropower station at Makali to provide a renewable supply of electricity, and posted teams at all three stations to lead extension work with outlying farmers. Their work explains how Lambayama was still functioning during the war, more than twenty years after its initial construction. This was purely aid, Yin told me – a donation. The Chinese government paid for all the costs: salaries for the Chinese, seeds from China, agrochemicals, fertilizer, equipment, even transport.

The war drove the Chinese teams out of Lambayama and Makali in 1993, and China finally suspended the project for almost thirty months in 1997 when the war reached Freetown. But the Wuhan experts returned to Lumley in September 1999, almost three years before peace was officially declared. The Chinese ambassador arranged for the water supply system at Lambayama to be repaired (again), and funded several agricultural officers to attend three-month training courses in China. In 2001, they also returned to a fourth station, on the outskirts of the southern town of Bo.

On my way back from the trip to Lambayama, I spent the night in a small hotel in Bo frequented by local diamond dealers. At two in the morning a drunken fellow guest rattled my locked door, rousing me from a fitful sleep plagued by mosquitoes and the raucous sounds of a party in the hotel's bar. I slipped out early the next morning to visit the former Chinese station. When I arrived, the agricultural officer in charge, Sumaile Massaquoi, and his counterpart Yang Sanhai, were standing on the edge of the demonstration plots in the irrigated area, issuing instructions to the station workers. When they finished, we walked over to the station offices, past a building filled with a set of enormous industrial-size rice-processing machines donated by the Chinese government.

China is promoting *hybrid* seeds in Sierra Leone. Under the right conditions, hybrids have what is called hybrid *heterosis*, or "hybrid vigor." Like mules, they are stronger and more productive than either parent. But hybrids do not breed true from seeds. Yields fall dramatically if farmers try to save some of the harvest for planting. To keep yields high, they need to buy new seeds, creating a steady market. Hybrids also require more fertilizer and pesticides, and some doubt that hybrid seeds are appropriate for small-scale African farmers, particularly if they need to borrow to buy the seeds. Yet many small-scale farmers in East Africa have been eager to adopt hybrid maize, which suggests that they may find hybrid rice attractive.[32]

"Conventional seed is better for the long term," Massaquoi said. The Chinese were giving hybrid seeds away at the time, and they were naturally very popular. Moreover, some farmers were using them for three seasons, despite the reduced yields. "But even in China, they use hybrids to combat acute hunger," he told me, pointing out that his country was still recovering from the war. Massaquoi had traveled to China twice for training courses on hybrid rice: three months each at the Hunan Academy of Agricultural Science and the privately owned Yuan Longping High-Tech Agriculture Company in Hunan. Perhaps his country could multiply the Chinese seed; in time, they might be able to do hybridization themselves, he ventured, although the weak scientific capacity made this a long shot, at best.

The Wuhan team would finally wind down the project in September 2008, Massaquoi said. A separate team from Hubei province was now conducting trials of Chinese hybrid rice seed at the government rice research station. The former Minister of Agriculture, Sama Monde, described the trials as an experiment, a joint venture between the Hubei team and the Sierra Leone government. "But after the third year," he said, "we expect the private sector to become interested." In a small way, as we shall see below, Sierra Leone and next door neighbor Liberia were going to fit into China's strategic plan for "going global" in agriculture.

The Father of Hybrid Rice

Dr. Yuan Longping is elderly now, but he still rides a motorcycle to his research fields twice a day. Famous in China as the "father of hybrid rice," Yuan runs Hunan province's Hybrid Rice Research Center. Long ago, Yuan dreamt of rice grains as big as peanuts, rice stalks as tall as trees. He went on to become the first scientist to crack the difficult secret of hybrid rice.[33] In 1979, China's patent on the hybrid rice developed by Yuan was the first agro-technology patent registered to China in the US. Further patents followed. By the start of the new millennium, Chinese farmers were using hybrids in more than half of their rice area. In Africa, hybrid rice has been as scarce as hens' teeth.

Yuan's research made him a wealthy man with multiple accolades. He was the winner of the State Scientific and Technological Award jointly bestowed by the Communist Party and the State Council. He won the 2004 World Food Prize (co-awarded with Dr. Monty Jones, a native of Sierra Leone, honored for his work in cross-breeding Asian and African rice varieties). And he sat between Jackie Chan, the Hong Kong kung fu star, and Gong Li, one of China's most beautiful actresses, when all three were winners of the 2007 "You Bring Charm to the World" award for outstanding Chinese citizens. But all of these may have paled beside the $12 million value of the 5 percent of shares transferred to Yuan in 2001 when he agreed to lend his name to a consortium: Yuan Longping High-Tech Agriculture Company.

Patents are the foundation of today's global seed business, worth billions of dollars annually. Until recently, many African countries kept seed supply as a state monopoly, partly out of concern for quality control, and partly for the extra profit. Liberalization of African agricultural markets under structural adjustment programs created openings for agribusiness. US-based Pioneer, and Monsanto, the Swiss firm Syngenta, and Germany's Bayer Crop Science began to market their hybrid maize across much of east and southern Africa. A farmer can now visit a tiny shop in a remote area of Malawi and buy soap, cooking oil, and her choice of hybrid maize seeds. China had no comparative advantage in hybrid maize, but they did in rice.

Hybrid seed is multiplied from the pure parent stock (foundation or breeder seed) to produce certified seed, with only the latter actually used by ordinary farmers. Rather than importing tons of certified seed, the foundation stock could be imported from China and multiplied in Africa to get certified seed. Yao Xiangjun, the deputy director of the Department of International Cooperation at the Ministry of Agriculture, told *China Daily* in 2007: "We believe there will be great potential for trading cooperation between China and Africa in small and medium-sized farming equipment and hybrid rice seeding." Involving Chinese companies in hybrid seed multiplication in Africa would help provide a smooth transition out of the old model of aid. It would also fit neatly into Beijing's global strategy for agribusiness.

China's Agrotechnology Centers: Sustainability and Business

The May 2006 Africa investment roadmap developed by forty domestic and international experts for China's strategic planners pointed to agricultural technology and seed cultivation as two areas where China could be competitive. The experts recommended that China establish cutting-edge agricultural technology demonstration parks across Africa. "This will create a lot of opportunities for China's agricultural enterprises," Shi Yongxiang, one of the team's leaders, told *China Daily*.[34]

China's top leaders liked the idea. Chinese President Hu Jintao pledged to construct ten agricultural demonstration centers for Africa. He also promised to train an average of 5,000 Africans per year in agriculture. Training creates contacts and networks. (Recall that Yuan Longping High-Tech Agriculture Company offered the hybrid rice training course taken by

Sierra Leone's Sumaile Massaquoi and other African agriculturalists.) But the agricultural demonstration farms would be equally important for the new model of mixing aid and business.

The experience of Koba Farm in Guinea showed how China's aid could segue into the business of hybrid rice. In 1979, China built an irrigated rice promotion center at Koba, a two-hour drive southeast of Conakry. The farm did poorly after it was handed over in 1982. Under the consolidation program, China paid for the renovation (1989–92) and then in 1996, as part of the experiments in aid reform, China State Farm Agribusiness Corporation signed a contract establishing a joint venture with the Guinean Ministry of Agriculture at Koba.

With the Chinese holding 80 percent of the shares and supporting the project, Koba rapidly expanded into a large, diversified agribusiness. In 2003, CSFAC launched a new experiment, inviting experts from Yuan Longping's Hybrid Rice Research Center to conduct hybrid rice trials at Koba. The trials worked well, with the top variety yielding more than 9 tons per hectare, compared with an average of 1.5 tons on farmers' traditional fields.[35] Hybrid rice provided a good basis for mutual benefit, CSFAC concluded: "a hybrid rice cultivation center in Guinea will alleviate grain shortages in Africa and also bring the CSFAC good economic returns."[36]

After the 2006 FOCAC Summit wrapped up, the Ministries of Agriculture and Commerce sent five teams of experts to Africa to finalize the locations, design, and size of the ten proposed agrotechnology demonstration centers.[37] At the end of 2007, Ministry of Commerce deputy minister Wei Jianguo announced that there would now be *fourteen* centers. There had been "constant debates" about the implementation of the agricultural centers, Wei said.[38] The two ministries invited experts and Chinese companies with experience in agriculture overseas to attend a series of workshops in Beijing and in some of the provinces to help develop the design of the new centers.

In Beijing, in late November 2008, as a biting wind swept down from the steppes of Mongolia, I went to meet with an official in the International Cooperation department of the Ministry of Agriculture in Beijing to ask him about these centers. The Ministry, old and sitting in a distinctly unfashionable district, was worlds away from the shining new buildings of China's Ministry of Commerce and the sweeping boulevards near Tiananmen

Square. Men with baggy trousers and chapped cheeks sat in the waiting room joking with the two receptionists and looking curiously at me.

"Our discussions focused on sustainability," the official, Wang Jinbiao, told me when we met across a long table in a room lined with photographs of smiling peasants and officials. "The effects of our projects are good, but they don't last. They are often not supported well by the local governments. We wanted to find a model that would allow the benefits to continue."

The winning plan was this: the centers would be delegated to Chinese enterprises to run. China National Agricultural Development Corporation (now the parent company of China State Farm Agribusiness Corporation) would run the centers in Benin and South Africa. Eleven other centers were delegated to strong agricultural provinces, which would each select a leading company to carry out the project (Figure 9.1). One would be run by a government institute: the Hainan island-based Chinese Academy of Tropical Agriculture Sciences would build the center in Congo, Brazzaville.[39]

The Ministry of Commerce would give three years of grant support to the enterprises and institutes, which would use this period to "explore how to operate in a commercial, sustainable, and mutually beneficial way."[40] And then they would be pushed out, and expected to fly on their own. They had to commit to run the centers for a minimum of five to eight more years, if the recipient country agreed. (The South Africans said firmly that three years of Chinese management would be enough, and that *they* would run the centers after that.) This plan, the Chinese hoped, would give the centers a better chance at sustainability, and their companies a head start in agribusiness.

Mozambique, with its vast unrealized potential for irrigation, was selected as the first country to receive one of the centers, at Umbeluzi agricultural station near Maputo. Not long after, Yuan Longping High Tech signed a contract to develop a center at the Central Agricultural Research Institute (CARI) in Bong County, Liberia, not far from China's earlier rice project at Kpatawee Farm. Chongqing Seed Corporation said it would work with outgrowers and use "its own intellectual property" to develop 300 hectares in Tanzania for seed multiplication.[41] In September 2008 at the United Nations, Chinese Premier Wen Jiabao announced that China planned to build thirty of these centers worldwide. "We need these organizations to distribute the seed," a Chinese official told me two months later, in Beijing.

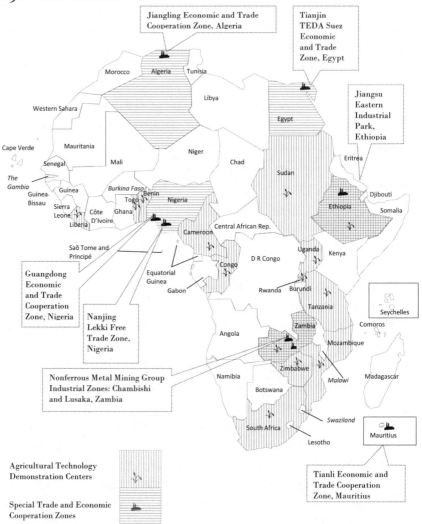

Fig. 9.1. Map of China's African Agricultural Demonstrations Stations and Special Economic Cooperation and Trade Zones, 2006–2009

In September 2006, the Bill and Melinda Gates Foundation joined the Rockefeller Foundation to establish AGRA, Alliance for a Green Revolution in Africa. What Africa needs, they argued, was better farming practices, water control systems, improved seeds and fertilizer, and networks of small shops to sell them. From what we have seen in this chapter, many aspects of

China's business-driven aid and engagement in rural Africa parallel the AGRA initiative. What impact is it likely to have on poverty and development in Africa?

Under the Chinese plan, local food supply will almost certainly increase, a positive outcome for poor consumers and countries that use scarce foreign exchange to import grain. Many of the countries that are hosting Chinese agricultural demonstration stations – Mozambique, Liberia, Senegal, for example – are among the rice importers whose total bill amounts to some $2 billion annually. Yet both models – Chinese companies using African labor, or Chinese companies using outgrowers – have risks. There is very little arable land in Africa that is not already claimed by individuals or traditional communities. African governments have not always obtained permission from local communities before turning their land over to investors. In addition, as I found many years ago in The Gambia, the introduction of potentially profitable new crops into systems where men traditionally grow crops for the market, but women are responsible for producing food, runs the risk of women losing access to the land they depend on for family food production.[42] Chinese aid workers had little knowledge of local farming systems in the places where they were working, and Chinese companies may be equally ill-prepared.

On another note, Chinese importers are already setting up networks of small shops in many countries, a need identified by the AGRA plan. In Sierra Leone, for example, Henan Guoji has branches in Makeni and Bo, "and they are setting up in Kono and Kabalah," Jack Jalloh, an official at the Ministry of Agriculture told me. "In the past three or four years we have been buying a lot of agricultural equipment from them. They have promised to open branches in all twelve districts" to serve local farmers (and make money). Although it would be better for poverty reduction if these small shops were owned and operated by local people, this is precisely the problem: the private sector never picked up the agricultural input market that had been abandoned by African governments. Hence the Chinese presence might help in the effort to increase production.

Finally, the impact of this aspect of China's engagement in rural Africa may depend in part on where one sits with regard to the green revolution in Asia, and its potential in Africa. Some are fervent believers in an African green revolution, and are frustrated because what they deem a success in

Asia has not spread to Africa. Others take the opposite view, pointing to Asian problems: higher pollution and health risks from agrochemicals, increased debt and landlessness, and reduced biodiversity.

In general, improved seeds help reduce poverty. In Mozambique, for example, researchers estimated in 2001 that rural households could earn an average $97 more per year, nearly half the per capita income, if farmers simply had access to improved seeds already tested by the national research service. Yet China's focus on hybrid seeds could have less certain results. Gates and Rockefeller have put their money into improved maize seeds that are *not* hybrid, arguing that hybrids breed farmer dependence and are not resilient enough for the uncertain conditions that face small farmers. China's fledgling agribusiness companies are looking at African farmers as potential customers. The Chinese government's plan is that, with a little help, Chinese companies will gain a foothold in a promising new market. Meanwhile, as Chinese seed companies ventured out to Africa, the German agrochemical company Bayer announced that it planned to expand its own hybrid rice seed operations into China.[43] The Chinese were clearly playing by the rules of global competition. But would African countries benefit?

CHAPTER 10

Foreign Farmers: Chinese Settlers in Rural Africa

To the Chinese, Africa appears to be vastly underused. At the end of my conversation with Wang Yibin, team leader of the South–South Cooperation project, he spread his arms wide and said: "Land plenty in this country, no one use it!" But like Chinese investments in minerals, or oil-backed loans for infrastructure, some of China's proposed agricultural ventures created waves. "China's Coming Land Grab" was a typical blog headline. In several cases, the alarm outpaced the reality. As we will see, many of the huge Chinese land "deals" trumpeted in the media, such as the reports of millions of Chinese farm laborers working in Africa, were greatly exaggerated.[1] But the Chinese interest in land overseas *is* very real. They have a fifth of the world's population, and only 7 percent of its arable land.

The crowded islands of Japan may again be a model. By 1996, the Japanese owned 12 million hectares of farmland overseas, triple the size of the arable land at home.[2] But overseas investment in farming is a common strategy for pioneers from all wealthy countries where the cost of land is high. And as Wang Yibin noticed, Africa's low population density makes it particularly attractive. In 2008, with global food prices at record highs, Lonrho, the company founded by the Rhodesia-born tycoon "Tiny" Rowland, began trying to buy up 200,000 hectares of productive land across Africa. Chiquita Banana visited Angola in March that year, on the lookout for land. Korea's Daewoo corporation began to negotiate with Madagascar over a land concession of a million hectares. In October, Jacques Diouf, the Senegalese diplomat who heads the UN's Food and Agriculture Organization, warned that investments like these posed risks of a new colonization.[3]

China is not a newcomer to overseas farming. In 1987, a peasant collective from Wuxi, a town west of Shanghai, spent $800,000 to buy a remote 4,400 hectare Australian sheep farm described by a local as being "at the end of the bloody earth."[4] China State Farm Agribusiness Corporation also stepped out first in Australia, acquiring a 43,000 hectare farm in Queensland two years after the Wuxi purchase.[5] In Africa, Zambia was an early trial destination for China's state-sponsored agricultural investment. Unlike many African countries, Zambia allowed foreigners to own land.

China State Farm Agribusiness Corporation purchased a tract of land to set up the China–Zambia Friendship Farm in Zambia in 1990. Two years later, they bought land for the larger Zhongken Farm, an hour outside the capital, Lusaka. Wang Chi, a teacher at an agricultural college in Beijing, organized a team of 100 Zambians to cut the thick brush that covered the area, and began to raise chickens, dairy cows, and pigs. In 2005, Wang was killed in a car accident on the Lusaka road. His forty-two-year-old widow Li Li took over the management of the farm, now employing 200 workers. "I was a nurse in Beijing," Li Li told me when I met her in 2008. "When we came here, I knew nothing about farming." CSFAC invested $600,000 to buy the farm, and then another $1.6 million to develop it. It is now worth $6 million, Li said.

Located 10 kilometers down a dirt road, the 3,573 hectare property had been used as a country retreat by the previous owner. "Trees, flowers," she smiled. "It looked like a national park." The farm house had three bedrooms, no electricity, and no running water. Wang Chi brought home 200 day-old chicks in the first few weeks after they had moved in. They put 100 chicks in each of the two spare bedrooms while they made their own concrete blocks and built poultry housing. The 200 chicks multiplied into 20,000 and then 200,000. Is the farm profitable? I asked. The farm has a contract to repay CSFAC $100,000 every year, she said, "but we reinvest it instead of sending it to Beijing. That is fine with them. They have a long-term view. Our headquarters always looks how far we are going, not how much we make and send back."[6]

By 2009, there were anywhere between fifteen to twenty-three state-owned and private Chinese farms in Zambia.[7] Some were spin-offs from farms sponsored by China's government. Si Su, an expert from Jiangsu province who came to work for a state-owned company in 1992, stayed on after his contract to set up his own "Sunlight Farm." In 2007, Si was managing fifty Zambian employees.[8] By then, CSFAC had agricultural investments not only in Zambia, but in Tanzania, South Africa, Gabon, Togo, Ghana, Mali, Guinea, and Mauritania. They were in the first wave of Chinese "going global" in agriculture.

Going Global in Agriculture

The Chinese government encouraged overseas agricultural investment under its general "going global" policies. But, as noted in Chapter 3, outward investment in agriculture and related activities (Figure 10.1) remained far smaller than in mining or manufacturing. In 2007, agricultural investments were only $272 million, just over 1 percent of the total for that year ($26.5 billion). China's policy guidance catalogs began offering specific incentives for Chinese companies to grow rubber, oil palm, and cotton overseas.[9] They were encouraged to invest in aquaculture and poultry-raising, agricultural machinery assembly and fertilizer production.

The government-sponsored seminars and even television programs encouraged Chinese investors to take the plunge. At a 2002 seminar organized by the Chinese government, a manager from China State Farm Agribusiness

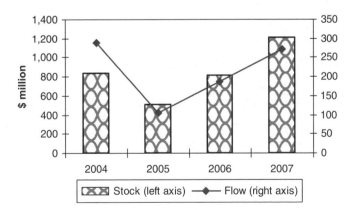

Fig. 10.1. Chinese outward FDI, agriculture ($ million)

Source: Chinese Ministry of Commerce.

Note: Data refers to agriculture, forestry, husbandry, and fisheries.

Corporation told a Chinese audience: "Ten years of experience in Africa has made me more confident."[10] Many were inspired to go and see for themselves. "In China now," the energetic Wang Yibin told me in Sierra Leone, "many Chinese companies want to come and develop agriculture in Africa." The "father of hybrid rice" Yuan Longping sent a delegation from his Hunan research institute to Mozambique to explore hybrid rice production possibilities in Chókwe, where more than 20,000 hectares had been developed for irrigation under the Portuguese, but largely abandoned during the long civil war.

In November 2006, the China Development Bank and the Chinese Ministry of Agriculture announced an agreement to work together to encourage projects using land and water resources overseas.[11] China Exim-bank promised to offer support for agricultural projects in Africa.[12] Finally, in 2008, the media reported that the Ministry of Agriculture had submitted a draft plan to the State Council outlining policies that would encourage five major Chinese state-owned farming companies to obtain land abroad for agricultural use on a large scale.[13] Asked repeatedly about this, Chinese officials categorically denied that such a plan existed.[14]

As this suggests, Chinese interest in African land became a hot-button issue. Many regions of Africa had unhappy experiences of European settlement during the colonial period. Others worried about rising land inequality. So far, much of Africa has avoided the sharp land disparities found in Latin America with its haciendas and squatters, but this is not the case everywhere (Zimbabwe and South Africa come to mind here). Some were against foreign investment more generally. Hearing rumours that Zimbabwe was inviting Chinese companies to invest in agriculture, a local activist, decried the idea. This would "turn the land holders and their workers into labour tenants and subject them to exploitation."[15] Three other issues made headlines: the potential conflict between China's food security and Africa's, the sheer size of some of the proposed investments, and concerns about Chinese farmers settling in Africa.

Food Security: China and Africa

In 2000, a Chinese economist published an article on Chinese investment in African agriculture. China's main goal should be to contribute to food security in Africa, he said. However, additional land offshore might aid

China's own food security. "If the international situation turns against us –
for example, if North American countries were to exert pressure using food
as a weapon – we could, if necessary, use this 'food storage'."[16]

China became a net food importer in 2003. The risk of embargoes aside,
the inevitability of urbanization and the shrinking of arable land point to a
day soon when China will need to import far more food. Already, almost 70
percent of the soybeans it consumes are imported, mainly from the US,
Brazil, and Argentina.[17] So far, the Chinese have relied on the global market
for these supplies.

Chinese farms in Africa are mainly producing for local sale. A small
number – Chinese producers of sugar in Togo and Sierra Leone, organic
vegetables in Senegal, vanilla in Uganda – export to Europe or even America,
taking advantage of duty-free incentives. A Chinese producer of sesame seed
in Senegal plans to export to China, as I noted in Chapter 3. But even with
the high grain prices of 2008, shipping costs were simply too high to ship
grain to China, as an official from Chongqing Seed Corporation said: "We
hope our (overseas) production could be a choice for the country, as our
farmland is decreasing and the population is growing. But not now."[18]
"There is a saying in Chinese, another official said, 'Don't transport grain
further than a thousand miles.' It's not cost-efficient."[19]

Xie Guoli, a senior official at the Minister of Agriculture, put his finger on
the shaky politics of the idea: "It is not realistic to grow grains overseas,
particularly in Africa or South America. There are so many people starving
in Africa, can you ship the grains back to China?"[20] In addition, the
incentives offered by the Chinese state did not seem to reflect a strategy of
producing food in Africa to ship back to China. As China State Farm
Agribusiness Corporation's director of overseas development complained,
the Ministry of Commerce gave no special incentives for the kind of
products already being produced in Africa by his company: wheat, corn,
rice, soybeans, and sisal.[21] However, some Chinese companies began to
explore agricultural mega-projects even without these incentives.

Mega-Projects

The first signs of huge Chinese agricultural projects overseas arose not in
Africa, but closer to home in the Philippines. In January 2007, Fuhua, a

company owned by the Jilin provincial government, signed a memorandum of understanding with the Philippines government to lease one million hectares for hybrid rice, maize, and sorghum (they planned to begin with a more modest 50,000 hectares, still a huge area in a country with South American-style land inequality).[22] The agreement was later thrown out after protests from Filipinos, but concessions of a similar size were being discussed by Chinese firms in Indonesia and Papua New Guinea, along the lines of earlier Japanese investments.[23]

Later in 2007, the newspaper *Africa Confidential* circulated a report that ZTE, one of China's largest state-owned telecommunications companies, planned a joint venture in an oil palm biofuels project of *three million* hectares in the Democratic Republic of the Congo.[24] Oil palm was one of the overseas investment areas given incentives from China's National Reform and Development Commission. As it turned out, however, the true story in the DRC was slightly less alarming. Approved by the DRC Council of Ministers in August, the ZTE project would involve 100,000 hectares.[25] One widely circulated "fact" that turned out to be fiction was a story that China had promised to invest $800 million to modernize Mozambican agriculture. In Mozambique, I spoke to local journalists, NGOs, the head of the national peasants association, the Chinese, and top officials in the Ministry of Agriculture. I even hired an assistant to search through four years of local newspapers, but found no sign of this pledge. The Chinese *had* promised to build one of their fourteen African agro-technical stations in Mozambique: a training center on 30 hectares, at a cost of RMB 55 million ($8 million). Could this have been the origin of the rumor?

In a now familiar pattern, some of the other reports on Chinese farm investments that buzzed through the media turned out to be less concrete on a second glance. In Zimbabwe, for example, China International Water and Electric Corporation (CIWEC) was said to have obtained the right to farm more than 100,000 hectares of maize. But the real story was that the government of Zimbabwe awarded CIWEC a contract simply to clear the land and build an irrigation system. Mugabe's chaotic and brutal takeover of large, white-owned farms severely disrupted grain production in Zimbabwe. The quixotic maize project was an attempt to compensate for the failure of production on the parched plots where inexperienced black settlers were eking out a living. CIWEC began the project, but when the Mugabe government was unable to make its payments, CIWEC withdrew its construction crews and suspended activities.

Reports also circulated that the China State Farm Agribusiness Corporation had taken over some of the farms formerly owned by white Zimbabweans in a joint venture with Zimbabwe's Agricultural Rural Development Agency (ARDA). Mugabe's government did offer the farms to CSFAC. But as I learned after traveling to Zimbabwe, CSFAC turned down the offer. An official in the Zimbabwe Ministry of Agriculture reported that the Chinese determined that security issues and a poor business environment made Zimbabwe too risky.[26] Zimbabwe had no credible plan to bring its agricultural sector back to life, CSFAC negotiators concluded. They were not willing to risk the investment.

In the North, There is Only Magbass

China's Magbass sugar project in Sierra Leone shows some of the challenges African communities are likely to face from large-scale Chinese agricultural investment in Africa. Built by China between 1977 and 1982, Magbass was the first aid project to transition directly into Chinese management after completion. After 1982, the state-owned Complant managed the 1,280 hectare complex for the government until the war drove them out in 1996. In 2003, just after the end of the war, Sierra Leone tried to privatize many state-owned assets. There were few takers, but Complant – now listed on the Shanghai stock exchange and one of China's 100 top state-owned companies – signed a lease to renovate, expand, and manage the remote sugar complex, this time for profit.

Did the Chinese government direct Complant to make this investment? "Complant did the research, they made the decision," China's ambassador in Freetown, Cheng Wenju, asserted. "We can't order them to come." Complant's experience illustrates the rocky road traveled by Chinese companies carrying out the policy that former aid projects now be sustained by enterprises, not by aid. It also foreshadows some of the conflicts that are likely to arise for China's less experienced investors, when they "go down to the countryside" in Africa.

Former Minister of Agriculture, Dr. Sama Monde, recalled that his government was delighted at Complant's interest. "We thought for any investor to come at that time, it would be a boost, send the right signals. Magbass was in a rebel stronghold. The rebel leader Foday Sankoh was from that area. If we could get the Chinese there, it would be good economically and politically." They moved quickly to finalize the project, something that would later come back to haunt them.

George Guo, who became the managing director of Magbass, told me that he had first seen the complex late in 2002, when he was asked by Complant to check out the feasibility of the renovation. "The farm was empty. The factory was almost fully destroyed. Everything that could be moved was gone." he recalled. When the rebels took over the area in 1993, the Chinese managers left. Rebel leader Foday Sankoh was from the area, Guo told me. "His people tried to keep the factory going. They asked the workers to run it, and they did, for one season. But it was too hard, and then the rebels moved on. There was a power vacuum, nobody was in charge, and the local people began to take things. When I visited, there was the mill, a small housing compound, some very heavy things that they couldn't move, but everything else was gone, it was totally empty. Complant had successful experiences running sugar companies in Togo and Madagascar [also former aid projects], but it was nothing like this. You can imagine." It took Guo two years to rehabilitate the complex, with the help of Chinese experts, local workers, and cane stock imported from their Togo operation. "Every year it gets better," Guo told me. "Maybe next season we will make a profit."

Magbass provided a lot of benefits for the country. In the high season, the complex had the capacity to employ up to 1,500 people from the district of Tonkolili, a rare opportunity for paid work in the hinterland. Several hundred skilled people found permanent jobs as electricians, plumbers, carpenters, and clerks, and local people reported that they had acquired new skills.[27] The top jobs at Magbass were held by about thirty-three Chinese staff, although in 2007 the factory sent six of the more senior local employees to China for training, to support a planned reduction in the Chinese staff.

But basic wages were low. The contract signed with the government stipulated that Magbass would respect the country's labor laws, but that they would set wages based on "the lowest wage standard in the region."[28] In 2006, the second full year of operation, participants in a focus group organized for a World Bank study said that the Chinese paid only $1.62 per day. This was actually higher than the $1.26 paid by local farms, but the youth in the focus groups reported that they were being asked to pay "tips" of about $18 to land a position at Magbass.[29]

After a series of strikes in the third year, Complant raised wages to about $2.19 per day. "Now the workers are happy," K. B. J. Conteh, vice-president of the Sierra Leone Labour Congress told me. "During the production season, some will earn 300,000 leones [$101] a month." When I asked him about wildcat strikes at Magbass, Conteh elaborated: 'Formerly there was thieving, even on the managing board. Now, there is no thieving. It is too difficult. They employ a security company. The people were saying: if you don't want us to thieve, pay us better. That was the whole problem," Conteh said. The people had expectations of those days returning. As an aid project, the Chinese had a clinic and a doctor who treated local villagers. They supplied housing for local workers. They were more generous with bags of sugar for the local chiefs. But "those who are here now, they are businessmen. These Chinese have come to find money."

Sierra Leone's Ministry of Foreign Affairs negotiated the right for Magbass to export nearly 6,000 tons of raw sugar to Europe duty-free, under the Everything But Arms initiative, earning scarce foreign exchange for the country. ("This is big for us," Sama Monde, the former Minister of Agriculture, told me with some pride, "to be exporting an industrial product to Europe from the third world.")

But there were strains at Magbass. In early 2007, the Nobel-prize winning organization Médicins Sans Frontiers complained that runoff from the Magbass complex and its hundreds of workers ran straight into the Rokel River, contributing to an outbreak of cholera.[30] Some landowners argued that the sugar company had a responsibility to provide more social benefits for the community. And local people were deeply concerned about their government's having agreed to give the Chinese company another 1,000 hectares of land.[31]

In December 2008, on my way to a meeting at the Ministry of Agriculture, I passed a man addressing a group of farmers milling outside the deputy permanent secretary's office. Later, I learned that this delegation represented some of the landowners from the villages near the sugarcane plantation and factory at Magbass. The next day, the farmers were still there, and I eventually met with them. A landowner from Rochain village explained to me, "We have come to tell the government what we want: schools and scholarships for the children, medical facilities, water supply, and roads. *The Chinese should do that*. They should also clear farms for the landowners." Another farmer cut in: "It is forbidden to cut sugarcane without their permission! You will go to prison, even though the land was taken without our consent."

The villagers were asking that the Chinese be better corporate citizens, invest in social development projects, deliver social services that the local government was failing to provide. But they were also concerned about their land. The Chinese managing director, George Guo, told me bluntly: "This farm needs to run at 12,000 metric tons of sugar to be economical. This year we were at 9,000 metric tons. *We need to expand the farm area*. This is in the lease contract." But who spoke for the landowners? Who agreed to give up land for the expansion, and with what compensation for local villages? Who was actually receiving the rent paid annually for the land by Complant?

One of the landowners, who was also a senior civil servant in the Ministry of Agriculture, told me that they were genuinely concerned about the expansion: "We are afraid now that all of our villages will have to move. We have our ancestral areas there, our cemeteries where our grandfathers are buried, our loved ones. We don't want to lose them. The Chinese think the government is the owner of the land all over the country, so they don't have to deal with the landowners."

When I asked the former minister Sama Monde about the landowners' complaints, he sighed and replied: 'The landowners are telling me that land is the last inheritance they have. It's like taking a child away from their mother. My tribe doesn't put so much premium on land." He admitted that they had moved quickly to get the new lease signed, concerned that Complant might change its mind. They had asked the village councils to establish a committee of landowners. But perhaps they had not consulted widely enough on the expansion. However, he continued, the responsibility for providing the land *does* lie with the government. According to the constitution, the state can requisition land by eminent domain, with compensation.

"We guide the process so that the villages are left intact, with most of their farms," he told me. "We leave a two-mile perimeter around each village. But these people always want more. I'm not saying they don't deserve more. But the landowners committee has to be responsible. The land lies fallow for years because they don't have the wherewithal to develop it." He suddenly looked tired. "For the last three years, I have been to Magbass nine times. President Kabbah even went once. It has all been negotiated. Most of the payment for the extension of the land has been made. The landowners committee has signed off on it. The Chinese are paying an annual rent to the landowners – it will soon be more than $150,000. By our standards, these figures are good. But now there are family squabbles and politics at play."

M. A. Tarawalla, the newly elected representative from Tonkolili District, explained to me: "What is happening now is complicated. The Chinese pay the rent to the government, then it goes to the landowners committee, which is dominated by the Sierra Leone People's Party, and from there to the villages. But since the election there are now *two* landowners committees, the second is allied with the All People's Congress. They don't trust each other. And now both have come to Freetown."

George Guo added to this when I spoke with him. "Before the election we had finalized a deal with the landowners' committee, through the Ministry. We had worked out compensation for the economic trees.[32] We started work. But after the election, some of the villagers came out to stop the work. In their minds, the agreement was with the former government. Now, with a new government, they think there should also be a new landowners' committee. But now the situation is calming down," he added.

Politics was clearly involved. But different understandings about the complex social requirements of land rights had cropped up early in the history of Magbass. In 1980 a ministry official warned his superiors that the Chinese at Magbass wanted to "start surveying the area without awaiting the usual agreement with the local heads in the area. A move of this nature will certainly kindle trouble."[33]

In project files archived from the 1970s, I came across eviction notices sent to the Chinese aid teams in Sierra Leone. A letter from local landowners at Makali Station said, "May this give notice of our intention to sue these Chinese farmers for Criminal Trespass." The local landowning family at the Rolako station wrote to demand compensation for the use of the Rolako hill after the Chinese left. "When the Chinese were here they were not paying for the hill too, but the working was nice with us but since the Chinese left here the working is not well with us," they said.[34] Most of the problems involved rents that were not being paid by the government. Since Magbass *was* paying, perhaps this time it would be different, if the villages could ensure that government and their committee actually distributed them fairly.

"In the north," George Guo told me, "there is only Magbass." As the goose that laid the golden eggs, Magbass was caught up in the 2007 election. Candidates flung charges against the politicians who had made the original agreement. Those from the winning party tried to revisit the arrangements made by the losing party. "What if Magbass closes again?" I asked Conteh, the union leader. "No one else will come," he said flatly. "Magbass is the only industry there. It is the duty of the government to set things right."

I remembered the parting comments of the high-level civil servant, a native of the Magbass area: "When our parents were farming on that land they could educate us, send us to university, but since they came in 1977 and took our land, no one can say: *That is the house I have built. That is the child I have educated.* I have been to China. I went on a seminar for one month. I saw how they are judiciously managing their resources. They are very careful there. We would not like them to come here and exploit us."

The view from the new Chinese embassy on Signal Hill embraces the rusted zinc rooftops and the sun-faded buildings of Freetown. Distance softens the squalor and poverty, and the pockmarks of bullet holes in the buildings below. Vultures circle lazily on the warm updrafts. In the evening, waves of bats explode from the city's remaining trees in search of night insects. At the end of our conversation, the Chinese ambassador, Cheng Wenju, told me: "The project is still at an early stage. We believe it will be successful. But if they want to make the project succeed," he continued, "there needs to be understanding from the government, from the people."

Some months later, after I returned to Washington, I saw a notice that Complant had sold its interest in Magbass and its three other African sugar projects to Hua Lien, a private Chinese leather company.[35] After many decades, the Chinese government was finally giving up responsibility for keeping these aid projects alive. It was not clear how profitable Hua Lien would find its investment. As we will see now, many Chinese were well aware that it would be difficult to profit from their involvement in rural Africa.

Not a Good Chew on the Bones

As the tale of Magbass makes clear, the risks of investment were not small for all concerned. Not every Chinese entrepreneur will have to manage the challenges of a post-conflict environment, but in other respects the Magbass saga shows how the triangle of interests – African governments, local landholders, Chinese investors – are likely to clash. The fate of Chongqing Seed Corporation's venture in China's neighbor Laos – like much of Africa, a land-locked, relatively sparsely populated, and very poor country – provides another cautionary tale.

In 2004, the Chinese newspaper *People's Daily* reported on a Chinese project in Laos that intended "to lease overseas farmland to solve the food problem."[36] The Chongqing municipal government was going to set up a 5,000 hectare "agricultural park" to produce hybrid rice in Laos. They planned to import 10,000 Chongqing workers. Both governments offered supportive tax policies and preferential loans to bolster the project. "Through cooperating with countries with abundant water and soil resources and exporting labor force and advanced agricultural technology, China expects a win-win result for both sides," a senior official in Chongqing's Municipal agricultural bureau said.

But four years later Chongqing Seed Corporation's deputy general manager Huang Zhonglun told *Reuters* that they had "given up on Laos."[37] Huang explained their decision. "The system there doesn't have any leverage over farmers, so labour is not very efficient. But we can't send Chinese workers to plant there. They charge a lot for land rent, and there's no irrigation infrastructure so we have to rely on the rainy season." Companies like Chongqing are likely to find very similar conditions in Africa, where farmers (as in Sierra Leone) generally resist the kind of weeding and leveling Chinese farmers expect to do in their paddies. As we saw in Chapter 9, Chongqing planned a different model in Tanzania: working with existing farmers as outgrowers, who would be able to choose how much work and how much reward they wanted to seek.

In denying reports that China planned to make a major push for large-scale acquisitions of overseas farmland, a Ministry of Agriculture official commented, "As [grain] prices rise, offshore farming projects might become profitable. But so far, companies operating them [are] still struggling to repay their investments."[38]

Going global in Africa would be a challenge, as Xia Zesheng, a director of China State Farm Agribusiness Corporation, pointed out. Many of China's agricultural investments and development projects in Africa had problems: "low economic efficiency, great risks, a shortage of funds, difficult conditions, and difficulty maintaining benefits. Some enterprises that are implementing agricultural projects in Africa are walking with difficulty... China–Africa agricultural cooperation is by no means 'a good chew on the bones.' "[39] But despite this, many individual Chinese were being persuaded to try their luck overseas.

As I was preparing to travel back to Africa in 2007, I received an email from a friend at the Rockefeller Foundation. She sent me a newspaper article that claimed thousands of Chinese farmers were settling in dozens of "Baoding villages" around Africa. Do you know anything about these, she asked me. I did not, but I tried to find out.

Liu Jianjun's "Baoding Villages"

In 1996, the story goes, a Beijing-based engineering company recruited eighty workers from Dingzhou, a town in the Baoding area, to help build a dam along the Zambezi River in Zambia. They saw the vast lands (which looked idle to them) and rich agricultural potential. When their two-year contract was finished, the Dingzhou workers decided to recruit their families and relatives to buy land in Zambia.

Baoding native Liu Jianjun was appointed the head of the Hebei province Bureau of Foreign Trade Promotion in 1999, and he heard about the Dingzhou farmers. By then, or so Liu Jianjun contends, the farmers had formed a small Zambian colony of some 380 people. Hebei was suffering from the impact of the 1997 Asian economic crisis, and Liu decided to promote African migration as one solution.

Like European migration into Africa and the lands of new settlement, Asian migration overseas has a long history. Chinese economic migrants populated many of the countries of Southeast Asia beginning in the fifteenth century. Singapore is almost entirely Chinese, of course, while ethnic Chinese make up 26 percent of the population in Malaysia and about 14 percent in Thailand. In Africa, Chinese migration began in the nineteenth century with Chinese miners, plantation workers, and traders who settled in Mauritius, Madagascar, and South Africa as early as 1821. By the 1950s, the thousands of Chinese living in Madagascar had established more than 1,600 Chinese shops. More than 20,000 Chinese were living in Mauritius by then, nearly 3 percent of the population, and more than 4,000 in South Africa. In the late 1980s, as noted earlier, the isolated apartheid government also invited a number of wealthy Taiwanese families to invest and settle in designated regions of South Africa.[40]

Few of this wave of Chinese set out to be farmers, unlike Japan's experience with early out-migration. Late in the nineteenth century, pushed off the land by the higher taxes and restructuring of the Meiji Restoration (1868–1912) a wave of young Japanese ventured out of their cramped island. Because of restrictions placed on Asian immigration by the United States and other wealthy countries and their colonies, they headed to the independent countries of Latin America. Some worked on the coffee plantations of Brazil, others in the sugar plantations of Peru. Most eventually saved enough money to buy small farms, and they grouped together, establishing modest agricultural colonies. They planned to return to Japan one day, dressed in the "golden brocade" of wealth, but fewer than 10 percent ever did.[41] Today there are some 1.5 million people of Japanese descent living in Latin America. The grandson of one Japanese settler, Alberto Fujimori, would eventually become President of Peru. He was given a nick-name by Peruvians: "El Chino" – "The Chinese."

Suspended during the strict emigration controls of the Maoist period, migration from mainland China has started up again, accelerating in recent years. Chinese settlers in Africa are resuming the diaspora pattern. The farming area of Baoding in Hebei province, less than three hours by train from Beijing, may illustrate these recent migrants' experience and the factors that drive it.[42]

By 2007, Liu Jianjun had left the government and was bringing multiple delegations of Hebei farmers on trips to Africa. He founded the China Baoding Africa Business Council to negotiate agricultural investments and the resettlement of Chinese farmers.[43] A flamboyant promoter, fond of dressing for interviews in African garb, Liu presented wildly optimistic accounts of his successes. The original Baoding village in Zambia was so wealthy, he reported, that they sent home remittances of more than $9 million during the Chinese New Year of 2002. Liu sometimes claimed that 15,800 Baoding farmers had moved to Africa; other times he said "7,000" or "maybe 10,000." Between 400 and 2,000 Chinese were now living in each of twenty-eight "Baoding villages" in seventeen African countries, he told one reporter.[44] Perhaps, he said, people found them hard to find because he had located the Baoding villages far from cities, to keep them distant from urban violence and "tribal conflicts."

I tried to find the fabled original Baoding village when I was in Zambia in 2008. First, I asked Li Qiangmin, the Chinese ambassador. "We have also heard about this," he said, shaking his head. "I have gotten so many emails, even phone calls, from China. Some Chinese companies have investments in agriculture in Zambia, like China–Zambia Friendship Farm, but we don't know anything about these 'Baoding farmers'."

At Zambia's Ministry of Agriculture, I asked Imataa Akayombokwa, director of agriculture, about the mysterious, wealthy Baoding farmers. "This is a fairy tale," he told me. "There is nowhere on the Zambezi where 380 Chinese farmers can be settled without causing a serious displacement of local inhabitants. Someone is trying to create an impression that Zambia is ready to accommodate Chinese farmers in large numbers, which I can safely say is not true."

Li Qiangmin and Imataa Akayombokwa were not the only people to be skeptical about the mythical Baoding villages. In August 2007, a blogger on a Chinese-language website devoted to issues of China in Africa, africawindows.com, issued a challenge: "Baoding Farmers: Where Are You?" He asked Chinese living in Africa to do their own investigations. Could anyone find a "Baoding village"? Chinese living in fifteen countries, including Kenya, Uganda, Cameroon, South Africa, Sudan, Libya, Ethiopia, Zambia, Mozambique, Rwanda, Ghana, Gabon, and Angola, reported that they could not find Baoding villages in their countries.

People were suspicious in particular about Liu Jianjun's claim to have been allocated more than 500 square kilometers of land in Uganda, an area twenty times the size of the Chinese territory of Macao. Liu claimed that he would use the area, near Lake Victoria, to develop a private, multifunctional East Africa Free Trade Zone, with 10 million *mu* (over 600,000 hectares) allocated to farming. Yet in November 2008 Liu Jianjun surprised people with a press conference in Beijing announcing the official signing of the agreement. Ugandan President Museveni sent a high-level delegation of ten people; the Ugandan ambassador attended. Perhaps most importantly, the economist Hu Deping, son of Hu Yaobang (former secretary-general of the Chinese Communist Party), gave a speech at the signing. Hu was deputy head of the All-China Federation of Industry and Commerce, but, like his father, he was also a high-ranking officer in the Communist Party and a classmate of Chinese President Hu Jintao. This convinced many of the skeptical Chinese bloggers that Liu Jianjun and his Baoding villages may have had more official support than it seemed on the surface. Perhaps, as Tang Xiaoyang suggested to me, this was a way for the government to experiment, without being visibly in the lead, another example of "crossing the river by feeling the stones."

If Liu Jianjun represented the private face of Chinese agricultural resettlement in Africa, Li Ruogu, the outspoken president of China Exim-bank, came to represent its public face. In September 2007, Li Ruogu spoke to an audience at a meeting on the planned rapid urbanization of the steeply picturesque city of Chongqing along the Yangtze River. Millions of farmers would be displaced, he warned, but his bank was ready to offer full support, including "capital investment, project development and product-selling channels," to Chongqing's displaced farmers, to help them go to Africa.[45]

Some reports of Li Ruogu's speech quoted him as saying that Chongqing's labor exports would really "take off" if the government could convince Chinese farmers "to become landlords overseas."[46] Li's office later said he had not really used the word "landlords," a point that may seem immaterial, but which is important for Chinese views of their role in Africa. In 1950, the victorious Communist Party dispatched thousands of work teams to break up the landlord system and rapidly redistribute the farms to China's poor peasants. Perhaps a million or more landlords and "rich peasants" who had held 80 percent of the land died at the hands of Party cadres and vengeful peasants. For decades to be called a "landlord" was a vile insult, or worse, and that history still resonates for many who grew up in the years after 1949.

Whether as landlords or not, the idea that Chinese farmers might *settle* in Africa, with state support, was deeply worrying to many in Africa. The number of Chinese that have recently migrated to Africa remains a mystery, with wildly different estimates. In 2006, for example, Michael "King Cobra" Sata estimated that Zambia had 80,000 Chinese, while the Zambian government claimed the number was closer to 3,000. The longstanding Chinese communities in Mauritius, South Africa, the French island of Réunion, and Madagascar had significant longstanding Chinese communities, close to a combined total of 100,000 at the end of the twentieth century. As I noted in Chapter 5, some estimate that anywhere from 300,000 to 750,000 mainland Chinese have migrated to Africa since the early 1990s, with perhaps a third in South Africa alone.[47] Everything I have seen leads me to believe the figure of Chinese who have actually *settled* permanently in Africa over the past decade or so (as opposed to moving back and forth as traders or working for a Chinese company) to be less than 750,000. Yet no matter the number, many in Africa would agree with Sama Monde, the former Minister of Agriculture in Sierra Leone, who told me: "Our country is small. We are uneasy with the idea of them coming to settle."

The competition posed by Chinese farmers selling in African markets was also a concern. I met Cecilia Makota, national coordinator of Zambian Women in Agriculture, by chance at the Zambian National Farmers Union (ZNFU) headquarters, where she is a board member. Feisty, loud, seventy-nine years old, and dressed for the cool rainy weather in a combination of knee-high Wellington boots, a cotton dress, and a man's suit jacket, she stood out in the foyer of the building. We agreed to meet the next day at her office in Lusaka.

Mrs. Makota told me that a Chinese delegation came to talk to the board of the ZNFU in 2001 about investing in agriculture and helping the small-scale farmers emerge from subsistence. She asked what their vision was, and they replied (she said), "we will use them as laborers, this will generate income, then with this finance they can start their own economic activities." She told them: "this seems to me to be exploiting people who are already overworked. What our women farmers need is animal draft power, tools, finance to secure inputs. *That* would be their springboard to emerge from subsistence."

Then, she told me, "the president of the Zambia National Farmers Union, Guy Robinson, said: 'Mrs. Makota, these people are here to talk about investment.' I said, Dear Mr. President. We know these Chinese investors, there is no level playing field. They are mechanized. They sell their produce very cheap in our market because they use very cheap labor. I have visited some of their farms. Their vegetables grow enormously big. They use human feces!" She shuddered. "We would prefer them to sell wholesale, and leave the retail market to local people."

The issues raised in this chapter are not likely to go away. As food prices rose after the millennium, so rose investor interest in land, something many African countries still have in relative abundance. Indeed, many African governments have welcomed foreign investment in agriculture. Some of Zimbabwe's displaced white farmers moved to Zambia, Mozambique, and Nigeria to set up farms. The land squeeze in China and the underdevelopment of African agriculture create both demand and supply. What is the impact likely to be?

Chinese techniques could still be adopted by African farmers, making more intensive use of existing farmland. Chinese farmers could take on the risks of experimentation, providing models of more intense production, encouraging a natural technology transfer through imitation. Competition with Chinese farmers might sharpen local skills and upgrade existing practices. The agro-technical demonstration projects described in the previous chapter are designed in part to help make this happen, with their emphasis on demonstration and training. Some Chinese investors plan to work with local smallholders as outgrowers: the aid-supported Chongqing Seed Company in Tanzania, for example. Others who are investing purely for profit (Magbass, today) believe it would take too long to bring smallholder skills up to the necessary level. This provides a possible entry point for cooperation with other donors.

But, on the other hand, access to land is central to the well-being of poor farmers. Vast areas may seem to be waiting for development, but what appears to be untouched bush is often providing important economic and social benefits for local communities, particularly those with poor soils and systems of shifting cultivation that depend on long fallow periods for the land to recoup its nutrients. Customary land tenure rules are often unclear or still changing in many places. Land-related corruption and local abuse of power can all too easily deter progress. African governments (and their civil societies) need to protect the rights of local communities to say no – or to seek adequate compensation and rents when investors, Chinese and others, come calling. Failing this, more African countries could end up like Zimbabwe at an earlier point in time, or South Africa, with displaced and unemployed rural citizens migrating to the cities, while prosperous minority farmers occupy vast stretches of land. The historical record here is not encouraging, and the weak governance in much of Africa makes the current land rush worrisome.

CHAPTER 11

Rogue Donor? Myths and Realities

Oil-rich Angola is a country deeply cursed with natural resources – a tropical paradise laced with landmines and hemorrhagic fever, bauxite and gold. Angola also features as one of the prime exhibits in the chorus of condemnation about China's engagement in Africa. We start this chapter with a closer look at this relationship. Unpeeling its many layers can lay bare some of the myths and realities of China's engagement in Africa.

First, a brief history. Angola's war for independence became an East–West conflict after Portugal abruptly gave up power in 1975. The Soviet Union and Cuba stepped in to support the new socialist government. The United States and apartheid South Africa aided the rebels. With the end of the Cold War, Angola's proxy struggle morphed into a fight for control over blood diamonds, natural gas, and oil. The death in battle of the sixty-seven-year-old rebel leader Jonas Savimbi in 2002 finally allowed Angolans to end more than forty years of war and limp toward something resembling normalcy.

The Angolan government financed the war with a shadowy system of off-budget accounts that sometimes sloshed with oil revenues and sometimes ran dry. Over the years, the once Marxist leadership grew wealthy on a toxic diet of oil money and kickbacks from weapon sales. "Corruption is widespread throughout society," the IMF wrote in a report leaked to the press.[1] Ten out of every fifty infants born in Angola died before reaching their fifth birthday.

As the war drew to an end, Angola was badly behind on its debts. They owed more than two billion dollars to the Paris Club, the nineteen wealthy creditor nations that meet informally to decide on bilateral debt issues. But they also owed more than eight billion to other creditors, some (such as a group of Russians) even shadier than the Angolan government itself. These moneylenders were clamoring for payment; some tried to seize government assets outside the country.

Enter China. The story that follows has some of the flavor of the classic 1950 film *Rashomon*, in which an encounter in the woods is retold, very differently, through the eyes of each participant.[2] The conventional wisdom goes something like this. After the war, the IMF and the West decide to clean up Angola. The IMF insists that Angola improve oil revenue transparency and open its tangled accounts for inspection. Backed into a corner by 2004, the Angolans are about to agree, when China steps in, offering Angola billions of dollars of aid. Flush with cash, Angola turns its back on the IMF, taking China's offer, which comes with no strings attached. "Angola is avoiding pressure to clean up corruption thanks to aid from China," concludes a typical news item.[3] Reports on China in Africa rarely fail to mention this cautionary tale. It is always obvious who plays the villain.

Rashomon is a film about truth and perception. Let us complicate this simple tale by telling it again, from a different point of view. In this story, José Eduardo dos Santos, Angola's president since 1979, begins using the state-owned oil company Sonangol as a "cash cow" to finance the war, political payoffs, and other state expenses. By the end of the war, Angola has taken out an estimated *forty-eight* oil-backed loans, nearly all arranged, very profitably, by respectable Western banks: BNP Paribas of France, Standard Chartered of the UK, Commerzbank of Germany, and so on.

The IMF tries to wean Angola off its risky diet of expensive short-term loans. They ask Angola to commit to a host of reforms. For example, Angola's April 2000 reform program contains forty-four conditions and benchmarks, including raising income taxes and liberalizing trade. If they keep on track for six months, they earn a seal of approval that could *then* make them eligible for debt rescheduling through the Paris Club, and international aid.

Angola negotiates at least four IMF programs between 1995 and 2004, but fails to stick with any of them. In 2001, with the war still ongoing, Angola again promises the IMF it will reform: create greater transparency in oil revenues, turn over customs management to a British firm (Crown Agents), reduce fuel subsidies, raise water rates, rein in borrowing, and privatize several money-losing enterprises.

However, Angola again fails the test – not only on the transparency issue (which the IMF agrees is improving but still has far to go), but on the other conditions, particularly its unwillingness to stop borrowing. The international watchdog group Global Witness estimates that between September 2000 and October 2001 alone, international banks provided Angola up to $3.55 billion in seven secretive, high-cost, oil-backed loans.

For a while the Paris Club continues to present a united front to Angola's attempts to get relief on its overdue loans. They want Angola to successfully complete at least *one* IMF program. But then in 2003 the Germans break rank, settling a debt reduction deal unilaterally. This allows Germany's companies to return to Angola, and Germany to extend new export credits. Meanwhile, the French bank Société Générale helps Angola out with *another* large oil-backed loan for $1.15 billion.

Now we see China enter this crowded room with an oil-backed loan of its own. The $2 billion line of credit offered by China Eximbank in 2004 is unlike most other oil-backed loans, however. First, it costs less. Angola, a relatively high-risk country, has been borrowing at a premium of up to 2.5 percent over LIBOR (the London Inter-Bank Offered Rate, the benchmark interest rate for international finance). The Chinese loan is at LIBOR plus 1.5 percent. Second, it allows repayment over seventeen years, with a grace period, far longer than the European banks' normal term of four or five years, without any grace period. "This is not foreign aid," a senior Chinese diplomat tells me. "But it *is* a very good rate."

As we already know, the most unusual feature of the line of credit is that it will be used entirely for infrastructure projects, the same oil-for-infrastructure model Japan used in China three decades ago.[4] Four decades of war left Angola's road system "in a shocking state of disrepair," a World Bank team reports.[5] Bombs destroyed more than 300 bridges. Rural roads and farming fields were planted with landmines. Urban infrastructure "dramatically deteriorated," streets were "in a state of virtual collapse." Raw sewage spilled out of the open gutters during heavy rains and ran down the alleys of chaotic shanty towns. Angolans badly need infrastructure.

To get aid funding from the West, their leaders are being asked, not unreasonably, to end the cozy system of oil finance that served as a substitute for a proper budget and a central bank all these years.[6] The negotiations with the IMF did not even involve a loan. "We are not looking for money," the Angolan Finance Minister said about the IMF. "We are looking for a seal of approval that we can present to creditors in order to reschedule our debt."[7]

This alternative story is more complicated, but this brings it closer to reality than the first story, with its shadow play of good and evil. The first story also misses something else. There is a second act. Within months of the Chinese loan, a group of Western banks, including Barclays and Royal Bank of Scotland, arrange an even *larger* oil-backed loan for $2.35 billion, at 2.5 percent over LIBOR, with repayment over five years. "We were very excited," one of the bankers told a trade magazine, which called the deal "the largest oil backed transaction in the entire history of the structured trade finance market."[8] In late 2005, Angola asks the French group Crédit Agricole (Calyon) to arrange another $2 billion loan; sixteen international banks participate. The United States Eximbank provides credits of $800 million for Angola to buy six Boeing aircraft.[9] China Eximbank makes two more oil-for-infrastructure loans, of $2 billion and $500 million, between 2005 and 2007. Again, out of the crowd, only the Chinese loans make headlines.

Then, to the surprise of the Paris Club, the Angolans decide to simply pay off their debts with their booming oil revenues. Transparency improves, even without the conditionality of the Western donors: with technical assistance from the IMF, the Angolans finally begin to publish a fairly complete account of their oil revenues and expenditures on the website of their Ministry of Finance.[10] There is still enormous corruption, but roads, clinics, and schools are being built. Although some believed the Chinese loans arrived in cash, they were wrong, as we have seen from our study of China's unusual resource-backed infrastructure loans.[11] A second look reveals that it was *Western* banks that gave loans without requiring transparency, and *Western* companies that exported Angolan oil, providing cash flows for the ruling party. The Chinese deal was not without risks, but it was also revolutionary for the country: for the first time, there was a hope that some of Angola's riches might actually be translated directly into development projects.

Akira Kurosawa, the talented director of *Rashomon*, left his viewers pondering what really happened in the woods that day. They were sure of only one thing: the story was no longer so black and white, with a villain, a victim, and a clear verdict of *guilty*. Today, media headlines have shaped the conventional wisdom about China's engagement in Africa: "European Investment Bank Accuses China of Unscrupulous Loans," "Chinese Aid to Africa May do More Harm than Good, Warns Benn," "Wolfowitz Slams China Banks on Africa Lending," "How China's Taking Over Africa, and Why the West Should Be VERY Worried."[12] In varied form, these accusations reappear even in official reports from the European Parliament, for example.[13]

Is China the "rogue donor" we see in these headlines? In the rest of this chapter, I explore this last set of myths and realities in a Kurosawa-like manner, digging down into the most frequently repeated stories about China's aid and engagement on the continent.[14]

"Chinese Aid: It's All about Oil/Minerals/Resources"

Well, not really. Versions of this story spill across countless reports and media stories. A journalist writes that China is financing "hospitals, water pipelines, dams, railways, airports, hotels, soccer stadiums, parliament buildings – nearly all of them linked, in some way, to China's gaining access to raw materials."[15] China is trying "to establish firm control over Africa's natural resources," a Berlin meeting concludes.[16] The European Parliament argues that China's interest in Africa "seems confined to resource-rich (or "resource-cursed") countries, bypassing a large number of other African nations."[17] Even a World Bank study said "most Chinese government funded projects in Sub-Saharan Africa are ultimately aimed at securing a flow of Sub-Saharan Africa's natural resources for export to China."[18]

Relatedly, some assume that the infrastructure being built by Chinese companies across the continent follows a grand strategy: roads and railroads leading directly from mines and oil wells to ports, to ships, to China. From *The Economist*: "China is building a lot of infrastructure – presumably to help it procure all the natural resources its firms are gobbling up."[19] This belief in the "grand strategy" also underpins assumptions that the investments of Chinese companies are masterminded by Beijing, with the single-minded goal of channeling natural resources back to China.

It is easy to understand why these beliefs have arisen. China *is* very active in Africa's resource-rich areas, and the interest in these resources is very real. But the notion that aid is offered mainly as a quid pro quo exchange for resources, or that the Chinese are *only* interested in countries with resources ignores several facts. As Figure 11.1 makes clear, China gives aid to *every single country* in sub-Saharan Africa that follows the One China policy.[20] Even relatively wealthy South Africa and Mauritius are recipients of China's aid. Chinese officials point to this as a contrast between their approach and

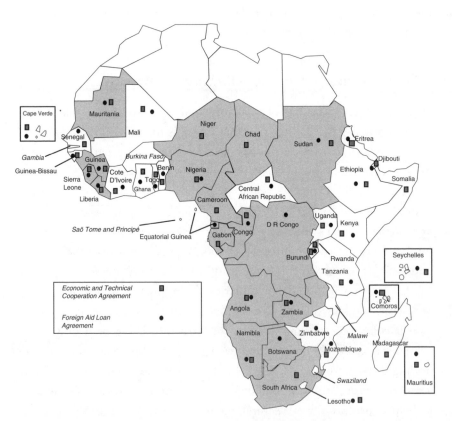

Fig. 11.1. China's Aid Agreements in Sub-Saharan Africa, 2006–2007

Note: "Resource-rich" countries are shaded. Countries recognizing Taiwan are in italics.

that of the international aid system, where some countries are more favored by the traditional donors.

Second, China does not seem to give more official development aid to countries with more resources. Grants and zero-interest loans from the Ministry of Commerce are distributed fairly evenly across countries for the kind of projects that won political kudos. As we have seen in earlier chapters, the Eximbank's concessional renminbi loans are given to credit-worthy *countries* with the ability to pay. In these countries, China Eximbank simply extends a line of credit and waits for a capable government to propose projects: sewers in Mauritius, for example, or public housing in Botswana. In less creditworthy countries, concessional loans can be given for *projects* that can earn money to repay the loan (a Kenyan cement telephone pole factory; a mobile telephone network in Eritrea or Sierra Leone).

On the other hand, as we have seen in Angola, the Democratic Republic of Congo, and Equatorial Guinea, China Eximbank has provided large, very competitive, but still commercial-rate loans to finance infrastructure, with payment guaranteed in oil (or other resources). Doesn't this show that *it really is all about oil* (you can substitute copper, iron ore, timber, etc.)?

Resources matter, but China's "mutual benefit" approach is about generating *business*. African resources are definitely part of this. But there is much more. Exports, for example: the Chinese exported more than *$50 billion* worth of equipment, consumer goods, and machinery to Africa in 2008. China's single largest Africa investment to date has been Industrial and Commercial Bank of China's purchase of 20 percent of South Africa's Standard Bank for $5.6 billion. Contracts for infrastructure are hugely important. In 2007 alone, Chinese construction companies earned revenues of *$12.6 billion* and signed contracts for more than *$29 billion* in Africa.[21] China's telecom firm Huawei, constructing phone systems across Africa, earned more revenues than any other Chinese engineering company world-wide in 2007.[22] As a Nigerian diplomat told me in Beijing: "The Chinese are trying to get involved in every sector of our economy. If you look at the West, it's oil, oil, oil, and nothing else."

Before commodity prices slumped in the global recession that began in 2008, many non-Chinese companies were also signing large mining con-tracts. In Madagascar alone, Canada's Dynatec signed a contract for $2.5 billion, and Rio Tinto (a major mining company founded in the nineteenth century by Europe's Rothschild family), for $650 million.[23] But the Chinese saw that Africa's infrastructure needs were enormous, just as China's were as they launched their "Four Modernizations" decades ago. Buried in debt, African countries had no way to finance these needs. They might jump at the chance to develop their resources both to secure and to repay the loans. Following the path carved out first by Japanese companies in India, and later in China, Chinese engineering companies would get the contracts that might earlier have gone to the German company Siemens, or the San Francisco-based Bechtel.

If you look again from this angle, you can understand why the loan for Ghana's Bui Dam was backed with cocoa export revenues deposited into an escrow account with China Eximbank. It is not that the Chinese are desperate to lock up Ghana's premium cocoa beans. But these resources allowed Ghana to guarantee repayment, enabling the country to move forward on a long-desired (if environmentally controversial) electric power project.

What about the assumption that the infrastructure China is building goes mainly from the mines to the ports, like the colonial infrastructure of old? A major project still under discussion for Gabon *would* involve building a port linked to a railway cutting deep into a pristine area of the central African rainforest to reach the mother lode of iron ore. Chinese companies have proposed a similar project in Guinea (and in Brazil), although the financial meltdown that began in 2008 put all of these on hold.

Yet the Angola projects do not fit this mold. China built hospitals, irrigation systems, and roads – but Angola's oil is found miles away from the coast, deep offshore. Likewise, the resource-backed projects in the DRC involve everything from universities to railroads. The reality is that Chinese engineering companies are rebuilding Africa, and they are doing it nearly everywhere. The World Bank team that used newspapers and internet sources to study China's infrastructure projects in Africa (they did not actually visit any African countries) said that most of them were aimed at securing flows of resources back to China.[24] Yet the list of projects they provided, comprising roads, bridges, sewer systems, and power plants built with Chinese finance in places such as Botswana, Kenya, Rwanda, Madagascar, Mauritius, and so on, do not map out to some kind of master plan for resource extraction.

Finally, what about the notion that the Chinese state is directing all of this from Beijing? Researchers who have investigated this question, rather than assuming the answer, continually report that Chinese companies have considerable freedom to operate.[25] A Japanese survey of Chinese oil companies operating overseas found that they were under no obligation to ship their oil back to China. They could sell it wherever the price was highest.[26] Likewise, the Chinese investors in Zambia's Chambishi copper mines were not required to send their copper output to China. As a Chinese mining supervisor told British researcher Dan Haglund: "China is so far away, expensive to get to. I would rather just deliver the money."[27]

"China Enables Sudan to Get Away with Murder in Darfur"

Yes, but China is changing. The pariah government of Sudan under Khartoum-based President Omar al-Bashir is China's most controversial partner in Africa. The relationship between China and Sudan was a central focus of human rights activism in the period leading up to the 2008 Beijing Olympics. Mia Farrow, George Clooney, and other celebrities targeted China as the main "enabler" of a situation labeled genocide by the United States. Their story was necessarily simple: China's purchase of Sudanese oil enabled Sudan to buy Chinese arms, which were used against the Darfur rebels. Further, in the words of one fund-raising appeal that crossed my desk in 2009, "China has thwarted international action to end the violence in Darfur which has enabled the Sudanese government to get away with murder."

Sudan has a history of conflict. A decades-long war between the north and southern Sudan came to an end with a peace agreement in January 2005, and a partial UN arms embargo that aimed to keep weapons out of the south. As that war was winding down, two rebel groups in the arid Darfur region, the Sudanese Liberation Army and the Justice and Equality Movement, started to attack government police and military outposts, drawing attention to their own history of neglect. Khartoum retaliated viciously, bombing villages in rebel-held areas in Darfur, a vast region the size of France. They provided arms and support to the brutal "janjaweed" militias, nomads that have swept into villages, burnt families alive in their huts, held women as sex slaves, and displaced millions of innocents.

What has China's role been? Mainly investment, arms sales, and political cover. Since Sudan's oil began blasting out of the ground, China has given relatively little official development assistance to Sudan.[28] But Chinese companies are the main players in Sudan's oil fields, seconded by countries such as Malaysia and India (all three provide considerable investment). For years, China purchased the bulk of Sudanese oil, although in 2006 Japan was Sudan's largest oil customer.[29] Beijing helped Sudan build its own arms factories, supplied the bulk of Sudan's small arms imports, sold military aircraft to Sudan and energetically defended its military cooperation with Sudan's government. There is some evidence that arms supplied by the Chinese to Khartoum have been used in Darfur, although Beijing claims its arms transfers to Khartoum are legal and follow the terms of the UN embargo.[30]

China also supported Khartoum diplomatically, insisting that the United Nations get Khartoum's permission before sending UN troops to help police Darfur. They watered down or abstained from Security Council resolutions to impose economic sanctions. "We don't believe in embargoes," a senior Chinese official said. "That just means that the people suffer. From a practical consideration, embargoes and sanctions can't solve problems, just like armed invasion cannot solve problems."[31] China's business-as-usual engagement with Khartoum continued, even as a chorus of criticism swelled. "There may be profit to China in turning a blind eye to all of this," a reporter for *The Economist* concluded, "but there is no honour."[32]

Then China began to change. During a state visit to Sudan in early 2007, Chinese President Hu Jintao held "frank" discussions with Sudan's President Bashir. "Usually China doesn't send messages, but this time they did," China's UN ambassador said, emphasizing: "it was a clear, strong message."[33] Sudan had to agree to the UN proposal to send joint UN–African Union peacekeepers to Darfur. China "never twists arms," the ambassador said, but Sudan "got the message."

China appointed a special envoy for Sudan, persuaded Khartoum to allow the hybrid peacekeeping force into Darfur, and supplied a contingent of some 300 military engineers for the peacekeepers. The Brussels-based International Crisis Group remarked optimistically: "Beijing is shifting in Sudan from being an obvious part of the problem to a significant part of the solution."[34] Andrew Natsios, the special envoy to Sudan appointed by former US President Bush, agreed: "China in my view has been very cooperative. The level of coordination and cooperation has been improving each month." As Brookings Institution scholar Erica Downs noted, the combination of China's quiet "good cop" approach to Sudan complemented the "bad cop" bluntness of the United States.[35]

If China had agreed to the West's sanctions efforts, would the Darfur crisis have been easier to resolve? Possibly, but (unfortunately) unlikely. Sanctions may be a potent expression of moral outrage. They may be the only acceptable response to an unfolding tragedy, short of going to war. But researchers suggest that despite their popularity, economic sanctions *usually do not work*.[36] Think of the impotence of decades of sanctions applied against Fidel Castro's regime in Cuba, for example, or against Iraq to force Sadaam Hussein to respect UN Security Council resolutions that followed Iraq's failed 1991 invasion of Kuwait. In the few celebrated cases where they were effective (South Africa under apartheid, Rhodesia under the last white ruler, Ian Smith) they were used in situations where governments had domestic business allies that were painfully aware of their international standing and its impact on the economy and wanted to re-engage with the world. This is hardly true in Sudan.

Furthermore, China was not the only outside player. Russia was Sudan's major supplier of military aircraft and conventional weapons.[37] Democratic Japan and India purchased Sudan's oil, as did Malaysia. A Canadian company, La Mancha Resources, was the main foreign player in Sudan's non-oil minerals and mining.[38] And, surprisingly, the website of the British official trade and investment agency encouraged British companies to consider Sudan as a location for business, noting the country's "sound and liberalised macro economy."[39]

By 2009 it was clear that even if it once had been in control, Khartoum probably no longer held all the keys to unlock the door to a negotiated peace. The sources of violence had expanded, now including bandits, intertribal fighting, and at least four major rebel groups, several of whom refused to attend peace talks or agree to periodic ceasefires.[40] One Darfur rebel group sent a thousand fighters to attack the African Union peacekeeping force sent to protect the people of Darfur, killing twelve peacekeepers.[41] And the violence had spread out of Darfur. An attack by a group of Darfur rebels (backed by Chad) brought the war to the gates of Khartoum, while a Chadian rebel group (backed by Sudan) swept across the desert to attack Chad's capital, N'Djemena.

Was China a scapegoat in the campaign to end Darfur's tragedy, as many in China believed? "China has been vilified over Sudan on the basis of inflated expectations about what they could do. Russia is in fact more significant in terms of being an aggressive ally," Alex de Waal, a Sudan expert, Harvard researcher, and program director at the Social Science Research Council, told me. But China did have influence, and was very slow to employ that influence. They needed to be pushed, and people in Beijing needed to start talking about the pros and cons of their policy of non-interference. Without the threat to the Olympics, Hu Jintao may not have been so keen to ensure that Khartoum "got the message." But, at the same time, the tactical decision to focus the Darfur advocacy campaign on China had a cost. It removed pressure on the United States, France, and other governments to mount a sustained, high-level, mediation effort, the only way a complicated crisis like Darfur is ever likely to be resolved.[42]

"China Hurts Efforts to Strengthen Democracy and Human Rights in Africa"

Less than you probably think. "We don't attach political conditions. We have to realize the political and economic environments are not ideal. But we don't have to wait for everything to be satisfactory or human rights to be perfect." China's special envoy for Africa, Liu Guijin, outlined China's stance on aid and engagement thus.[43] Much as with the Sudan case above, the conventional wisdom is that Chinese support enables rogue regimes to prevail despite international opposition. "China's growing foreign aid program creates new options for dictators who were previously dependent on those who insisted on human rights progress," the respected non-governmental organization Human Rights Watch argued.[44]

China's engagement in Zimbabwe under the oppressive rule of Robert Mugabe is central to this belief. Others point to Angola, Sudan, or even Equatorial Guinea. But to analyze realistically the impact of "the China option" on democracy and human rights in Africa we need to answer two questions. First: what would the situation be like without China? Has China's entry changed the playing field significantly, as Human Rights Watch suggested? Second (and more controversially): have political conditions attached by other donors to foreign aid been effective in improving human rights and democracy in Africa? Is China's lack of political conditionality thus rolling back a wave of progress?

Let us tackle the first question. China's rise has clearly given dictators additional financing options. But *finance* from China differs little from the other options readily open to most African dictators. As we saw at the start of this chapter, before and after China got involved, European banks, and even the United States Eximbank, gave loans to Angola. Chevron and Shell financed oil in Nigeria and Exxon Mobil in Equatorial Guinea. Other global mining corporations – Rio Tinto and the Australian–UK conglomerate BHP Billiton, for example – are significant sources of investment and revenues for dictators in places like Guinea and Zimbabwe. Although these firms are increasingly sensitive to sustained advocacy campaigns in places like Sudan or Burma, few yet apply any general democracy or human rights litmus test to their investment decisions.[45] African dictators in most resource-rich countries *do* have options. They were never very dependent on the champions of human rights. Beijing fits in with these other amoral financiers quite comfortably.

Surely *donors* have begun to withhold aid from countries with poor records on human rights and democracy, you might believe. While improvements have been made since the Cold War, the record here is also disappointing. Oil-rich Cameroon, ruled by the dictator Paul Biya since 1982 and ranked by the NGO Freedom House as one of the fourteen worst countries in Africa for political and civil liberties, received aid worth almost $1.7 billion in 2006.[46] Freedom House gave Ethiopia, another donor favorite, a dismal five out of seven on both civil and political liberties (with one being best). Between 2004 and 2006, donors gave Ethiopia $5.6 billion in aid. When we move from rhetoric to the reality of aid, it seems that in the less publicized cases the Chinese and the traditional donor community are not so far apart. Columbia University economist Jeffrey Sachs, a champion of increased aid to Africa, commented in 2006: "The idea that aid should be heavily conditioned with political conditions was a mistake. The best way to end conflict is to end poverty."[47]

Consider the World Bank. Like China, the World Bank lends to dictators without imposing political conditions. As *The Economist* noted, for most of its history, aid from the World Bank "added to the spoils by which feckless governments stayed in power."[48] Many believe that the World Bank and the

International Monetary Fund now demand good human rights records and use conditionality to promote democracy in their borrowers. After the Cold War ended, the World Bank did begin to impose governance conditions, but only on corruption, *not* on democracy or human rights.[49] The Bank has not offered new loans to some of Africa's worst governed countries, Sudan and Zimbabwe, in recent years. But officially at least, this was not due to their abuse of democracy and human rights, but because these countries fell into arrears on their Bretton Woods debts.[50]

It would be odd if the Chinese, who do not practice democracy at home, required it of others. Yet Chinese official views on democracy in their own country have softened in recent years. "We have to move toward democracy," Premier Wen Jiabao said in 2007. "We have many problems, but we know the direction in which we are going."[51] This strategy of political evolution rather than sudden democratization allows the Communist Party to remain in power, of course. It is also used to justify continuing restraints on freedom of the press, speech, assembly, and other political and civil rights. But the belief in the overriding importance of stability also influences Chinese responses to political turmoil outside.

In 2007, when the leaders of Burma (Myanmar) violently suppressed peaceful protestors, Beijing sent an envoy who reportedly urged the leaders of Burma to move more rapidly toward democracy.[52] They backed efforts by the United Nations to mediate in the Burmese crisis. The point here is that Beijing identified the *lack* of progress on democracy with political and economic instability. Similarly, the Chinese ambassador in Sierra Leone joined the other foreign ambassadors in an effort to persuade the incumbent president, defeated in the 2007 elections, to step down peacefully.[53] But when Kenya erupted into violence in early 2008 following a disputed election, an editorial in the *People's Daily* commented: "Western-style democratic theory simply isn't suited to African conditions, but rather carries with it the root of disaster."[54]

Not surprisingly, some African leaders with questionable credentials as democrats support China's refusal to impose political conditions: "I think it would be wrong for people in the west to assume that they can buy good governance in Africa," said Meles Zenawi, Prime Minister of Ethiopia. "Good governance can only come from inside; it cannot be imposed from outside. That was always an illusion. What the Chinese have done is explode

that illusion. It does not in any way endanger the reforms of good governance and democracy in Africa because only those that were home-grown
ever had a chance of success."[55]

Serge Mombouli, ambassador from Congo-Brazzaville to the United
States told National Public Radio that China provided tangible things,
while the West pushed for something less tangible: better governance.
"We need both. We cannot be talking just about democracy, transparency,
good governance. At the end of the day the population does not have
anything to eat, does not have water to drink, no electricity at night, industry
to provide work, so we need both. People do not eat democracy."[56]

"Chinese Support Kept Robert Mugabe in Power in Zimbabwe"

If only it was this simple. Zimbabwe was long one of Africa's most publicized
pariah regimes. Zimbabwe's aging dictator Robert Mugabe sanctioned brutal
gang violence against opposition parties, condoned the kidnapping and torture
of human rights activists and encouraged a chaotic land redistribution that
delivered many farms into the hands of politicians who coveted them, rather
than the landless poor. When the West imposed sanctions on his government,
Mugabe brushed this off. "We have turned East, where the sun rises," he
proclaimed, "and given our backs to the West, where the sun sets."

I traveled to Zimbabwe in September 2009. Outside Harare, we drove
past empty, brown, mismanaged farms shiveled by drought. A tenuous
power-sharing arrangement had not stopped the cycle of violence in the
countryside. One evening, I visited friends for a quiet dinner. As the sun
set, frogs and insects ratcheted up their evening sounds. Soon it was
dark. We sat on their verandah drinking South African wine. The
peacefulness contrasted with their tales of the brutality still being
inflicted by supporters of Robert Mugabe and his ZANU-PF party. As
human rights activists, our friends and many others remained vulnerable. Millions of Zimbabweans were living in exile, but the new unity
government was optimistically hosting a mining promotion. The next
day, I slipped into the convention. Hundreds of foreign businessmen
packed the hall, listening skeptically to Mugabe pledge to respect property rights and the rule of law.

My hosts believed that China's diplomatic and military support helped prolong their country's crisis. But they also repeated something I heard often in Harare: much of the conventional wisdom on China's economic role in Zimbabwe is right, a lot is wrong. First, *Chinese aid* has not been a lifeline to this rogue regime. Rumors of billions in Chinese aid turned out to be wishful thinking on Mugabe's part.[57] China's official development aid to troubled Zimbabwe has been even more limited than to Sudan.[58] Perhaps symbolic of this, where the Chinese financed a new presidential residence for Sudan's president, they supplied only blue Chinese tiles for the roof of Mugabe's Eastern-style residence (Malaysia supplied the remaining materials). In 2006, China Eximbank gave Zimbabwe a short-term export credit of $200 million for fertilizer and pesticides. These inputs could have been doled out to the regime's supporters but the credit itself was on completely commercial terms, with a platinum concession mortgaged as collateral. It would be difficult to document secret cash transfers, if they existed. Yet close observers of the situation such as the *Economist Intelligence Unit* report that ties between Zimbabwe and China "do not appear to have been translated into hard cash."[59] As another sign of this, before the regime finally abandoned the Zimbabwe dollar in 2009 inflation had risen to 79.6 billion percent, and the government had issued a $100 trillion note.[60] Governments bankrolled by outside powers do not need to print money at rates like this.

In 2005, after the US and the EU imposed an arms embargo and targeted sanctions on Mugabe and his cronies, Chinese companies and the Zimbabwe government signed eight wide-ranging agreements covering irrigation, roads, power plants, telecoms, and electric power.[61] These were not terribly friendly agreements. For one contract, the Chinese telecom firm Huawei reportedly demanded a 20 percent cash down payment, plus security in tobacco, chrome, or platinum exports.[62] An electricity project signed between the Zimbabwe Electricity Power Authority (ZESA) and China National Aero-Technology Import and Export Corporation (CATIC) required a down payment of $3.6 million, and tobacco exports as security.[63] Some projects started up – exporters delivered goods, engineers began construction – but most stalled or were suspended when Zimbabwe failed to hold up its end of the deals.[64] "It now appears our government negotiated in bad faith," a senior government official told a reporter.[65] Zimbabwe's unreliability, rather than any Chinese reticence, kept the Chinese from deeper investment in a deteriorating situation.

Despite this, several major Chinese foreign investors did conclude deals, although fewer than reported by the media.[66] Sinosteel paid more than $200 million for Zimasco, a private ferrochrome producer formerly owned by Union Carbide.[67] The China–Africa Development Fund became a shareholder in Sinosteel's chromium-processing venture. Other deals that went forward were far smaller than originally announced. For example, China Jingniu Group was widely reported to have launched a "$400 million" glass production and processing complex in Kadoma, in the center of Zimbabwe. They actually began prudently with a single much more modest project, a $13 million plate glass factory.[68]

Chinese traders are a growing presence in Zimbabwe's markets. People in Zimbabwe widely believe rumors that a series of forced evictions that destroyed shanty towns and informal markets in May 2005 known as Operation Murambatsvina ("drive out filth") were done to protect Chinese traders from informal sector competition. The Catholic archdiocese of Bulawayo concluded that the evictions were actually done to punish the urban-based supporters of the opposition Movement for Democratic Change, and to push newly arrived rural migrants back into the country-side where they would be kept from finding common cause with the opposition, and be "utterly reliant on government-controlled food aid for survival."[69]

What about military support? The US and the EU refused to allow their own companies to sell arms to Zimbabwe after the failed 2002 elections. But Chinese companies were not so constrained. Zimbabwe bought twelve Chinese trainer jets and other military equipment on credit in 2004. China's military exporters also seem to have secured their loans through mineral concessions.[70] Despite the country's dangerous turmoil and economic instability, Chinese companies also supplied Zimbabwe with at least $28 million in conventional arms between 2005 and 2007.[71]

Just after Zimbabwe's disputed March 2008 elections, a Chinese freighter, the An Yue Jiang, was returned to China after unions in South Africa and neighboring countries refused to offload the cargo. Four of the thirty-six containers contained ammunition and rocket-propelled grenades (RPGs) intended for trans-shipment to landlocked Zimbabwe.[72] Later that year,

United Nations experts monitoring arms transactions in the Democratic Republic of the Congo reported that fifty-three tons of ammunition had been flown to Zimbabwe from the DRC in August.[73] Many people assumed that at least some of this cargo was from the thwarted Chinese shipment, although Jason Stearns, the leader of the UN monitoring team, denied that the UN team had found any evidence for this. "It's possible, but we have no clues," he said.[74]

How might these military deals have helped keep Mugabe in power? Mugabe's thugs did their brutal work with clubs. They did not use fighter jets or RPGs. But to forestall disgruntlement that could lead to a coup, Mugabe needed to ensure that his military had enough toys. Soldiers guarding without ammunition, a grounded air force – these signs of hollowing out would have been unacceptable to the military. Arms also allowed Mugabe to keep the threat of even more violent suppression a reality. "If only that ship had been carrying food and medicine," a Kenyan newspaper editorialized. "How much more legitimate China's interests in Africa would have looked."[75] But we can speculate that there is probably more.

In 2004, the orders for Chinese jets placed by Zimbabwe's military went behind the backs of Zimbabwe's parliament and its government procurement board. Arms exports are notorious for lucrative commissions and kickbacks. Let us imagine how this might have worked in Zimbabwe by looking at the system as it apparently worked in the UK.

In 2003, a whistleblower accused BAE Systems (formerly state-owned British Aerospace, the UK's major weapons producer) of keeping a multimillion pound slush fund to supply gambling trips, sports cars, prostitutes, and yachts for the Saudi royal family. For nearly twenty years, he said, this fund greased the wheels for tens of billions of pounds in sales of British Hawk jets and other armaments in a barter arrangement known as the "Al-Yamamah" deal. (Saudi Arabia paid for the jets in barrels of oil.) In 2006, the British government abruptly terminated a criminal investigation into the scandal by its own Serious Fraud Office, on the grounds of national security.[76]

There is no public evidence regarding corruption in Chinese arms sales in Zimbabwe, but the pattern of scandal illustrated above suggests that arms deals often rest on expectations of illicit enrichment of various kinds. These patronage opportunities could also be useful for someone like Mugabe trying to keep himself in power. Mugabe's two main constituencies are the military (including ex-combatants) and rural farmers. This military boost would have complemented Chinese credits supplied for agricultural machinery and fertilizer.

But we also need to keep in mind that the finger pointed, with justification, at the Chinese obscures the fact that other companies remained active in Zimbabwe. For instance, Ukraine supplied Zimbabwe with weapons worth $12 million between 2005 and 2007. The vice-president of a US tobacco company that remained in Zimbabwe commented: "All kinds of deals [are] going on down there to pay bills...I don't like the situation but we have a factory in Harare to run."[77] Two British banks, Barclays and Standard Chartered, retained branches in Zimbabwe.[78] A French bank provided a loan for fuel imports, using Zimbabwe's nickel resources as a guarantee; a South African mining company loaned Zimbabwe $100 million as part of a platinum investment.[79] In 2008 Anglo-American announced plans to invest close to $400 million to develop a new chromium mine.[80] (Responding to criticism, Anglo-American sent out a press release: "The responsible development of the Unki mine will create a long-term viable business which will be important to the economic future of Zimbabwe for years to come." This might easily have been uttered by a Chinese spokesman.)

As happened with Sudan, we can also see signs of a change in China's support of Zimbabwe. Beijing has consistently indicated that it will follow the lead of African organizations like the African Union or the regional Southern African Development Community (SADC) on Zimbabwe. In July 2008, China joined Russia in vetoing a UN Security Council resolution that would have imposed an arms embargo and targeted sanctions on Zimbabwe's leadership. (South Africa also opposed the measure.) All three took the stance that Chapter VII of the UN Charter authorized the Security Council to impose sanctions only in situations that threatened international security. Zimbabwe's troubles were domestic, they maintained.[81]

Early in 2009, as a cholera epidemic and economic chaos spread Zimbabwe's tragedy further beyond its borders, South Africa declared that it would withhold aid until Mugabe agreed to form a national unity government with the opposition. China's Foreign Ministry spokesman followed by publicly expressing "concern with the current constant deterioration of the economic and political situation in Zimbabwe," and urging the formation of a government of national unity.[82] Shortly after this, Mugabe and opposition leader Morgan Tsvangirai formed a national unity government. Soon the two rivals were each claiming credit for securing a very large Chinese loan for their bankrupt government.[83] China Eximbank *was* interested in a major resource-backed credit, a Chinese official told me, but they were struggling to convince skeptics in Beijing that the new Zimbabwe government could now overcome its long history of defaults on Chinese loans.

In Zimbabwe and Sudan, the Chinese were opportunistic. They took advantage of situations of stark, government-sponsored repression that have horrified and mobilized many to protest. They could have done much more, much earlier, to exercise their growing ability to be a persuasive and responsible stakeholder. To their credit, the US, Britain, and their allies played an active role in putting pressure on Mugabe. Yet we would do better in pushing China to change if we had more evidence that our own tactics, including sanctions, embargoes, and even armed intervention, as in Iraq, resulted in social justice, stability, and prosperity for the people our governments mean to help.

"China is Making Corruption Worse"

Probably not *worse,* but definitely not better, either. China has partnered with Mauritius, South Africa, and Botswana, Africa's best-governed countries. But as we have seen, China has also partnered with Angola, Equatorial Guinea, and the Democratic Republic of Congo, countries regarded as some of Africa's most corrupt. Is Chinese engagement making corruption *worse?*

Researching corruption is always difficult, for obvious reasons: how often will people readily admit the existence, let alone the size, of kickbacks and embezzlement? Even the annual rankings released by Transparency International rely on *perceptions* of corruption rather than hard data. That said, concerns about China, Africa, and corruption fall into three categories. First, huge new sums of money from China might be tempting targets for embezzlement. Second, Chinese firms with looser attitudes about corruption might cheat, winning contracts away from more honest companies. Finally,

China's willingness to lend in countries without imposing broad conditions about transparency might make those countries turn away from other financiers with stronger safeguards. This could halt hard-won gains in fighting corruption or even spur a "race to the bottom" as some have warned.

The first concern is, fortunately, almost entirely misplaced. Many do not understand how Chinese loans usually work. For instance, Stephen Muyakwa, a civil society activist in Zambia, told a newspaper that China's loans "could fuel corruption, as African governments are free to use the money as they wish...You can't just hand over a blank cheque to the Minister of Finance and assume everything will be okay."[84] Civil society in Nigeria worried that some $4 billion in Chinese "aid" (actually investments and export credits) on the table in 2006 and 2007 would "end up in the ruling party's coffers."[85] An opposition member of parliament in Malawi asked what had happened to the "40 billion kwacha" ($280 million) she had heard that Malawi's president "brought back" from China "in a suitcase" after a state visit. (Malawi's Minister of Finance explained to her that he "did not bring a bag full of money from China" but rather a pledge of $280 million in aid that would be used over three years for development projects.)[86] Purchases of state assets would provide cash to governments, but in the Chinese system of aid and resource-backed infrastructure loans, as we saw in Chapter 5, their governments would likely never lay eyes on the money, unless of course some of it surfaced via kickbacks.

Aid so tightly tied to goods and services from the donor country has many critics, for good reason, as I have noted earlier. But a development loan that is managed entirely by the lender is not necessarily a bad thing, as some Africans will attest. "The Chinese knew very well that if the funds had been handed over to the government of Madagascar, they would have been used for totally different ends," a Malagasy journalist said, explaining why the Chinese were constructing a sports complex themselves in Madagascar.[87] Pointing to the parliament building built by China, a resident of Guinea Bissau said: "In a corrupt country, it's better to come and build something big like this. At least this is something we can see. Other countries give us money, but the politicians eat it, and so people like me never see any of it."[88] These people understood that China's system of aid and development finance does not work the way a loan works from the IMF or the World Bank, or for that matter, from a private bank: deposited straight into a government account, from where, despite safeguards and crossed fingers, it might simply disappear. Government revenues from oil and natural resources exported to the West are exposed to the same risks.

The fact that China Eximbank loans are not usually disbursed to the borrowing government in weak states helps reduce corruption. Some journalists write that China does not demand "proper accounting of funds."[89] That is not what I have seen. There is plenty of accounting – all done in China, where the money stays (Chapter 5). "The Chinese have proved much more relaxed about what their billions are used for," said one journalist. "Much of it goes straight into the pockets of dictators."[90] Ironically, this is also wrong: the Chinese actually appear *more* concerned about their billions being well used. This is not out of the goodness of their hearts, but because these billions can essentially be used twice: to finance the import of oil or resources, *and* to pay Chinese construction companies to build infrastructure.

Keeping the money in China and using escrow accounts filled by receipts from natural resource exports as guarantees, means that there is also a little less opportunity for the kind of wholesale embezzlement sadly common in some resource-rich countries. For instance, former Nigerian dictator Sani Abacha was alleged to have skimmed off as much as $20 billion from oil revenues into offshore accounts during his five years in power. In the wake of the multibillion minerals-for-infrastructure deal in the Democratic Republic of the Congo, Congolese worried that their government would "line its own pockets" with Chinese funds instead of investing in infrastructure.[91] But on learning more about the Chinese approach, a BBC reporter investigating the Congo deal concluded that the money would actually bypass the government's "sticky hands." Congo's rich resources might actually begin to pay for its development.

What about the second concern, the potential for padding of expenses, sweetheart deals, collusion and bid-rigging, and kickbacks? Are these now likely to increase? Seventy-nine percent of China Eximbank loans in Africa are given for government infrastructure investments, a sector notorious for corruption and kickbacks in most countries.[92] In 2009, for example, two American companies, Halliburton and Kellogg Brown and Root, paid $579 million in fines after being found guilty of breaking US laws by paying bribes to Nigerian officials between 1998 and 2006 in pursuit of construction contracts worth $6 billion.[93] If Chinese engagement leads to an increase, it will be on top of levels that some Western firms have already helped make sky-high.

That said, Chinese companies overseas do not enjoy a good reputation. Transparency International's 2006 Bribe Payer's Index ranked Chinese companies twenty-ninth from the top, out of thirty countries surveyed, for their propensity to bribe overseas. We also have some harder evidence from the World Bank's effort to enforce integrity in the bidding and procurement for Bank-financed projects. In January 2009 the World Bank announced that it was blacklisting four major Chinese firms after almost six years of investigation into multiple allegations of bid rigging in tenders for Bank-financed road projects in the Philippines.[94] These four were the first Chinese firms to be sanctioned for corruption on World Bank projects, joining 339 other companies and individuals sanctioned since 1999, including twenty-five British firms, and eleven from Sweden.[95]

China State Construction Engineering Corp., debarred for eight years by the World Bank, is China's single largest contractor operating overseas. China Road and Bridge Corporation, debarred for six years, had already won contracts worth almost $400 million for at least fifteen World Bank projects in various countries. China Geo-Engineering Corporation, debarred for five years, was ranked in the top twenty-five of overseas Chinese companies in 2007. These are major Chinese companies. Their blacklisting may speak to the general acceptance of these practices among Chinese firms, and the real dangers this poses to efforts to reduce corruption on infrastructure contracts.

The US action in Nigeria outlined above was an unusual conclusion for an anti-bribery case. Wealthy countries have only recently agreed to crack down on their own companies' bribery overseas, through legislation such as the OECD's Anti-Bribery Convention (1997), itself based on the US Foreign Corrupt Practices Act of 1977. From China we see mixed messages on the issue of corruption overseas, leading to the conclusion that it will be some time before these practices are even made illegal, a necessary first step.

On the one hand, during his 2006 visit to Africa, Premier Wen Jiabao met with a large group of Chinese entrepreneurs in Zambia and laid down clear expectations about corporate governance: "Our enterprises must conform to international rules when running businesses, must be open and transparent, should go through a bidding process for big projects, forbid inappropriate deals and reject corruption and kickbacks."[96] China was also a sponsor of, and has signed and ratified, the UN Convention Against Corruption, which stipulates that bribery overseas be made a crime.

In June 2008, the Central Committee of the Chinese Communist Party included the prohibition of commercial bribery overseas in their work plan for anti-corruption legal reforms over the next five years.[97] A Chinese official reported that checks and balances and transparency characterize China's domestic bidding for aid projects: "The bidding evaluation committee is a group of experts who are each time chosen at random. Bribery is impossible, and bidding evaluations will not be influenced by personal relations. You can't join such a committee based on your own will. These experts have no prejudices against any enterprise. Evaluation is performed openly, fairly, and justly."[98] Still, corruption seems to exist. In 2006 China's Ministry of Commerce pledged to blacklist for at least two years companies implicated in bribery or collusion in the tender process for the supply of materials and equipment under China's foreign aid program.[99]

On the other hand, like many other export credit agencies, China's Export Import Bank (Eximbank) is not averse to funding contracts awarded under the kind of no-bid arrangements Wen Jiabao warned against in Zambia. In Japan, the corruption that accompanied a similar system created a societal backlash against corporate involvement in aid. This kind of pressure is unlikely to happen anytime soon in China. When queried in 2007 about his bank's policies on transparency, Eximbank's president, Li Ruogu commented: "In China, we have a saying: If the water is too clear, you don't catch any fish."[100]

Chinese views on corruption are shaped by their experience at home. Corruption is widespread in China and many other Asian countries such as Korea, yet it has not derailed economic development. Aside from the impact it might have on business, imposing economic sanctions or conditionality to combat corruption is seen as harmful to Africans because it hurts their opportunities for growth. Li Ruogu stated his views bluntly at a meeting of the World Economic Forum in South Africa: "We spend most of the time discussing issues such as transparency and good governance. And that would not help because they are part of a development process. I do not think that Britain was as transparent as it is today some 200 years ago, let alone the United States a hundred years ago."[101]

China does not require recipient countries to have good governance in order to receive its aid or loans. But will this non-conditional finance option from China roll back efforts to improve transparency and corruption? As with the arguments we reviewed earlier on democracy and human rights, this assumes that the rich world's multinational banks, oil companies, and aid agencies are now holding back their billions from the world's most corrupt countries.

This is not the case. True, several new, voluntary programs are trying to change the normative climate. Most importantly, the Extractive Industries Transparency Initiative (EITI) launched in 2003 has helped establish global standards for accountability. Yet it is natural resource exporting countries whose governments commit to EITI responsibilities. Companies have no independent requirement to "publish what they pay." The continued eagerness of Western banks and oil companies to do business in non-transparent, corrupt countries suggests that they are not waiting for governance to improve.

As for donors, a study published in 2008 by New York University economists Bill Easterly and Tobias Pfutze showed that donors were *still* giving an average of 68 percent of their aid to countries ranked at the bottom of the corruption scale.[102] Some donors (Greece, Australia, Portugal, Ireland, the European Bank for Reconstruction and Development, and New Zealand) gave more than 80 percent of their aid to the most corrupt countries. With examples like this from the West, it is difficult to point to China as the odd man out.

"Chinese Aid and Loans are Part of a System of 'Unfair' Subsidies"

True. OECD countries have reined in similar subsidies. Chinese President Hu Jintao's announcement in 2005 that China would provide developing countries with $10 billion in preferential loans and export credits heightened concerns about China's subsidized export credits. Europe, the US, Canada, and Japan used to regularly fight trade battles with each other using heavily subsidized export credits, or mixing official development aid with other kinds of credits.

Led by the United States, OECD members moved to level the playing field. Under the voluntary 1978 Arrangement on Officially Supported Export Credits, concessional export credits from OECD governments were supposed to be limited to projects that were not commercially viable: the construction of public goods like primary schools or health clinics. Members agreed to offer export credits for things like bulldozers, ships, or airport construction at standard commercial rates. This was done mainly for the benefit of the exporters, avoiding a race to the bottom, rather than recipient countries, which would pay more. This was a step toward untying aid, by separating it from the system of export promotion.

Under the Arrangement, members report their offers of export credits to the OECD. These offers can be challenged or matched by other members if they believe the offers violate the voluntary agreement. While the need to protect commercial concerns means that the system is not transparent to the outside world, it has, in theory, helped ensure that aid is used for non-commercial ends and that countries can select projects and goods that they need on the basis of price, technology, and quality, not subsidized credit.

As Chinese engineering companies ratchet up the competition for projects in Africa, and as Chinese exporters move into the aircraft and military markets formerly monopolized by European and American companies, many believe that their low bid prices on commercial projects are influenced by the preferential lines of credit available from the Chinese policy banks (China Eximbank, China Development Bank). There is no question that these subsidized loans do help, and they are clearly part of the portfolio of instruments rolled out to support the "going global" push. But their role should not be exaggerated. Most private Chinese companies active in Africa cannot get access to subsidized loans. At the same time, Chinese savings rates mean that finance in China is relatively low-cost, even for firms without access to preferential loans.

In some instances, Chinese engineering companies that are relatively new to a country will be directed by their home office to offer a cut-rate price as a "loss leader" simply to break into the market, often competing against other Chinese companies. In other instances, Chinese companies *are* simply more competitive. Their profit margins are slim, as I noted in Chapter 5. Many have been working in Africa for decades and know their market well. And their costs are far lower: a Chinese engineer earns about $19,000 per year, compared with a minimum of about $110,000 in Germany.[103]

A conversation among several Chinese researchers with experience in Africa gives a Chinese view on how their companies compare with those from the US:

> The USA has drilled oil in Africa for many years, but has not brought lots of benefits for African people. African countries are well aware of this. The US companies' bidding price for extraction projects is very high, and they make the costs as high as possible. Everything required for the projects, even mineral water and screws, is imported from the USA. Chinese companies costs are relatively low and relatively fair. African countries are seeking diversification in resource extraction. This provides China with an opportunity.[104]

China Eximbank and Sinosure are well aware of the evolving norms for export credits. Several years ago, the Chinese translated the text of the OECD Arrangement into Chinese.[105] Eximbank's website stresses that its export buyer's credits "generally" follow the Arrangement, even though China is not a member of the OECD. At the same time, the Chinese believe that companies in wealthier countries got a head-start with assistance from their governments, under rules that were changed before Chinese firms became global players. The United States' Eximbank was established in 1934; China's only in 1994. They are unlikely to agree to put their companies on a level playing field without spending a few more years learning how to "go global." This issue will continue to be a bone of contention.

"China Gains Business with Low Environmental and Social Standards"

True, but this may be changing, at least for China's policy banks. In 2006, European Investment Bank president Philippe Maystadt famously complained to the *Financial Times* that Chinese banks had "snatched projects from under the EIB's nose" with their lack of social and environmental conditions.[106] The Chinese are notoriously lax about labor standards, as I have noted throughout this book. Hydropower dams, concessions for tropical hardwood and large rainforest plantations, roads, and large-scale mining all pose risks for the environment in Africa. They also all require that people affected by the project be consulted, compensated, and properly resettled. As the case of the expansion of Sierra Leone's Magbass sugar complex indicated (Chapter 10), Chinese investors are way behind the curve on all of this. So are many African governments.

"China Lets Child Workers Die Digging in Congo Mines for Copper," charged one headline.[107] The article pointed out that private Chinese smelters in the Democratic Republic of Congo's Katanga province were buying copper ore from Congolese middlemen who collected it from children and others who dug in extremely unsafe conditions. One of those children was Adon Kalenga, a homeless, barefoot, thirteen-year-old orphan. Adon worked for a Congolese middleman, Patrick Nsumba, who paid him a flat rate of $3 a day to fill sacks with ore and wash them in a nearby stream. Nsumba said that Adon asked him for work; he needed money to buy food. "The conditions are too tough," he agreed. Private Chinese companies bought the ore from Nsumba. Neither party felt morally responsible for ensuring that it was produced under tolerable conditions. Moving beyond the harsh realities of poverty in Katanga province will require solving dilemmas much more complicated than simply enforcing labor laws.

That said, however, one of the most enduring critiques of Chinese engagement in Africa concerns exploitative labor practices. For example, a careful study of Chinese construction companies in Namibia found that they repeatedly violated local minimum wage laws and affirmative action training requirements, while failing to pay social security and allowances.[108] Complaints by African workers in Chinese shops, factories, and construction sites are legion, and it is not only African workers that have problems. In March 2008 in Equatorial Guinea, some 200 Chinese construction workers allegedly went on strike in the frontier town of Mongomo, leading to a violent clash with local security forces in which two Chinese were killed.

Part of the problem lies in Chinese ignorance of local labor regulations. To combat this, Mozambique translated its labor laws from Portuguese into Chinese. But more typically, Chinese companies in Africa apply the same low standards that have been common in many parts of China, particularly in the "town and village enterprises." These are also standards typical among smaller, local African employers. For example, the Namibia study also found that more than 80 percent of the small and medium-sized companies owned by Namibians failed to follow local labor laws. World

Bank researchers found that small informal factories in Africa frequently paid wages only a quarter of the level paid by large formal firms.[109]

Some firms get around their obligations to workers by giving contracts to local firms to provide temporary labor services, shifting responsibility to the broker to pay benefits required under local law. It is not only the Chinese who do this. Subcontracting is common practice among non-Chinese firms in the mining areas of Zambia, for example. As researcher Dan Haglund has pointed out, non-Chinese companies such as Mopani Copper Mines actually subcontracted far more Zambian workers under "unacceptably poor conditions" than did the Chinese company at the Chambishi mine.[110]

Are these practices simply exploitative? Participants in a Namibia focus group believed that Chinese employers in their country were "creating more poverty" rather than providing opportunities.[111] In Chinese shops, "women work long hours for only N$300 or 400 [$30–40] a month. What will a person do with that wage?" On the other hand, Chinese official toleration of many of these practices also reflects a stark difference in development models – what we might call the "trade union consensus" versus the "Beijing Consensus." The advice given by China's economic and commercial counselor to Namibia, Liu Kungyuan, reflected Beijing's perspective. China's own development success began with similarly low wages that allowed more people to find jobs, he said. "If you sacrifice on labour costs now for future generations, then Namibia will develop. Let people be paid lower wages now and attract more FDI and set up manufacturing so that the future generation will reap the benefits of the sacrifices."

Turning to the environment, Chinese companies are clearly implicated in illegal harvesting of old-growth timber and illegal fishing, and in obtaining concessions without regard to the rights of local communities.[112] In August 2007, China's State Forestry Administration and the Ministry of Commerce released guidelines that Chinese logging companies are expected to use abroad; these include an emphasis on consulting and compensating local communities. There are no sanctions for not following the guidelines, however, and without much civil society activism in China to hold Chinese companies accountable, progress will be slow here. In addition, ethnic Chinese companies from Malaysia, Taiwan, and Hong Kong are also active in these areas, which would create additional difficulties for any effort from Beijing to police "Chinese" firms. But since all generally ship their timber straight to China, the buck of environmental responsibility ultimately stops there.

Hydropower dams are at the center of much of the social and environmental critique of China's role in Africa. China's Eximbank has financed a small number of hydropower projects since the turn of the millennium: on the border between Benin and Togo (Adjarala Dam), in Congo (Imboulou), Ethiopia (Tekeze), Ghana (Bui), and Sudan (Merowe). Many others are under discussion. Sudan's Merowe Dam across the Nile is a bitter, and so far extreme, example of a problem project. In 2006, Sudanese police shot and killed several farmers during a protest over forced resettlement in arid conditions far from the lush banks of the Nile.

Over the years, global activists succeeded in stopping the World Bank and other aid agencies from financing major hydropower dams in poor countries. They argued that most large dams have social and environmental costs that planners fail to incorporate. Europe and North America built their hydropower dams before there were many concerns about resettlement and the environment. Rivers were dammed, salmon migrations permanently altered. From the Appalachian mountains of the Tennessee Valley Authority to the Alqueva mountains of Portugal, people lost their land and livelihoods. Some joined the exodus to the city slums. Others stayed, switching their oil lanterns to electric lights. Up to 70 percent of the hydropower potential in the wealthy West was exploited in the era when a dam was seen as a sign of progress, not a badge of social and environmental devastation.

Africa came late to the development of hydropower. It then ran headlong into rising concerns about environmental and social impact. Consequently, only about 8 percent of the continent's renewable energy hydropower potential was ever developed. A study led by Vijaya Ramachandran at the Washington-based Center for Global Development reported that 500 million Africans still rely on kerosene and firewood for light, cooking, and heating.[113] Even those connected to a grid suffer repeated power outages. In the Congo, they can expect more than 170 days with power cuts per year; in Tanzania, an average of 120. Only nine African countries have fewer than fifty days with power cuts each year.

"We have seen probably three decades now of extreme underinvestment in power projects in Africa," Ramachandran said.[114] The potential for hydropower is "enormous," she told an interviewer for the *Voice of America* radio program. "There are large rivers in central Africa which can be harnessed to provide a massive amount of power to multiple African countries." These are the projects now being targeted by big Chinese companies like Sinohydro. Peter Bosshard, policy director of the California-based advocacy group International Rivers, told the *Wall Street Journal* in 2007, "China is promoting dams around the world based on an analysis which doesn't recognize the true cost."[115] Is this still true?

At home, China has been on a steep learning curve on environmental issues and corporate social responsibility – part of President Hu Jintao's pledge to build a "harmonious society." In March 2008 China established a new Ministry of Environmental Protection, reflecting leaders' growing concerns about the impact of pollution, energy consumption, and global warming. China Eximbank published new guidelines for social and environmental impact assessments in July 2008, aligning the bank's approach with the central government's "Green Credit" policy, and including land rights and resettlement as new concerns.[116] The Chinese Academy for Environmental Planning began drafting environmental guidelines for Chinese companies involved in aid and overseas investment that same summer.[117] China Eximbank president Li Ruogu told me late in 2008 that his bank was now using European consultants, for example the Swiss subsidiary of the Finnish company Pöyry, for almost all of their final environmental impact assessments: "We do not hire Chinese agencies for these now. Foreign agencies are more credible. We do not want the environment to be an issue," he said. China Eximbank's multi-billion dollar agreement in the DRC required each project to spend 3 percent of the investment on environmental mitigation, 1 percent on community projects, and 0.5 percent on skills training for Congolese staff.[118]

In Washington DC, along the broad expanse of Pennsylvania Avenue, a few blocks down from the White House, a small team of corporate social responsibility (CSR) experts staff an office at the World Bank's International Finance Corporation (IFC). They help manage the process of publicizing and training banks in the "Equator Principles," a voluntary set of social and environmental principles agreed in 2002 that the IFC hopes will shape new norms for lending.

In 2007, the IFC and China Eximbank signed a memorandum of understanding to work together on these issues. Chinese banks and ministries were surprisingly eager to get training on the Equator Principles, which the IFC helped to translate into Chinese. "There is demand left and right, we can't fully meet it," one of the experts told me as we met for tea in the IFC's combined handicraft shop and café. "We never thought we would get this far. It's unprecedented."

The concept of social responsibility was still very new in China itself, let alone among Chinese companies operating overseas. "In the past ten or fifteen years," an experienced IFC mining expert told me, "Western companies have improved immensely. They now see their requirements for social responsibility very differently. But the Chinese still see CSR as building schools and clinics. They have no concept of the human rights core of these issues. It's a big gap. We are trying to educate them about these issues."

He told me about the controversial Ramu nickel concession in the South Pacific islands of Papua New Guinea (PNG), a joint venture between an Australian company and China Metallurgical Construction Company (MCC). The first Chinese to visit the area traveled up the Ramu River by dugout canoe, mosquitoes whining in their ears. They hired local men to cut a trail through the dense jungle to the mine site on a remote mountainside. Within three years, they had built Papua New Guinea's longest bridge, biggest wharf, a road, and a 135 mile slurry pipeline as part of a planned $1.4 billion investment.

The president of the Ramu joint venture, Luo Shu, is an engineer with an MBA from the University of Maryland. The company did not get off on the right foot. In early 2007, as national elections were heating up, fifty PNG workers went on strike to protest poor working conditions. The PNG Labour Minister, David Tibu, visited the site unannounced and declared that local workers were underpaid, sleeping in barracks filled with mosquitoes, their canteen "not fit for pigs." The toilets were so bad that workers were using bushes. "The Chinese developer does not seem to have any standards, and I will not allow my countrymen and women to be used as slaves," he told a local newspaper.[19]

Pushed perhaps by the Australian partners, the joint venture asked the IFC for help with corporate social responsibility, the mining expert told me in his Pennsylvania Avenue office. "The Chinese didn't understand that you need to engage with the community, get their permission. They are struggling with this. Their attitude was: we'll bring in jobs, build schools. They were out of their depth. They are desperately wanting to do the right thing. If we had gotten there earlier, we could have helped. The manager was definitely forward-thinking. She saw the value we could bring."

With advice from the IFC, the company decided to give 2.5 percent of the venture to landowner groups. They began to meet with local representatives and invest in community development: microfinance loans, rice projects, small business training. They hired a group of local university graduates and sent them to Beijing to learn Chinese. Environmental consultants were brought in from Australia and the US to evaluate the company's plans. Public relations consultants wrote newsletters and disseminated information, and the Chinese themselves underwent training on local culture.

In 2008, Wang Chun, the chief engineer, told a reporter: "Everyone has to understand the importance of the land to the people here. Our first two years here were very difficult, and we had many cultural misunderstandings."[120] The Chinese tried to work fast, to finish the project on time, using two twelve-hour shifts, typical in China. "But we understand that that model won't work here." The project fell behind schedule by almost a year. But Wang said this did not matter. "We are the young generation and we understand the international rules. If we don't follow the best world standards, China could suffer from the failure of this project. It would shut down opportunities for China in other parts of the world."

As China's state-owned companies move to develop global reputations, they may learn from experiences like this. MCC is planning to go public, with stock listings and disclosure requirements. Corporate social responsibility will help them avoid expensive reputational risks. Anglo-American and Rio Tinto, two major multinational mining companies now partnering with Chinese companies, announced in March 2008 that they had adopted high social, environmental, and governance standards and expected joint ventures with their Chinese partners to "maintain similarly high standards," adding that they were "happy to work with them to help them adopt these."[121] China's interest in partnering with firms that have more experience, better technology, or more assets makes these avenues of influence promising, as long as the global expectation for better social and environmental performance remains strong.

I thought of these complicated environmental and social challenges when I got an inside look into how it works in Sierra Leone. My Freetown hotel was also the temporary home for members of a timber company, waiting for the newly elected government to authorize the release of their bulldozers from containers in the harbor. They were confident that work would soon begin, since they had made the vice-president a shareholder in the venture. They planned to build the area's first road along a track where villagers still carried their goods to and from markets on top of their heads. They told me of their past experience logging the rainforest in Liberia, and their forays to the area where they would be logging the last remaining old growth rainforest in Sierra Leone. "The trees are enormous," they said, arms wide to show the girth of tropical hardwoods that may have started to grow in the early days of the colonial period. The company had contracts to ship the timber to China, not surprisingly, but the company cutting down Sierra Leone's rainforest was not Chinese: it was American.

Engaging China

Is China a "rogue donor," as pundit Moisés Naím argued in the pages of the *New York Times*? I do not believe so. China's rise in Africa is cause for some concern, but it need not evoke the level of fear and alarm raised by some who have condemned China's aid and engagement as destabilizing, bad for governance, and unlikely to help Africa to end poverty. Many of the fears about Chinese aid and engagement are misinformed, the alarm out of proportion. First of all, China's aid is *not* huge; the traditional donors give far more aid to Africa. China's export credits are much larger than its aid, but not as large as commonly believed. Their novel approach in Angola, the Congo, and elsewhere applies the system China learned from Japan: using very large credits, at competitive market rates, tied to Chinese machinery, equipment, and construction services, with repayment in oil or other resources. This is the essence of the "win-win" approach.

These credits are by no means risk-free. Debt sustainability is an issue, a concern that deepened as the global financial crisis washed over Africa. The credits are tied to Chinese goods and services, reducing choice. Although in Angola at least three Chinese firms bid on each project, it is not clear how transparent bidding will be elsewhere. Still, this approach provides a new opening for the construction of badly needed infrastructure. Chinese banks can act as "agencies of restraint" for African leaders beset by patronage demands. These agreements can directly channel mineral riches into development projects. This is a practical way to address the "natural resource curse" that plagues so many African countries.

The Chinese say: "to end poverty, build a road." The "Four Modern-izations" China launched in the 1970s emphasized infrastructure. They built roads, ports, and rural power plants, modernized agriculture, invited in factories. They experimented with different approaches: special economic zones, for example. China's "Beijing Consensus" may simply be about embracing experimentation (what works?) and avoiding easy certainties. The deals they offer Africa are based on similar deals Japan and the West offered China decades ago, and which the post-Mao Chinese accepted in the belief that they could also win from an approach that was not about aid, but business. Where the West regularly changes its development advice, pro-grams, and approach in Africa (integrated rural development in the 1970s, policy reform in the 1980s, governance in the 1990s, and so on) China does not claim to know what Africa must do to develop. China has argued that it was wrong to impose political and economic conditionality in exchange for aid, and that countries should be free to find their own pathway out of poverty. Mainstream economists in the West today are also questioning the value of many of the conditions imposed on aid over the past few decades. Exchanging views, rather than lectures, on lessons learned and approaches to aid and cooperation could lead to more useful engagement between China and the West.

Concerns about Chinese exports crushing African manufacturing are very real. Although Africa still represents only 4 percent of China's overall trade, this is 4 percent of an economic juggernaut. African wax print fabric industries in Nigeria, many based on an import substitution model with outmoded equipment and hampered by poor roads and "epileptic" electricity supplies, are rapidly going out of business. Yet some industries in some countries – leather, shoes and plastics, consumer appliances, for example – seem to be competing with Chinese imports. Indeed, these are the industries now attracting investment from China, even in Nigeria. The overseas economic zones Chinese firms are building in Nigeria and elsewhere in Africa are intended to foster Chinese invest-ment in African manufacturing, enabling China's mature industries to move offshore in groups. Contrary to popular belief, they are creating employment for Africans. There has been almost no attention in the West to the role African countries might play in attracting investment from these Chinese firms.

China's early aid to African industry and agriculture was not sustainable. Getting Chinese companies involved to consolidate the projects helped sustain the benefits in some instances, but not in others. The new "win-win" initiatives are only just starting, but we can see that Chinese companies have already served as industrial catalysts for some African firms, just as Japanese and Korean firms have done for decades in South and Southeast Asia. The flying geese model has a long way to go, but it has proven its potential, in the "miracle" environment of Mauritius, and even in the tough conditions of Nigeria.

On agriculture, I am less sanguine. African lands may seem empty, but signing over large tracts of land to foreign concessionaries without the informed consent of local communities is a strategy unlikely to end poverty in Africa, even if it does boost domestic food production. Patented hybrid seeds as the entry point for Chinese seed companies may help more modern farmers, but present risks to the subsistence farmers eking out a precarious existence in rural Africa. Using smallholders as voluntary outgrowers, as Chongqing Seed Company is doing in Tanzania, may be a socially and economically sustainable compromise. At the same time, however, out-grower systems shift many of the risks of farming directly onto the contract farmers. China's own rural development strategy focused first on land reform, then incomes for rural farmers, only much, much later opening up to foreign investment in agribusiness. Were more African countries to shift toward the land inequalities of South Africa, Zimbabwe, or even Brazil, it would be a tragedy.

As I was researching and writing this book, China was already changing rapidly, with Chinese leaders moving away from old alliances (Mugabe in Zimbabwe) and stepping into an unaccustomed new role as a mediator in Sudan. Chinese naval patrols were rescuing European ships in the pirate-infested waters off the coast of Somalia. New domestic pressures for corporate social responsibility and environmental and social protections were growing inside China. New laws were put in place for labor rights in China, new guidelines published outlining the environmental and social responsibilities of banks and forestry companies overseas. This is a practical move, even if these norms are not yet taken to heart. As China's state-owned companies move to develop global reputations, they are learning that corporate social responsibility will help them avoid expensive reputational risks.

The Chinese are many things in Africa: touring presidents delivering grand promises for partnership, provincial companies with very long names, huge global corporations, resource-hungry and profit-motivated. They are factory managers demanding long hours of work, tough businesswomen, scrap metal buyers, traders. They offer frank deals that they expect to work well for China, but also for Africa: roads, broadband, land lines, high-tech seeds. They bring aid workers: vocational teachers, agricultural specialists, water engineers, youth volunteers, and others who have come, as so many from the West have done, out of curiosity, a sense of adventure, or a desire to help the poor. And they have not just arrived on the scene. Some Chinese families came to Africa in the 1820s. Sino-Africans – Eugenia Chang, Jean Ping, Jean Ah-Chuen, Manuel Chang, Fay King Chung, and others – have served African governments as parliamentarians, finance ministers, and ministers of foreign affairs.

Their long history in post-independence Africa gives China legitimacy and credibility among many Africans. Arriving after independence, they never really left. The West simply did not notice the Chinese teams laboring upcountry building small hydropower stations and bridges, repairing irrigation systems, managing state-owned factories, all usually without the kind of billboards other donors favored to advertise their presence. Today, Africa fits into the strategy of "going global," not simply for its natural resources, but for opportunities in trade, construction, industry: *business*. The Chinese are linking business and aid in innovative ways. Aid subsidizes Chinese companies to set up agro-technical demonstration stations, or economic cooperation and development centers. The Chinese are experimenting, hoping that the profit motive will make these efforts sustainable, releasing the Chinese government from having to return again and again to resuscitate its aid projects. They will continue to change, and grow, and learn from these experiments, and we would do well to follow this progress and learn from it too.

By Western standards, China is secretive about its aid and export credits. This lack of transparency understandably raises suspicion and concern. Beijing could easily address this by using reporting standards adopted long ago by the OECD. But, on the other hand, private banks and corporations in the West have long maintained secrecy about their deals with African leaders. Transparency is good, but the West should lead the way.

It would be unrealistic to expect Chinese corporations to be the first to publish their own business contracts.

The United States, Europe, and Japan should continue to engage China as a "responsible stakeholder" in Africa, while recognizing that the traditional donor countries have their own credibility gaps as development partners. Aid pledges made by Western leaders go unfunded by Western parliaments. Promises to untie aid are hedged by simply not counting some areas – technical assistance, for example. As the Center for Global Development points out in its annual Commitment to Development index, several OECD countries (France, the UK, the US, Belgium) continue to profit from arms sales to undemocratic, militaristic governments. A shared commitment to improve in all these areas would do much to make similar demands of China more credible.

China is now a powerful force in Africa, and the Chinese are not going away. Their embrace of the continent is strategic, planned, long-term, and still unfolding. The global economic recession created a pause in this engagement, but the Chinese government still lived up to the pledges they made in Beijing in November 2006: to double aid, to set up agro-technical stations and special economic zones. Ambitious Chinese companies used that pause to buy assets at bargain prices, as they first began to do in the 1990s.

Ultimately, it is up to African governments to shape this encounter in ways that will benefit their people. Many will not grasp this opportunity, but some will. The West can help by gaining a more realistic picture of China's engagement, avoiding sensationalism and paranoia, admitting our own shortcomings, and perhaps exploring the notion that China's model of consistent non-intervention may be preferable to a China that regularly intervenes in other countries' domestic affairs, or uses military force to foster political change.

At the end of the day, we should remember this: China's own experiments have raised hundreds of millions of Chinese out of poverty, largely without foreign aid. They believe in investment, trade, and technology as levers for development, and they are applying these same tools in their African engagement, not out of altruism but because of what they learned at home. They learned that their own natural resources could be assets for modernization and prosperity. They learned that a central government commitment to capitalist business development could rapidly reduce poverty. They learned that special zones could attract clusters of mature industries from the West and Japan, providing jobs and technologies. These lessons emphasize not aid, but experiments; not paternalism, but the "creative destruction" of competition and the green shoots of new opportunities. This may be the dragon's ultimate, ambiguous gift.

APPENDICES

Appendix 1: Eight Principles for China's Aid to Foreign Countries (1964)

1. The Chinese Government always bases itself on the principle of equality and mutual benefit in providing aid to other countries. It never regards such aid as a kind of unilateral alms but as something mutual.

2. In providing aid to other countries, the Chinese Government strictly respects the sovereignty of the recipient countries, and never attaches any conditions or asks for any privileges.

3. China provides economic aid in the form of interest-free or low-interest loans and extends the time limit for repayment when necessary so as to lighten the burden of the recipient countries as far as possible.

4. In providing aid to other countries, the purpose of the Chinese Government is not to make the recipient countries dependent on China but to help them embark step by step on the road of self-reliance and independent economic development.

5. The Chinese Government tries its best to help the recipient countries build projects which require less investment while yielding quicker results, so that the recipient governments may increase their income and accumulate capital.

6. The Chinese Government provides the best-quality equipment and material of its own manufacture at international market prices. If the equipment and material provided by the Chinese Government are not up to the agreed specifications and quality, the Chinese Government undertakes to replace them.

7. In providing any technical assistance, the Chinese Government will see to it that the personnel of the recipient country fully master such technique.

8. The experts dispatched by China to help in construction in the recipient countries will have the same standard of living as the experts of the recipient country. The Chinese experts are not allowed to make any special demands or enjoy any special amenities.

Source: Speech by Chinese premier Zhou Enlai, Accra, Ghana, January 15, 1964.

Appendix 2: Zhao Ziyang's Four Principles of Economic and Technological Cooperation (1983)

1. In carrying out economic and technological cooperation with African countries, China abides by the principles of unity and friendship, equality and mutual benefit, respects their sovereignty, does not interfere in their internal affairs, attaches no political conditions and asks for no privileges whatsoever.

2. In China's economic and technological cooperation with African countries, full play will be given to the strong points and potentials of both sides on the basis of their actual needs and possibilities, and efforts will be made to achieve good economic results with less investment, shorter construction cycle and quicker returns.

3. China's economic and technological cooperation with African countries takes a variety of forms suited to the specific conditions, such as offering technical services, training technical and management personnel, engaging in scientific and technological exchanges, undertaking construction projects, entering into cooperative production and joint ventures. With regard to the cooperative projects it undertakes, the Chinese side will see to it that the signed contracts are observed, the quality of work guaranteed and stress laid on friendship. The experts and technical personnel dispatched by the Chinese side do not ask for special treatment.

4. The purpose of China's economic and technological cooperation with African countries is to contribute to the enhancement of the self-reliant capabilities of both sides and promote the growth of the respective national economies by complementing and helping each other.

Source: *Beijing Review*, January 24, 1983, p. 19.

Appendix 3: Chinese President Hu Jintao's Five Measures For Assisting Other Developing Countries (2005)

1. Zero tariff treatment to some products from all the thirty-nine least developed countries (LDCs) having diplomatic relations with China, which covers most of the China-bound exports from these countries.

2. Further expand aid program to the Heavily Indebted Poor Countries (HIPCs) and LDCs and, working through bilateral channels, write off or forgive in other ways, within the next two years, all the overdue parts as of the end of 2004 of the interest-free and low-interest governmental loans owed by all the HIPCs having diplomatic relations with China.

3. Within the next three years, China will provide $10 billion in concessional loans and preferential export buyer's credit to developing countries to improve their infrastructure and promote cooperation between enterprises on both sides.

4. China will, in the next three years, increase its assistance to developing countries, African countries in particular, providing them with anti-malarial drugs and other medicines, helping them set up and improve medical facilities and training medical staff.

5. China will train 30,000 personnel of various professions from the developing countries within the next three years so as to help them speed up their human resources development.

Source: Hu Jintao, "Promote Universal Development to Achieve Common Prosperity," written statement by Chinese President Hu Jintao at the High-Level Meeting on Financing for Development at the 60th Session of the United·Nations, New York, September 14, 2005.

Appendix 4: China's Overseas Economic and Trade Cooperation Zones

ZONES SELECTED FOR MOFCOM SUPPORT IN 2006

1. Pakistan — Haier-Ruba Home Appliance Industrial Zone
2. Zambia — Chambishi Nonferrous Metal Mining Group Industrial Park
3. Thailand — Luoyong Industrial Zone
4. Cambodia — Taihu International Economic Cooperation Zone (Sihanouk Harbour)
5. Nigeria — Guangdong Ogun Economic and Trade Cooperation Zone
6. Mauritius — Tianli Economic and Trade Cooperation Zone
7. Russia — St. Peterburg Baltic Economic and Trade Cooperation Zone
8. Russia — Ussuriysk Economic and Trade Cooperation Zone

ZONES SELECTED FOR MOFCOM SUPPORT IN 2007

1. Venezuela — Lacua Tech and Industrial Trade Zone
2. Nigeria — Lekki Free Trade Zone
3. Vietnam — Chinese (Shenzhen) Economic and Trade Cooperation Zone
4. Vietnam — Longjiang Economic and Trade Cooperation Zone
5. Mexico — Ningbo Geely Industrial Economic and Trade Cooperation Zone

6. Ethiopia   Eastern Industrial Park (Jiangsu Qiyaan Investment Group)
7. Egypt   Tianjin TEDA Suez Economic and Trade Cooperation Zone
8. Algeria   Chinese Jiangling Economic and Trade Cooperation Zone
9. S. Korea   Chinese Industrial Zone
10. Indonesia   Chinese Guangxi Economic and Trade Cooperation Zone
11. Russia   Tomsk Siberia Industrial and Trade Cooperation Zone

Source: Author's research.

Appendix 5: Medical Teams: Chinese Provinces Twinned with African Countries

Chinese Province	African Country (or Territory)
Beijing	Guinea
Fujian	Botswana, Senegal
Gansu	Madagascar
Guangdong	Equatorial Guinea, Ghana
Guangxi	Comoros, Niger
Hebei	Democratic Republic of the Congo
Heilongjiang	Mauritania
Henan	Eritrea, Ethiopia, Zambia
Hubei	Algeria, Lesotho
Hunan	Sierra Leone, Zimbabwe
Inner Mongolia	Rwanda
Jiangsu	Zanzibar
Jiangxi	Tunisia, Chad
Jilin	Somalia
Ningxia	Benin
Qinghai	Burundi
Shaanxi	Guinea, Sudan
Shanghai	Morocco
Shanxi	Cameroon, Djibouti, Togo
Sichuan	Guinea Bissau, Mozambique, Cape Verde, Angola
Tianjin	Gabon, Republic of Congo
Yunnan	Uganda
Zhejiang	Central African Republic, Mali, Namibia

Source: Ministry of Health, *China Health Almanac* (Beijing, 1991–2008).

Appendix 6: Chinese Aid (US$ million)

	A. China official budget for external assistance RMB mil	IMF annual average exchange rate, RMB/US$	B. China official budget for external assistance $ mil	C. Eximbank concessional loans, annual $ mil	D. Chinese debt cancellation $ mil	E. Total Chinese aid, annual $ mil	Budgeted aid to Africa, percent	F. Official budget for external assistance (Africa portion) $ mil	G. Eximbank concessional loans to Africa $ mil	H. Debt relief to Africa $ mil	I. Total Chinese aid to Africa	J. Accumulated Eximbank concessional loans, based on C $ mil	K. Accumulated Eximbank concessional loans, Africa only $ mil
1996	**3212**	8.3	**387**	**23**	..	*410*	..						11
1997	**3552**	8.3	**428**	**71**	..	*499*	..						47
1998	**3720**	8.3	**449**	**66**	..	*516*	..					**160**	80
1999	**3920**	8.3	**474**	**80**	..	*553*	..					240	120
2000	**4588**	8.3	**554**	**91**	..	*645*	..					331	166
2001	**4711**	8.3	**569**	**128**	450	*1147*	44	**250**	64	375	689	**459**	230
2002	**5003**	8.3	**604**	173	450	*1227*	44	**266**	86	375	727	632	316
2003	**5223**	8.3	**631**	233	450	*1314*	44	**278**	117	375	769	865	433
2004	**6069**	8.3	**733**	315	450	*1498*	30	220	158	375	753	1181	590
2005	**7470**	8.2	**912**	425	450	*1787*	30	273	213	375	861	1606	803
2006	**8200**	8.0	**1028**	693	450	*2172*	30	309	347	375	1030	2299	1150
2007	**11154**	7.6	**1466**	1130	450	*3046*	31	440	565	375	1380	3429	1715
2008	n/a	6.7	n/a	*1842*	450			515	921	375	1811		
2009	n/a	n/a	n/a	*3003*				600	1501	375	2476		

Note: Figures in bold are from Chinese published sources. Figures in italics are author's estimates. Eximbank concessional loans are estimated between 2002 and 2005 on the basis of reported 35 percent annual growth rate (China Eximbank *Annual Report 2005*). Debt relief ($3.6 billion total, and $3.0 billion for Africa) are allocated evenly across the affected periods and are assumed to continue in 2008 and 2009. The percentage of official aid expenditure allocated to Africa is based on Chinese official estimates, 2002–2004. Thereafter, the percentage is extrapolated from information derived from author's interviews. Half of Eximbank concessional loans are estimated to go to Africa.

Sources: China Statistical Yearbook; China Eximbank *Annual Reports*, Qi Guoqiang, "China's Foreign Aid," for figures in bold. Author's estimates for the rest.

ENDNOTES

Prologue: The Changing Face of Chinese Engagement in Africa

1. "Address by Hu Jintao at the Opening Ceremony of the Beijing Summit of the Forum on China–Africa Cooperation," Beijing, China, November 4, 2006.
2. Deborah Brautigam, *Chinese Aid and African Development: Exporting Green Revolution* (New York: St. Martin's Press, 1998).
3. Mu Xuequan, "Financial Collaboration a New Focus in China–Africa Economic Co-op," May 17, 2007, *Xinhua* (the official Chinese news agency), May 17, 2007. All dollar figures in this book refer to United States dollars unless otherwise specified.
4. World Bank data applies to Fiscal Years 2005–6 to 2007–8. World Bank, *Annual Report* (various years).
5. Moisés Naím, "Help Not Wanted," op-ed, *New York Times*, February 15, 2007.
6. RMB 880 million yuan.
7. Based on interviews with Mauritian Finance Minister Rama Sithanen, Washington DC, April 17, 2007; Ambassador Paul Chong Leung, Beijing, July 26, 2007; and various articles in *L'Express* (Mauritius), October 19, 2006–July 16, 2007 (translations by the author).
8. The government of Zambia retained 15 percent of the shares. "Zambia: Non-Ferrous Metals Pumps $59m into Chambishi Mine," *The Post* (Lusaka), February 12, 2002.
9. Kingsley Kaswende, "Zambia: Chinese Firms Invest $150 Million in Mining," *The Post* (Lusaka), July 8, 2005.
10. The Chambishi story is based on the author's interviews, Zambia, January 2008, and on these articles: "Zambia: Chambishi Mines Launches Social Responsibility Plan," *The Times of Zambia* (Ndola), July 10, 2007; Jackie Range, "Zambia's Miners Pay High Price For Copper Boom," *Dow Jones Newswire*, October 12, 2005; Yaroslav Trofimov, "In Africa, China's Expansion Begins to Stir Resentment," *Wall Street Journal*, February 2, 2007; John Reed, "China's

African Embrace Evokes Memories of the Old Imperialism," *Financial Times*, September 28, 2006.

11. Isabel Chimangeni, "Zambia: Is China Sneaking in Deals Through the Back Door?," *Inter Press Service* (Johannesburg), March 27, 2007.

12. Chris McGreal, "Thanks, China, Now Go Home: Buy Up of Zambia Revives Old Colonial Fears," *The Guardian*, February 5, 2007.

13. SADC is the Southern Africa Development Community, and COMESA is Common Market for Eastern and Southern Africa. Potipher Tembo, "Chambishi Mines Launches Social Responsibility Plan," *The Times of Zambia* (Ndola), July 10, 2007.

14. Tembo, "Social Responsibility Plan."

15. The early literature on this theme posited a uniformly negative relationship. See Walter Rodney, *How Europe Underdeveloped Africa* (Washington DC: Howard University Press, 1982); Samir Amin, *Accumulation on a World Scale: A Critique of the Theory of Underdevelopment*, trans. Brian Pearce (New York: Monthly Review Press, 1974).

16. Daniel Kaufmann, Aart Kraay, and Massimo Mastruzzi, "Governance Matters VI: Governance Indicators for 1996–2006," World Bank Policy Research Working Paper No. 4280 (July 2007).

17. Shaohua Chen and Martin Ravallion, "China's (Uneven) Progress Against Poverty," *Journal of Development Economics*, 82(1) (2007): 1–42.

18. For a thorough treatment of these environmental issues, see Elizabeth C. Economy, *The River Runs Black: The Environmental Challenge to China's Future* (Ithaca, NY: Cornell University Press, 2004).

19. Sarah Gertrude Millin, *Rhodes* (London: Chatto and Windus, 1933), p. 138.

20. Joaquim Alberto Chissano, "Why We Should Rethink Aid," Conference on New Directions in Development Assistance, Oxford University and Cornell University, Center for Global Economic Governance, June 11–12, 2007.

21. For an excellent review and analysis of this experience, see Roger C. Riddell, *Does Foreign Aid Really Work?* (New York: Oxford University Press, 2007).

22. Transcript of IMF press conference of African finance ministers, International Monetary Fund, Washington DC, April 14, 2007, available at: http://go. worldbank.org/QWSCW31S50 (accessed September 20, 2007).

23. Françoise Crouigneau and Richard Hiault, "Wolfowitz Slams China Banks on Africa Lending," *Financial Times*, October 24, 2006.

24. Paul Collier, *The Bottom Billion: Why the Poorest Countries Are Failing and What Can Be Done About It* (Oxford: Oxford University Press, 2007), p. 86. Emphasis added.

25. An official government website spells out their mission to assist US firms "by providing access to World Bank facilities and personnel, by advocating for US commercial interests, and by elaborating effective strategies to pursue Bank-related business opportunities." The Advocacy Center's Liaison Office to the World Bank Group, available at: www.buyusa.gov/worldbank/ (accessed May 4, 2008).

26. There is a vast literature on the topic. Some highlights: Alberto Alesina and David Dollar, "Who Gives Foreign Aid to Whom and Why?" *Journal of Economic Growth*, 5(1) (2000): 33–63; Samuel P. Huntington, "Foreign Aid for What and For Whom," *Foreign Policy*, 1 (1970–1); Peter J. Schraeder, Steven W. Hook, and Bruce Taylor, "Clarifying the Foreign Aid Puzzle: A Comparison of American, Japanese, French, and Swedish Aid Flows," *World Politics*, 50 (2) (1998): 294–323. Schraeder, Hook, and Taylor identify six factors that might prompt aid: humanitarian need, strategic importance, economic potential, cultural similarity, ideological stance, and region.

27. China's currency is the renminbi. The unit of account is the yuan.

28. Joshua Cooper Ramo, "The Beijing Consensus," The Foreign Policy Centre, London, May 2004. The alternative "Washington Consensus" was dubbed by John Williamson, in his chapter "What Washington Means by Policy Reform," in John Williamson, ed., *Latin American Adjustment: How Much Has Happened?* (Washington DC: Institute for International Economics, 1990).

29. Chalmers Johnson, *MITI and the Japanese Miracle: The Growth of Industrial Policy, 1925–1975* (Stanford, CA: Stanford University Press, 1982). See also Meredith Woo-Cumings, ed., *The Developmental State* (Ithaca, NY: Cornell University Press, 1999).

30. This question was also asked by L. Rieffel, in "Why Bad Loans Are Good For Africa." *The Globalist*, February 13, 2007.

31. China's Ministry of Commerce was part of the Ministry of Foreign Economic Relations and Trade (1982–93), and the Ministry of Foreign Trade and Economic Cooperation (1993–2003). It was renamed the Ministry of Commerce in 2003. I use the Ministry of Commerce name most of the time in this book for simplicity's sake.

1 Missionaries and Maoists: How China's Aid Moved from "Red" to "Expert"

1. Their story was chronicled by Grace Nies Fletcher: *The Fabulous Flemings of Kathmandu: The Story of Two Doctors in Nepal* (New York: Dutton, 1964).

2. George C. Abbott, "A Re-Examination of the 1929 Colonial Development Act," *Economic History Review*, new series, 24(1) (1971): 68–81. To the extent possible, all equipment purchased under these programs was to be procured in the UK, a precursor of tied aid.

3. For a sample of the many econometric studies exploring the question of the impact of different colonizers on their ex-colonies, see Daron Acemoglu, Simon Johnson, and James A. Robinson, "The Colonial Origins of Comparative Development: An Empirical Investigation," *American Economic Review*, 2001, 91(5): 1369–1401; Michael Bernhard, Christopher Reenock, and Timothy Nordstrom, "The Legacy of Western Overseas Colonialism on Democratic Survival," *International Studies Quarterly*, 2004, 48: 225–50. For non-econometric analyses, see Atul Kohli, *State-Directed Development: Political Power and Industrialization in the Global Periphery* (New York: Cambridge University Press, 2004); and Matthew Lange and Dietrich Rueschemeyer, eds., *States and Development: Historical Antecedents of Stagnation and Advance* (Basingstoke, UK: Palgrave Macmillan, 2005).

4. Louise Levanthes, *When China Ruled the Seas* (Oxford: Oxford University Press, 1994).

5. "Kenyan Girl Traces Chinese Roots Over 600 Years Later," press release, Embassy of the People's Republic of China in Kenya, July 21, 2005.

6. Albert Feuerwerker, "Chinese History and the Foreign Relations of Contemporary China," *Annals of the American Academy of Political and Social Science*, 402(1) (1972): 1–14; Kenneth Pomeranz, "Empire and 'Civilizing' Missions, Past and Present," *Daedalus*, 134(2) (2005): 34–45.

7. Alan Beattie, "Loans that Could Cost Africa Dear: The Money China is Pouring into Africa Could Damage the Economics and Politics of the Continent," *Financial Times*, April 22, 2007.

8. Harry S. Truman, "Inaugural Address," January 20, 1949.

9. Carl Eicher, "Flashback: Fifty Years of Donor Aid to African Agriculture," Conference Paper No. 16 presented at the InWEnt, IFPRI, NEPAD, CTA Conference "Successes in African Agriculture," Pretoria, December 1–3, 2003, p. 6.

10. Truman, "Inaugural Address."

11. Walter Rostow, *The Stages of Economic Growth: A Non-Communist Manifesto* (Cambridge: Cambridge University Press, 1960). For helpful overviews of thinking at this time, see Roger C. Riddell, *Does Foreign Aid Really Work?* (Oxford: Oxford University Press, 2007).

12. Theotonio dos Santos, "The Structure of Dependence," *American Economic Review*, 60 (1970): 233.

13. Devesh Kapur, John P. Lewis, and Richard Webb, *The World Bank: Its First Half Century*, vol. 1: *History* (Washington DC: Brookings Institution, 1997).

14. This was the case in Cameroon, Uganda, and Kenya. Sanjay Pradhan, "Evaluating Public Spending: A Framework for Public Expenditure Reviews," World Bank Discussion Paper No. 323, 1996; Riddell, *Foreign Aid*, p. 37.

15. William R. Cotter, "How AID Fails to Aid Africa," *Foreign Policy*, 36 (1979): 107–19, at p. 107.

16. The first fifteen countries to formally receive aid from China were North Korea, Albania, North Vietnam, Romania, Mongolia, Indonesia, Nepal, Egypt, Cambodia, Burma, Sri Lanka, North Yemen, Algeria, Guinea, and Cuba. Teh-chang Lin, "The Foreign Aid Policy of the People's Republic of China: A Theoretical Analysis," unpublished dissertation, Northern Illinois University, DeKalb, IL, 1993, p. 148, reported that, between 1953 and 1963, North Vietnam, North Korea, and Mongolia received an estimated 82 percent of China's aid.

17. "Vive l'Independance!" *Time Magazine*, February 16, 1959.

18. Wolfgang Bartke, *China's Economic Aid* (New York: Holmes and Meier, 1975), p. 116.

19. "Communist Aid Contrasts: Guinea," Radio Free Europe, September 19, 1960, accessed online through the Open Society Archives: http://files.osa.ceu. hu/holdings/300/8/3/test/90-3-144.shtml (accessed September 13, 2008).

20. Jan S. Prybyla, "Communist China's Economic Relations with Africa 1960–1964," *Asian Survey*, 4(11) (1964): 1136.

21. The ten countries were the United Arab Republic (currently Egypt), Algeria, Morocco, Tunisia, Ghana, Mali, Guinea, Sudan, Ethiopia, and Somalia. Daniel Large's excellent article "Beyond 'Dragon in the Bush': The Study of China–Africa Relations," revisits this earlier period of alarm. *African Affairs*, 107(426) (2008): 45–61.

22. These are listed in Appendix 1.

23. Shi Lin, editor in chief, *Dangdai Zhongguo de Duiwai Jiingji Hezuo* ("China's Economic Cooperation with Foreign Countries Today") (Beijing: China Social Sciences Press, 1989), p. 42. The quotations in the next sentences are also from this source.

24. Bartke, *China's Economic Aid*, p. 120.

25. The title comes from George Yu, "Dragon in the Bush: Peking's Presence in Africa," *Asian Survey*, 8(12) (1968): 1018–26; also used by Large, "Dragon in the Bush."

26. The Mediterranean (Egypt, Algeria, Morocco), the Horn of Africa near the oil-rich Gulf (Ethiopia, Somalia, and Sudan), and Guinea and Ghana. Bartke, *China's Economic Aid*, pp. 20–3.

27. *Xinhua*, February 6, 1964, cited in Yu Fai Law, *Chinese Foreign Aid* (Fort Lauderdale, TX: Breitenbach, 1984), pp. 47–8.

28. "From a Little Trickle to a Mighty Gush," *People's Daily*, October 8, 2004.

29. "Learn from Dazhai," *China Now*, 72 (1977): 2, available at: www.sacu.org/learntachai.html (accessed May 5, 2008). The poem reproduced in the article is from "Songs of Dazhai," by Liang Laiqeng, *Chinese Literature*, 2 (1976).

30. Marsh S. Marshall, Jr. "Red and Expert at Tachai [Dazhai]: A Sources of Growth Analysis," *World Development* (1979): 424.

31. Hans-Helmut Taake, "Promoting Non-Alignment and Self-Reliance: China's Development Policy," *D&C Development and Cooperation* (Germany), 5/6 (1994). On the Benin project, see also Law, *Chinese Foreign Aid*.

32. Snow's account of Zhou Enlai in Algeria is from *Beijing Review*, January 3, 1964, p. 94.

33. "Stevens the Tactician (1905–1988)," *West Africa*, June 6, 1988, p. 1019.

34. D. A. Brautigam, "Foreign Assistance and the Export of Ideas: Chinese Development Aid in The Gambia and Sierra Leone," *Journal of Commonwealth and Comparative Politics*, 32(3) (1994): 324–48.

35. Brautigam, "Export of Ideas," pp. 332, 338.

36. Letter, Senior health education officer to Minister of Health, Chinese Project Files, Ministry of Agriculture and Natural Resources, Freetown, Sierra Leone, September 11, 1979.

37. W. E. S. Smith, *We Must Run While They Walk* (New York: Random House, 1971).

38. *Ujamaa*'s failure in Tanzania is expertly analyzed in James Scott's *Seeing Like a State: How Certain Schemes to Improve the Condition Have Failed* (New Haven, CT: Yale University Press, 1998), pp. 223–61, and Goran Hyden, *Beyond Ujamaa in Tanzania* (London: Heineman, 1980).

39. Jonathan Unger, "Remuneration, Ideology, and Personal Interests," in William L. Parish, ed., *Chinese Rural Development* (New York: M. E. Sharpe, 1985), p. 124.

40. On the World Bank: Trevor Parfitt, "The First Lomé Convention and its Effects on Sierra Leone," unpublished Ph.D. dissertation, University of Manchester, 1983. The World Bank explained their selection of chiefs as necessary to gain the approval of local authorities and to be accepted in the communities.

41. The Tan-Zam railway has been far and away the most studied of China's aid projects in Africa. George T. Yu, "Working on the Railroad: China and the Tanzania–Zambia Railway," *Asian Survey*, 11(11) (1971), pp. 1101–17; Richard Hall and Hugh Peyman, *The Great Uhuru Railway: China's Showpiece in Africa* (New York: Gollancz, 1976). American professor Jamie Monson has returned to the project with her well-documented *Africa's Freedom Railway: How a Chinese Development Project Changed Lives and Livelihoods in Tanzania* (Bloomington, IN: Indiana University Press, 2009). This section draws on this work, and also on Philip Snow, *The Star Raft: China's Encounter with Africa* (New York: Weidenfeld and Nicolson, 1988), pp. 150–4, and Bartke, *China's Economic Aid*, p. 16.

42. "Tanzania–Zambia Railway symbolizes Sino-African Friendship," *Xinhua*, June 23, 2006, available at: www.chinaview.cn (accessed May 7, 2008).

43. Shi Lin, *Zhongguo Jingji Hezuo*, p. 61. Cooperation agreements made in the 1970s but not fully utilized were extended in Burkina Faso (Upper Volta, 1984), Burundi (1987), Mauritius (1982), Mozambique (1985), Sudan (1987). Lin, "Foreign Aid Policy," pp. 344–65.

44. Shi Lin, *Zhongguo Jingji Hezuo*.

45. Ai Ping, "From Proletarian Internationalism to Mutual Development: China's Cooperation with Tanzania, 1965–95," in Goran Hyden and Rwekaza Mukandala, eds., *Agencies in Foreign Aid: Comparing China, Sweden and the United States in Tanzania* (New York: Macmillan, 1999), pp. 167–9; citing Shi Lin, *Zhongguo Jingji Hezuo*.

46. Shi Lin, *Zhongguo Jingji Hezuo*, pp. 61–3.

2   Feeling the Stones: Deng Xiaoping's Experiments with Aid

1. Senegalese Minister of Finance Jean Collin, January 1969, quoted in Catherine Boone, *Merchant Capital and the Roots of State Power in Senegal* (New York: Cambridge University Press, 1992), pp. 172–3.

2. Shi Lin, editor in chief, *Dangdai Zhonguo de Duiwai Jingji Hezuo* ("China's Economic Cooperation with Foreign Countries Today") (Beijing: China Social Sciences Press, 1989), p. 68.

3. Tomozo Morino, "China–Japan Trade and Investment Relations," *Proceedings of the Academy of Political Science*, 38(2) (1991): 92.

4. Japan's foreign aid loans provided through the Overseas Economic Cooperation Fund (now the Japan Bank for International Cooperation), generally had

interest rates ranging from 0.7 to 2.5 percent, with grace periods of ten years and repayment over thirty years. Tsukasa Takamine, *Japan's Development Aid to China: The Long Running Foreign Policy of Engagement* (New York: Routledge, 2006), p. 97.

5. David Arase, *Buying Power: The Political Economy of Japan's Foreign Aid* (Boulder, CO: Lynne Rienner, 1995), pp. 39–40.

6. Arase, *Buying Power*, p. 40.

7. Kevin Conway, "Case Study: India. Tracking Health and Well-being in Goa's Mining Belt," International Development Research Centre, Canada, available at: www.idrc.ca/en/ev-29129–201–1-DO_TOPIC.html (no date; accessed July 9, 2008).

8. Takamine, *Japan's Development Aid*, p. 89.

9. "Bu Ming on Banking Contacts with Abroad," *Xinhua*, February 6, 1980.

10. "Japan and China: Aid Precedes Trade," *The Economist*, December 8, 1979.

11. Nicholas R. Lardy, *Foreign Trade and Economic Reform in China, 1978–1990* (New York: Cambridge University Press, 1992), p. 42.

12. "Trade and Cooperation," Peking for abroad [sic] *BBC Summary of World Broadcasts*, April 11, 1979; "Chinese Import-Export Commission Vice-Minister on Economic Cooperation," *Xinhua*, April 10, 1980.

13. "Chinese Import-Export Commission Vice-Minister on Economic Cooperation," *Xinhua*, April 10, 1980.

14. Some reported that the French had signed a seven-year, two-way trade agreement for 30 billion French francs ($7.9 billion); others claimed it was a $13.6 billion agreement over ten years, and would finance French exports (including two nuclear power plants) with subsidized export credits. "China Trade: Peking Dips a Toe in the Credit Pool," *The Economist*, December 9, 1978. See also François Godemont, "Between the Gold Rush and Political Trade: France's Approach to the China Market," in Ost-West-Kolleg der Bundeszentrale für Politische Bildung, Friedrich Ebert Stiftung, ed., *China's International Role: Key Issues, Common Interests, Different Approaches* (Bonn: Friedrich Ebert Stiftung, 1997), pp. 81–93.

15. "Vice-Minister on Economic Cooperation," *Xinhua*, April 10, 1980.

16. "More Heat on Eximbank over Non-Performing Loans to China, Cuba," *International Trade Finance*, June 1, 1989.

17. "An American Edge in China's Hydro Plans," *The Economist*, September 17, 1979.

18. The Italian and French deals are from these sources: *Almanac of China's Foreign Economic Relations 1989* (Beijing: 1990), "Chinese Foreign Trade Minister Signs Financial Agreement with France," *Xinhua*, October 25, 1988.

19. "Cooperation Between China, Sweden, Can Reach New Level: Tian," *Xinhua*, May 27, 1992.

20. Haruo Ozaki, "Cheap Loans Give Edge to Europeans in China: Nations Back Firms' Bidding," *Nihon Kezai Shimbun* (The Japan Economic Journal), March 26, 1988.

21. Shi Lin, *Zhongguo Jingji Hezuo*, pp. 68–73.

22. The trip is described in Foreign Broadcast Information Services – China Report (FBIS-CHI-83), January 3, 1983; *People's Daily*, January 15, 1983; *Beijing Review*, January 24, 1983, p. 19; *Daily Intelligencer*, January 10, 1983.

23. These principles are set down in Appendix 2.

24. *Beijing Review*, September 5, 1983, p. 18 (emphasis added).

25. George T. Yu, "Africa in Chinese Foreign Policy," *Asian Survey*, 28(8) (1988), p. 850.

26. China's aid commitments to developing countries in 1984, as estimated by the OECD, were $289 million. OECD, "The Aid Program of China," Paris, W.2196D/Arch.0792D 3434, Paris, March 1987, p. 8. This excluded debt relief, scholarships, and medical teams.

27. Author's calculations based on annual data on percentage of aid to Africa reported annually in *Almanac of China's Foreign Economic Relations and Trade* (Beijing: Ministry of Foreign Economic Relations and Trade, various years).

28. Chinese Sugar Survey Team, "The Brief Survey Report on the Rehabilitation of Production of the Barrake Cane and Sugar Complex," Ministry of Agriculture, LIBSUCO (Liberia Sugar Company) files, Monrovia (n.d.: circa 1982). It probably did not help Liberia's case that the project had originally been built by Taiwan.

29. These economic cooperation loans typically had higher interest rates and shorter repayment and grace periods than regular aid loans, which were always zero interest in this period.

30. Emphasis added. "In nearly every case the recipient countries are allowed to make repayments in domestically produced commodities." Teh-chang Lin, "The Foreign Aid Policy of the People's Republic of China: A Theoretical Analysis," unpublished dissertation, Northern Illinois University, DeKalb, IL, 1993, p. 131.

31. "Opinions on Consolidating Results of Complete-Set Projects of Assistance," October 1983, summarized in Shi Lin, ed., *Zhongguo Jingji Hezuo*, pp. 220–9. The policy shift was formalized at the Sixth National Foreign Aid Conference in 1983.

32. Ai Ping, "From Proletarian Internationalism to Mutual Development: China's Cooperation with Tanzania, 1965–95," in Goran Hyden and Rwekaza Mukandala, eds., *Agencies in Foreign Aid: Comparing China, Sweden and the United States in Tanzania* (New York: Macmillan, 1999), p. 198.

33. Shi Lin, *Zhongguo Jingji Hezuo*, pp. 220–9.

34. "Sierra Leone – Farming Co-Operation," *Xinhua*, November 4, 1979.

35. *Almanac* (1988), pp. 73–4.

36. William Easterly, *The White Man's Burden: Why the West's Efforts to Aid the Rest Have Done So Much Ill and So Little Good* (New York: Penguin Books, 2006), pp. 189–90.

37. Ai Ping, "China's Cooperation with Tanzania," p. 181.

38. *Daily Mail* (Freetown), February 21, 1984.

39. Wan Yingquan, "A Brief Report on the Kpatawee Agricultural Cooperation Project," Ministry of Agriculture, Monrovia, Liberia, 1986.

40. Deborah Brautigam, "Doing Well by Doing Good: China's New-Style Foreign Aid Projects Now Emphasize Mutual Benefit," *China Business Review* (September–October 1983), pp. 57–8.

41. Shi Lin, *Zhongguo Jingji Hezuo*, pp. 453–4; Deborah Brautigam, *Chinese Aid and African Development: Exporting Green Revolution* (New York: St. Martin's Press, 1998).

42. He Xiaowei, Director General of Department of Foreign Aid, MOFTEC, "Continuously Pursue the Reform of Aid Forms, and Strictly Implement the Aid Agreements," *Almanac* (1997), p. 69.

43. Lucy Corkin, "Chinese Multinational Corporations in Africa," *Inside Asia*, 3 and 4 (October/December 2006): 10–14.

44. Li Lu, "How 7 Chinese Firms Have Won Nearly $1.4 Billion in International Construction Contracts," *China Business Review* (September–October 1983), p. 58.

45. As the deputy director of the Department of Foreign Aid explained in a 1987 report, because of the economic crisis China's new contracting business was "in a difficult situation. To promote the contracting business ... [China will adopt a] combination of foreign aid and contracting." *Almanac* (1988), p. 74.

46. *Xinhua*, February 26, 1991.

47. *Almanac* (1989–90), p. 64.

48. *Almanac* (1988–9), p. 74; Department of Foreign Aid, Ministry of Foreign Economic Relations and Trade, "China's Economic and Trade Relations with African Countries," *Almanac* (1988), p. 427.

49. OECD, "China's Aid," p. 13. In 1987, the OECD estimated that about 95 percent of Chinese assistance was in the form of projects, with about 5 percent in emergency aid, grants, and cash.

50. Philip Snow, *The Star Raft: China's Encounter with Africa* (New York: Weidenfeld and Nicolson, 1988), p. 183.

51. He Xiaowei, deputy director, Department of Foreign Aid, Ministry of Foreign Economic Relations and Trade, "China's Economic Aid to Foreign Countries in 1990," *Almanac* (1991), p. 62.

52. Source: Author's research and William Chung-lian Jiang, "Beijing and Taipei, the African Challenges," unpublished paper, available at: www.african-geopolitics.org/show.aspx?articleid=3584 (n.d.) (accessed February 16, 2008).

53. *Almanac* (1992), p. 755.

54. "UK Companies Sell African Investments," *Financial Times*, June 28, 1990, p. 4, cited in Li Anshan, "The Transformation of China's Policy Towards Africa," paper presented at conference on China–Africa links, Hong Kong University of Science and Technology, November 11–12, 2006, p. 9.

55. The Second Department for Regional Affairs, Department of Foreign Aid, Ministry of Foreign Economic Relations and Trade, "China's Economic and Trade Relations with African Countries," *Almanac* (1988), p. 426.

3   Going Global: Foreign Aid in the Toolkit of a Rising China

1. Gail A. Eadie and Denise M. Grizzell, "China's Foreign Aid, 1975–78," *China Quarterly*, 77 (1979): 228.

2. "A Large Chinese Stadium for Tanzania," *Indian Ocean Newsletter*, 1109, November 6, 2004.

3. These stages of Chinese policy are well outlined in an article by Peter J. Buckley, L. Jeremy Clegg, Adam R. Cross, Xin Liu, Hinrich Voss, and Ping Zheng, "The Determinants of Chinese Outward Foreign Direct Investment," *Journal of International Business Studies*, 38 (2007): 499–518.

4. World Bank, "Aid Architecture: An Overview of the Main Trends in Official Development Assistance Flows," International Development Association, Resource Mobilization (FRM) February 2007, p. 11; International Food Policy Research Institute (IFPRI), "The 10 percent That Could Change Africa," *IFPRI Forum* (October 2008), p. 9.

5. Pei Shanqin, "Chinese Premier's Visit Surely to Inject Vigor to Sino-Tanzanian Friendly Relations," *Xinhua*, May 11, 1997.

6. *Almanac of China's Foreign Economic Relations and Trade 2001* (Beijing, 2002), p. 560. The other statistics in this paragraph are also from this source.

7. The name of China's Ministry of Commerce in this period was Ministry of Foreign Trade and Economic Cooperation (MOFTEC).

8. On Chinese foreign policy thinking around the issue of China's rise, see Bonnie Glaser and Evan S. Medeiros, "The Changing Ecology of Foreign Policy-Making in China: The Ascension and Demise of the Theory of 'Peaceful Rise'," *China Quarterly*, 190 (2007): 291–310.

9. "Beijing Notches up Points," *Indian Ocean Newsletter*, 724, June 22, 1996.

10. Wu Yi, "Seizing Opportunities, Accelerating the Development and Pushing China's Foreign Trade and Economic Cooperation to a New Stage," *Almanac* (1993–4), preface (no page number). The translation was smoothed a bit to improve the English.

11. Zhang Chixin, deputy director, Department of Foreign Aid, MOFTEC, "The Foreign Aid Work Develops in the Course of the Reform," *Almanac* (1996–7), p. 69.

12. Vinaye Ancharaz, "David v. Goliath: Mauritius Facing Up to China," Scoping Study prepared for the Africa Economic Research Consortium, November 2007 (draft), p. 28. Loans from the credit were to be offered at 4 percent interest, over twelve years, with grace periods to be determined in the case of each joint venture.

13. *Almanac* (1995), p. 469.

14. *Almanac* (1997–8), p. 69. Although the situation would soon change, at this point the Chinese were simply joining Canada, Sweden, and other wealthier countries, all interested in the promise of Sudan's oil potential, and all using their own ways of smoothing the pathway of their country's firms.

15. Shi Heqiu, "China's Foreign Aid Developed in the Adjustment and Reformation," *Almanac* (1993), p. 66; Li Guoqing, "China's Foreign Aid Work in 1998," *Almanac* (1999/2000), p. 75.

16. *People's Daily*, April 9, 2000.

17. Another of the Ministry's companies, the China National Overseas Engineering Corporation (COVEC), opened a center in Bamako, Mali, where they also operated a textile mill and other companies. In Egypt the new center was operated by China National Service Corporation for Personnel Working Abroad. Provincial Economic and Trade Commissions from Gansu, Hubei, and Liaoning opened centers in Côte d'Ivoire, Cameroon, and Gabon, respectively. Changzhou Machinery Equipment Import and Export Group from Jiangsu province opened the center in Tanzania. China Jiangxi Corporation for International Economic and Technical Cooperation established the Zambia center (which cost $2.6 million). Centers were also established in Mozambique,

Nigeria, Benin, and possibly in Kenya, Tunisia, and Sudan. Author's interviews; "China Builds Trade Centre," *Xinhua*, January 27, 1999; and *Almanac* (various years).

18. "Benin China Economic and Trade Development Center Was Launched," Zhejiang Foreign Trade and Economic Cooperation Bureau, January 12, 2009. The figures were RMB 17 million yuan, and RMB 5 million yuan, respectively. See: www.zzftec.gov.cn/english/PoliciesRegulations/FFE/T222487.shtml (accessed February 1, 2009).

19. "Chinese Premier Interviewed on Purpose of African Tour," *Xinhua*, May 4, 1997.

20. *Radio Tanzania*, July 20, 1995.

21. "China Denies Aid for Tanzanian-Zambian Railway Will Stop if it is Privatized," *Xinhua*, July 25, 1995.

22. The Berg Report is mentioned in Chapter 2.

23. Gregor Dobler, "Cheapness and Resentment: Chinese Traders and Local Society in Oshikango, Namibia," paper given at ASC Seminar, Leiden, March 27, 2008.

24. "Chinese 'Investors' Selling Groundnuts in Suburbs," *Mwananchi* (Dar es Salaam, Tanzania, in Swahili) on July 16, 2005.

25. For more on the "peaceful rise" see Bonnie Glaser and Evan S. Medeiros, "The Changing Ecology of Foreign Policy-Making in China: The Ascension and Demise of the Theory of 'Peaceful Rise', " *China Quarterly*, 190 (2007): 291–310.

26. These measures are listed in Appendix 3.

27. Dennis Pamlin and Long Baijin, "Rethink: China's Outward Investment Flows," World Wildlife Fund, Trade and Investment Policy Program, 2007, p. 20. Other examples in this section are from Hu Yuanyuan, "CSCEC Deal Propels 'Go Global' Scheme," *China Daily*, December 29, 2005; "CNOOC Ltd. Signs Loan Agreement with China EXIM Bank," company press release, available at: www.secinfo.com/drjtj.v44d.htm (accessed July 24, 2008). Fu Jin, "Overseas Investment Encouraged with Loans," *China Daily*, November 4, 2004.

28. "Circular of the Ministry of Finance and the Ministry of Commerce on Relevant Issues Concerning Financial Interest Subsidy to Loans for Foreign Contracted Projects in 2005," *Cai Qi*, 5 (2006). Circulars like these are usually published in the Ministry of Commerce, *China Economic Cooperation and Trade Gazette*.

29. "Policy Guidance for Overseas Investment," July 5, 2006 (attachment). Available at: www.tech110.net/policy/html/article_382215.html (accessed August 24,

2008). Richard McGregor, "Iran, Sudan and Nigeria off China Incentive List," *Financial Times*, March 2, 2007.

30. Yang Yao and Yin He, "Chinese Outward Investing Firms, A Study for FIAS/IFC/MIGA," China Center for Economic Research, Peking University, August 2005.

31. "SA in Talks To Swap Minerals for New Factories with China," *Business Report* (South Africa), October 1, 2007.

32. "Guiding Opinions Special Funds of 'Going Global' Used to Support Textile Enterprises," Ministry of Finance and Ministry of Commerce; Wu Xilin, "Implementation of the Strategy of 'Going Global' in China in 2006," *China Commerce Yearbook* (Beijing, 2007), p. 419; China Textile and Apparel Industry, "Annual Report on Social Responsibility," 2006, p. 17.

33. "Trade Policy Review Report by China," World Trade Organization, Trade Policy Review Body, WT/TPR/G/199, May 7, 2008.

34. Jiang Wei, Zhan Lisheng, and Lillian Liu, "Thousands of HK Firms Face Risk of Shutdown," *China Daily*, August 2, 2007.

35. "Africa Fund Will Benefit People's Lives," *Shanghai Daily*, July 25, 2007.

36. "World Bank Lending to Borrowers in Africa by Theme and Sector, Fiscal 2002–2007," World Bank, *Annual Report 2007*, and OECD/DAC Statistics www.oecd.org/dac/stats/data (accessed September 12, 2008).

37. Calculated by author from International Finance Corporation, *Annual Reports* (various years).

38. Paul S. Bennell, "British Manufacturing Investment in Sub-Saharan Africa: Corporate Responses During Structural Adjustment," *Journal of Development Studies*, 32(2) (1995): 193–217; Paul Bennell, "Industrial Restructuring in Africa During the 1990s: Outcomes and Prospects," background paper prepared for the *African Development Report 1998*, p. 16.

39. Office of the US Trade Representative, "2008 Comprehensive Report on US Trade and Investment Policy Toward Sub-Saharan Africa and Implementation of the African Growth and Opportunity Act," May 2008; Bureau of Economic Analysis, US Government, 1995–2007.

40. Stephen Hayes, president, Corporate Council on Africa, "Testimony on the Africa Growth and Opportunity Act (AGOA) to the United States Senate Committee on Foreign Relations," June 25, 2003.

41. "Guidelines to Assure USAID Programs Do Not Result in the Loss of Jobs in the US," Subpart 726.71 – Relocation of US Businesses, Assistance to Export Processing Zones, Internationally Recognized Workers' Rights," 726.7101 Policy Determination (PD) 20, Title 48, Federal Acquisitions Regulations System, US Code of Federal Regulations.

42. Dominique Patton, "Projects in Ghana, Ethiopia Benefit From China Fund," *Business Daily* (Nairobi), November 21, 2007.

43. "China's Eight-Measure Economic Policy on Africa Well-Implemented, Says Chinese Minister," *Xinhua*, January 20, 2009.

44. Over the past thirty-five years, a total of between $2.5 and $4.8 billion. Personal communication, Alison Germak, OPIC, March 14 and 17, 2008; "OPIC Highlights: OPIC Supports US Investment and Development Needs in Africa," April 2006, p. 1.

45. "China–Africa Development Fund Delegation Visits Liberia," Chinese Embassy, Monrovia, Liberia, April 24, 2008.

46. Lucian Cernat, Sam Laird, Luca Monge-Roffarello, and Alessandro Turrini, "The EU's Everything But Arms Initiative and the Least-Developed Countries," WIDER Discussion Paper No. 203/47, June 2003; Garth Frazier and Johannes van Biesebroeck, "Trade Growth under the US Growth and Opportunity Act," NBER Working Paper No. 13222, July 2007.

47. "China's Eight-Measure Economic Policy on Africa."

48. Adam Minson, "China's Preferential Trade Policy for Africa," South Africa Institute of International Affairs, China in Africa Briefing No. 1, February 2008.

49. Minson, "Preferential Trade Policy," p. 3.

50. Mark George, "China–Africa Two-Way Trade: Recent Developments," unpublished paper, Department for International Development, Beijing, January 30, 2009, pp. 5–6.

51. "Zhongguo Jiang Jianli 50 Ge Jingwai Jingmao Hezuoqu, Jianshao Maoyi Moca," ("China Will Establish 50 Foreign Economic and Trade Cooperation Zones to Reduce Trade Friction"), *Xinhua*, June 20, 2006.

52. Both kinds of zones had low taxes of 15 percent (with full tax exemption in the first two years and a 50 percent reduction in the following three years) and infrastructure at an international standard.

53. List of incentives based on author's interviews with Chinese economic counselors in Zambia, January 16, 2008 and Mauritius, June 26, 2008, and on "Investing Environment and Favorable Policies," on the website of the Mauritius Tianli Trade and Economic Zone, available at: www.mtetzone.com.

54. Fu Ziying, "International Strategy and a Harmonious World for the Financial Industry and Businesses," speech at China Financial Forum, February 12, 2007; Bo Xilai, speech at National Meeting of Foreign Economic and Trade Cooperation Zones held in Beijing, Department of Information Technology, Ministry of Commerce, Beijing, August 1, 2007.

55. See Appendix 4 for a list of the first zones selected.
56. Xu Weizhong, interviewed in "Economic Salon: The Chances and Risks of Investing in Africa," *Foreign Investment and Foreign Export Credit*, March 2006.
57. China Nonferrous Metal Mining (Group) Company Ltd. and China Association of Development Zones, "Master Plan for the Zambia–China Economic and Trade Cooperation Zone," June 2007.
58. Anil Gayan, "Tianli: Danger pour notre sécurité," *L'Express*, February 18, 2008.
59. Alain Barbé, "Coopération Sino-Mauricienne, quinze companies chinoises arrivent en prospection," *L'Express*, November 17, 2006.

4 Eastern Promises: An Aid System with Chinese Characteristics

1. "African Scramble: China Ups the Aid Stakes with its Thrust into Congo," *Financial Times*, September 29, 2007.
2. For the first decade after 1950, decisions on aid were made directly by the central government and simply assigned to related departments to implement, as part of the system of central planning. The Ministry of Finance managed cash aid. The Ministry of Trade (established in 1952) managed material aid (aid-in-kind) and assigned state-owned, import-export corporations to transfer the goods. When China began to do "turn-key" aid projects in 1954, the State Planning Commission assigned them to be done by different technical bureaus or ministries, which organized the work.
3. This discussion of the history of China's aid bureaucracy draws on Shi Lin, *Dangdai Zhonguo de Duiwai Jiingji Hezuo* ("China's Economic Cooperation with Foreign Countries Today") (Beijing: China Social Sciences Press, 1989).
4. Turn-key projects and technical assistance for the same project would frequently be assigned to different offices. For example, China's Mbarali farm project in Tanzania was constructed by a bureau under the Ministry of Construction, while the Jiangsu provincial government's Agriculture and Forestry Department was assigned to provide a team of agro-technicians to direct the planting and cultivation. Ai Ping, "From Proletarian Internationalism to Mutual Development: China's Cooperation with Tanzania, 1965–95," in Goran Hyden and Rwekaza Mukandala, eds., *Agencies in Foreign Aid: Comparing China, Sweden and the United States in Tanzania* (New York: Macmillan, 1999), p. 177.
5. Robert D. Dennis, "The Countertrade Factor in China's Modernization Plan," *Columbia Journal of World Business* (Spring 1982): 72.

6. Li Xiaoyun, "China's Foreign Aid to Africa," China Agricultural University, paper presented at workshop on "Managing Aid Effectively: Lesson for China?" International Poverty Reduction Center in China, Beijing, March 27–28, 2008.

7. Eight divisions for regions, including five for Africa, and five administrative divisions (human resources, financial management and planning, laws and regulations, information systems, and overall coordination).

8. Nicholas Lardy reports that "China began competitive bidding for projects financed by the World Bank in the 1980s. The practice then spread to major domestically funded infrastructure projects. By the mid-1990s, government administrative units in some regions began, on a trial basis, to use open, transparent bidding procedures for purchases." *Integrating China into the Global Economy* (Washington DC: Brookings Institution Press, 2002), p. 59. The announcements on projects and tenders are made in *China Construction News*, *China Daily*, or at www.chinabidding.com.cn.

9. For example, Special Fund for External Economic and Technical Cooperation; Overseas Economic and Trade Cooperation Zone Development Funds.

10. Quoted in Chris Buckley, "China Reviews Aid Policy as its Global Might Grows," *Reuters*, June 7, 2007.

11. New buildings for Ministries of Foreign Affairs were built for governments in Uganda, Côte d'Ivoire, Djibouti, Sierra Leone, Mozambique, and Rwanda, while Namibia's Ministry of Foreign Affairs received an in-kind donation of RMB 1 million, and Equatorial Guinea's foreign affairs building was expanded.

12. Export seller's credits have a long maturity and a preferential interest rate, and are provided to selected Chinese companies to help them export or invest overseas. China Eximbank's website lists six kinds of loans under the export seller's category: export seller's credits for ships, equipment, high- and new-tech products, and general mechanical and electronic products, as well as loans for overseas construction contracts and overseas investment projects (including joint ventures in which the Chinese partners have a majority share). China Eximbank, "Export Seller's Credit," available at: http://english.eximbank.gov. cn/business/credit.jsp (accessed December 14, 2008). As of March 2005, the bank had lent more than $2.4 billion for Chinese overseas investment, with a quarter of these loans going into manufacturing projects. The foreign investment loans were about 14 percent of the bank's total loans. Wang Zhi, "Supporting Chinese Enterprises to 'Go Global' in Every Way," *Economic Daily*, available at: www. eximbank.gov.cn/upload/13ecwang.doc (accessed August 29, 2008).

13. "The operations generally follow the Arrangement on Guidelines for Officially Supported Export Credits as developed by OECD...The interest rate could be either a fixed interest rate on the basis of the Commercial Interest Reference Rate (CIRR) as monthly announced by OECD, or a floating interest rate on the basis of London Interbank Offered Rate (LIBOR) plus a certain interest rate spread. For special cases, the interest rate could be negotiated and decided between the lender and the borrower." China Eximbank, "Export Buyer's Credits," available at: http://english.eximbank.gov.cn/business/buyer.jsp (accessed December 14, 2008).

14. In 2008, the Eximbank merged the staff of the preferential buyer's credit program and the foreign aid concessional loan program to enable the two relatively small programs to better manage the increase in their workload. The two instruments themselves remained separate.

15. China Import and Export Bank, "Zhongguo Zhengfu Duiwai Youhui Daikuan Jianjie" ("Introduction to Chinese Government Foreign Concessional Loans"), *Guoji Jingji Hezuo* ("International Economic Cooperation"), 6 (1997).

16. China Export Import Bank, *Annual Report 2006*, p. 17 (emphasis added).

17. "Chinese Bank-Financed Housing Project Kicked Off in Kenya," Xinhua, May 31, 2008.

18. According to both institutions' annual reports for 2007, the total assets of the CDB reached nearly $381 billion at the end of 2007, making it much larger than the Eximbank, whose total assets were only $69 billion. At the end of 2007, CDB loans outside mainland China accounted for 0.92 percent of the total portfolio (China Development Bank, *Annual Report 2007*, p. 9).

19. "China approves China–Africa Development Fund," *Xinhua* (Shanghai), May 14, 2007. Some were relatively small. CDB gave a $30 million line of credit to the East African Development Bank to fund productive enterprises, for example. "EADB Receives Credit from China," *The Monitor* (Kampala), June 11, 2008. The project manager, Robert Wabbi, said that at least half of the funds for any loans under the line of credit needed to be used to purchase goods or services from China.

20. "$1.5 Billion China Telecoms Deal," *Ethiopian News*, 5(2) (September and October 2006). International Financial Law Review Guide to the World's Leading Financial Law Firms, www.iflr1000.com/JurisdictionFirm/795/9/White–Case.html (accessed February 26, 2009).

21. Michelle Chan-Fishel, "Time to Go Green: Environmental Responsibility in the Chinese Banking Sector," Friends of the Earth and Bank Track, May 2007.

22. As a news report stated, "ZTE and China Exim Bank will join to establish a financing platform to support ZTE and its holding subsidiaries in overseas market activities, including export seller's credit, export buyer's credit, import credit, preferential foreign loans, transferred loans of foreign governments and trade financing, as well as other premium financial services." "ZTE Secures US $10 Billion Deal for Vendor Financing Contracts," *Cellular News*, available at: www.cellular-news.com/story/37622.php?source=rss (accessed May 25, 2009).

23. Huang Meibo, "Chinese Foreign Aid System and its Trend," unpublished paper, June 2007; Buckley, "China Reviews Aid Policy as its Global Might Grows."

24. Ai Ping, "China's Cooperation with Tanzania," p. 192.

25. C. Veilette, "Foreign Aid Reform: Issues for Congress and Policy Options," Congressional Research Service Report RL 34243 (November 7, 2007). On the large number of agencies involved in French aid, see Carol Lancaster, *Foreign Aid: Diplomacy, Development, Domestic Politics* (Chicago: University of Chicago Press, 2007), pp. 148–50.

26. According to Huang, "Chinese Foreign Aid System," p. 9, the institutions involved in these mechanisms are as follows. Inspection or evaluation (MOF, MOFCOM, MOFA); emergency humanitarian aid (MOFA, MOFCOM, Ministry of Civil Affairs, People's Liberation Army); human resources and training (MOFCOM, MOF, MOFA, Ministry of National Defence, Ministry of Education, Ministry of Public Security, Ministry of Land and Resources, Ministry of Information Industry, Ministry of Agriculture, Ministry of Health). The implementation committee for FOCAC is made up of twenty-seven ministries, including the Foreign Ministry, MOFCOM, Ministry of Finance, NRDC, Ministry of Education, Ministry of Health etc. See www.fmprc.gov.cn/zflt/chn/zt/default.htm. The office of the committee is located in the Africa Department of the Foreign Ministry. But the tendering in MOFCOM was organized by MOFCOM's Executive Bureau of International Economic Cooperation, Office for Foreign Aid Project Tenders.

27. "China's 16th Medical Team Leaves for Madagascar," *Xinhua*, November 4, 2006; "Chinese Medical Team Leaves for DR Congo," *Xinhua*, October 11, 2007.

28. "PRC Improves Medical Aid to Foreign Countries," *Xinhua*, October 11, 1999.

29. "PRC Improves Medical Aid to Foreign Countries."

30. Li Baoping, "On the Issues Concerned with China–Africa Education Cooperation," unpublished paper, Beijing University, 2006. Li reported that at least eight of these students are now holding ministerial posts (or higher), another

eight are at the level of ambassador or counselor, and six are serving "as premier or their secretaries."

31. Organization for Economic Co-Operation and Development, "The Aid Programme of China," W. 2196D/Arch. 0792D, Paris, March 1987, p. 21. According to a circular from the Ministry of Finance, scholarships do not appear to be paid out of the foreign aid budget. "Guanyu Yinfa 'Duiwai Yuanzhu Zhichu Yusuan Zijin guanli Banfa' de Tongzhi" (Ministry of Finance, "Measures for Oversight and Management of the Foreign Aid Budget," Ministry of Finance, China, June 24, 1998, available at: http://law.chinalawinfo.com/newlaw2002/slc/slc.asp?db=chl&gid=84478 (accessed May 22, 2009).

32. Gail A. Eadie and Denise M. Grizzell, "China's Foreign Aid, 1975–78," *China Quarterly*, 77 (1979): 230.

33. "Sierra Leone Students in China Demand to Go Back Home by Ship," *Standard Times* (Freetown), June 16, 2001.

34. Higher Education for Development, *Annual Report 2007*, p. 20, available at: www.hedprogram.org/Portals/0/PDFs/2007_AnnualReport.pdf (accessed May 22, 2009); BIFAD (Board for International Food and Agricultural Development), "Renewing USAID Investment in Global Long-Term Training and Capacity Building in Agriculture and Rural Development," Washington DC: BIFAD, June 2003, cited in Carl Eicher, "Flashback: Fifty Years of Donor Aid to African Agriculture," revised version of a paper presented at the InWEnt, IFPRI, NEPAD, CTA conference on Successes in African Agriculture, Pretoria, South Africa, December 1–3, 2003.

35. *China Commerce Yearbook* 2004, p. 78: "The increase of China's emergency humanitarian aid further demonstrated its image as a responsible major power."

36. "China Starts Largest Foreign Disaster Relief," MOFCOM press release, Beijing, January 5, 2005. See Huang, "Chinese Foreign Aid System," p. 9.

37. United Nations Development Program, "Tsunami Response: A Review of China's Contribution to the United Nations Response to the 2004 Indian Ocean Tsunami," UNDP, Beijing, January 2007.

38. Qi Guoqiang, "China's Foreign Aid: Policies, Structure, Practice and Trend," paper delivered to Oxford University Conference on New Directions in Foreign Aid, Oxford, June 2007, p. 5.

39. This section draws on these articles: "China Sends First Group of Volunteers to Africa," *China Daily*, August 4, 2005; Danna Harman, "Young Chinese Idealists Vie to Join their 'Peace Corps' in Africa," *Christian Science Monitor*, June 27, 2007; "Hundreds of Chinese Volunteers to Teach Mandarin in Thailand," *Xinhua*, June 4, 2007; "More Volunteers to Venture Abroad," *China Daily*,

September 6, 2006; "First 20 Volunteers Leave China for Seychelles," *Xinhua*, January 27, 2007, available at: www.Chinagate.com.cn/English/wb/49926.htm (accessed April 8, 2007), Li, "China–Africa Education Cooperation," pp. 3, 8, *China Commerce Yearbook 2006*, p. 111, and interviews with returned volunteers.

40. The first volunteers to Africa were actually sent to Mauritius by the Volunteer Program for International Chinese Teachers, Office of Chinese Language Council. Li "China–Africa Education Cooperation," pp. 2, 8.

41. Ai Ping, "China's Cooperation with Tanzania, 1965–95."

42. Rumors of political cash transfers at the presidential level have surfaced from time to time in the diplomatic tug of war between Beijing and Taipei. So far in Africa there has been no "smoking gun" or evidence provided for allegations like these, which are plausible but difficult to prove. In Latin America, scandals have surfaced of relatively small amounts transferred from Taiwan to presidents in the region ($1 million to the Panamanian President Mireya Moscoso, 2004; $1.5 million to Guatemala's President Alfonso Portillo, 2005). Johanna Mendelson Forman and Susana Moreira, "Taiwan–China Balancing Act in Latin America," Analysis of the Real Instituto Elcano (ARI) No. 154/2008, Real Instituto Elcano, Madrid, November 26, 2008, p. 3.

43. Li Xiaoyun, "China's Foreign Aid to Africa," p. 20.

44. "Establecimiento de relaciones diplomáticas con la República Popular China ha resultado beneficioso para el país" ("Establishment of Diplomatic Relations with the People's Republic of China Has Resulted in a Beneficial Outcome for the Country"), Ministry of Foreign Relations, Government of Costa Rica, September 7, 2008, available at: www.rree.go.cr/1243-RPCH-beneficios.doc (accessed February 6, 2009). For the full text of the agreement, see "Memorando de Entendimiento entre el Gobierno de la República de Costa Rica y el Gobierno de la República Popular China," *Nación*, September 10, 2008.

45. The Chinese also agreed that their State Administration of Foreign Exchange would buy $300 million of Costa Rica's bonds at a very preferential interest rate. This would also involve an element of subsidy, estimated by one source to amount to nearly $90 million. US–China Economic and Security Review Commission," 2008 Report to Congress," Washington DC, November 2008, p. 44.

46. The Foreign Ministry in Taiwan said that the sum was intended as a pledge of development aid, and that the PNG government had asked for it to be deposited as a guarantee while discussions were going on about recognition.

"Taiwan Control Yuan Impeaches Two MOFA Officials in Papua New Guinea Scandal," *Taiwan News* (Taipei), February 14, 2009.

47. "President Ma Defines 'Flexible Diplomacy'," *China Post*, November 11, 2008.

48. Stéphanie Giry, "China's Africa Strategy," *New Republic*, November 15, 2004. Giry speculated that China's interest must have been somehow related to oil-rich Chad next door.

49. The UN reported that the CAR "had completed a return to constitutional rule through transparent elections and had started to show its resolve to fight endemic corruption and to strengthen respect for human rights." "Central African Republic Needs Immediate Support to Prevent Renewed Conflict, Says UN Official," UN News Center, July 11, 2005.

50. The European Union provided some budget support to pay civil servant salaries. *Economist Intelligence Unit*, "Country Report: Central African Republic," February 2006, p. 7.

51. "US $3 Million Lands in Government Hands," *The News* (Monrovia), January 9, 2004; "Sustaining China–Liberia Relations – One Year of Renewed Ties," *The News* (Monrovia), October 21, 2004; "President EJS Travel Deliverables," available at: www.emansion.gov.lr/doc/travelanalysis.pdf (accessed November 21, 2007).

52. "China helps Guinea Bissau Pay Public Sector Workers," *Macauhub*, June 15, 2007, available at: www.macauhub.com.mo/en/news.php?ID=3512 (accessed January 15, 2008). Another source said it was $3.7 million. Panafrica News Agency (PANA) Daily Newswire, November 20, 2005.

53. "Seychelles: Five Agreements Signed with China During President Hu Jintao's Visit," *Seychelles Nation* (Victoria), February 7, 2007; "Zimbabwe Treasures China's Help in Difficult Times," *People's Daily*, July 1, 2009, and interviews, Harare, Zimbabwe, September 2009. Several countries have received cash grants of $100,000 to $500,000.

54. Huang, "Chinese Foreign Aid System," p. 9.

55. The first loan was for about $12.1 million in 1997 (at 4 percent interest). A second loan of about $5.8 million (at 3 percent) in 2000 expanded the plant; both loans had eight-year grace periods. "Zimbabwe: IDC Repays U.S.$2,8 m to Chinese Eximbank," *The Herald* (Harare), March 18, 2008.

56. Stephanie Hanson, "China, Africa, and Oil," Council on Foreign Relations, Backgrounder, June 6, 2008.

57. Premier Wen Jiabao, Speech at UN High Level Meeting on the MDGs, New York, September 25, 2008, *China Daily*, September 26, 2008, available at: http://english.gov.cn/2008–09/26/content_1106949.htm (accessed May 22, 2009).

5 Orient Express: How Does Chinese Aid and Engagement Work?

1. Constantine Michalopoulos, "Assistance for Infrastructure Development," in Anne O. Krueger, Constantine Michalopoulos, and Vernon W. Ruttan, *Aid and Development* (Baltimore, MD: Johns Hopkins University Press, 1989), p. 125.

2. Abdoulaye Wade, "Time for the West to Practice What it Preaches," *Financial Times*, January 24, 2008.

3. Andrew Grieve and Thomas Orr, seminar notes, "China's Involvement in Africa's Infrastructure Development," Centre for Chinese Studies Seminar, Shanghai, May 12, 2007, p. 2.

4. "The Future of Aid: A Scramble in Africa," *The Economist*, September 6, 2008, citing an Oxfam study.

5. "Review of World Bank Conditionality: Issues Note," Operations Policy and Country Services, World Bank, Washington DC, January 25, 2005.

6. Wade, "Time for the West to Practice What it Preaches."

7. "The Future of Aid," *The Economist*.

8. William Wallis and Geoff Dyer, "Lending Rattles the Traditional Donors," *Financial Times*, January 24, 2008.

9. List of Participants, Consultative Group Meeting for Sierra Leone, Freetown, November 29–30, 2006.

10. For example, on October 17, 2005, the two countries signed an AETC that offered an interest-free loan of 20 million RMB (about $2.4 million), which would be good for five years). The grace period would begin in 2010, and repayment would be from 2015 to 2025. Ministry of Foreign Affairs, Government of Sierra Leone, "Agreements/Contracts/Memoranda of Understanding with the Chinese Government," Freetown, Sierra Leone (no date).

11. The bid on the stadium project was won on August 25, 2006. Seventeen enterprises bid. Notification No. 22, 2006 of the Tendering Board for Foreign Assistance Projects of the Ministry of Commerce of the People's Republic of China, October 27, 2006.

12. Cheng Wenju, Ambassador of China to Sierra Leone, "Speech at the Symposium to Mark the 35th Anniversary of the Establishment of Diplomatic Relations between China and Sierra Leone," July 28, 2006.

13. The loan was for RMB 133 million. The turn-key contract was signed on July 28, 2006, and the final loan agreement on April 10, 2007. The terms of the loan were 2 percent interest, 1 percent management fee, a commitment fee of 0.75

percent on each year's balance, a grace period of five years, and maturity of twenty years (including the grace period). "Details of China's Loan to Sierra Leone," Ministry of Finance, Sierra Leone (no date).

14. *Almanac of China's Foreign Economic Relations and Trade 2001* (Beijing: Ministry of Foreign Trade and Economic Cooperation, 2002), p. 111.

15. Shi Heqiu, "China's Foreign Aid Developed in the Adjustment and Reformation," *Almanac 1992/1993* (Beijing, 1993), p. 66.

16. Carol Lancaster, *Foreign Aid: Diplomacy, Development, Domestic Politics* (Chicago: University of Chicago Press, 2006), pp. 112–15.

17. David Arase, *Buying Power: The Political Economy of Japan's Foreign Aid* (Boulder, CO: Lynne Rienner, 1995), pp. 109–10.

18. Arase, *Buying Power*, p. 114. OECF is Overseas Economic Cooperation Fund.

19. Wei Hong, "Woguo Duiwai Yuanzhu Fangshi Gaige de Jingyan yu Wenti" ("Experiences and Issues in the Reform of China's Method of Giving Foreign Aid"), *Guoji Jingji Hezuo* ("International Economic Cooperation"), 5 (1999): 4–8 (emphasis added).

20. President Alhaji Dr Ahmad Tejan Kabbah, "Address on the Occasion of the Special Session of the Second Parliament of the Second Republic of Sierra Leone," June 19, 2007.

21. United Nations, Office for the Coordination of Humanitarian Affairs, Sierra Leone Humanitarian Situation Report, October 2003, p. 9.

22. Cheng, "Speech."

23. Kabbah, "Special Session of Second Parliament."

24. Another possibility suggested by a foreign consultant was that the Sierra Leone government wanted to use the Chinese to put pressure on Sierra Leone Diamond Corporation (SLDC), which it believed was actually doing mining in areas where it only held licenses for exploration. SLDC had refused to hand over information gained from its exploration on the grounds that the Sierra Leone government could not secure the proprietary information.

25. John Mansaray, "Parliament Kicks Out Chinese Mining Agreement in Sierra Leone," *Awareness Times* (Freetown), June 25, 2007. The vague terms of the MOU, which mentioned a future royalty rate of 12.5 percent, would have been firmed up if the Henan survey led to actual exploration, and eventually mining. But to put it in perspective, the future royalty rate would have been more than double the 5 percent imposed by the Canadian province of Ontario to encourage diamond mining in their own hinterlands. This suggests that the proposal by Henan Guoji may not have been terribly exploitative. (The Ontario royalty

applied until March 2007.) "Diamond Royalty Concerns," available at: http://diamondconsultants.ca/mediacontent/DiamondRoyalty%20Concerns.pdf (accessed April 15, 2007).

26. This review is based primarily on "Contribution by the Minister on the Occasion of the Accords Signed Between the Government of the Democratic Republic of the Congo and the People's Republic of China," Ministry of Infrastructure, Public Works, and Reconstruction, Government of the Democratic Republic of the Congo, May 9, 2008.

27. John Vandaele, "China Outdoes Europeans in Congo," Inter Press Service (Johannesburg), February 8, 2008.

28. Vines and Campos, "Angola and China: A Pragmatic Partnership," p. 9.

29. "OP 7.20 – Security Arrangements," in *World Bank Operational Manual* (Washington DC: World Bank, 2002). See also World Bank, "IBRD's Negative Pledge Policy with Respect to Debt and Debt Service Reduction Operations," (R90–151), July 19, 1990.

30. Yet as some staff at the IMF told me in private, this prospect does not worry them. Further, they noted, the joint venture would involve only a very small fraction of the DRC's resources.

31. "A Reward for Promoting Foreign Aid Projects," *China Daily*, available at: www.chinagate.com/cn/english/wb/50018.htm (no date; accessed April 8, 2007).

32. "A Reward for Promoting Foreign Aid Projects."

33. Joaquim Alberto Chissano, "Why We Should Rethink Aid," statement by former President of Mozambique at Conference on New Directions in Development Assistance, Oxford University and Cornell University, Center for Global Economic Governance, June 11–12, 2007.

34. Christopher Swann and William McQuillen, "China to Surpass World Bank as Top Lender to Africa," available at Bloomberg.com, November 3, 2006.

35. William Easterly, "What Did Structural Adjustment Adjust? The Association of Policies and Growth with Repeated IMF and World Bank Adjustment Loans," Center for Global Development, Working Paper 11, October 2002. Even a major World Bank study on aid and reform in Africa concluded that "conditionality as an instrument to promote policy reform has been a failure." Shanta Devarajan, et al., eds., *Aid and Reform in Africa: Ten Case Studies* (Washington DC: World Bank, 2001).

36. This does not mean they are indifferent to unfavorable policy environments for their aid projects. They just go about it differently. As one Chinese analyst noted, "While China has a set of effective preferential policies for agriculture, African countries often lack these measures. When we start to negotiate

agricultural aid projects with the authorities in recipient countries, we should try to convince them to adopt preferential and supportive policies to ensure a better environment for the smooth implementation of the project." Zhou Jianjun and Wang Qiang, "Xin Xingshi Xia Dui Feizhou Nongye Yuanzhu de Tantao" ("Discussion and Exploration on Agricultural Aid for Africa under the New Situation"), *International Economic Cooperation* 3 (1997): 9–11.

37. Reserve Bank of Zimbabwe, "Investment Proposals and Financing Plan for the Projects in the Power Sector," Legal Department, Supplement 4 (no date, circa 2005), p. 19. The project was never implemented.

38. This story is based on my interviews in Zambia, including with Michael Sata, January 2008, and Chinese ambassador to Zambia, Li Baodong, January 2008. "Zambia: Michael Sata Riles China," *The Times of Zambia*, August 29, 2006; "Zambia: Sata Has a Deal With Taiwan – Li Baodong," *The Post* (Lusaka), September 3, 2006; "Zambia: China Threatens to Cut Ties," *The Times of Zambia*, September 5, 2006. "Chinese Envoy Challenges Zambian Opposition Leader over Taiwan Issues," *Xinhua*, September 5, 2006.

39. Joshua Kurlantzick, "Beijing Envy," *London Review of Books*, July 5, 2007, p. 11.

40. Catrinus J. Jepma, "The Tying of Aid," OECD Development Centre Studies, Paris, 1991, p. 15.

41. United States Agency for International Development, "Why Foreign Aid?" public relations pamphlet (circa 1995). For current data on aid-tying, see the Millennium Development Goals Indicators, Goal 8, available at http:mdgs.un.org/unscl/molg/ (accessed July 25, 2009).

42. See, for example, "Interim Measures for the Administration of Foreign Assistance Material Projects," Decree No. 5, Ministry of Commerce, July 7, 2006, available at: http://english.mofcom.gov.cn/aarticle/policyrelease/announcement/200804/20080405491354.html (accessed February 12, 2009). Brief announcements of the results of tenders are provided in English, for example: "Notification No. 7, 2008 of the Tendering Board for Foreign Assistance Projects of the Ministry of Commerce of the People's Republic of China," available at: http://english.mofcom.gov.cn/aarticle/policyrelease/gazettee/200805/20080505515160.html (accessed May 22, 2009).

43. "...no less than 50 percent of the procurements shall come from China." China Eximbank, "Chinese Government Concessional Loan," available at: http://english.eximbank.gov.cn/business/government.jsp (accessed January 24, 2009).

44. Under new rules, the OECD also allows up to 30 percent of an export credit to be used for local costs (site preparation or local construction), with 70 percent for

foreign costs. This was a change from an earlier limit of 15 percent. "Ex-Im Bank Increases Support for Local Costs on US Export Contracts From 15 Percent To 30 Percent," press release, United States Ex-Im Bank, April 7, 2008, available at: www.exim.gov/pressrelease.cfm/29910564-ED03-0A4D-41B576F7409E571C/ (accessed January 24, 2009).

45. John Vandaele, "China Outdoes Europeans in Congo," Inter Press Service (Johannesburg), February 8, 2008.

46. Ashraf Ghani and Clare Lockhart, *Fixing Failed States* (Oxford: Oxford University Press, 2008), p. 94.

47. Horizon Research Consultancy Group, "Current Status of and Future Prospects for Sino-African Cooperation," Beijing, September 2007, p. 124.

48. "Diplomacy Through Aid," *Time Magazine*, October 18, 1968.

49. Jamie Monson, "Liberating Labour? Constructing Anti-Hegemony on the Tazara Railway in Tanzania, 1965–76," in Christopher Alden, Daniel Large and Ricardo Soares de Oliveira, eds., *China Returns to Africa* (New York: Columbia University Press, 2008), p. 212.

50. Fox Butterfield, "Company Ready to Bring Peasants from China to US," *New York Times*, September 25, 1987.

51. Ministry of Commerce, *China Commerce Yearbook 2008*, pp. 217–18. All the figures on labor are from this source, except the total of 743,000 which comes from "MOFCOM Holds a Regular Press Conference on January 24, 2008," available at: http://english1.mofcom.gov.cn/aarticle/newsrelease/significantnews/200801/20080105362145.html (accessed November 6, 2008).

52. "The Economic and Trade Relations Between China and African Countries in 2007," *China Commerce Yearbook 2008*, p. 488. The Ministry of Commerce reported that 67,000 Chinese workers were sent to Africa in 2007, joining other Chinese workers who were already there, making the total 114,000.

53. In 2006, the Chinese ambassador to South Africa estimated that South Africa had around 100,000 resident Chinese, including long-time Chinese citizens. "Business Week Interviews Ambassador Liu Guijin (excerpts)," Embassy of the People's Republic of China in South Africa, July 17, 2006, available at: www.chinese-embassy.org.za/eng/znjl/t263487.htm (accessed February 24, 2008).

54. See http://chrisblattman.blogspot.com/2008/08/international-white-man-alert.html (accessed May 22, 2009).

55. Henry Lee and Dan Shalmon, "Searching for Oil: China's Oil Strategies in Africa," in Robert I. Rotberg, ed., *China into Africa: Trade, Aid and Influence* (Washington: Brookings Institution Press, 2008), p. 135, n. 32.

56. Tang Xiaoyang, "Bulldozer or Tow Tractor? Chinese Enterprises' Impact on the Local Employment Market in Angola and the DRC," New School, New York, unpublished paper, p. 13.

57. Center for Chinese Studies, "China's Interest and Activity in Africa's Construction and Infrastructure Sectors," Stellenbosch University, 2006, p. 69, and personal communication.

58. Chris McGreal, "Thanks China, Now Go Home: Buy-Up of Zambia Revives Old Colonial Fears," *The Guardian*, February 5, 2007.

59. The number of Chinese workers also depends on the host government policies on work visas. For instance, a South African company working in Zambia gave two construction contracts to Chinese firms because their bids came in lowest. Part of the deal was that the South African company had to guarantee to the Zambian government that the Chinese workers would return to China when the contract was finished. Personal email communication, David Hirschmann, March 20, 2007.

60. Keynote presentation at the Opening of the Round Table on Reforming Technical Co-operation for Capacity Development, Accra, Ghana, February 11, 2002, available at: www.minbuza.nl/nl/actueel/speeches,2002/02/reforming_technical_co_operation_for_capacity_development.html (accessed January 23, 2009).

61. "Welcoming PRC's Medical Team," *The Analyst* (Monrovia), August 3, 2005.

62. Deborah Brautigam, "State Capacity and Effective Governance," in Benno Ndulu and Nicolas van de Walle, eds., *Agenda for Africa's Economic Renewal* (New Brunswick: Transaction Publishers for the Overseas Development Council, 1996), pp. 81–108.

63. Action Aid, "Real Aid 2: Making Technical Assistance Work," May 7, 2006, available at: www.actionaid.org.uk/doc_lib/real_aid2.pdf (accessed May 22, 2009).

64. Speech by Chinese Premier Wen Jiabao, UN High-Level Meeting on the Millennium Development Goals, New York, September 25, 2008. The construction of schools and hospitals was part of the original FOCAC pledge made in Beijing, November 2006.

65. "Largest China–Foreign Joint School Founded in Ethiopia," *Xinhua*, December 24, 2008.

66. "First, as early as possible, inform recipient country staff of the time when Chinese experts will be leaving, so that they can prepare. Second, Chinese experts should gradually transfer to the second line, letting the recipient country staff work independently and practice solving problems on their

own. Third, instruct recipient country's staff in repair and maintenance of major equipment, and focus on areas of weakness. Fourth, help staff organize blueprints and drawings about gas lines, etc., and the operating instructions for equipment. Fifth, make a booklet of the various standard parts, and their categories. Draw simple pictures of non-standard parts so that they can be ordered as needed." Shi Lin, *Zhongguo Jingji Hezuo*, pp. 220–9 (translation by Zu Yiming).

67. Brautigam, "State Capacity and Effective Governance," p. 97.

68. Wan Yingquan, "A Brief Report on the Kpatawee Agricultural Cooperation Project," Ministry of Agriculture, Monrovia, Liberia, 1986. See also Deborah Brautigam, *Chinese Aid and African Development: Exporting Green Revolution* (New York: St. Martin's Press, 1998), pp. 164–6.

69. "Youyi is a Challenge," *Sunday We Yone* (Freetown), September 4, 1983, p. 3.

70. Thabiso Mochiko, "Huawei Continues African Expansion with Training Centre in Angola," *Business Report* (South Africa), October 27, 2008.

71. "ZTE Taps Overseas Market with Quality Service," *Market Avenue* (China), August 11, 2008.

6   Apples and Lychees: How Much Aid Does China Give?

1. Dianna Games, "Funds Alone Won't Take Mozambique to Next Level," *Business Day* (South Africa), February 12, 2007.

2. China Railway Construction Company, "China's Fastest Developed Overseas Project Contractor," CRCC website: www.crcc.cn/Page/210/Default.aspx (accessed October 24, 2008).

3. Moises Naim, "Help Not Wanted," *New York Times*, February 15, 2007.

4. Tim Whewell, "China to Seal $9bn DR Congo Deal," *BBC Newsnight*, April 14, 2008.

5. US Agency for International Development, Statistics and Reports Division, November 17, 1975, available at: www.marshallfoundation.org/about_gcm/marshall_plan.htm (accessed May 22, 2009).

6. "Growing More Corrupt," *Economist Intelligence Unit Views Wire*, October 17, 2008.

7. See the discussion in Roger Riddell, *Does Foreign Aid Really Work?* (Oxford: Oxford University Press, 2007), pp. 17–21.

8. At the OECD, an interest rate of 10 percent is assumed for commercial loans, for calculating the grant element of other loans. The IMF uses a different rate, the Commercial Interest Rate of Reference (CIRR).

9. Emphasis added. OECD, "Glossary," available at: www.oecd.org/document/19/ 0,3343,en_21571361_39494699_39503763_1_1_1_1,00.html (accessed May 22, 2009).

10. Wen Jiabao, Speech at the UN High Level meeting on MDGs, New York, September 25, 2008; Zhang Hongming, "China Policy of Assistance Enjoys Popular Support," *People's Daily*, June 23, 2006. The respective figures in renminbi were 206.5 billion yuan (total), of which 90.8 billion yuan was in the form of grants. For Africa, the amount of grants for 2008 was 2.3 billion yuan, plus 700 million yuan of interest-free loans, while the total amount of aid since 1956 was 44 billion yuan (2006). The inputs into these sums are unlikely to have been adjusted for inflation.

11. Du Daobin, "Opinion: China's Foreign Aid Should Be Public Knowledge," *Epoch Times*, September 10, 2003, available at: www.theepochtimes.com/news/ 3-9-19/6353.html (accessed April 8, 2007).

12. China's official *Xinhua* news agency sometimes includes figures for aid packages signed at meetings of senior Chinese leaders and their African counterparts. The Ministry of Commerce frequently circulates information about individual concessional loans and aid agreements to its provincial branches to encourage provincial companies to compete in tenders. But this seems to be done on an ad hoc basis. The Chinese have never provided annual figures on official development aid, country by country, as do OECD members.

13. "Guanyu Yinfa 'Duiwai Yuanzhu Zhichu Yusuan Zijin guanli Banfa' de Tongzhi" (Ministry of Finance, "Measures for Oversight and Management of the Foreign Aid Budget"), Ministry of Finance, China, June 24, 1998; Takaaki Kobayashi, "Evolution of China's Aid Policy," JBIC Institute Working Paper No. 27, April 2008, pp. 2–3, and author's interviews.

14. However, the mission statement of the United States Trade and Development Agency (USTDA) describes how it uses foreign aid to advance "US commercial interests in developing and middle income countries...USTDA's strategic use of foreign assistance funds...creates an enabling environment for trade, investment and sustainable economic development...In carrying out its mission, USTDA gives emphasis to economic sectors that may benefit from US exports of goods and services." United States Trade and Development Agency, "Mission Statement," available at: www.tda.gov (accessed April 8, 2007).

15. Foreign Ministry of the People's Republic of China, "China Pledges to Grant More Aid to Africa," press release, December 5, 2007, available at: www.fmprc. gov.cn/zflt/eng/zxxx/t387066.htm# (accessed May 22, 2009).

16. This budget differs from the OECD Development Assistance Committee's rules for official development assistance (ODA) in several ways. Most importantly, it counts military goods, but does not include some humanitarian aid expenses, or scholarships. Until we know further, I assume these cancel each other out.

17. The Export-Import Bank of China, *Annual Report 2005* (Beijing), p. 27.

18. In 2006, as we have seen, Chinese leaders pledged that they would provide $3 billion in concessional loans to Africa between 2007 and 2009. To meet this pledge to Africa, China's concessional loans would have to grow at an annual rate of around 63 percent.

19. The total of debt cancelled up to June 2008 was RMB 24.7 billion yuan ($3.6 billion at the exchange rate prevailing in June of RMB 6.86 = $1.00). Wen Jiabao, Speech at U.N. High-Level Meeting on MDGs. (This is also the speech where Wen reported a figure of RMB 206.5 billion ($30.8 billion) for China's aid, since the beginning.)

20. *Almanac* (various years). The average for this period was 57 percent. Information was not reported every year.

21. Li Zhaoxing, "Report by H. E. Mr. Li Zhaoxing, Minister of Foreign Affairs of the People's Republic of China to the Second Ministerial Conference of the China–Africa Cooperation Forum," Addis Ababa, December 15, 2003.

22. I have seen no official announcements of the percentage of the concessional loans that go to Africa. I have used a simple average of 50 percent, which may be an underestimate. As noted below, at the end of 2005, concessional loans to Africa probably came to an accumulated $800 million, while total concessional loans were around $1.116 billion. This would make the share in Africa close to 70 percent.

23. Figures announced by the Chinese were RMB 2.377 billion yuan ($349 million) in grants, and RMB 700 million yuan ($102 million) in interest-free loans. Converted by author at an exchange rate of RMB 6.8 to $1.00. See http://english.gov.cn/2008-09/26/content_1106949.htm (accessed May 22, 2009).

24. Harry Broadman, *Africa's Silk Road: China and India's New Economic Frontier* (Washington DC: World Bank, 2007), p. 274.

25. The figure given was RMB 11.3 billion. Chinese embassy official, statement at a conference organized by American University's School of International Service and Johns Hopkins University School of Advanced International Studies, Washington DC, April 6, 2007.

26. Standard and Poor's, Bank Credit Report: Export-Import Bank of China, August 2006, p. 5 (calculations by author).

27. Yang Zilin, Chairman And President, China Eximbank, "Strengthening Cooperation on Export Credit Activities Promoting Joint Development of Asian Countries," speech at the opening ceremony of the tenth Annual Meeting of Asian ECAs, May 11, 2004.

28. The Pakistan side contributed $50 million in local currency. "Gwadar Port," *Pak Tribune* (no date; circa 2001). This was for Phase I of the project. See www. paktribune.com/exclusive/gwadarport.shtml (accessed August 23, 2007).

29. Eximbank *Annual Report 2006*, p. 39.

30. The first export credit had a variable interest rate of CIRR plus 0.75 percent, a five-year grace period when only the interest would be paid, and a maturity of seventeen years (the period from the start of disbursement to full repayment). Ministry of Finance and Economic Planning, Government of Ghana, 2008 Budget, Appendix Tables. The second loan had a maturity of twenty years, and a five-year grace period. The grant element of the mixed credit was calculated by the Ghanaian Ministry of Finance and Economic Planning to be only 22 percent. This was just below the level of 25 percent (and up) required for a loan to be considered as ODA.

31. "For special cases, the interest rate could be negotiated and decided between the lender and the borrower." http://english.eximbank.gov.cn/business/buyer.jsp.

32. Alex Vines and Indira Campos, "Angola and China: A Pragmatic Partnership," Center for Strategic International Studies, Washington DC, p. 4.

33. "There is no question of this loan qualifying as ODA." Personal email communication, Simon Scott, director, Statistics, OECD, Paris, July 16, 2008.

34. Minister of Infrastructures, Public Works, and Reconstruction, "Contribution by the Minister on the Occasion of the Presentation of the Accords Signed Between the Government of the Democratic Republic of the Congo and the People's Republic of China," Kinshasa, Democratic Republic of the Congo, May 9, 2008.

35. These credits could be used for any projects negotiated by the two governments. A Chinese official at the embassy in Abuja told me that the Nigerians were unable to offer oil blocks outside of their relatively well-institutionalized system of oil block tenders, and that the offer of $2 billion, which had expired, was unlikely to be renewed. The $500 million preferential buyer's credit was still available. Interviews, Chinese embassy, Abuja, Nigeria, May 15, 2009; "Transcript of a Press Conference by African Finance Ministers," IMF, Washington, October 20, 2007; IMF, Nigeria Country Report No. 07/20, January 2007 (Second Review under the Policy Support Instrument).

36. "Transcript of a Press Conference."

37. Vivien Foster, William Butterfield, Chuan Chen, and Nataliya Pushak, "Building Bridges: China's Growing Role as Infrastructure Financier for Sub-Saharan Africa," World Bank, Trends and Policy Options No. 5, Washington DC, 2008, p. 8.

38. Salah Nasrawi, "China looks to Africa with an Eye to Reaping Financial and Political Gains," Cairo, Egypt, carried by AP Newswire, June 18, 2006. Wen had actually announced that China's assistance to Africa between 1957 and 2006 totaled *RMB* 44.4 billion ($5.7 billion). Zhang Hongming, "China Policy of Assistance Enjoys Popular Support," *People's Daily*, June 23, 2006.

39. Danna Harman, "China Takes up Civic Work in Africa," *Christian Science Monitor*, June 27, 2007, pp. 1–13. The figure on aid from the OECD and multilateral agencies is from the OECD/DAC.

40. The grant was for RMB 30 million ($4.4 million), the interest-free loan of RMB 40 million ($5.9 million) and the preferential export buyer's credit was $260 million at 2 percent interest. "Hu Signs Mauritius Accords," *China Daily*, February 18, 2009.

41. President Hu Jintao's visit to Namibia in February 2007 led to an aid pledge of RMB 1 billion ($131.6 million) of concessional loans, 100 million US dollars of preferential export buyer's credit, RMB 30 million yuan ($3.9 million) of grants and RMB 30 million ($3.9 million) of interest-free loans. "China–Namibia Relations," website of the Chinese embassy in Namibia, October 2007 available at: http://na.china-embassy.org/eng/zngx/t410246.htm (accessed May 22, 2009).

42. For example, Nigerian officials were undecided about how to allocate the $2.5 billion in Eximbank credit lines extended in 2006. At various times they sought to apply them to the Lagos–Kano railway, the Abuja mass transit project, and the Mambilla hydropower project. But the World Bank researchers mistakenly added all three of the projects to their list of "confirmed Chinese financing commitments" for a total of $4.5 billion. Foster et al., "Building Bridges," p. 74.

43. "Protocole d'Accord Entre le Gouvernement de Madagascar et la Société China CAMC Engineering Co., Ltd.," Ministre de l'Énergie et des Mines, Madagascar, June 22, 2006.

44. Foster et al., "Building Bridges," mentions this as "being developed" by the Chinese, p. 16. As a World Bank representative told me in Lusaka, in January 2008: "Kafue Lower Gorge has been through a lot of phases. There was a Nordic consortium in the late 1990s. They seemed to be doing a negotiated deal, but the government then decided to go for an open tender. In 2002 there were

six consortia on the short list, Eskom from South Africa, Scanska from Sweden, a US company, and so on. But then the government announced that Sinohydro would do the project faster. But that also didn't happen."

45. "Forget Mao, Let's Do Business: China and Africa," *The Economist*, February 7, 2005, p. 58.

46. Joshua Eisenman and Joshua Kurtlanzick, "China's Africa Strategy," *Current History*, 105 (May 2006): 219–24; on the source for this, personal communication, Joshua Eisenman, September 8, 2007.

47. Broadman, *Africa's Silk Road*, p. 274.

48. "The last officially reported flows are for 2002, when the Chinese government reported that it provided US$1.8 billion in economic support to Africa." Jian-Ye Wang, "What Drives China's Growing Role in Africa?" International Monetary Fund Working Paper, WP/07/211 (August 2007), p. 8.

49. Ministry of Commerce, "Turnover of Economic Cooperation with Foreign Countries or Regions," *China Statistical Yearbook*, 2004.

50. Comment by James Adams, World Bank vice-president for East Asia and the Pacific, "World Bank Says China Can Teach African Countries How to Develop," *Asian Economic News*, December 11, 2006.

51. Christopher Swann and William McQuillen, "China to Surpass World Bank as Top Lender to Africa," available at: Bloomberg.com (accessed November 3, 2006). The journalists told readers that China committed "$8.1 billion" just to Angola, Mozambique, and Nigeria in 2006, compared to the World Bank's pledge of "$2.3 billion" to all of sub-Saharan Africa.

52. The World Bank's commitments for sub-Saharan Africa in fiscal year 2006 were $4.8 billion, and loans to North Africa were $573 million. *Annual Report 2006*, Washington DC, p. 30. The previous year, World Bank commitments to Africa were $5.4 billion ($3.9 billion and $1.5 billion, respectively).

53. IDA is International Development Association, the zero-interest loan window of the World Bank.

54. Source for World Bank data: World Bank *Annual Report*, 2008. Figures are for the World Bank's financial year, not the calendar year.

55. China Eximbank had approved an accumulated $6.5 billion in export credits (non-concessional) for 260 projects in thirty-six African countries by the end of 2005, according to Chinese sources cited by Garth le Pere, "The Geo-Strategic Dimensions of the Sino-African Relationship," in Kweku Ampiah and Sanusha Naidu, *Crouching Tiger, Hidden Dragon? Africa and China* (Scottsville, South Africa: University of KwaZulu-Natal Press, 2008), p. 28. By the end of 2006, the Eximbank had approved more than 280 African loans, totaling more than RMB

92.5 billion ($11.6 billion). Li Ruogu, "Deepening Sino-African Cooperation and Promoting Common Development," *Overseas Investment and Export Credits*, special issue for the 2007 African Development Bank Annual Meetings, February 2007, p. 5. The difference between these two figures is $5.1 billion, which would be the loans approved during 2006.

56. "By this June, the total value of loans to Africa approved and signed by China Eximbank has topped over RMB 100 billion [$13.5 billion] while the outstanding stood at RMB 50 billion [$6.58 billion], accounting for 20 percent of the total business volume of the Bank." "The Export-Import Bank of China hosted a Symposium on Financing and Export Cooperation in Africa," Eximbank news release, July 24, 2007, available at: http://english.eximbank.gov.cn/info/Article.jsp?a_no=2001&col_no=84 (accessed May 22, 2009).

57. These figures aggregate my estimate above of the proportion of Eximbank's total export credits and guarantees extended to Africa, together with my estimates from Figure 6.2 of China Eximbank's concessional loans (which are not included in the totals published in Eximbank's annual reports). The figures for China Eximbank include loans to North Africa, which in 2006 made up about 31 percent of China Eximbank's Africa portfolio. China Eximbank *Annual Report*, 2006, p. 39. World Bank figures also include North Africa loans.

58. "China Approves China–Africa Development Fund," *Xinhua* (Shanghai), May 14, 2007. Some of the large Chinese companies financed to "go global" with large policy loans from China Development Bank (the telecommunications firms Huawei and ZTE, for example) have been able to offer attractive supplier's credits to win business in Africa. My research suggests that supplier's credits remain relatively rare. I have left them out of these estimates, as well as the relatively modest amounts offered by China's Department of Foreign Aid.

59. Swann and McQuillen, "China to Surpass World Bank."

60. "Official Export Credits, and Other Official Flows," in the OECD online database, OECD.Stat (accessed February 14, 2009).

61. "Private Flows to all of Africa (Total Banks)," from the OECD online database, OECD.Stat (accessed February 14, 2009).

62. A. Beattie and E. Callan, "China Loans Create 'New Wave of Africa Debt'," *Financial Times*, December 7, 2006.

63. International Monetary Fund, "Sudan: Staff Report for the Article IV Consultation and Staff-Monitored Program," EBS/06/59, Washington DC, April 19, 2006, cited in Ben Leo, Seth Searls, and Lukas Kohler, "Achieving Debt Sustainability in Low-Income Countries: Past Practices, Outstanding Risks,

and Possible Approaches," Occasional Paper No. 5, Department of the Treasury, Office of International Affairs, USA, November 2006.

64. Leo et al., "Achieving Debt Sustainability."

65. Michael M. Phillips, "G-7 to Warn China Over Costly Loans to Poor Countries," *Wall Street Journal*, September 15, 2006, p. A-2.

66. Henrique Almeida, "EU Will Not Cover Chinese Loans to Africa," *Reuters*, July 30, 2007.

67. Helmut Reisen and Sokhna Ndoye, "Prudent versus Imprudent Lending to Africa: From Debt Relief to Emerging Lenders," OECD Development Centre Discussion Paper No. 268, January 2008.

68. "World Bank President Robert B. Zoellick's Press Conference in China," transcript, December 18, 2007, available at: http://web.worldbank.org/WBSITE/EXTERNAL/COUNTRIES/EASTASIAPACIFICEXT/CHINAEXTN/0,,print:Y~isCURL:Y~contentMDK:21590904~pagePK:141137~piPK:141127~theSitePK:318950,00.html (accessed May 22, 2009).

69. Li Ruogu, "A Proper Understanding of Debt Sustainability in Developing Countries," *Shijie Jingji Yu Zhangzhi* ("World Economics and Politics"), 4 (2007): 63–72.

70. Li Ruogu, "Debt Sustainability and Sustainable Development," presentation at the OECD, Paris, November 14, 2006.

71. "Interview with African Development Bank President Donald Kaberuka," *Africa Confidential*, January 2007.

72. "China Never Imposes Its Will on Ethiopia By Way of Assistance," interview with Chinese Ambassador to Ethiopia Gu Xiaojie, *WALT* (Addis Ababa) August 19, 2008.

73. In early 2007, Ethiopian exporters were required by their government to channel all payments received for exports to China through the National Bank of Ethiopia. Centre for Chinese Studies, "China's Engagement of Africa: Preliminary Scoping of African Case Studies: Angola, Ethiopia, Gabon, Uganda, South Africa, Zambia," report prepared for the Rockefeller Foundation, University of Stellenbosch, September 2007, pp. 53–9, passim.

74. "$1.5 billion China Telecoms Deal," *Ethiopian News*, 5(2) (September and October 2006). The Chinese consortium led by ZTE won over seven other bidders on the initial tender, including German company Siemens, Finland's Nokia, France's Alcatel, and the Swedish firm Eriksson. "Chinese Firms to Invest $1.5 Billion Updating Ethiopia's Telephone Network," *Wireless News*, September 17, 2006.

75. Reisen and Ndoye, "Prudent versus Imprudent Lending," p. 30.

76. The real story turned out to be that the Chinese promised to consider co-financing some portions of the Malawi government's long desired Shire–Zambezi canal project, a $6 billion plan to link the landlocked country with the Indian Ocean. In 2006 the government claimed to have financing pledges for the mammoth project from the European Union, the World Bank's International Finance Corporation, the Development Bank of Southern Africa, the Amalgamated Bank of South Africa, and the governments of Egypt and Qatar. The aid package that welcomed Malawi to Beijing was more in the order of $280 million. Frank Phiri, "Budget-busting Canal," *The Nation* (Malawi), June 4, 2006. Deborah Nyangulu-Chipofya, "Windfall: K40bn Aid from China," *Malawi Times*, April 2, 2008.

77. This includes $11.6 billion in Eximbank exposure to Africa as of December 2006, and the $20 billion projected by the end of 2009, plus concessional loans of $1.115 billion as of the end of 2006, and projected concessional loans of $3 billion by the end of 2009, for a total of $35.7 billion. These figures do not include the relatively modest figures for other areas of external assistance.

7 Flying Geese, Crouching Tiger: China's Changing Role in African Industrialization

1. Richard Behar, "Special Report: China Invades Africa," Fast Company, Issue 126, June 2008, available at: www.fastcompany.com/magazine/126/special-report-china-in-africa.html (accessed July 15, 2008).

2. G. A. Donovan and Mike McGovern, "Africa: Risky Business," *China Economic Quarterly*, Q2 (2007): 24.

3. Raphael Kaplinsky, "What Does the Rise of China Do for Industrialization in Sub-Saharan Africa?," *Review of African Political Economy*, 35(1) (March 2008): 20.

4. Olukoya Ogen, "Contemporary China–Nigeria Economic Relations: Chinese Imperialism or South–South Mutual Partnership?" in *China in Africa: Who Benefits?* special issue of *China Aktuell*, 3 (2008) (from abstract).

5. Isiyaku Ahmed, "Northern Nigerian Businessmen Debate the Effects of Chinese Investments," *Voice of America News*, February 22, 2007.

6. Michael Chege, "Economic Relations Between China and Kenya: 1963–2007," Center for Strategic and International Studies, Washington DC, June 4, 2008, p. 23.

7. World Bank, "Patterns of Africa–Asia Trade and Investment, Potential for Ownership and Partnership," Washington DC (based on data from UNCTAD),

p. 63. This almost certainly does not include investment from Hong Kong, which is usually calculated separately.

8. Harry G. Broadman, *Africa's Silk Road: China and India's New Economic Frontier* (Washington DC: World Bank, 2007), pp. 98–9.

9. Cao Guochang, "Hebei Baoding: 7000 duo nongmin feizhou chuangye" ("More than 7000 Farmers Start Undertakings in Africa"), *New China Net*, Shijiazhuang, October 20, 2006.

10. This case is based on: "Sino-South African Economic and Trade Relations" (no date, probably around 2001), available at: http://en.chinagate.com.cn/english/380.htm (accessed March 15, 2008); "Hisense to Increase TV Production in South Africa," *Xinhua*, January 22, 2007; and Hisense S. A. Development Enterprise (Pty) Ltd website http://product.hisense.com/en/about/sub_inc/safrica.htm (accessed September 5, 2008).

11. Data from World Bank, *World Development Indicators*, 2007.

12. Paul Bennell, "Industrial Restructuring in Africa During the 1990s: Outcomes and Prospects," background paper prepared for the *African Development Report 1998*, Africa Development Bank.

13. Peter Lawrence, "Explaining Sub-Saharan Africa's Manufacturing Performance," *Development and Change*, 36(6) (November 2005): 1129.

14. Public opinion surveys conducted by Afrobarometer document still reveal a widespread skepticism about the private sector, especially in formerly socialist countries. In Ghana, for example, 70 percent of those surveyed in 1999 agreed with the statement: "The government should retain ownership of its factories, businesses and farms." Michael Bratton, Peter Lewis, and E. Gyimah-Boadi, "Attitudes to Democracy and Markets in Ghana," Afrobarometer Working Paper No. 2, 1999, p. 29.

15. Walden Bello, "Beijing's Diplomacy in Africa Sparks Debate at World Social Forum," *Focus on the Global South*, February 6, 2007.

16. My discussion here draws heavily on Nuno Crespo and Maria Paula Fontoura, "Determinant Factors of FDI Spillovers: What Do We Really Know?" *World Development*, 35(3) (2007): 410–25, and Arne Bigsten and Mans Soderbom, "What Have We Learned from a Decade of Manufacturing Enterprise Surveys in Africa?" *World Bank Research Observer*, 21(2) (Fall 2006): 241–66.

17. "The Problem with Made in China," *The Economist*, January 13, 2007.

18. Yung Whee Rhee, "The Catalyst Model of Development: Lessons from Bangladesh's Success with Garment Exports," *World Development*, 18(2) (February 1990): 333–46.

19. Paul Collier and Anthony J. Venables, "Rethinking Trade Preferences: How Africa Can Diversify its Exports," *World Economy*, 30(8) (August 2007): 1331.

20. K. Akamatsu, "A Historical Pattern of Economic Growth in Developing Countries," *Journal of Developing Economies*, 1(1) (March–August 1962): 3–25; S. Kasahara, "The Flying Geese Paradigm: A Critical Study of its Application to East Asian Regional Development," United Nations Conference on Trade and Development, Discussion Paper No. 169, April 2004.

21. Alan Rix, *Japan's Foreign Aid Challenge: Policy Reform and Aid Leadership* (London: Routledge, 1993), p. 149; Robert J. Orr, *The Emergence of Japan's Foreign Aid Power* (New York: Columbia University Press, 1990), pp. 77–8.

22. Kunio Yoshihara, The Rise of *Ersatz Capitalism in South East Asia* (Oxford: Oxford University Press, 1988).

23. Akira Suehiro, "Capitalist Development in Postwar Thailand: Commercial Bankers, Industrial Elite, and Agribusiness Groups," in Ruth Thomas McVey, ed., *Southeast Asian Capitalists* (Ithaca, NY: Cornell University Southeast Asian Program Publications, 1992), pp. 54–5.

24. For a list of projects between 1975 and 1987, see Gail Eadie and Denise M. Grizzell, "China's Foreign Aid, 1975–78," *China Quarterly*, 77 (March 1979): 217–34.

25. Xue Hong, "Discussions on Some Theoretical Questions of Setting up Joint Ventures Abroad," in *Almanac of China's Foreign Economic Relations and Trade 1986* (Beijing, 1987), pp. 803–4.

26. Quotation is from Hu Zhaoqing, "PRC: MOFTEC official on Foreign Economic Assistance," *Xinhua*, January 30, 1996. The other points are from Ministry of Foreign Trade and Economic Cooperation, "The Economic and Trade Relations between China and African Countries in 1998," *Almanac* (1999), p. 466.

27. *Almanac* (various years).

28. "Peking Builds Largest Tanzania Textile Mill," *Black Panther*, January 15, 1969, p. 3.

29. "Tanzania: Dar Employers Against Minimum Wage Increase," *East African* (Nairobi), January 11, 2008.

30. Wei Hong, "Woguo Duiwai Yuanzhu Fangshi Gaige de Jingyan yu Wenti," (Experiences and Issues in the Reform of China's Method of Giving Foreign Aid), *Guoji Jingji Hezuo* ("International Economic Cooperation"), 5 (1999): 4–8.

31. "Adding Value to our Exports Without Partisanship," *The Statesman* (Ghana), July 24, 2007.

32. Dela Tsikata, Ama Pokuaa Fenny, Ernest Aryeetey, "A Draft Scoping Study Prepared for the African Economic Research Consortium, Institute of Statistical, Social and Economic Research," University of Ghana, January 2008.

33. This account is based on "A Briefing on Sino-Namibian Relations," Chinese Embassy, Windhoek, Nambia, available at: http://na.china-embassy.org/eng/zngx/t144075.htm (accessed September 15, 2008); "Namibia: Northern Tannery Falters," *New Era* (Namibia), January 16, 2006; "Namibia: $50N Million Tannery Another White Elephant," *New Era* (Namibia), March 16, 2007; "Namibia: Millions for Gov't Tannery Down Drain," *The Namibian* (Namibia), June 29, 2007.

34. Figure given by Chinese source was RMB 3.9 billion. Zhang Dingmin, "Bank Finances Plant in Mali," *China Daily*, March 22, 2000.

35. The loan was for RMB 100 million ($12 million). Interview, Chinese official, Dar es Salaam, Tanzania, January 8, 2008.

36. Melanie Yap and Diane Leong Man, *Colour, Confusion and Concessions: The History of the Chinese in South Africa* (Hong Kong: Hong Kong University Press, 1996), p. 421.

37. L. M. Lim, "Hong Kong and the Free Zone," *L'Express* (Mauritius), July 11, 1997.

38. This story is based in part on research later published in Deborah Brautigam, "Substituting for the State: Institutions and Industrial Development in Eastern Nigeria," *World Development*, 25(7) (1997): 1063–80.

39. Boladale Abiola, "Knowledge, Technology and Growth: The Case Study of Nnewi Auto Parts Cluster in Nigeria," Knowledge for Development Program, World Bank Institute, Washington DC, World Bank, April 2006, p. 20.

40. "Virgin business terrain – Chukwuma,"*Daily Champion* (Lagos), December 25, 2007.

41. Wuling's website states that the company is following the directive of China's eleventh five-year plan to move into overseas markets through establishing a "leading position" in the international automotive industrial chain. Wuling Auto, "About Us," available at: http://wulingauto.com.cn/en/About_Us.aspx (accessed May 30, 2009).

42. Data supplied to author by Tanzania Investment Commission, Dar es Salaam, January 2008.

43. "Angola: Dongfeng-Nissan Auto Plant Opens in April," *Macauhub.com*, March 12, 2008; *East African*, November 26, 2007.

44. Abiola, "Nnewi Auto Parts Cluster in Nigeria," p. 20.

8 Asian Tsunami: How a Tidal Wave Can also Be a Catalyst

1. For example, tax rebates for lightly processed leather exports were removed in 2006 to encourage movement up the value chain in China. In 2007, tax rebates were removed for all leather products, specifically to reduce pollution and energy consumption. "China Cut Export Rebates on all Leather Products Since July 1st (2007)," available at: www.leather.com.cn/eng/zhengce/index. htm (accessed September 21, 2008).

2. Hazan Shoe Company, available at: www.madeinchina.com/261994/aboutus. shtml (accessed September 20, 2008).

3. Dominique Patton, "Chinese Company Plans to Open Tannery," *Business Daily* (Nairobi), March 4, 2008.

4. Participants came from Kenya, Tanzania, Eritrea, Ethiopia, Zimbabwe, Zambia, Sierra Leone, and Nigeria. Dominique Patton, "China Breaks New Ground in Leather Technology," *Business Daily* (Nairobi), June 1, 2008.

5. This case is based on author's research and these articles: "China–Uganda Trade Deficit Hits $120 m," *New Vision* (Uganda), February 28, 2007; Doreen Musingl, "Jinja Factory Closed over Pollution," *New Vision* (Uganda), November 22, 2007; "NWSC Seals Sewage Lines from Leather Industries," *The Monitor* (Uganda), March 25, 2008; Joseph Mazige, "Leather Firms Lose Millions of Shillings after Closure," *The Monitor* (Uganda), May 13, 2008.

6. Tegegne Gebre-Egziabher, "Impacts of Chinese Imports and Coping Strategies of Local Producers: The Case of Small-scale Footwear Enterprises in Ethiopia," *Journal of Modern African Studies*, 45(4) (2007): 647–79. Local tanneries were exporting 86 percent of their output, with only minimal processing.

7. Muluken Yewondwossen, "Chinese Factory to Produce Gloves, Footwear in Ethiopia," *Capital* (Ethiopia), August 12, 2008.

8. R. W. Johnson, "China's Empire-Builders Sweep up African Riches," *Sunday Times*, July 16, 2006.

9. See http://zambian-economist.blogspot.com/2008/05/chinas-impact-in-zambia-bbc-report.html (accessed February 21, 2009).

10. These cotton spinning mills were located in Benin (Lokossa), Burundi (Complexe Textile de Bujumbura, or COTEBU), Congo (Société des Textiles du Congo or SOTEXCO), Ethiopia (Awassa), Mali (COMATEX), Tanzania (Friendship), Zambia (Mulungushi), Sudan (Friendship). Clothing factories but not mills were established in Mauritania and Zimbabwe. A Chinese cotton spinning aid project in Ghana is mentioned in Gail A. Eadie and Denise

M. Grizzell, "China's Foreign Aid, 1975–78," *China Quarterly*, 77 (1979). Mozambique also had a cotton textile project.

11. Manufacturers Association of Nigeria, 1995, p. 3, in Paul Bennell, "Industrial Restructuring in Africa During the 1990s: Outcomes and Prospects," unpublished background paper prepared for the African Development Report, 1998.

12. UNCTAD, "Asian Foreign Direct Investment in Africa: Towards a New Era of Cooperation among Developing Countries," United Nations, New York, 2007, p. 56.

13. Tanzania (Friendship), Zambia (Mulungushi), Benin (Lokossa), and Mali (Segou/COMATEX). The Burundi government offered COTEBU for privatization in 1992, and asked for more technical assistance from China in 2002, but COTEBU was still 100 percent state-owned in 2007, when production was suspended. Africa Business Development, "Cotebu – Burundi Textile Company," available at: www.africabusiness.se/countries/burundi_/Cotebu_info.aspx (accessed September 2, 2008). A brief mention on a blog suggested that China's former aid project SOTEXCO in Congo had closed down.

14. In 1997 Shanghai Huayuan Group bought 80 percent of Sonitextil, a privatized factory in Niger, in a joint venture with a Nigerien entrepreneur who had studied in China (they renamed the company Enitex). In 2002, according to China's Ministry of Commerce, a Chinese company from Shandong bought a Guinean textile factory, Sanoyah, constructed in the 1960s by a Belgian-French venture, nationalized, and later privatized, by the Guinean government. "Guinée Complexe Textile Linmian Shandong Chine," February 18, 2005, available at: http://gn2.mofcom.gov.cn/aarticle/bilateralvisits/200502/20050200017566.html (accessed October 7, 2008).

15. Since 2000, Chinese concessional aid loans have funded upgrading of textile industries in Benin (Lokossa), Burundi (COTEBU), Niger (Enitex), Ethiopia (Awassa), Tanzania (Friendship), Zambia (Mulungushi), and Sudan (Friendship).

16. Omoh Gabriel and Victor Ahiuma-Young, "How Nigerian Textiles Failed to Tap into the $31bn US Booming Export Garment Market," *Vanguard* (Lagos), April 14, 2008.

17. Employment between 2004 and 2005 fell 9 percent in Kenya, 29 percent in Lesotho, 12 percent in South Africa, and 56 percent in Swaziland. Raphael Kaplinsky and Mike Morris, "Do the Asian Drivers Undermine Export-Oriented Industrialization in SSA?" *World Development*, 36(2) (February 2008).

18. Muntazir Zaidi, "Textile and Clothing Sectors Recover from Slump, Swaziland," July 8, 2007, available at: www.tg-supply.com/article/view.html?id=16048 (accessed September 2, 2008).

19. Vinaye Ancharaz, "Mauritius: Benefiting from China's Rise," *The China Monitor*, Issue 39, Center for Chinese Studies, University of Stellenbosch (April 2009), p. 6; see also Amédée Darga, "The Rebound of the Mauritian Textiles Industry," International Centre for Trade and Development, *News and Analysis*, 11(5) (August 2007).

20. Ministry of Economy, Finance and Budget, Government of Madagascar, as reported by World Bank, "Madagascar," 2008, p. 20; Jean-Pierre Cling, Mireille Razafindrakoto, and François Roubaud, "Export Processing Zones in Madagascar: The Impact of the Dismantling of Clothing Quotas on Employment and Labour Standards," Working Paper, DIAL, Paris, September 2007.

21. Calculated by author from Manufacturing Index of Production 2003–7, Kenya National Bureau of Statistics, available at: www.cbs.go.ke/.

22. Lawrence Edwards and Mike Morris, "An Evaluation of the Employment Trends in the Clothing and Textile Industry," University of Cape Town, South Africa, October 23, 2006.

23. The International Textile, Garment, and Leather Workers Federation's African chapter, quoted in *Business Day*, September 27, 2005, in Ian Taylor, *China's New Role in Africa* (Boulder, CO: Lynne Rienner, 2009), p. 84.

24. Phil Alves, "It's Time to Stop Blaming China Alone over Textiles," *Business Day* (South Africa), June 12, 2006.

25. E-TV interview with Zhou Yuxiao, chargé d'affaires, Chinese embassy, South Africa, April 13, 2006.

26. Sanusha Naidu, "Balancing a Strategic Partnership? South Africa–China Relations," in Kweku Ampiah and Sanusha Naidu, *Crouching Tiger, Hidden Dragon? Africa and China* (Scottsville, South Africa: University of KwaZulu-Natal Press, 2008), p. 188.

27. J. Van Eeden and T. Fundira, "South African Quotas on Chinese Clothing and Textiles: 18 Month Economic Review," Tralac Working Paper No 08/2008.

28. "Africa: China's Great Leap into the Continent," *Reuters*, March 23, 2006.

29. Mathabo Le Roux, "South Africa; State Plan to Beef up Clothing and Textiles," *Business Day* (Johannesburg), August 11, 2008.

30. E-TV interview with Zhou Yuxiao.

31. Ibid.

32. Textiles, spinning, knitwear, garments, home appliances, pharmaceuticals, shoes, building materials, and electrical appliances are among the Chinese industries encouraged to establish production bases overseas. "Industrial Catalog for Foreign Investment," Policy Guidance for Overseas Investment, jointly issued

by the National Development and Reform Commission, Ministry of Commerce, Ministry of Foreign Affairs, Ministry of Finance, General Administration of Customs, State Administration of Taxation, and State Administration of Foreign Exchange, July 5, 2006, available at: www.tech110.net/policy/html/article_382215.html (accessed August 26, 2008).

33. Cling et al., "Export Processing Zones in Madagascar," pp. 10, 15, 17.

34. Mathabo Le Roux, "Lesotho Shows Textile Woes Are about More than China," *Business Day* (South Africa), July 1, 2006.

35. Personal email communication, Mark S. Bennett, former ComMark adviser to the Lesotho textile industry, September 7, 2008.

36. UNCTAD, *World Investment Report*, 2007, p. 38.

37. See, for example: "Convenient transportation, perfect infrastructure, low labor price and extensive market in South Africa will be used *to export more parts, accessories and materials* for electronic machinery and textile and clothing. Domestic enterprises will be encouraged to cooperate with potential black entrepreneurs." "Sino-South African Economic and Trade Relations," (no date; circa 2001), available at: http://en.chinagate.com/cn/english/380.htm (emphasis added).

38. Nnamdi Duru, "HPZ Builds First Ozone Friendly Factory in Africa," *This Day* (Lagos), May 22, 2005; F. Bonaglia, A. Goldstein, and J. A. Mathews, "Accelerated Internationalization by Emerging Markets' Multinationals: The Case of White Goods Sector," *Journal of World Business*, 42(4) (2007): 369–83.

39. Tagu Zergaw, "ZTE, Janora to Build Mobile Assembly," *Capital* (Ethiopia), September 4, 2008.

40. Pharmaceutical projects based on: Jean Razafindravonona, Eric Rakotomanana, and Jimmy Rajaobelina, "Étude sur les Échanges entre Chine et Madagascar," Africa Economic Research Consortium, Nairobi, January 2008, p. 18; "$4 million Pharmaceutical Joint Venture Inaugurated," available at: http://gh.chineseembassy.org/eng/xwdt/t200166.htm (accessed May 22, 2009). "Madagascar Invites More Investment from China," CRIEnglish webcast, July 4, 2008, available at: http://english.cri.cn/4026/2007/07/04/1361@245587.htm (accessed September 19, 2008); "Sichuan Drug Maker Starts Construction of Anti-Malarial Factory," *China Pharmaceuticals and Health Technologies Weekly*, August 22, 2007; "Tasly Plans to Set Up Factory in Kenya," *Xinhua*, January 25, 2007.

41. Examples in this paragraph are from author's interviews and Yang Yao and Yin He, "Chinese Outward Investing Firms," A Study for FIAS/IFC/MIGA,

China Center for Economic Research, Peking University, August 2005, p. 53; Alan Odhiambo, "Asian Firms Flock to Kenya in Search of Big Deals," *Business Day* (Nairobi), April 1, 2008;

42. Andualem Sisay, "Ethiopia – Billion Birr Steel, Cement Factories Underway," *Capital* (Ethiopia), September 4, 2007 (the four Chinese partners were Jiangsu Yonggang Group, Panhua Group, Jiangsu Qiyuan Group and Zhangjiang Pipe-making Ltd).

43. Harry Broadman, *Africa's Silk Road: China and India's New Economic Frontier* (Washington DC: World Bank, 2007), pp. 52–6.

44. Author's calculations from data supplied by the Tanzania Investment Commission, January 2008.

45. "Chinese Shops and the Formation of an Expatriate Community in Namibia," paper delivered at conference on China and Africa, School of Oriental and African Studies, London, September 26, 2008.

46. Andrew Child and David White, "Chinese Investors Target Virgin Markets," *Financial Times*, March 15, 2005.

47. Sechaba Consultants, "Report on Employee Attitudes and Satisfaction in Textile Factories in Lesotho," prepared for ComMark Trust, Lesotho, March 2004, p. 1.

48. Personal email communication, Mark S. Bennett, former ComMark adviser to the Lesotho textile industry, September 9, 2008.

49. Joseph Onjala, "A Scoping Study on China–Africa Economic Relations: The Case of Kenya," African Economic Research Consortium (AERC), Nairobi, March 2008, p. 23.

50. Walden Bello, "Beijing's Diplomacy in Africa Sparks Debate at World Social Forum," *Focus on the Global South*, February 6, 2007.

51. O. Cadot and J. Nasir, "Incentives and Obstacles to Growth: Lessons from Manufacturing Case Studies in Madagascar," Regional Program on Enterprise development, RPED Working Paper No. 117 (2001), World Bank, Washington DC.

52. George Clarke, David E. Kaplan, Vijaya Ramachandran, James Habyarimana, and Mike Ingram, "An Assessment of the Investment Climate in South Africa," World Bank, May 2007, p. 17.

53. Mike Morris and Leanne Sedowski, "Report on Government Responses to New post-MFA Realities in Lesotho," Institute for Global Dialogue, South Africa, May 2006, p. 15, available at: www.saldru.uct.ac.za/prism/lesotho_clothingrept.pdf (accessed May 22, 2009).

54. Broadman, *Africa's Silk Road*, pp. 251–6.

55. "Hisense To Increase TV Production in South Africa," *Xinhua*, January 22, 2007.

56. Companies in Mauritius also employ foreign workers from a variety of other Asian countries. Government of Mauritius, Central Office of Statistics.

57. Paul Collier and Anthony J. Venables, "Rethinking Trade Preferences: How Africa Can Diversify its Exports," *World Economy*, 30(8) (August 2007): 1341.

58. International Finance Corporation, *Annual Report*, 2007, p. 37.

59. Morris Aron, "Kenya: 1,200 EPZ Jobs Lost to Asian Firms Since 2005," *Business Daily* (Nairobi), November 6, 2007.

9   Exporting Green Revolution: From Aid to Agribusiness

1. Yun Wenju, "Cong Guoji Yuanzhu de Fazhan Kan Zhonguo dui Fei de Yuanzhu" ("The Development of International Aid and China's Agricultural Aid to Africa"), *West Asia and Africa*, 2 (2000): 17–23.

2. *The Economist*, April 19, 2008, p. 54.

3. "15 Mln Farmers to Lose Land over Next 5 Years," *Xinhua*, July 24, 2006.

4. Albert Keidel, "China's Social Unrest; The Story Behind the Stories," Carnegie Endowment Policy Brief No. 48, September 2006.

5. Figures from Tony Peacock, Christopher Ward, and Gretel Gambarelli, "Investment in Agricultural Water for Poverty Reduction and Economic Growth in Sub-Saharan Africa Synthesis Report," Collaborative program of ADB, FAO, IFAD, IWMI, and World Bank, 2007 (draft), cited in World Bank, "World Bank Assistance to Agriculture in Sub-Saharan Africa, An Independent Evaluation Group Review," Washington DC, 2007, p. 121.

6. Agriculture here includes aid to fisheries and forestry. Africa received only 3 percent of all World Bank funding for irrigation and drainage between 1994 and 2004. World Bank, *Annual Report*, 2007, Eicher, "Flashback," p. 35; World Bank, "World Bank Assistance," p. 28.

7. World Bank, "World Bank Assistance," p. 34. Irrigation poses environmental and health risks. Without proper management, standing water can breed mosquitoes and other pests that carry tropical diseases, while better water control and drainage can affect the wetlands that are important refuges for bird and animal species.

8. Carl Eicher, "Flashback," p. ii. Eicher also pointed out that US food aid in Ethiopia alone in 2003 was larger than the budget for all US aid to agricultural development across the world in 2001 ($354 m).

9. For an overview of this aid, see my earlier book, Deborah A. Brautigam, *Chinese Aid and African Development: Exporting Green Revolution* (New York: St. Martin's Press, 1998).

10. "Chinese President: Food Issue Concerns World's Development, Security," *Xinhua*, July 9, 2008.

11. Between 2003 and 2008, China built fourteen turn-key agricultural aid projects in Africa. "Chinese President: Food Issue Concerns World's Development, Security."

12. Chen Shun and John Karanja, "Africa Focus: China–Africa Agricultural Cooperation Reaches New Heights," *Xinhua*, November 6, 2007; "Agricultural Cooperation," FOCAC Summit website, September 21, 2006: http://english. focacsummit.org/2006-09/21/content_905.htm (accessed May 22, 2009).

13. They continue to get their regular salary at home, plus a stipend of about $800 per month, he said (October 2007).

14. Government of Tanzania, Presidential Parastatal Sector Reform Commission, "Invitation for Outright Purchase of Assets of Mbarali Rice Farm," Dar es Salaam, Tanzania, 2004; Ai Ping, "From Proletarian Internationalism to Mutual Development: China's Cooperation with Tanzania, 1965–95," in Goran Hyden and Rwekaza Mukandala, *Agencies in Foreign Aid: Comparing China, Sweden and the United States* (New York: St. Martin's Press, 1999), pp. 177–8.

15. "Diplomacy Through Aid," *Time Magazine*, 18 October 1968. Taiwan also built some large sugar plantations and factories: Liberia Sugar Company in southeastern Liberia, for example.

16. Most of this was rice (35,700 hectares). Like Taiwan, Beijing also developed a sideline specialty in sugarcane (11,800 hectares). Shi Lin, editor in chief, *Dangdai Zhongguo de Duiwai Jiingji Hezuo* ("China's Economic Cooperation with Foreign Countries Today") (Beijing: China Social Sciences Press, 1989), pp. 140–56.

17. Zhou Jianjun and Wang Qiang, "Xin Xingshi Xia Dui Feizhou Nongye Yuanzhu de Tantao" ("Discussion and Exploration on Agricultural Aid for Africa under the New Situation"), *International Economic Cooperation* 3 (1997): 9–11, emphasis added.

18. The rate applied to the period between 1965 and 1986. World Bank, *Rural Development: World Bank Experience* (1988), in Eicher, "Flashback."

19. Mahmud Duwayri, Dat van Tran, and Van Nguu Nguyen, "Reflections on Yield Gaps in Rice Production: How to Narrow the Gaps," available at: www. fao.org/docrep/003/x6905e/x6905e05.htm (accessed May 22, 2009).

20. Deborah Brautigam, "Chinese Agricultural Aid in West Africa: A Technical, Institutional, and Economic Analysis," unpublished Ph.D. dissertation, Fletcher School of Law and Diplomacy, Tufts University, 1987.

21. Technical Assistant's Report, Ministry of Agriculture and Natural Resources Files, Makali Station, Sierra Leone, June 1977.

22. "Minutes of Meeting at Tower Hill," Ministry of Agriculture and Natural Resources, Chinese Project Files, Tower Hill, Freetown, January 3, 1979.

23. Han Baocheng, "China Proposes Aid Plan for Africa," *Beijing Review*, 29, July 21, 1986, p. 26. See also "More Effective Aid to Foreign Countries," *Xinhua* in Chinese, March 1, 1984, Foreign Broadcast Information Service, Part 3, The Far East; Weekly Economic Report; A. Economic and Scientific; China; FE/W1277/A/15.

24. China AGRICON, "Rolako Rice Production Feasibility Study," prepared for Mr. Jamil Said Mohammed, September 7, 1985.

25. Interview, Lei Shilian, manager, China Agricon, Freetown, Sierra Leone, June 16, 1988. A March 1, 1984 *Xinhua* article, "More Effective Aid to Foreign Countries," said that "China is devoting efforts to increasing the economic results of its various forms of agricultural aid to foreign countries." It mentioned the Magbass project, and also mentioned that China Agricultural, Animal Husbandry, Fishery, Engineering Services Export Company "sent people to five countries including Rwanda, Uganda, and Libya to assume contracted responsibilities for growing paddy-rice and breeding freshwater fish...In addition, progress has been made in its talks with some Asian and African countries on making joint investment in agricultural undertakings." China Agricon also won an FAO contract for sericulture (rice cultivation) in Madagascar in 1986. See www.undp.org/execbrd/archives/sessions/gc/34th-1987/DP-1987-12-Add5-PARTI.pdf (accessed May 22, 2009).

26. "Co-operation Agreement between China and Sierra Leone," *Xinhua*, March 28, 1985. "Under the agreement, the Chinese government will provide 30m yuan to a number of Chinese companies to use in joint projects with Sierra Leone. The two sides will also explore possibilities of expanding co-operation in agriculture, water conservancy, forestry and sugar production."

27. Yun Wenju, "Cong Guoji Yuanzhu de Fazhan Kan Zhongguo dui Fei de Yuanzhu" ("The Development of International Aid and China's Agricultural Aid to Africa"), *West Asia and Africa*, 2 (2000): 17–23.

28. Zhou Jianjun and Wang Qiang, "Xin Xingshi Xia Dui Feizhou Nongye Yuanzhu de Tantao" ("Discussion and Exploration on Agricultural Aid for Africa under the New Situation"), *International Economic Cooperation* 3

(1997): 9–11 (emphasis added); Si Liang, "Special Article: China's Two New Forms of Aiding Foreign Countries," *Zhongguo Tongxun She*, May 8, 1996, translated in Foreign Broadcast Information Service, FBIS-CHI-96-102, May 29, 1996 (emphasis added).

29. FOCAC, "Agricultural Cooperation," September 21, 2006, available at: http://english.focacsummit.org/2006-09/21/content_905.htm (accessed October 15, 2007).

30. "Senegal Welcomes Chinese Investment in Agriculture," *China Daily*, July 23, 2008.

31. Xia Zesheng, "Quanmian Tuijin Zhong Fei Nongye Hezuo Zhengfengqishi" ("It is the Right Time for the Serious Promotion of China–Africa Agricultural Cooperation"), *Guoji Shangbao* ("International Business Daily"), November 20, 2006.

32. Elizabeth Nambiro, Hugo de Groote, and Willis Oluoch Kosura, "Market Structure and Conduct of the Hybrid Maize Seed Industry, a Case Study of the Trans Nzoia District in Western Kenya," proceedings of the seventh Eastern and Southern Africa regional maize conference, February 11–15, 2001, pp. 474–9. See also James C. McCann, *Maize and Grace: Africa's Encounter with a New World Crop, 1500–2000* (Cambridge, MA: Harvard University Press, 2005).

33. Li Jinhui, "Yuan Longping – Father of Hybrid Rice," china.org.cn, May 3, 2001.

34. "Energy Partnership with Africa Based on Equality," *China Daily*, June 22, 2006.

35. Peng Jiming, "Studies on the Use of Chinese Hybrid Rice with Modified SRI in Guinea," China National Hybrid Rice Research and Development Centre, Changsha, Hunan, China (no date).

36. "Fruitful Agricultural Cooperation," December 10, 2003, available at: www.china.org.cn/english/features/China-Africa/82040.htm (accessed July 31, 2007).

37. Chen Shun, "New Impetus to China–Africa Agricultural Cooperation," *Xinhua*, December 22, 2007.

38. Wei Jianguo, "Speech at the Progress Briefing on the Implementation of the 8 Africa-Targeting Measures of the Beijing Summit of the Forum on China–Africa Cooperation," available at: mofcom.gov.cn, November 13, 2007 (accessed May 22, 2009).

39. Wei Jianguo, "Speech." For more on these centers, see Deborah Brautigam and Tang Xiaoyang, "China's Agricultural Engagement in Africa: 'Going Down to the Countryside'," *China Quarterly*, 199 (September 2009).

40. Wei Jianguo, "Speech"; Chinese embassy in Liberia, "Chinese ambassador Zhou Yuxiao Attends the Agreement Signing Ceremony for the China-aided Agricultural Technology Demonstration Center," March 30, 2008, www.fmprc.gov/cn.eng/wjb/zwig/zwbd/t419551.htm (accessed August 22, 2008).

41. "Firm Will Grow Rice in Africa," *China Daily*, May 9, 2008.

42. Deborah Brautigam, "Land Rights and Agricultural Development in West Africa: A Case Study of Two Chinese Projects," *Journal of Developing Areas*, 25(4) (October 1992): 21–32. I thank Jamie Monson for this point.

43. Sameer Mohindru, "Bayer CropScience Plans to Expand Global Rice Hybrid Opportunities," *Dow Jones Newswires*, October 10, 2006.

10   Foreign Farmers: Chinese Settlers in Rural Africa

1. A careful study by Lorenzo Cotula, Sonja Vermeulen, Rebecca Leonard and James Keeley, "Land Grab or Development Opportunity? Agricultural Investment and International Land Deals in Africa," International Institute for Environment and Development (IIED), Food and Agriculture Organization (FAO), and International Fund for Agricultural Development (IFAD), London/Rome, 2009, concluded "as yet there are no known examples of Chinese land acquisitions in Africa in excess of 50,000 hectares where deals have been concluded and projects implemented" (p. 37).

2. Akira Yamauchi, "Toward Sustainable Agricultural Production Systems: Major Issues and Needs in Research," Proceedings of the Forum on Sustainable Agricultural Systems in Asia, Nagoya, Japan, June 2002, p. 53; See also: "Japan Mitsui Affiliate Buys Brazil Farmland," *Reuters*, November 13, 2007.

3. Tom Burgis, "Africa: Angola Launches $6bn Agricultural Expansion," *Financial Times*, October 6, 2008; "UN Warns of Food Neocolonialism," *Financial Times*, August 19, 2008; "US Investor Buys Sudanese Warlord's Land," *Financial Times*, January 9, 2009.

4. Peter Fray, "A Slice of China Comes to the Murray," *Sydney Morning Herald* (Australia), June 16, 1989.

5. Rowan Callick, "Chinese Firms Eye Aussie Farmland," *The Australian*, May 12, 2008.

6. Recently, she said, they obtained a loan from the Zambia National Commercial Bank to expand into irrigated wheat.

7. "Zambia Welcomes Chinese Agricultural Know-How," *People's Daily*, March 21, 2006, and author's research.

8. Andreas Lorenz and Thilo Thielke, *Der Speigel*, May 30, 2007.

9. "Policy Guidance for Overseas Investment, Directive Catalog for Foreign Investment," National Development and Reform Commission, July 5, 2006.

10. "Africa: Top Option for China's Agricultural Investment," *Xinhua*, September 28, 2002.

11. "China Agri Ministry, Development Bank Support Agri Projects," sinocast. com, Comtex News Network, November 23, 2006.

12. "Zhongguo Jinchukou Yinhang: Chongqing Qing Nonghu ke Qu Feizhou Kai Nongchang" ("China Eximbank: Chongqing Peasant Households May Go to Africa to Set Up Farms"), *Chongqing Chenbao* (Chongqing Morning News), September 18, 2007.

13. Li Ping, "Food Security: Hopes and Strains in China's Overseas Farming Plan," *Economic Observer*, 374 (June 2008), eeo.com.cn (translated by Zuo Maohong).

14. "Nongyebu Fouren Woguo Haiwai Duntian" ("Ministry of Agriculture Denies China to Occupy Land Overseas"), *Xinhua*, July 4, 2008; "Gaifawei: Wu Haiwai Duntian Jihua" ("National Development and Reform Commission: No Plan to Occupy Land Overseas"), *Xinhua*, November 13, 2008.

15. Parsing this comment can leave a reader confused. Presumably the workers were not already "being exploited" by the land holders! Chapter in Firoze Manji and Stephen Marks, *African Perspectives on China in Africa* (Cape Town: Fahamu Networks for Social Justice, 2007), p. 97.

16. Yun Wenju, "Cong Guoji Yuanzhu de Fazhan Kan Zhonguo dui Fei de Yuanzhu" ("The Development of International Aid and China's Agricultural Aid to Africa"), *West Asia and Africa*, 2 (2000): 17–23.

17. Chinese domestic soybean production in 2007 was estimated at 14 million tons, and imports at 30.8 million tons. "China Commodities Report: Grains and Softs," Interfax News Service, Ltd., April 2008.

18. Huang Zhonglun, deputy general manager of Chongqing Seed Corp. (which has launched a small hybrid rice operation in Nigeria as well as the center in Tanzania), told Niu Shuping, "China Overseas Food Push Not Realistic," *Reuters*, May 9, 2008.

19. Callick, "Chinese Firms Eye Aussie Farmland."

20. Ibid.

21. Xia Zesheng, "Quanmian Tuijin Zhong Fei Nongye Hezuo Zhengfengqishi."

22. "Memorandum of Understanding on Construction of Agricultural Technology Transfer Center and Grain Production and Processing Base in the Philippines," January 15, 2007, available at: http://newsbreak.com.ph/index.php?option= com_

remository&Itemid=88889273&func=startdown&id=139 (accessed May 22, 2009).

23. Li Ping, "Food Security: Hopes and Strains in China's Overseas Farming Plan."

24. *Africa–Asia Confidential*, 1(2) (December 14, 2007).

25. "Le Ministère de l'Agriculture et la Coopération ZTE ont signé une convention de partenariat," *Documentation et Information pour l'Afrique*, November 2, 2007; "L'ambassadeur Wu Zexian: La Chine n'a pas de visées Impérialistes," *Le Potential*, January 14, 2008 (posted on the website of the Chinese embassy of the DRC).

26. "Zimbabwe: China Turns Down Zimbabwe Farm Offer," *Zim Online*, October 12, 2005, available at: www.Zimonline.co.za (accessed May 22, 1009).

27. World Bank, "Consultations with Youth in Sierra Leone" (draft), background report for the *World Development Report 2007: Youth and Development* (no date). Field wages had started at Le 2,500/day, risen to Le 4,500/day at the time the research for the World Bank report was done (probably 2006), and were at Le 6,500/day at the time of my visit at the end of 2007.

28. "Lease Contract on Magbass Sugar Complex of Sierra Leone," Government of Sierra Leone, Ministry of Agriculture, January 23, 2003, p. 5.

29. There was no suggestion that they paid the Chinese. World Bank, "Consultations with Youth in Sierra Leone."

30. I asked K. B. J. Conteh, the labor leader, about the cholera issue, and he said, "It is so political. You should meet with the Minister." When I asked the former minister Monde about it, he said, "The Chinese invited us to test the water. We found that there has been no change in the quality."

31. The lease signed in 2003 specified that the Government of Sierra Leone would provide "another 800–1000 hectares of land (adjacent to or neighboring the Complex)" and take care of all legal formalities for this by 2004. "Lease Contract on Magbass Sugar Complex," p. 3.

32. Economic trees can be planted, or they can be growing wild, but are valuable to those who have the right to harvest their fruits or tap them for palm wine.

33. Memo from Ministry of Agriculture and Natural Resources, Agricultural Officer, Magbass, to MANR office, Magburuka, Magbass Sugar Cane Project Files, Tower Hill, July 3, 1980.

34. Pa Santiagie Lima Kanu to Paramount Chief, Makari Gbanti Chiefdom, November 29, 1980, Rolako Station, Chinese Project Files, Principle Agricultural Office, MANR, Makeni.

35. Hualien, a leather products company based in southern China, bought all four, including one in Benin and two separate companies in Madagascar. "Letter from the Board," Hua Lien International Company Ltd., January 23, 2009, available at: www.hkexnews.hk/listedco/listconews/sehk/20090122/LTN 20090122532.pdf (accessed May 22, 2009).

36. "China to Lease Overseas Farmland to Solve Food Problem," *People's Daily*, May 24, 2004.

37. "China Overseas Food Push Not Realistic," *Reuters*, May 9, 2008.

38. Callick, "Chinese Firms Eye Aussie Farmland."

39. Xia Zesheng, "Quanmian Tuijin Zhong Fei Nongye Hezuo Zhengfengqishi."

40. Live Yu-Siou, "Madagascar," and Huguette Ly-Tio-Fane Pineo, "Mauritius," both in Lynn Pan, ed., *The Encyclopedia of the Chinese Overseas* (Cambridge, MA: Harvard University Press, 1999), pp. 350, 353. The other Africa experiences in this paragraph are also from this book.

41. Figure applies to those who arrived between 1908 and 1933. Daniel M. Masterson with Sayaka Funada-Classen documents their experience in a fascinating book, *The Japanese in Latin America* (Evanston, IL: University of Illinois Press, 2004).

42. This tale is based on my assistant Tang Xiaoyang's interviews with Liu Jianjun in Baoding, China, November 21 and 22, 2008, and on "Hebei Baoding: 7000 Duo Nongmin Feizhou Chuangye" ("Hebei Baoding: 7000 Plus Farmers Set Up in Africa"), *Xinhua*, October 20, 2006; Xin Li, "China Digs in on a Struggling Continent," *Washington Times*, May 11, 2006; Michael Bristow, "China's Long March to Africa," *BBC Online*, November 29, 2007; Richard Spencer, "Chinese Workers Seek Fortunes in Africa," *Daily Telegraph*, February 26, 2008; Dominique Patton, "China Eyes Idle Farmland In Kenya," *Business Daily Africa* (Kenya), April 7, 2008.

43. Many who subsequently picked up on this report mistakenly linked Liu to the China–Africa Business Council, an organization jointly established by the United Nations Development Program and the Chinese government.

44. In various reports, Mr. Liu has said that these villages are located in Kenya, Nigeria, Sudan, Zambia, Uganda, Côte d'Ivoire, Ghana, and Senegal.

45. "Chongqing Peasant Households May Go to Africa to Set Up Farms."

46. Susan Ramsay, "China Sees the Continent as an Ideal Source of Raw Materials and Oil – With Farmland Aplenty for Displaced Peasants," *South China Morning Post*, November 25, 2007.

47. Spencer, "Chinese Workers Seek Fortunes in Africa"; Emmanuel Ma Mung Kuang, "The New Chinese Migration Flows to Africa," *Social Science Information*, 47(4) (2008): 643–59.

11 Rogue Donor? Myths and Realities

1. Henri E. Cauvin, "I.M.F. Skewers Corruption in Angola," the *New York Times*, November 30, 2002.

2. *Rashomon* was directed by the legendary Akira Kurosawa. This tale of Angola is based on author's interviews with IMF staff, Washington DC, November 2008; China Eximbank, Beijing, November 2008; and interviews conducted in Angola in 2007 by Tang Xiaoyang, who generously agreed to share summaries with me. It relies as well on the following materials: Government of Angola, "Memorandum of Economic and Financial Policies," April 3, 2000, available at: www.imf.org/external/NP/LOI/2000/ago/01/index.htm (accessed May 22, 2009); Government of Angola, "Memorandum of Economic and Financial Policies," February 7, 2001, available at: www.imf.org/external/NP/LOI/2001/ago/01/INDEX.HTM (accessed May 22, 2009); *Angola Country Reports*, *Economist Intelligence Unit* (various issues); "Angola: Oil-backed Loan Will Finance Recovery Projects," UN Integrated Information Networks, February 21, 2005. For excellent overviews of the Angola case, see Manuel Ennes Ferreira, "China in Angola: Just a Passion for Oil?" in Chris Alden, Daniel Large and Ricardo Soares de Oliveira, eds., *China Returns to Africa: A Rising Power and a Continent Embrace* (New York: Columbia University Press, 2008), pp. 295–317; Lucy Colhin, "All's Fair in Loans and War: The Development of China–Angola Relations," in Kweku Ampiah and Sanusha Naidu, eds., *Crouching Tiger, Hidden Dragon? Africa and China* (Scottsville, South Africa: University of KwaZulu-Natal Press, 2008), pp. 108–23.

3. Christopher Swann and William McQuillen, "China to Surpass World Bank as Top Lender to Africa," Bloomberg.com, November 3, 2006.

4. Repayment begins separately as each project is finished, using a designated escrow account funded by proceeds from oil exports, at market rates. The loan funds remain in China (in the pattern described in Chapter 5), with Eximbank disbursing them directly to the Chinese companies doing the work.

5. World Bank, "Angola: Broad-Based Growth and Equity," Washington DC, 2007, p. 85.

6. Why did China negotiate such a relatively generous deal? The huge block of guaranteed business for Chinese construction companies made it "win-win" for the Chinese. But the Chinese also knew that in 2004 Royal Dutch Shell was preparing to sell its 50 percent share of Block 18, one of thirty-four concessions in the Atlantic waters off the coast of Angola. Shell was about to accept an Indian offer: $620 million plus $200 million for railway reconstruction by

Indian companies. Instead, Angola's national oil company Sonangol unexpectedly arranged for the block to be sold to a joint venture between itself and the Chinese oil company Sinopec. The timing of the $2 billion Eximbank loan may have been connected to the unexpected entry of Sinopec into its first ownership stake in Angolan oil (a direct quid pro quo was never established). Henry Lee and Dan Shalmon, "Searching for Oil: China's Strategies in Africa," in Robert I. Rotberg, ed., *China into Africa: Trade, Aid and Influence* (Washington DC: Brookings Institution Press, 2008), p. 120. The subsequent loans offered in 2007 did not seem to be connected to investment.

7. "Angola: Birthday Blues," *Africa Confidential*, 46(23) (November 2005): 5.
8. "Angola: Standard Chartered Draws Fire," *Mail and Guardian* (South Africa), June 8, 2005.
9. "Angola: Birthday Blues."
10. A final character deserves a story of its own: China International Fund (CIF), a private Hong Kong company. CIF is connected to China-Sonangol, a Chinese-Angolan joint venture in oil trading, and Beiya International Development Company, a shadowy property development and construction firm. Beiya is chaired by Xu Jinghua, a Russian military academy classmate of the Angolan President, Dos Santos. CIF has also set up oil-for-infrastructure lines of credit in Angola. These were rumored to be many times higher than the Eximbank loans. But in October 2007 Aguinaldo Jaime, a graduate of the London School of Economics, former governor of Angola's Central Bank and a key architect of Angola's reforms, released an official figure of $2.9 billion for the CIF loans, and even these have not been forthcoming as planned. In 2007, the Angolan government itself had to issue treasury bonds to finance some of the projects planned under the CIF arrangement. (Alex Vines and Indira Campos, "Angola and China: A Pragmatic Partnership," Center for Strategic International Studies, Washington DC, p. 10.) The Hong Kong-based CIF has a bad reputation among Chinese mainland companies: "So far, half a dozen contractors have had unpleasant experiences with the CIF, which stands accused of routinely delaying payment for completed work and keeping rates as low as possible." Zhou Jiangong, "Africa Frenzy Feeds China Stock Bubble," *Asia Times Online*, March 27, 2007, available at: www.atimes.com/atimes/China_Business/IC27Cb01.html (accessed May 22, 2009). While the smaller Eximbank projects moved ahead, many of the large projects being funded by the CIF loan – the Benguela Railway renovation, a new airport, a massive housing complex – stalled over the course of 2007 and 2008. Chinese bloggers believe

that the CIF program must have been approved by the Chinese government; the Chinese embassy in Angola denied any knowledge of the CIF venture. For excellent reviews of the CIF saga, see Lee Levkowitz, Malta McLellan Ross, and J. R. Warner, *The 88 Queensway Group: A Case Study in Chinese Investors' Operations in Angola and Beyond*, US-China Economic & Security Review Commission, July 2009; and Alex Vines, Lillian Wong, Markus Weimar and Indira Campos, "Thrist for African Oil: Asian National Oil Companies in Nigeria and Angola," A Chatham House Report, August 2009.

11. For example, Ana Maria Gomes, "Report on China's Policy and its Effects on Africa," Report of the European Parliament, A6-0080/2008 (2007/2255(INI)), Brussels, April 2008, p. 11, claimed that China's $2 billion loan was "a cash flow which represents a financial boost to the ruling party in the run up to forthcoming elections." What the Angolan government got from the Chinese loan was the political benefit of very rapid, very visible improvements in infrastructure.

12. George Parker and Alan Beattie, "EIB Accuses China of Unscrupulous Loans," *Financial Times*, November 28, 2006; Chris McGreal, "Chinese Aid to Africa May Do More Harm than Good, Warns Benn," the *Guardian*, February 9, 2007; Françoise Crouigneau and Richard Hiault, "Wolfowitz Slams China Banks on Africa Lending," *Financial Times*, October 24, 2006; Andrew Malone, "How China's Taking Over Africa, and Why the West Should Be VERY Worried," *Daily Mail (UK) Online*, July 18, 2008.

13. Gomes, "Report on China's Policy."

14. I use the style of the "Think Again" pieces in the magazine *Foreign Policy*. I thank Erica Downs for the idea of doing this. Her article "The Fact and Fiction of Sino-African Energy Relations," *China Security*, 3(3) (Summer 2007): 42–68 is a model of this kind of analysis. I have also drawn on her excellent analysis for the section below on Sudan.

15. Richard Behar, "Endgame: Hypocrisy, Blindness, and the Doomsday Scenario," *China in Africa* (Part 6), available at: www.fastcompany.com/magazine/126/endgame-hypocrisy-blindness-and-the-doomsday-scenario.html (accessed May 9, 2008).

16. "Africa at Risk or Rising? The Role of Europe, North America, and China on the Continent," summary of a May 4–6 conference co-organized by the Stanley Foundation and the Aspen Atlantic Group, Berlin, Germany, Stanley Foundation, Policy Dialogue Brief, p. 8.

17. Gomes, "Report on China's Policy."

18. Vivien Foster, William Butterfield, Chuan Chen, and Nataliya Pushak, "Building Bridges: China's Growing Role as Infrastructure Financier for Sub-Saharan Africa," World Bank, July 2008, p. 64.

19. "Oil, Politics and Corruption," *The Economist*, September 20, 2008, p. 20.

20. Country aid allocations in Figure 11.1 come from the database constructed by my assistants. Resource-rich countries are those assigned to this category in John Page, "Rowing Against the Current: The Diversification Challenge in Africa's Resource Rich Economies," Global Working Paper No. 28, Brookings Institution, December 2008. Furthermore, I reclassified several countries that were not categorized as "resource-rich" by Page, but that exported more than $100 million in minerals to China in 2007 or 2008 (DRC, Mauritania, South Africa) or where Chinese investors planned significant mineral investments (Liberia, Niger, Zimbabwe).

21. Ministry of Commerce, *China Commerce Yearbook 2008* (Beijing: China Commerce and Trade Press, 2008), p. 488. The figure aggregates labor services and design services, which are relative small percentages.

22. *China Commerce Yearbook 2008*, p. 256.

23. "Mining: New Frontiers," *The Economist*, March 17, 2007.

24. Foster et al., "Building Bridges," p. 8.

25. See Downs, "Fact and Fiction."

26. Mika Takehera, "Why Chinese Oil Majors Rush to Africa," *Oil and Gas Review*, 40(6) (2006), cited in Takaaki Kobayashi, "Evolution of China's Aid Policy," Japan Bank for International Cooperation (JBIC) Institute Working Paper No. 27, April 2008, p. 44, n. 89.

27. Dan Haglund, "In it for the Long Term? A Comparative Perspective on Emerging Issues Around Chinese FDI in Africa," paper delivered at *China Quarterly*/School of Oriental and African Studies Conference on China and Africa, London, October 2008, p. 26. See also Pieter Snyman, "The Rising Tide of Chinese Investment in SADC Mining and Metals," *China Analyst*, 5(3) (March 2007), p. 3.

28. Aid is limited to modest loans, grants for humanitarian assistance, and several small infrastructure projects such as schools, clinics, and agricultural demonstration. In 2007 China provided a new aid package to Sudan: an interest-free loan of 100 million yuan ($12.8 million), a grant of 40 million yuan ($5.1 million), and an Eximbank concessional line of credit of 600 million yuan ($77 million) for infrastructure projects, and also canceled a second round of overdue debt of 470 million yuan ($60.6 million). As of February 2008, the Chinese had provided RMB 80 million (about $12 million) in five shipments of

humanitarian aid for Darfur. "China Envoy: More Humanitarian Aid to Darfur," *Xinhua*, February 26, 2008.

29. Daniel Large, "From Non-Interference to Constructive Engagement? China's Evolving Relations with Sudan," in Alden et al., *China Returns to Africa*, pp. 275–94. I am grateful to Daniel Large for sharing his expertise on Sudan with me, but absolve him of any responsibility for my interpretations.

30. For an excellent discussion of China's arms transfers in Sudan and elsewhere, as well as China's new peacekeeping efforts, see Ian Taylor, *China's New Role in Africa* (Boulder, CO: Lynne Rienner, 2009), pp. 113–59.

31. "Africa: China's Great Leap into the Continent," UN Office for the Coordinator of Humanitarian Affairs, Humanitarian News and Analysis, March 23, 2006, available at: www.irinnews.org/Report.aspx?ReportId=58530 (accessed May 22, 2009).

32. "Mr. Hu's Mission to Khartoum," *The Economist*, February 3, 2007.

33. "China told Sudan to Adopt UN's Darfur Plan – Envoy," Bloomberg.com, February 7, 2007, cited in Large, "From Non-Interference to Constructive Engagement?" pp. 275–6.

34. Gareth Evans and Donald Steinberg, "Signs of Transition," June 11, 2007, available at: http://commentisfree.guardian.co.uk/gareth_evans_and_donald_steinberg/2007/06/signs_of_transition.html (accessed May 22, 2009).

35. Downs, "Fact and Fiction," pp. 58–62.

36. Jon Hovi, Robert Huseby, and Detlef F. Sprinz, "When Do (Imposed) Economic Sanctions Work?" *World Politics* 57(4) (July 2005): 479–99; Jacob Weisberg, "Thanks for the Sanctions: Why Do We Keep Using a Policy that Helps Dictators?" August 2, 2006, available at: www.slate.com/id/2147058/ (accessed May 22, 2009).

37. Belarus supplies aircraft and armored combat vehicles, and Iran, tanks. Human Rights First, "Arms Transfers to Sudan, 2004–2006," available at: www.humanrightsfirst.org/pdf/CAH-081001-arms-table.pdf (accessed May 22, 2009); SIPRI, "Arms Imports to Sudan, 2000–2007," Arms Transfers Database, available at: www.sipri.org/contents/armstrad/output_types_TIV.html (accessed January 4, 2009).

38. La Mancha Resources, "Responsible Development in Sudan," available at: www.lamancharesources.com/servlet/dispatcherservlet?selectedContentID=1131 &lang=2&action=2 (accessed December 20, 2008). US company Marathon Oil retains exploration rights in a concession in southern Sudan. France's Total and Sweden's Lundin retain rights to large oil blocks. Several European engineering companies profit from large construction projects, including Lahmeyer

International and Siemens of Germany, France's Alstom, and ABB of Switzerland (several of these companies have pledged to withdraw from Sudan after completing their contracts).

39. UK Trade and Investment, "Sudan," available at: www.uktradeinvest.gov.uk/ukti/appmanager/ukti/countries?_nfls=false&_nfpb=true&_pageLabel=CountryType1&navigationPageId=/sudan (accessed December 21, 2008).

40. "Sudan Ousts Aid Groups After Court Pursues President," *Washington Post*, March 5, 2009; "Q & A: Darfur's Conflict," *BBC News Online*, available at: http://news.bbc.co.uk/2/hi/africa/3496731.stm (accessed March 5, 2009).

41. "ICC Wants Three Darfur Rebels Arrested: Attacks on Peacekeepers Will Not Be Tolerated," available at: www.rnw.nl/internationaljustice/icc/Sudan/081120-sudan-icc (accessed December 21, 2008).

42. Morton Abramowitz and Jonathan Kolieb, "Why China Won't Save Darfur," Foreignpolicy.com, June 2007 (accessed May 22, 2009).

43. Harvey Morris, "China Defends Africa Aid Stance," *Financial Times*, July 2, 2008.

44. Human Rights Watch, *World Report 2007*, February 5, 2007, p. 3.

45. Since the millennium, several voluntary corporate social responsibility initiatives such as the United Nations' Global Compact (launched in 2004) and the Equator Principles, launched in 2003 by a group of international banks, have raised the profile of human rights, the environment, anti-corruption and labor standards. The Global Compact is a set of very general principles: "Businesses should support and respect the protection of internationally proclaimed human rights (Principle 1); and make sure that they are not complicit in human rights abuses (Principle 2)." There is no independent monitoring or sanctions. Over time, however, these voluntary efforts are likely to contribute to the development of new norms for businesses increasingly conscious of their "social" bottom line.

46. World Bank, *World Development Indicators 2007*; Freedom House, *Freedom in the World 2008* (Washington DC: Freedom House, 2008). None of this was from China, whose foreign aid is not included in these databases.

47. "China Could Help Lift Africa From Poverty – UN Adviser," *Marketplace News*, Namibia Business Report, South Africa, August 16, 2006.

48. "Foreign Aid: Right to Bear Alms," *The Economist*, May 3, 2007.

49. See Heather Marquette, "The Creeping Politicisation of the World Bank: The Case of Corruption," *Political Studies*, 52(3) (2004): 413–30.

50. In Sudan, for example, the World Bank suspended programs in 1993 because Khartoum fell into arrears on its World Bank loans. At the end of 2007, Sudan

still owed a lot of money – about $28 billion – to various creditors, including the IFIs, and more than 80 percent of this was overdue.

51. John L. Thornton, "Long Time Coming: The Prospects for Democracy in China," *Foreign Affairs*, January/February 2008. See also "China Urges Faster Myanmar Reforms," November 17, 2007, available at: http://english.aljazeera.net/news/asia-pacific/2007/11/200852514465386617.html (accessed May 22, 2009).

52. "China Urges Faster Myanmar Reforms."

53. David K. Leonard and Titi Pitso with contributions from Anna Schmidt and Mark Smith, "The Political Economy of Democratisation in Sierra Leone: Reflections on the Elections of 2007 and 2008," Brighton, UK, Institute of Development Studies, 2009.

54. "Chinese Editorial Says Kenya Violence Proof That Western Democracy Unsuitable," *Associated Press*, January 14, 2008.

55. William Wallis, "Ethiopia Looks East to Slip Reins of Western Orthodoxy," *Financial Times*, February 6, 2007. The report noted that the United States provides about $600 million in aid annually to Ethiopia, despite its questionable record on governance.

56. Tom Gjelten, "Congo and China Forge Economic Partnership," *National Public Radio*, July 11, 2007.

57. In 2005, the Chinese allegedly refused Mugabe's request for $1 billion in aid. "China Refuses Aid Money to Zimbabwe," China Corporate Social Responsibility, available at: www.chinacsr.com/en/2005/08/02/272-china-refuses-aid-money-to-zimbabwe/ (accessed January 6, 2009). In late 2006 the Chinese took the unusual step of publicly denying rumors that they were planning to loan Mugabe's government $2 billion, saying this was "anything but true." Ministry of Foreign Affairs, "Foreign Ministry Spokesman Qin Gang's Regular Press Conference on 26 December 2006," Beijing, China, available at: www.chinese-embassy.org.za/eng/fyrth/t285463.htm (accessed January 6, 2009).

58. Estimated official development aid from China to Zimbabwe averaged around $17 million per year between 2004 and 2009, a total of about $103 million. Zimbabwe received several rounds of food aid, including a cash-for-food contribution sent through the World Food Program ($5 million); cash aid for salaries ($5 million); the renovation of the Harare stadium (about $5.8 million); grants for several FOCAC project: an agricultural demonstration center (estimated to cost 50 million RMB), two primary schools (20 million RMB), and a hospital (70 million RMB); and two concessional Eximbank loans of 200 million RMB ($25 million, in 2006) and 300 million RMB ($42 million, in 2008) to

finance imports of Chinese agricultural machinery. CATIC financed the sale of two of Xi'An Aircraft Industry's MA-60 passenger planes and donated a third in a "buy-two-get-one-free" deal. Nepal was offered a similar deal. This was not aid, however, but a supplier-financed export credit, similar to another Zimbabwe deal financed by Chinese auto giant FAW for 55 buses. "Sino-Zimbabwean Partnership Presents Rosy Picture," Xinhua, October 23, 2006; "Donated Plane to Zimbabwe by China Expected Next Year," Xinhua, October 10, 2005; interviews, Harare, September 2009.

59. Economist Intelligence Unit, "Zimbabwe Country Profile 2008," p. 9.

60. Karin Bruilliard, "As Zimbabwe Dollar Dies, So Does a Lucrative Career," *Washington Post*, February 21, 2009.

61. Report by Secretary General Xu Jinghu of Chinese Follow-up Committee of Forum on China–Africa Cooperation (FOCAC), at the fourth Senior Officials' Meeting of FOCAC, August 22, 2005.

62. "Huawei Tech Wins African Contracts," November 12, 2004, available at: www.redorbit.com/news/technology/102640/huawei_tech_wins_african_contracts/ (accessed January 6, 2009).

63. Reserve Bank of Zimbabwe, "Investment Proposals and Financing Plan for the Projects in the Power Sector," Legal Department, Supplement 4 (no date, probably 2005), p. 24. CATIC would supply electricity generating equipment to ZESA. ZESA would buy tobacco from new black tobacco farmers in local currency. An American tobacco company, Zimbabwe Leaf Tobacco, would receive the tobacco and export it, paying ZESA with US dollars deposited into the escrow account. CATIC would receive the US dollars. The plan broke down when the Zimbabwe government was unable to supply ZESA with local currency to pay for the tobacco. "Transmission and Distribution Supply Credit Facility," Megawatt Bulletin (Harare), January–May 2005, p. 6; interviews, Harare. September 2009.

64. "Go East, Old Man," *Africa-Asia Confidential*, reprinted in *The Zimbabwean*, December 19, 2008.

65. Gavin du Venage, "Harare's Ties With Beijing Begin to Falter; China Unhappy as Unpaid Bills Mount Up for Aircraft, Engineering Work and Construction Projects across Zimbabwe," *South China Morning Post*, May 19, 2006.

66. In 2008, a widely circulated story reported that Chinese investments in Zimbabwe totaled $1.6 billion. The source seems to have been a report on the Zimbabwe visit of deputy Minister of Commerce, Gao Hucheng: Nelson Banya, "Some Foreign Investors Gamble on Zimbabwe," *Reuters*, March 25, 2008. The original story on Gao's visit was published in Zimbabwe's official government newspaper, *The Herald*. "Zimbabwe: Sino-Zim Trade Continues Bearing Fruit," *The Herald* (Zimbabwe), February 25, 2008. After reporting on

trade volumes between the two countries, Gao went on to discuss other areas of cooperation: "Chinese companies have also invested a further US$1.6 billion in engineering and related contracts," he said. He then added that Chinese companies had also "invested about $US50 million into Zimbabwe." The "investment" of $1.6 billion seems to have been the value of engineering and machinery export contracts signed by Chinese companies, the same contracts Zimbabwe had been unable to honor.

67. "Zimbabwe: Sinosteel to Bid for Higher Zimasco Stake," *Financial Gazette* (Harare), November 29, 2007. *Businessweek* reported that Sinosteel initially agreed to buy 50 percent of Zimasco for $200 million. Sinosteel later raised this to 67 percent, and the purchase was apparently completed on December 13, 2007. See http://investing.businessweek.com/research/stocks/private/snapshot. asp?privcapId=26167800 (accessed February 8, 2009). As of September 2009, most other investments mentioned in the media had not taken off. For example, CATIC pursued a joint venture of $1.3 billion in coal power generation for six years before finally giving up.

68. "African Largest Glass Center under Construction in Zimbabwe," *People's Daily*, November 20, 2006.

69. P. Ncube, R. Bate, and R. Tren, "State in Fear: Zimbabwe's Tragedy is Africa's Shame: A Report on Operation Murambatsvina – 'Operation Drive Out the Filth' – and its Implications," Catholic Archdiocese of Zimbabwe, Bulawayo, cited in Taylor, *China's New Role*, p. 103.

70. Zimbabwe Defense Industries, Norheo (a major Chinese military exporter) and Nor subsidiary, Wanbao Mining, have established joint ventures to explore for chrome and other minerals. "Zimbabwe signs Deals with China's Wambao [sic], Norinco," Bloomberg, July 12 2006.

71. Stockholm International Peace Research Institute, "TIV of Arms Exports to Zimbabwe, 2003–2007," available at: http://armstrade.sipri.org/arms_trade/values.php (accessed January 19, 2009).

72. "Dockers Refuse to Unload China Arms Shipment for Zimbabwe," *The Times* (UK), April 18, 2008.

73. Jason Stearns, Dinesh Mahtani, Mouctar Kokouma Diallo, Peter Danssaert, and Sergio Finardi, "Final Report of the Group of Experts on the Democratic Republic of the Congo," United Nations Security Council S/2008/773, December 12, 2008, pp. 34–5.

74. Reports that Zimbabwe received Chinese arms via Sudan and the DRC were "incorrect," Stearns cautioned. "UN: No Proof China Provided Arms to Zimbabwe," *Mail and Guardian* (South Africa), December 24, 2008; Stearns et al., "Final Report," pp. 34–5.

75. Ken Kamoche, "Zimbabwe Does Not Need Chinese Arms," *Daily Nation* (Kenya) April 27, 2008.

76. Sasha Lilley, "BAE System's Dirty Dealings," *CorpWatch*, November 11, 2003; "Saudi Arabia and the BAE Arms Scandal," *Middle East Monitor*, 2(1) (June/ July 2007).

77. Roger Bate, "The Shell Game Comes to Zimbabwe: Mugabe Shuffles Around Farms to Curry Favor with the Chinese," *Weekly Standard*, May 27, 2005.

78. "Tobacco Firm has Secret North Korean Plant," the *Guardian* (UK), October 17, 2005.

79. Dumisani Muleya, "Zimbabwe Signs Mining and Power Deals with China," *Business Day* (South Africa), June 15, 2006; Central African Mining and Exploration Company (CAMEC), Notice of General Meeting, May 8, 2008, available at: http:// investors.camec-plc.com/pdf/CAM_circular_080508.pdf (accessed May 22, 2009).

80. David Robertson and Philip Webster, "Outrage over £200 m UK Investment in Zimbabwe," *The Times* (UK), June 25, 2008.

81. "Zimbabwe: Russia, China Veto UN Sanctions on Mugabe," July 13, 2008, available at: www.talkzimbabwe.com/news/117/ARTICLE/2921/2008-07-12. html (accessed October 7, 2008).

82. Chris Buckley, "China Offers Zimbabwe Aid, Urges National Unity," *Reuters*, December 9, 2008.

83. "Storm Brews Over China Deal, *The Zimbabwe Independent*, August 21, 2009."

84. Miriam Mannak, "Africa: Concerns over Chinese investment and Working Conditions," *Inter Press Service* (Johannesburg), June 16, 2008.

85. Comment made by participant, Workshop on China and Africa, Northeastern University, Boston, MA, April 3, 2008.

86. Deborah Nyangulu-Chipofya, "Windfall: K40bn Aid from China," *Malawi Times*, April 2, 2008; "Malawi Finance Minister Explains K40 Billion Chinese Money," *Nyasa Times*, August 14, 2008. Some sources I interviewed believed that the package of aid contained $30 million in cash, as in Costa Rica (Ch. 4).

87. "Jean Razafindambo (Canada/Madagascar)," *Indian Ocean Newsletter* No. 766, May 24, 1997.

88. Rukmini Callimachi, "China Courts Africa with Aid, Projects," *Associated Press*, January 5, 2007.

89. Andreas Lorenz and Thilo Thielke, "China's Conquest of Africa," *Der Spiegel Online*, May 30, 2007 (translated from German by Christopher Sultan).

90. Andrew Malone, "How China's Taking Over Africa, and Why the West Should Be VERY Worried," *Daily Mail* (UK), July 18, 2008.

91. Stephanie Wolters, "DRC, China Unveil 'Marshall Plan'," *Mail and Guardian* (Johannesburg), May 23–29, 2008.

92. Charles Kenny, "Construction, Corruption, and Developing Countries," World Bank Policy Research Working Paper 4271, June 2007.

93. The companies made payments to high-ranking Nigerian officials using a United Kingdom agent, and a Japanese agent for payments to low-ranking Nigerian officials. "SEC Charges KBR and Halliburton for FCPA Violations," press release, Securities and Exchange Commission, United States Government, February 11, 2009.

94. The four firms are China Road and Bridge Corp., China State Construction Engineering Corp. (CSCEC), China Wu Yi Co. Ltd., and China Geo-Engineering Corp. Three Filipino companies and a Korean firm were also barred, with one of the Filipino companies and its owner receiving a permanent debarment. "World Bank Debars Seven Firms and One Individual for Collusive Practices Under Philippines Road Project," World Bank press release No. 2009/200/INT, January 14, 2009. See also Bob Davis and Glenn R. Simpson, "World Bank Seeks Right Balance," *Wall Street Journal*, November 19, 2007.

95. The number listed for firms registered in Britain does not include additional firms registered in the Channel Islands or the British Virgin Islands. World Bank, "List of Debarred Firms," Vice Presidency for Institutional Integrity, Washington DC, available at: http://web.worldbank.org/external/default/main?contentMDK=64069844&menuPK=116730&pagePK=64148989&piPK=64148984&querycontentMDK=64069700&theSitePK=84266 (accessed January 22, 2009).

96. "Zhongguo Zai Feizhou, Xin Juese Shi Shenme" ("What is the New Role of China in Africa?"), *Nanfang Zhoumo* ("Nanfang Weekend"), November 2, 2006, available at www.nanfangdaily.com.cn/zm/20061102/xw/tx1/200611020011.asp (accessed July 28, 2008).

97. Central Committee of the Chinese Communist Party, "Work Proposal of Establishing and Improving the Anti-Corruption System 2008–2012," June 2008. The quoted clause is from Paragraph VII, point 2, "Prohibit Chinese-funded enterprises and other organizations with income to commit commercial bribery overseas."

98. Horizon Research Consulting Group, "Current Status of and Future Prospects for Sino-African Cooperation," Beijing, September 2007, p. 121.

99. Ministry of Commerce, People's Republic of China, "Provisional Measures on Administration of Foreign Aid Material Projects," Decree No. 5, September 1, 2006, available at: www.mofcom.gov.cn/aarticle/b/c/200607/20060702671822.html&11185797=92550171 (accessed May 22, 2009).

100. This comment was made in response to a question posed after a talk by Li Ruogu sponsored by the Center for Strategic and International Studies, Washington DC, April 2007.

101. "Bank of China President Clashes With Western World Over Africa," *Sunday Standard*, June 23, 2007.

102. Data in the study referred to 2004. William Easterly and Tobias Pfutze, "Where Does the Money Go? Best and Worst Practices in Foreign Aid," *Journal of Economic Perspectives*, 22(2) (Spring 2008): 16.

103. Engineers earn about RMB 150,000 per year. Tom Leander, "ZTE: National Champion," *CFO Asia* in Economist Intelligence Unit, Global Technology Forum, available at: http://globaltechforum.eiu.com/index.asp?layout=rich_story&doc_id=10757&title=ZTE%3A+National+champion&categoryid=1&channelid=3 (accessed February 26, 2009). See also Lucy Corkin et al., "China's Interest and Activity in Africa's Construction and Infrastructure Sectors," Centre for Chinese Studies, Stellenbosch University, South Africa, 2006.

104. Interview with Xu Weizhong, Li Zhibiao, and Wang Hongyi, "Economic Salon: The Chances and Risks of Investing in Africa," *Foreign Investment and Export Credit*, 3 (2006): 1–10 (Wang Hongyi speaking).

105. Interview, Janet West, OECD, Paris, June 7, 2007.

106. Alan Beattie and G. Parker, "EIB Accuses Chinese Banks of Undercutting Africa Loans," *Financial Times*, November 29, 2006.

107. Simon Clark, Michael Smith, and Franz Wild, "China Lets Child Workers Die Digging in Congo Mines for Copper," Bloomberg.com, July 23, 2008.

108. Herbert Jauch and Iipumbu Sakaria, "Chinese Investments in Namibia: A Labour Perspective," Labour Resource and Research Institute, Windhoek, Namibia, March 2009. Except when otherwise noted, all Namibia examples in this section come from this excellent study, pp. 18–32 *passim*.

109. Francis Teal, "Efficiency Wages and Rent Sharing: A Note and Some Empirical Evidence," World Bank, Africa Regional Program on Enterprise Development, Working Paper n. 113, Washington DC, December 1, 1995.

110. "Chinese 'Push Factors' and the EITI in Zambia," July 4, 2008, available at: www.minewatchzambia.com/2008/07/chinese-push-factors-and-eiti-in-zambia.html (accessed February 23, 2009).

111. All quotations in this paragraph are from Jauch and Sakaria, "Chinese Investments," pp. 18–22.

112. For comprehensive, fieldwork-based reports on Chinese activities in forestry, see Catherine Mackenzie, "Forest Governance in Zambézia, Mozambique:

Chinese Takeaway!," Final Report for FONGZA, Mozambique, April 2006, and Simon Milledge, Ised Gelvas, and Antje Ahrends, "Forestry, Governance and Natural Resources: Lessons Learned From a Logging Boom in Southern Tanzania," TRAFFIC East/Southern Africa, May 1, 2007.

113. Vijaya Ramachandran, "Power and Roads for Africa," Center for Global Development Essay, March 2008.

114. Darren Taylor, "US President-Elect Urged to Build Power and Roads in Africa," *Voice of America News*, November 4, 2008.

115. Shai Oster, "China: New Dam Builder for the World," *Wall Street Journal*, December 28, 2007.

116. Adina Matisoff and Michelle Chan, "The Green Evolution: Environmental Policies and Practice in China's Banking Sector," Friends of the Earth/Bank Track, November 2008, p. 47.

117. Li Jing, "Environmental Guidelines for Firms Investing Abroad," *China Daily*, September 12, 2008.

118. John Vandaele, "China Outdoes Europeans in Congo," Inter Press Service (Johannesburg), February 8, 2008.

119. Geoffrey York, "Papua New Guinea and China's New Empire," *Globe and Mail*, January 3, 2009. This story is also based on Rowan Callick, "Ramu Nickel, 'Challenging, Exciting, but Manageable'," *Sydney Morning Herald*, September 8, 2008 and Hamish McDonald, "China's Offering May Be a Fool's Paradise," *Sydney Morning Herald*, July 14, 2007.

120. York, "China's New Empire."

121. Helen Power, "British Miners Get Tough with China," *Daily Telegraph*, March 3, 2008.

INDEX